T0210852

Communications
in Computer and Information Science   1283

Commenced Publication in 2007
Founding and Former Series Editors:
Simone Diniz Junqueira Barbosa, Phoebe Chen, Alfredo Cuzzocrea,
Xiaoyong Du, Orhun Kara, Ting Liu, Krishna M. Sivalingam,
Dominik Ślęzak, Takashi Washio, Xiaokang Yang, and Junsong Yuan

More information about this series at http://www.springer.com/series/7899

Audrius Lopata · Rita Butkienė ·
Daina Gudonienė · Vilma Sukackė (Eds.)

Information and Software Technologies

26th International Conference, ICIST 2020
Kaunas, Lithuania, October 15–17, 2020
Proceedings

Springer

Editors
Audrius Lopata
Kaunas University of Technology
Kaunas, Lithuania

Rita Butkienė ⓘ
Kaunas University of Technology
Kaunas, Lithuania

Daina Gudonienė ⓘ
Kaunas University of Technology
Kaunas, Lithuania

Vilma Sukackė
Kaunas University of Technology
Kaunas, Lithuania

ISSN 1865-0929 ISSN 1865-0937 (electronic)
Communications in Computer and Information Science
ISBN 978-3-030-59505-0 ISBN 978-3-030-59506-7 (eBook)
https://doi.org/10.1007/978-3-030-59506-7

This Springer imprint is published by the registered company Springer Nature Switzerland AG
The registered company address is: Gewerbestrasse 11, 6330 Cham, Switzerland

Preface

We are happy to present to you the proceedings of the 26th International Conference on Information and Software Technologies (ICIST 2020). This yearly conference was held during October 15–17, 2020, in Kaunas, Lithuania.

The present volume includes three chapters, which correspond to the three major areas that were covered during the conference, namely, Business Intelligence for Information and Software Systems, Software Engineering, and Information Technology Applications. According to the four special sessions of the conference, the proceedings and the three areas are subdivided into the following sections:

(i) Intelligent Methods for Data Analysis and Computer Aided Software Engineering
(ii) Intelligent Systems and Software Engineering Advances
(iii) Smart e-Learning Technologies and Applications
(iv) Language Technologies

Conference participants not only had the opportunity to present their rigorous research in more specialized settings, but also had the possibility to attend high-quality plenary sessions. This year, we had the pleasure of hearing the keynote presentations by Prof. Dr. Vladimir Trajkovkij (The Ss. Cyril and Methodius University in Skopje, North Macedonia) on "Big Data, Internet of Things and Health: May the Force Be with You," Prof. Dr. Adel S. Elmaghraby (University of Louisville, USA) on "The AI Journey: A Vision into the Future Guided from the Past," and Dr. Ajith Abraham (MIR Labs) on "Industry 4.0 and Society 5.0: Challenges from a Data Science Perspective."

We would like to express our deepest gratitude to the special session chairs Prof. Dr. Audrius Lopata (Kaunas University of Technology, Lithuania), Dr. Maria Dolores Afonso Suárez (SIANI University Institute), Assoc. Prof. Marcin Wozniak (Silesian University of Technology, Poland), Prof. Dr. Christian Napoli (University of Rome, Italy), Assoc. Prof. Danguolė Rutkauskienė (Kaunas University of Technology, Lithuania), Prof. Dr. Radu Adrian Vasiu (Politehnica University of Timisoara, Romania), Prof. Dr. Jurgita Kapočiūtė-Dzikienė (Vytautas Magnus University, Lithuania), and Peter Dirix (KU Leuven, Belgium). We acknowledge and appreciate the immense contribution of the session chairs not only in attracting the highest quality papers but also in moderating the sessions and enriching discussions between the conference participants.

The entire team working on organizing the conference is proud that despite the uncertainties of the pandemic period, the conference maintained and attracted the interest of numerous scholars across the globe. This year, we received 78 submissions from approximately 20 countries. This indicates that over the years the conference has truly gained international recognition as it brings together a large number of brilliant experts who showcase the state of the art of the aforementioned fields and come to discuss their newest projects as well as directions for future research.

As we are determined not to stop improving the quality of the conference, only 30 scientific papers were accepted to be published in this volume (thus accumulating to 38% acceptance rate). Each submission was reviewed by at least two reviewers, while borderline papers were evaluated by three or more reviewers. Reviewing and selection was performed by our highly esteemed Program Committee, who we thank for devoting their precious time to produce thorough reviews and feedback to the authors. It should be duly noted that this year, the Program Committee consisted of 54 reviewers, who represent 33 academic institutions and 17 countries.

In addition to the session chairs and Program Committee members, we would also like to express our appreciation to the general chair, Prof. Dr. Audrius Lopata (Kaunas University of Technology, Lithuania), who took up the responsibility of steering the wheel of ICIST after the conference celebrated its 25th anniversary in 2019. Moreover, we would like to thank the Local Organizing Committee, the Faculty of Informatics at Kaunas University of Technology, as well as the Research Council of Lithuania—the conference would not have been a success without their tremendous support.

The proceedings of ICIST 2020 are published as an issue of the *Communications in Computer and Information Science* series. This would not be possible without the kind assistance that was provided by Aliaksandr Birukou, Amin Mobasheri, Sanja Evenson, and Alla Serikova from Springer, for which we are extremely grateful. We are very proud of this collaboration and believe that this fruitful partnership will sustain for many more years to come.

July 2020

Vilma Sukackė
Audrius Lopata
Daina Gudonienė
Rita Butkienė

Organization

The 26th International Conference on Information and Software Technologies (ICIST 2020) was organized by Kaunas University of Technology and was held in Kaunas, Lithuania (October 15–17, 2020).

General Chair

Audrius Lopata   Kaunas University of Technology, Lithuania

Local Organizing Committee

Daina Gudonienė (Chair)	Kaunas University of Technology, Lithuania
Vilma Sukackė	Kaunas University of Technology, Lithuania
Romas Šleževičius	Kaunas University of Technology, Lithuania
Lina Repšienė	Kaunas University of Technology, Lithuania
Rita Butkienė	Kaunas University of Technology, Lithuania
Gintarė Lukoševičiūtė	Kaunas University of Technology, Lithuania

Special Session Chairs

Audrius Lopata	Kaunas University of Technology, Lithuania
Maria Dolores Afonso Suárez	SIANI University Institute, Spain
Marcin Wozniak	Silesian University of Technology, Poland
Christian Napoli	University of Rome, Italy
Danguolė Rutkauskienė	Kaunas University of Technology, Lithuania
Radu Adrian Vasiu	Politehnica University of Timisoara, Romania
Jurgita Kapočiūtė-Dzikienė	Vytautas Magnus University, Lithuania
Peter Dirix	KU Leuven, Belgium

Program Committee

Audrius Lopata	Kaunas University of Technology, Lithuania
Daina Gudonienė	Kaunas University of Technology, Lithuania
Ilona Veitaitė	Vilnius University, Lithuania
Vytenis Punys	Kaunas University of Technology, Lithuania
Martynas Patašius	Kaunas University of Technology, Lithuania
Aleksandras Targamadzė	Kaunas University of Technology, Lithuania
Carsten Wolff	Dortmund University Applied Sciences and Arts, Germany
Dalia Krikščiūnienė	Vilnius University, Lithuania

Alexander Mädche	Karlsruhe Institute of Technology, Germany
Sanjay Misra	Atilim University, Turkey
Jurgita Kapočiūtė- Dzikienė	Vytautas Magnus University, Lithuania
Rolf Engelbrecht	European Federation for Medical Informatics-Health Information Management Europe, ProRec, Germany
Andrzej Jardzioch	West Pomeranian University of Technology, Poland
Armantas Ostreika	Kaunas University of Technology, Lithuania
Jakub Swacha	University of Szczecin, Poland
Jorge Esparteiro Garcia	Business School of Polytechnic Institute of Viana do Castelo, Portugal
Danguolė Rutkauskienė	Kaunas University of Technology, Lithuania
Radu Vasiu	Politehnica University of Timisoara, Romania
Ramūnas Kubiliūnas	Kaunas University of Technology, Lithuania
Vytautas Rudžionis	Kaunas University of Technology, Lithuania
Tomas Krilavičius	Vytautas Magnus University, Lithuania
Rytis Maskeliūnas	Kaunas University of Technology, Lithuania
Yuh-Min Tseng	National Changhua University of Education, Taiwan
Zbigniew Banaszak	Warsaw University of Technology, Poland
Sanda Martincic-Ipsic	University of Rijeka, Croatia
Juan Manuel Vara	Kybele Research Group, Rey Juan Carlos University, Spain
Eduard Babkin	LITIS Laboratory, INSA Rouen, France, and TAPRADESS Laboratory, State University - Higher School of Economics, Russia
Justyna Patalas- Maliszewska	University of Zielona Góra, Poland
Kęstutis Kapočius	Kaunas University of Technology, Lithuania
Emiliano Tramontana	University of Catania, Italy
Sandro Leuchter	Hochschule Mannheim University of Applied Sciences, Germany
Janis Stirna	Stockholm University, Sweden
Virgilijus Sakalauskas	Vilnius University, Lithuania
Marisa Gil	Polytechnic University of Catalonia, Spain
Peter Dirix	KU Leuven, Belgium
Damjan Vavpotic	University of Ljubljana, Slovenia
Rimantas Butleris	Kaunas University of Technology, Lithuania
Rita Butkienė	Kaunas University of Technology, Lithuania
Prima Gustienė	Karlstad University, Sweden
Dominykas Barisas	Kaunas University of Technology, Lithuania
Christophoros Nikou	University of Ioannina, Greece
Kristina Šutienė	Kaunas University of Technology, Lithuania
Saulius Gudas	Vilnius University, Lithuania
Rimvydas Simutis	Kaunas University of Technology, Lithuania
Lina Čeponienė	Kaunas University of Technology, Lithuania
Marcin Wozniak	Silesian University of Technology, Poland
Milena Krumova	Technical University of Sofia, Bulgaria

Andre Schekelmann   Hochschule Niederrhein - University of Applied
                                Science, Germany
Martin Gaedke   Chemnitz University of Technology, Germany
Beata Gavurova   Technical University of Kosice, Slovakia
Vira Shendryk   Sumy State University, Ukraine
Karin Harbusch   University of Koblenz-Landau, Germany
Marcin Paprzycki   Systems Research Institute, Polish Academy
                                of Sciences, Poland
Evelina Stanevičienė   Kaunas University of Technology, Lithuania

Co-Editors

Audrius Lopata   Kaunas University of Technology, Lithuania
Rita Butkienė   Kaunas University of Technology, Lithuania
Daina Gudonienė   Kaunas University of Technology, Lithuania
Vilma Sukackė   Kaunas University of Technology, Lithuania

Contents

Business Intelligence for Information and Software Systems - Special Session on Intelligent Methods for Data Analysis and Computer Aided Software Engineering

Software Engineering - Special Session on Intelligent Systems and Software Engineering Advances

Information Technology Applications - Special Session on Smart e-Learning Technologies and Applications

Information Technology Applications - Special Session on Language Technologies

Business Intelligence for Information and Software Systems - Special Session on Intelligent Methods for Data Analysis and Computer Aided Software Engineering

Survey of Open-Source Clouds Capabilities Extension

Rita Butkiene[(✉)], Jaroslav Karpovic, Ricardas Sabaliauskas,
Laurynas Sriupsa, Mindaugas Vaitkunas, and Gytis Vilutis

Kaunas University of Technology, Kaunas, Lithuania
{rita.butkiene,gytis.vilutis}@ktu.lt

Abstract. In this paper, we present a survey, which would be beneficial to anybody considering private or hybrid cloud solution implementation or implementing custom scheduling optimization algorithm on popular cloud computing platforms. The cloud computing platform can be deployed as a private cloud on-premises or in dedicated data centre space, as a public service or as a combination of both. In this survey, we review similarities and differences of most popular private cloud implementation platforms and their compatibility with public cloud solutions. The survey reveals the prevalence of resource scheduling and service deployment algorithms within some popular open-source clouds.

Keywords: Open Cloud eXchange · Cloud · Scheduling algorithms

1 Introduction

Along with the growing availability in cloud computing services, different virtualization concepts are being developed in cloud computing systems to help cloud consumers and providers to achieve better usage and efficient management of the clouds with the least cost. Resource management in Cloud includes two stages: resource provisioning and resource scheduling. Resource provisioning is defined to be the stage to identify adequate resources for a given workload based on QoS requirements described by cloud consumers, whereas resource scheduling is mapping and execution of cloud consumer workloads based on selected resources through resource provisioning. Cloud consumer submits workloads while the cloud provider provides resources for the execution of workloads. Both the parties have different requirements: provider wants to earn as many profits as possible with the lowest investment and maximize utilization of resources while consumer wants to execute workload(s) with minimum cost and execution time. From the point of view of the consumer, higher efficiency of resource scheduling could be achieved by consolidating all available services into one multi-cloud environment, where multiple, independent and competitive service providers offer and deliver services to clients. The concept of such a system is called an Open Cloud Exchange [1]. The clients that wish to make use of these services can pick and

© Springer Nature Switzerland AG 2020
A. Lopata et al. (Eds.): ICIST 2020, CCIS 1283, pp. 3–13, 2020.
https://doi.org/10.1007/978-3-030-59506-7_1

choose between a diversity of offerings rather than being locked into the choices made by a single service provider. To achieve better accessibility of multi-cloud system resources, the process of cloning and migrating VMs from one source host to another within or beyond the cloud must be maximum simplified and automated. The overall control of migrated VMs needs to be assured through a compatible API. In this paper we will take a closer look at specifics of IaaS private cloud services implementation within some open-source clouds and possible avoidance of cloud vendor lock-in related issues: proprietary scheduling strategies, limited scheduling policy extension, different hypervisor implementations and native APIs.

2   Background and Related Works

Establishing service interoperability across different providers and clouds is still an open problem. The main challenges cloud consumers are facing lately are a large number of commercial cloud providers that have emerged in the market over the last years and a lack of standardization in the cloud services, which is inevitable in the early stages of the new technology. In cloud computing, the service interoperability is the ability to migrate and integrate services, which are deployed on different providers regardless of their location, their environment (single cloud or interconnected clouds), and the diversity of their hardware and software. Lack of interoperability is caused by several factors: heterogeneous virtualization technologies, non-standardized service descriptions and service-level agreement (SLA) definitions, diverse APIs, and non-standardized technologies for authentications and authorizations. A vendor lock-in is one of the outcomes induced by the lack of interoperability among cloud providers, which also means lack of ability to migrate application components and associated workload among multiple cloud providers. The majority of previous surveys declare the main focus of new approaches should be the avoidance of the vendor lock-in. To address these challenges, many researchers present their analytical surveys and practical solutions on how to use multiple clouds serially, when moved from one cloud to another, or simultaneously, when using services from different clouds and vendors.

Generally speaking, a collaboration of clouds may be from the user side (Multi-clouds or Aggregated services by Broker) [2,3] or the provider side (Hybrid clouds, Cloud federation, Inter-clouds and so on) [4,5]. Huynh et al. [6] highlight an ability for automatically porting cloud software components to other compatible cloud platforms which are provided by various cloud providers. They propose a concept of a Multi-cloud Marketplace, in which a consumer uses multiple cloud services (IaaS or PaaS) from more than one provider. Additionally, Juan-Verdejo [7], Long [8] and some other authors [9–11] denote the importance of vendor lock-in problem overcoming, which is a direct consequence of the lack of interoperability and portability between multiple clouds.

An important functionality of the Multi-cloud is to manage the deployments on various clouds. Several research and development collaborative projects that are dealing with deployable services on multiple clouds were started in 2010ths and going on [12–14]. Some worth mentioning among them are mOSAIC, Optimis, Cloud4SOA, PaaSage, Cloudify and a few others. Purpose of those projects is the development of an open-source platform that will serve as an environment for competition between cloud providers.

Also, many papers focus on the improvement of live Virtual Machine (VM) migration strategies [15,16]. Live migration is an essential feature of virtualization, which allows migrating VMs from one location to another without suspending VMs. A VM can be migrated seamlessly and transparently from one physical machine (source host) to another (destination host), while the VM is still running during migration. Researchers try to improve the migration process by minimizing total data transferred, total migration time and downtime. This might be significant when considering the next steps in the overall Open Cloud Exchange strategy.

3   Task Scheduling Implementation in Popular Private Cloud Systems and Its Extensibility Possibilities

IaaS private cloud services can be implemented by using many commercial and open-source software products. To implement resource scheduling strategies on IaaS cloud abstraction level, the algorithm should be integrated into cloud platform software stack. In this chapter architectures and task scheduling systems of three popular open-source projects, most often encountered in reviewed literature will be compared according to three aspects:

- Main components of cloud platform;
- Implemented task scheduling algorithms;
- Possibilities of implementation of custom task scheduling policies.

This chapter would be beneficial to anybody considering private or hybrid cloud solution implementation or implementing custom scheduling optimization algorithm on popular cloud computing platforms.

3.1   OpenStack Cloud Computing Suit

OpenStack cloud computing suit consists of six core services:

- Nova - compute instance lifecycle management;
- Neutron - network management;
- Swift - object storage;
- Cinder - block storage;
- Keystone - authentication and authorization token provider;
- Glance - image service.

In addition, there are 13 optional services, providing additional functionality, at the moment [17].

A new virtual machine resource request goes to Nova API service, then is forwarded to Nova scheduler and allocated on one of Nova compute nodes. Nova scheduler chooses host for VM allocation by simple, but extendable, two-step algorithm. On the first step, a list of all available hosts is filtered through pre-configured filter list. Filters can be based on available hypervisor resources (ComputeCapabilitiesFilter, RamFilter, DiskFilter), VM placement (DifferentHostFilter, SameHostFilter, AvailabilityZoneFilter) or flexibly configured (JsonFilter). JsonFilter supports comparison ($=, <, >, <=, >=$), boolean algebra (not, or, and) operators and variables, defining free and total ram, free disk space, total number and number of used virtual CPUs. On the second step, all hosts, complying requirements of all filters are sorted according to weights. By default six weighers are used: RAMWeigher, DiskWeigher, MetricsWeigher, IoOpsWeigher, ServerGroupSoftAffinityWeigher, ServerGroupSoftAntiAffinityWeigher. RAM and Disk weigher names are self-explanatory, metrics weight allows to evaluate expressions, defined by administrators, based on nova-compute host metrics, such as system CPU time, user CPU time, etc. Group affinity or anti-affinity weighers allow controlling distribution of virtual machine groups on hypervisor hosts. It allows to schedule VMs with high network traffic in between to the same host or to distribute members of application cluster in different hosts for high availability. With computed weights, Nova scheduler tries to provision resources from the start of the sorted list.

3.2 Eucalyptus Private Cloud

Eucalyptus private cloud consists of five main components:

- The Cloud Controllers - a central management service, providing EC2 compatible API and managing all private cloud.
- Walrus - a storage component, compatible with S3 standard.
- The Cluster Controller - a component acting as a front end of every cluster and managing virtual machine execution and SLAs per cluster.
- The Storage Controller - a service managing block volume storage and snapshots.
- The Node Controller - a component, managing single hypervisor.

In addition, there is one optional component - the VMware Broker, allowing to add VMware vSphere (vCenter or ESXI) to Eucalyptus cloud. Eucalyptus cluster controller implements greedy, roundrobin and powersave scheduling policies, also allows user-defined policy implementation through user scheduler [18]. Availability models of Eucalyptus architectures are analysed in [19].

3.3   OpenNebula Cloud

OpenNebula cloud consists of Front-End node, Hypervizor-enabled hosts, data-stores and physical networks. On the Front-End node there are three main services:

- Oned - management daemon of cluster nodes, virtual networks, virtual machines, users, groups and storage datastores.
- Mm_sched - OpenNebula's architecture defines this service as a separate process that can be started independently of oned (it is however started automatically when you start the opennebula service).
- Sunstone-server - web interface of OpenNebula.

In addition, some advanced services providing application provisioning, monitoring, EC2 API compatibility are available.

OpenNebula default scheduling algorithm consists of the following steps:

- If VM consumes more image datastore than is available, it will remain in 'pending' state.
- The hosts, that do not meet requirements or have not enough resources are filtered out. The same process is repeated for system datastores.
- Same process is repeated for system datastores;
- All remaining hosts and datastores are ranked according to configurable SCED_RANK and SCHED_DS_RANK expressions.
- Resources with higher rank are used first to allocate VMs.

In addition, OpenNebula supports resources rescheduling on demand. Also, the architecture allows replacing default scheduling service with third party implementation, because all services communicate through an XML-RPC interface [20].

3.4   Comparison of Open Source Cloud Platforms

All popular open-source cloud platforms implement a heuristical approach to resource scheduling, the default configuration does not implement more sophisticated algorithms Table 1. Basic algorithm extension for OpenStack and OpenNebula can be achieved by configuration of default scheduling subsystem, all platforms can support user redefined scheduling subsystems. Notable that only OpenNebula supports resource rescheduling on demand.

Table 1. Comparison of open source cloud platforms.

OpenStack	Eucalyptus	OpenNebula
Main services		
– **Nova: compute**[a] – Neutron: network – Swift: object storage – Cinder: block storage – Keystone: authentication and authorization – Glance: image service	– Cloud Controllers – Walrus: object storage – **Cluster Controller**[a] – Storage Controller – Node Controller	– Oned - management – **Mm_sched-scheduler**[a] – Sunstone-server: web interface
Implemented scheduling strategies		
Two step process: – Filtering out of unsuitable supervisors according to available resources and VM placement – Ranking of available hypervisors according to available resources and VM placement	Available heuristics: – Greedy – RoudRobin – Powersave	Two step process: – Filtering out of unsuitable supervisors according to available resources – Ranking according to configurable expressions
Scheduling policy extension method		
– JSON based custom filter – Custom user defined filters and weighters implemented on python	– Custom user scheduler, implemented on C language	– Default scheduler can be replaced with custom, implementing XML-RPG based interface

[a] *Components responsible for task scheduling*

4   Interoperability of Cloud Systems

The cloud computing platform can be deployed as a private cloud on-premises or in dedicated data centre space, as a public service or as a combination of both. In this section we will review similarities and differences of most popular private cloud implementation platforms and their compatibility with public cloud solutions based on two criteria:

– Compatibility of virtual machine images;
– Supported Application Programming Interfaces (API).

A provided comparison would benefit anyone, planning to implement hybrid cloud solutions, designing cloud-native systems or customising workloads for cloud computing environments. This particularly concerns those cloud consumers who are seeking for a possibility to extend computing resources by adding more VMs (horizontally scale) to the same cloud or embracing additional clouds. An extension would be available by using the existing cloud API or compatible API of the external cloud. Figure 1 illustrates the principle of VM migration.

For private cloud deployment, there are various options for software stacks. From open-source, a leader currently is an OpenStack project, backed up by

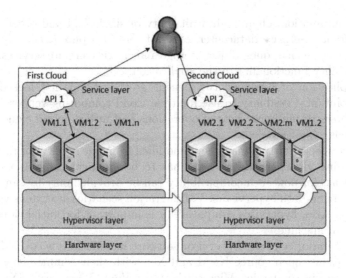

Fig. 1. Open-source clouds extension via VM migration functionality.

more than 150 companies. Also, private cloud implementation is possible using Apache CloudStack, OpenNebula and few others.

From commercial vendors, one of the leading implementations is VMware vCloud, based on leading VMware's virtualization technologies. Microsoft offers a virtualization platform Hyper V with integration with System Center services, offering some base private cloud functionalities. Many commercial vendors offer their supported versions of OpenStack.

The first company, which offered a public cloud service, was Amazon with AWS (Amazon Web Services). Now almost all leading IT infrastructure and service companies offer at least some public cloud-based services, such as Google APP platform, Microsoft Azure, RackSpace's OpenStack based services and many more to count.

A simple IaaS cloud architecture consists of management services and hypervisors, dedicated to run virtual machines of cloud customers. Modern cloud platforms can add much more services, such as network, storage virtualization, network load balancing, object storage, etc.

There are several initiatives to standardize cloud computing interfaces, one of most actively developed is Open Cloud Computing Interface [21], unfortunately, the support of open standards in cloud computing platforms is in a very early stage. Cloud standardization initiatives are also reviewed in corresponding [5] section, [4] discuss in detail scheduling of virtual machines in multiple providers and federated cloud environments.

Despite some common principles, architectures of cloud implementation can differ a lot. Starting from four hypervisor implementations (ESXi, HiperV, XEN, KVM), offering different virtual hardware interfaces to hosted VM's. Having different focuses and goals - some platforms extends usual enterprise architecture with automation, offers high availability of single VM and other services, expected from enterprise datacenter, others focus on a pure cloud application, offering services such as ques, object storage and elastic compute services, leaving high availability functionality to the application.

An application or workload can benefit greatly if it is not locked to one provider solution. Possibility to use multiple cloud computing vendors ar technologies allows to minimise costs of operations and utilise hybrid cloud deployment options.

To move specific virtual machine unmodified from one hypervisor to another, the underlying virtual hardware layer has to be identical. As it is mentioned above, at least for now such compatibility can be provided only by same hypervisor software on both hypervisors. VM migration scenarios are extensively analysed in [16]. Also, hypervisor compatibility is important for initial cloud image of the virtual machine.

The vast majority of the hypervisor software installations is covered by four implementations: open source KVM and Xen with their commercial modifications from various companies, Microsoft's Hyper-V and VMware's ESXi. In table Table 2 the support of these hypervisors in popular private cloud implementation platforms is presented.

Table 2. Supported hypervisors

Cloud environments	Hypervisors			
	KVM	Xen	Hyper-V	ESXi
Apache CloudStack [22]	+	+	+	
Eucalyptus [23]	+	−	−	+
OpenStack [24]	+	+	+	+
vmWare vCloud [25]	−	−	−	+
OpenNebula [26]	+	+	−	+
Nimbus [27]	−	+	−	−

VMware vCloud can be distinguished from other implementations as an only commercial private cloud platform, with closed architecture, all other five implementations are open source.

The direct migration of VM is not necessary for native cloud applications to migrate to another cloud provider or to balance load between two or more cloud infrastructures. If load balancing and elasticity are implemented in application logic, the application can utilise cloud service through web services and available APIs.

In the Table 3 supported APIs for computing and storage resources of most popular private cloud implementation platforms and three most popular commercial public cloud providers - Google, Amazon and Microsoft are presented. An API is important for cloud application and resource broker integration with

Table 3. Supported APIs

Cloud platform	Supported API
Apache CloudStack	– Native – AWS EC2 – AWS S3
Amazon Web Services API	– AWS EC2 – AWS S3
Eucalyptus	– AWS EC2 – AWS S3
Google Compute Engine	– Native
OpenStack API	– Native – AWS EC2 – AWS S3
VMware vCloud API	– Native
OpenNebula	– Native – EC2 through econe-server
Nimbus	– AWS EC2 – AWS S3
Azure	– Native

the platform because it is directly used for dynamic resource provisioning and management.

From presented comparison a conclusion can be drawn, that most commonly supported interfaces are Amazon's EC2 and S3 and they are implemented in most open-source private cloud implementations, but all three public cloud providers support only their native standards.

5   Conclusions and Future Works

The survey revealed the prevalence of resource scheduling and service deployment algorithms within some popular open-source clouds. To answer some end-user demand for making changes in the scheduling policies for the IaaS application, the possibility of resource scheduling algorithms customization was analyzed. The results show that all popular open-source cloud platforms implement a heuristic approach to resource scheduling, the default configuration does not implement more sophisticated algorithms. Basic algorithm extension for Open-Stack and OpenNebula can be achieved by configuration of default schedul-ing subsystem, all platforms can support user redefined scheduling subsystems. Notable that only OpenNebula supports resource rescheduling on demand.

Development of multi-cloud systems with shared services requires evalua-tion of the cloud service interoperability between different vendor clouds. It was important in our survey to find out whether the different clouds use the same hypervisor and what APIs could be used for automating VM migration tasks. From this point of view, both CloudStack and OpenStack are highly flexible and support multiple hypervisors and APIs. As to the diversity of hypervisors support, Nimbus seems to be the most restricted cloud. Selection of suitable API is less problematic since all popular clouds use AWS EC2 API.

Some good initiatives to standardise cloud computing interfaces were started, including the most prominent Open Cloud Computing Interface, which specifies a protocol and accompanying APIs for many kinds of cloud management tasks, including deployment, autonomic scaling, monitoring and more. However, the survey reveals that the major public cloud service providers (Amazon Web Services, Google Cloud Platform, and Microsoft Azure) don't support unification and standardisation efforts. By supporting native only APIs which are incompatible with other APIs, they further a vendor lock-in policy.

Future research will be focused on service deployment algorithms investigation, seeking for the best-suited algorithms individually for the end-user and service provide.

References

1. Demchenko, Y., et al.: Open Cloud eXchange (OCX): architecture and functional components. In: 2013 IEEE International Conference on Cloud Computing Technology and Science, pp. 81–87 (2013)
2. Ali, H., Moawad, R., Hosnil, A.A.F.: Cloud interoperability broker (CIB) for data migration in SaaS. Future Comput. Inform. J. 1(1–2), 27–34 (2017)
3. Chauhan, S.S., Pilli, E.S., Joshi, R.C., Singh, G., Govil, M.C.: Brokering in interconnected cloud computing environments: a survey. J. Parallel Distrib. Comput. 133, 193–209 (2019)
4. Rubio-Montero, A.J., Huedob, E., Mayo-García, R.: Scheduling multiple virtual environments in cloud federations for distributed calculations. Future Gener. Comput. Syst. 74, 90–103 (2017)
5. D'Agostino, D., Galizia, A., Clematis, A., Quarati, A.: A QoS-aware broker for hybrid clouds. Computing 95, 89–109 (2013)
6. Huynh, H.-L., Tran, V.-D., Nguyen, H.-D., Hu, Z., Le, T.-V., Huynh, Q.-T.: Auto-updating portable application model of multi-cloud marketplace through bidirectional transformations system. Front. Artif. Intell. Appl. Adv. Technol. Ind. Intell. Softw. Methodol. Tools Tech. 318, 11–24 (2019)
7. Juan-Verdejo, A., Surajbali, B.: XaaS multi-cloud marketplace architecture enacting the industry 4.0 concepts. In: DoCEIS 2016: Technological Innovation for Cyber-Physical Systems, pp. 11–23 (2016)
8. Long, H.H., Duc, N.H., Vinh, L.T.: Matchmaking for multi-cloud marketplace application. ICT Res. Res. Dev. Inf. Commun. Technol. 2019(1), 31–42 (2019)
9. García, A.L., Castillo, E.F., Fernández, P.O.: Standards forenabling heterogeneous IaaS cloud federations. Comput. Stand. Interfaces 47, 19–23 (2016)
10. Kaur, K., Sharma, S., Kahlon, K.S.: Interoperability and portability approaches in inter-connected clouds: a review. ACM Comput. Surv. 50(4) (2017). Article 49
11. Desnoyers, P., Hennessey, J., Holden, B., Krieger, O., Rudolph, L., Young, A.: Using open stack for an open cloud exchange (OCX). In: 2015 IEEE International Conference on Cloud Engineering (IC2E), vol. 48, no. 53, pp. 9–13 (2015)

12. Petcu, D.: Multi-cloud: expectations and current approaches. In: MultiCloud 2013: Proceedings of the 2013 International Workshop on Multi-Cloud Applications and Federated Clouds, pp. 1–6 (2013)
13. Saatkamp, K., Breitenbücher, U., Kopp, O., Leymann, F.: Topology splitting and matching for multi-cloud deployments. In: Proceedings of the 7th International Conference on Cloud Computing and Services Science (CLOSER 2017), pp. 247–258 (2017)
14. Saatkamp, K., Breitenbücher, U., Kopp, O., Leymann, F.: Method, formalization, and algorithms to split topology models for distributed cloud application deployments. Computing **102**(2), 343–363 (2019). https://doi.org/10.1007/s00607-019-00721-8
15. Noshy, M., Ibrahim, A., Ali, H.A.: Optimization of live virtual machine migration in cloud computing: a survey and future directions. J. Netw. Comput. Appl. **110**, 1–10 (2018)
16. Sun, G., Liao, D., Anandc, V., Zhaoa, D., Yua, H.: A new technique for efficient live migration of multiple virtual machines. Future Gener. Comput. Syst. **55**, 74–86 (2016)
17. OpenStack Homepage. https://www.openstack.org/software/project-navigator/. Accessed 14 Mar 2020
18. Eucalyptus github. https://www.openstack.org/software/project-navigator/. Accessed 7 Jan 2020
19. Dantas, J., Matos, R., Araujo, J., Maciel, P.: Eucalyptus-based private clouds: availability modeling and comparison to the cost of a public cloud. Computing **97**(11), 1121–1140 (2015). https://doi.org/10.1007/s00607-015-0447-8
20. Opennebula Homepage. http://docs.opennebula.org/4.12/administration/references/schg.html. Accessed 7 Jan 2020
21. Open Cloud Computing Interface Home page. http://occi-wg.org/
22. Cloudstack Homepage. http://docs.cloudstack.apache.org/projects/cloudstack-release-notes/en/4.6.0/compat.html. Accessed 7 Jan 2020
23. Eucalyptus Homepage. https://support.eucalyptus.com/hc/en-us/articles/205143059-Compatibility-Matrices. Accessed 7 Jan 2020
24. Openstack Homepage. https://wiki.openstack.org/wiki/HypervisorSupportMatrix. Accessed 7 Jan 2020
25. VMware Homepage. https://code.vmware.com/apis/72/vcloud-director. Accessed 7 Jan 2020
26. Opennebula Homepage. https://opennebula.org/about/faq/#toggle-id-8. Accessed 7 Jan 2020
27. Nimbus Homepage. http://www.nimbusproject.org/docs/2.2/faq.html. Accessed 7 Jan 2020

A Novel Model Driven Framework for Image Enhancement and Object Recognition

Yawar Rasheed[✉], Muhammad Abbas, Muhammad Waseem Anwar,
Wasi Haider Butt, and Urooj Fatima

Department of Computer and Software Engineering, College of E&ME, National University of
Sciences and Technology (NUST), H-12, Islamabad, Pakistan
{yawar.rasheed18,wasi,urooj.fatima}@ce.ceme.edu.pk,
{m.abbas,waseemanwar}@ceme.nust.edu.pk

Abstract. Modern technological trends like Internet of Things (IoT's) essentially require prompt development of software systems. To manage this, Model Driven Architecture (MDA) is frequently applied for development of different systems like industry automation, medical, surveillance, tracking and security etc. Image processing is an integral part of such systems. Particularly, image enhancement and classification operations are mandatory in order to effectively recognize objects for different purposes. Currently, such critical image processing operations are not managed through MDA and low level implementations are performed distinctly during system development. This severely delays the system development due to integration issues. Furthermore, system testing becomes problematic as few components of systems are developed through MDA and image processing operations are implemented in isolation. This article introduces a novel framework i.e. MIEORF – Model-driven Image Enhancement and Object Recognition Framework. Particularly, a meta-model is proposed, that allows modeling and visualization of complex image processing and object recognition tasks. Subsequently, an open source customized tree editor (developed using Eclipse Modeling Framework (EMF)) and graphical modeling tool/workbench (developed using Sirius) have been developed (both distributable via eclipse plugin). Consequently, the proposed framework allows modeling and graphical visualization of major image processing operations. Moreover, it provides strong grounds for model transformation operations e.g. Model to Text Transformations (M2T) using Acceleo for generating executable Matlab code. Furthermore, it systematically combines MDA and image processing concepts which are detailed enough to be easily integrated into wide variety of systems such as industrial automation, medical, surveillance, security and biometrics etc. The feasibility of proposed framework is demonstrated via real world medical imagery case study. The results prove that the proposed framework provides a complete solution for modeling and visualization of image processing tasks and highly effective for MDA based systems development.

Keywords: Digital image processing · Model Driven Architecture · Image enhancement · Graphical modeling · Object recognition · Meta modeling · Sirius tool · Model based systems

© Springer Nature Switzerland AG 2020
A. Lopata et al. (Eds.): ICIST 2020, CCIS 1283, pp. 14–25, 2020.
https://doi.org/10.1007/978-3-030-59506-7_2

1 Introduction

Digital Image Processing is the processing of digital images with the help of digital computers. Broadly, it encompasses Low-Level, Mid-Level and High-Level processing tasks while dealing with noise reduction, contrast setting and sharpening to attributes extraction, object recognition and 'making sense' of the recognized objects [1–3]. Image enhancement and object recognition are interesting areas of digital image processing due to the poor contrast and noise in most of the real life images obtained from various systems i.e. satellite imagery, medical imagery, biometrics, surveillance and security etc. Image enhancement primarily deals with improving the quality and bringing out obscured details for human perception as well as for automated processing of specific computer based applications. Object recognition, on the other hand deals with recognizing objects and making sense of the recognized objects and is generally preceded by some image enhancement tasks. Over period of time, various spatial and frequency domain techniques of image enhancement have evolved [6, 7]. Likely, accuracy of object recognition algorithms and classifiers have also improved tremendously. With the increasing sophistication of image enhancement and object recognition in digital image processing, the complexity of development of corresponding systems have also increased.

Essence of Model Driven Engineering (MDE)/Model Driven Architecture (MDA) lies in its capability of achieving abstraction and reducing complexity of software development via modeling. Models and transformations are considered as primary artifacts in MDE/MDA for automated design, development/implementation, testing and model based evolution of software systems [15, 16]. Model based development starts with developing a platform independent model (PIM)/Domain Specific Language (DSL)/Meta-model. Various domains have benefited from this powerful abstraction approach. For example, Iqra at el. [24] proposed a novel MDA framework for industrial automation. In another study [25], a novel MDA approach is introduced for embedded systems. Similarly, there exist several studies [26, 27] where MDA is applied to simplify the development of complex and larger systems. In addition to state-of-the-art approaches, there exist comprehensive MDA based industry oriented standards like Unified Architecture Framework (UAF) [28] for the development of diverse and large systems.

Image processing is an integral part of modern systems like industrial automation, medical, surveillance and security etc. The development complexity of such systems is frequently managed through MDA. However, for image processing operations like image enhancement and object recognition, the low level implementations are performed separately during system development. This severely delays the system development as few components of systems are developed through MDA and image processing operations are implemented in isolation. Although there exist few studies [19–22] where image processing is explored in the context of MDA, these solutions have very limited scope and cannot be applied/integrated in MDA development flow for larger systems. Consequently, the state-of-the-art MDA approach to effectively support the image processing operations for object recognition is hard to find in literature (Sect. 2). Therefore, there is a need of comprehensive MDA approach to perform critical image processing operations with simplicity. Furthermore, such approach should allow the seamless integration with other MDA based system development approaches/frameworks for the execution of image processing tasks.

This article introduces a novel framework i.e. MIEORF – Model-driven Image Enhancement and Object Recognition Framework, where MDA is utilized to perform major image processing operations. Particularly, a meta-model is proposed to represent core image enhancement and object recognition concepts at higher abstraction level. Subsequently, an open source tree editor (developed using EMF) and graphical modeling tool (developed using Sirius), distributable via eclipse plugin, have been developed. Consequently, the MIEORF allows modeling and visualization of major image processing operations with simplicity. Moreover, it provides strong grounds for model transformation operations. Furthermore, it systematically combines MDA and image processing concepts detailed enough to be easily integrated into wide variety of systems such as industrial automation, medical, surveillance, security and biometrics systems. The feasibility of proposed framework is demonstrated via real world medical imagery case study. The results prove that the proposed framework provides a complete solution for modeling and visualization of image processing tasks and highly effective for MDA based systems development. An overview of the development process of MIEORF is depicted in Fig. 1. Initially the selected literature (Sect. 2) was reviewed to get an insight of various concepts related to image enhancement/object recognition and Model Driven Software Engineering (MDSE). Integration of these concepts is achieved in the form of MIEORF (Sect. 3) which composes of a meta-model/M2 level Ecore model (Sect. 3.1), a tree editor and Sirius graphical modeling tool for M1 level Modeling (Sect. 3.2). MIEORF is validated via real world medical imagery case study (Sect. 4) by creating M1 level models of case study scenario using our tree editor and Sirius graphical modeling tool.

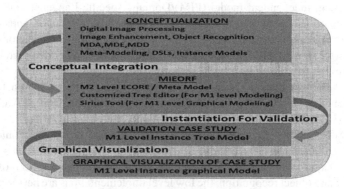

Fig. 1. Proposed methodology

2   Literature Review

The domain of digital image processing is characterized by processing of digital images with the help of digital computer. It encompasses low-level (noise reduction, setting contrast, sharpening), mid-level (features extraction) and high level processing (making sense of recognized objects) [1]. Image enhancement is one of the most common and interesting areas [1, 2] which deals with bringing out the obscured details for analysis

[1–3]. Due to the poor contrast and noise in most of the medical, satellite, aerial and real life images, actual information of interest may not be properly extracted from the images [4]. Hence image enhancement improves the quality of an image for visual perception as well as for automated processing of computer applications [5]. Primarily, enhancement techniques fall in two broad categories i.e. spatial and frequency domain enhancements [6, 7]. Various spatial enhancement techniques are highlighted by authors of [1, 6, 7] i.e. image negatives, thresholding, log transformations, power law transformations, contrast stretching, histogram equalization/matching, subtraction, averaging, Laplacian and Sobel filters. Some of the applications of image processing/enhancement are highlighted by authors of [6, 8–10] which are forensics, atmospheric sciences, satellite imagery, medical imagery, atmospheric sciences, astrophotography, surveillance and tracking systems, industrial automation, critical infrastructure security, biometrics and oceanography etc. Similarly recognition of targeted objects from an image [11], irrespective of various distortions (scale, rotation, and occlusion) and noise is a critical requirement [12]. Two broad categories have been reported i.e. appearance and feature based techniques for object recognition. These techniques are further categorized into variety of specialized techniques [1, 13]. Authors of [1] and [14] reported various classifiers for classifying objects that include KNN, Bayes Decision Theory and Neural Networks etc.

The advent of MDSE, in contrast to code centric approaches, is marked by achieving abstraction and reducing complexity of software systems through modeling [15]. Models and transformations are the primary artifacts and major corporate assets for automated design, development and other activities of the model based development of software [16]. The process of MDA/Model Driven Development (MDD) starts by defining/developing a formal model (Meta-model/Domain Model/Platform Independent Model) either using general purpose modeling language i.e. UML or defining a Domain Specific Language (DSL) using Ecore Modeling Framework. Various domains have benefited from this power abstraction approach including information systems [17], software enterprises [18], industrial automation [24] and embedded systems [25]. Combining the domains of modeling and image processing, authors of [19] integrated the techniques of digital water marking (an information hiding technique) to MDD life cycle for intellectual property protection of models. Authors of [20, 21] introduced a novel tool for extracting UML class models from images. 23 features are extracted by authors of [22] from images for classification of UML diagrams. Authors of [23] introduced a novel idea of model based shopping of various items from malls.

In summary, the reviewed literature reveals the necessity of image enhancement and object recognition tasks in the context of digital image processing for various domains. The reviewed literature also highlighted the importance of MDSE in reducing complexity of software development. Most of the reviewed literature focuses on the concepts of digital image processing and MDSE distantly and very little integration of the two domain have been noticed. The literature in no way, substantially or specifically proposes any meta-model or model driven approach for image processing operations. Although there exist few studies [19–22] where image processing is explored in the context of MDA, these solutions have very limited scope and cannot be applied/integrated in MDA development flow for larger systems. Consequently, the state-of-the-art MDA approach to effectively support the image processing operations for objective recognition is hard to find in literature. Therefore, there is a need of comprehensive MDA approach to perform critical image processing operations with simplicity. Furthermore, such approach should allow the seamless integration with other MDA based system development approaches/frameworks for the execution of image processing tasks.

3 MIEORF - Model-Driven Image Enhancement and Object Recognition Framework

MIEORF primarily composes a meta-model (M2 level Ecore Model) and its implementation in the form of tool support which includes a customized tree editor (for M1 level modeling in tree view) and a Sirius based graphical modeling workbench (for M1 level graphical modeling and visualizations).

3.1 Proposed Meta-Model

Proposed meta-model (Fig. 2, ieors.ecore) defines meta-classes which are required to model image enhancement and object recognition tasks in the context of digital image processing, computer vision and pattern recognition for wide variety of domains and applications. For better organization, it is further subdivided into two sub packages namely Spatial Image Enhancement and Object Recognition with concepts relevant to their names. Its possible integration with various systems such as Medical Imagery Systems, Surveillance and Tracking Systems, Critical Infrastructure Security System etc. has also been shown abstractly thorough composition relationships.

Description. IEORS (root level concept) composes of a working folder which further composes many images and datasets. The data set itself may composes many images. This means that for an image to be processed, it must be contained either by a data set or working folder itself. Image Buffer represents the concept of temporary storage for images for further processing and is composed by IEORS. Description of two sub-packages is as under:-

Spatial Image Enhancement. This package contains the concepts relevant to the enhancement of images in spatial domain (Primarily representing various transformation on images such as gamma correction). IES is the main concept of this sub-package. IEORS composes zero or one IES (Image Enhancement System) concept, which composes the concept of pre-processing (through zero or one relationship). Preprocessing is the major abstract class of this package and all other subclasses are directly or indirectly specialized from it. This class contains operations related to reading and showing of images, converting a color image to grey scale and resizing an image.

Due to the concepts of inheritance, all the attributes and operation of this class are available to its subclasses as well. Any Preprocessing task may be performed on individual image or a complete data set containing multiple images (as shown by the respective relationships). Similarly a partially processed image may be placed in an Image Buffer. The concept of Preprocessing is specialized by the abstract concepts of *Point* processing (representing pixel by pixel operation), *Histogram* Processing (representing processing

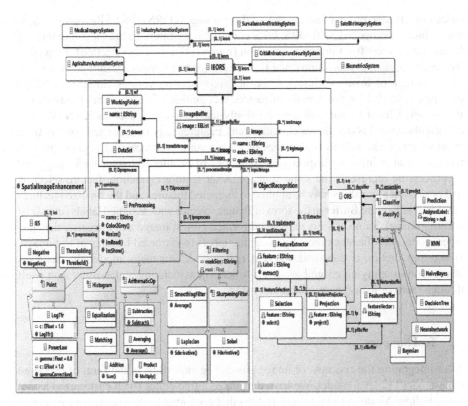

Fig. 2. Proposed meta model of MIEORF

on frequencies of occurrence of grey levels in images), *Arithmetic Op* (operation) and *Filtering* (representing application of filters/masks or kernel of specific size on images by sliding window operations). Corresponding to various point processing techniques, the concepts of *Point* processing is further specialized by the concepts of *Negative* (representing Image Negatives), *Thresholding* (assigning the minimum grey value to pixels with values lower than a certain threshold and vice versa), *Log Tfr* (transformation) and *Power Law* transformations for gamma correction of images. *Histogram* Processing is specialized by the concepts of Histogram *Equalization* and *Matching*. *Arithmetic Op* is specialized by Image *Subtraction* (for subtracting an image from the blurred version of itself for highlighting certain details) and *Averaging* (for removal of noise and smoothing of images). Out of various filters in use, our proposed meta-model has incorporated concepts of *Smoothing Filter* and *Sharpening Filter* which are specialized from Abstract class *Filtering*. The *Sharpening Filter* is further specialized by *Laplacian* and *Sobel* filters that uses second and first derivatives for the purpose of sharpening.

Object Recognition. This package contains concepts which may be used for automation/model based development of such systems which recognizes objects preceded by certain preprocessing of images. This package includes concepts pertaining to features based object recognition. Main concept of this package is ORS (Object Recognition System) which is composed by IEORS. ORS composes of Feature Extractor (for extracting features of interest from images), Selection (representing feature selection), Projection (representing feature projection), and Feature Buffer (for temporary storage of features or for storage of features vector), Classifier (representing various classifiers evolved over period of time in the context of pattern recognition). The concept of classifier is further specialized by some of the commonly used classifiers such as KNN (K nearest neighbors) and Naive Bayes classifiers etc. Features may be extracted directly from training images as well as test images or after certain preprocessing is performed on test and training images. Respective associations of Feature Extractor with Image and Preprocessing represents the same concept. After feature extraction, feature selection and projection algorithms may be applied to extracted features and the finalized features are stored in Feature Buffer in the form of features vector with assigned labels (in case of training image). Same process may be performed on test image and thereafter the classifier/model classifies the object by assigning labels to extracted features of test image. Hence a prediction is done and object is recognized. Our meta- model also achieves abstraction in applying ensembles of classifiers by associating a classifiers with itself through (zero or many) ensemble relationship.

3.2 Tool Support

After integrating the concepts of image processing and MDA in the form of proposed meta-model/M2 level model. We have developed a tree editor (with customized icons) using Eclipse Modeling Framework (EMF) that conforms to the concepts of proposed meta-model. Our tree editor allows M1 level modeling (with extension '*.ieors') and may be used for creating models for different scenarios of image processing tasks. This editor will be subsequently used for creating M1 level model of our case study scenario related to medical imagery domain (Sect. 4/Fig. 4). After creating tree editor, we have developed a Sirius based tool/work bench that allows graphical modeling and visualization (M1 level). Using this Sirius tool, the instance models (instance of our proposed meta-model) may be created and graphically visualized in a user friendly environment with drag drop palette facility. Case study scenario has also been modeled/visualized using our Sirius workbench (Sect. 4/Fig. 5). Our proposed meta-model, tree editor and Sirius tool are publically available at [29].

4 Case Study

We now intend to validate our meta-model via real world case study pertaining to medical imagery domain (Nuclear whole body bone scan) [1]. We have developed an M1 level instance model in runtime-New_Configuration of Obeo designer using our tree editor. This M1 level model maps the requirements of given case study by instantiating relevant concepts of our proposed meta-model and setting relationships amongst instances accordingly.

4.1 Case Study Narrative

Various image enhancement techniques are often used in combination to one another to highlight the features of interest. Figure 3A, shows an image of nuclear whole body bone scan which is used to diagnose tumors and infections in bones. As noticed, due to the high noise content and narrow dynamic range of grey levels, it is not possible for the medical staff to read the relevant details. Our aim is to use various image enhancement techniques for sharpening it, so that skeletal details can be brought out from the image for effective diagnosis. The technique involves steps i.e. *Step a*. Taking Laplacian of the original image. *Step b*. Adding the original and Laplacian image of step a. *Step c*. Sobel of original image. *Step d*. Sobel of image of step c to get a smoothed gradient image. *Step e*. Obtain a mask image by taking product of images of step b and d. *Step f*. Obtain a sharper image by adding original image and the image of step e. *Step g*. Applying power law transformations, with gamma = 0.5 and c = 1, to image of step f in order to obtain final result which is represented by Fig. 3B. We may notice a prominent enhancement of original image by comparing Fig. 3A and B.

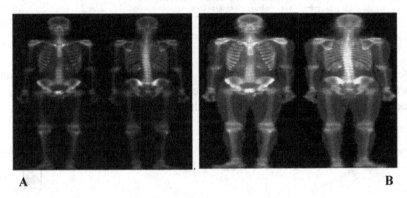

A   **B**

Fig. 3. Original image bone scan vs enhanced image

4.2 MIEORF in Action

Concepts of our proposed meta-model, which are instantiated to map the case study scenario may be noticed in Fig. 4. Attributes of these instances are also set as per the requirements of the case study. First of all an Instance of Medical Imagery System has been created which contains an instance of IEORS. Thereafter eight instances of Image created. Value of name attribute have been set to such strings that describes the task which has been performed on image. After that, instance of Laplacian Filter has been created which is associated with Image A (original image) as its input image and Image B as its processed image. Similarly instance of Addition Operation is associated with Image A and B as input images and Image C as processed image (this depicts that addition operation that performs pixel by pixel addition). Instance of Sobel Filter is associated with Image C as its input image and Image D as its Processed Images. A

5×5 Averaging Filter takes Image D as its input image and produces Image E. Product Operation produces Image F after multiplying images C and E. A second Addition Operation sums Images A and F and produces Image G. Finally Instance of Power Law takes Image G, as its input and produces Image H with gamma = 0.5 and C = 1. Image H i.e. enhanced image is visualized as Fig. 3B.

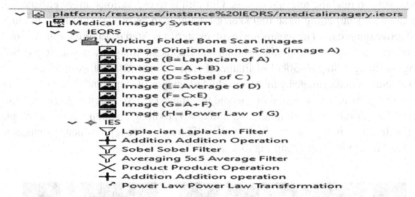

Fig. 4. M1 level instance model of case study scenario using tree editor

We have also graphically visualized this M1 level Instance Model via our Sirius workbench/tool as depicted in Fig. 5. This prototype tool allows the users to model/visualize any complex image enhancement scenario with the help of its palette.

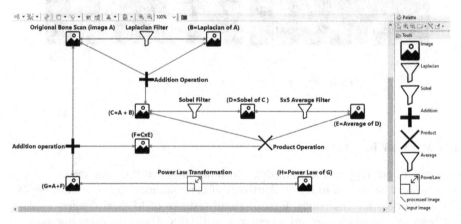

Fig. 5. M1 level instance model of case study scenario using Sirius workbench/tool

5   Discussion and Limitations

This article introduces MIEORF – Model-driven Image Enhancement and Object Recognition Framework to enable the execution of image processing operations through MDA development flow. This is a major milestone, as a comprehensive and open source model driven framework for image processing operations is hard to find in literature. There exist few well-known image processing solutions like Simulink image processing toolbox [30] and eclipse ImageN [31]. In contrast to Simulink toolbox, MIEORF deals with the pure Platform Independent Models (PIMs) that can be transformed to different target models as per requirements while Simulink toolbox is only effective in given environment. Furthermore, Simulink toolbox is proprietary while MIEORF is freely available. On the other hand, ImageN and MIEORF shares certain common features like both are based on object oriented approach and freely available. However, MIEORF operates on higher abstraction level while ImageN performs image processing tasks in java language at lower abstraction level. Therefore, MIEORF is more effective in terms of usability. Another significance of MIEORF with respect to Simulink toolbox and ImageN is that, it is highly interoperable and can be employed/integrated with other MDA frameworks. For example, the meta-model of MIEORF can be integrated easily with other MDA frameworks/MDA based systems for the execution of image processing tasks. For such integration, a particular Domain Specific Modeling Language (DSML) can be developed by using the concepts of proposed meta-model.

To summarize, MIEORF provides several benefits as follows: 1) Flexibility: It is highly flexible as it contains the concepts detailed enough to be easily integrated with other MDA frameworks for image enhancement and object recognition tasks. Moreover, it can be extended and enhanced to incorporate more detailed concepts related to image processing. 2) Model Transformation Support: MIEORF supports both Model to Model (M2M) and Text (M2T) transformations. Particularly, the meta-model of MIEORF may serve as source meta-model to perform M2M transformations in ATL (ATLAS Transformation Language). On the other hand, M2T transformation can be implemented in Acceleo using the concepts of MIEORF meta-model to transform M1 level models (developed using tree editor or Sirius tool) into low level implementations like Matlab code. 3) Tool Support: As part of MIEORF, a Sirius graphical modeling workbench/tool and a tree editor have been developed. Both the tool and tree editor are distributable via eclipse plugin and can be easily installed in any eclipse IDE/Obeo Designer.

Currently, MIEORF supports basic image processing tasks like image enhancement in spatial domain and feature based object recognition while advanced operations like frequency domain enhancements and correlation based object recognition are not supported. Such missing image processing concepts can be incorporated in MIEORF through the extension of meta-model. Similarly, no transformations (M2M/M2T) have currently been written for MIEORF to generate target low level implementations. However, such transformations can be conveniently written as per requirements because MIEORF supports both M2M and M2T transformations.

6   Conclusion and Future Work

This article introduces a novel MIEORF – Model-driven Image Enhancement and Object Recognition Framework, where MDA is utilized to perform major image processing operations. Particularly, a meta-model is proposed to represent core image enhancement and object recognition concepts at higher abstraction level. Subsequently, an open source tree editor (developed using EMF) and graphical modeling tool (developed using Sirius), distributable via eclipse plugin, have been developed. Consequently, MIEORF provides strong foundations to perform major image processing operations with simplicity by utilizing MDA development flow. The applicability of MIEORF is demonstrated via real world medical imagery case study by instantiating the concepts of proposed meta-model in tree editor and also graphically visualized via Sirius tool. The results reveal that MIEORF is highly effective for modeling and visualization of both simple as well as complex image processing tasks. It may be safely concluded that MIEORF is a major milestone, as a comprehensive MDA framework for image processing operations is hard to find in literature and industrial projects.

In Future, we intend to extend the proposed framework for incorporating concepts related to image enhancement in frequency domain and object recognition using co-relation filters and enhance our Tree editor/Sirius tool as well. Writing Acceleo transformation code in order to transform system models (M1 level models developed using our tool) into executable Matlab code is also a mile stone to be achieved.

References

1. Gonzalez, R.C., Woods, R.E., Eddins, S.L.: Digital Image Processing using MATLAB. Pearson Education India, Delhi (2004)
2. Solomon, C., Breckon, T.: Fundamentals of Digital Image Processing: A Practical Approach with Examples in Matlab. Wiley, Hoboken (2011)
3. Burger, W., Burge, M.J.: Principles of Digital Image Processing: Fundamental Techniques. Springer, London (2010). https://doi.org/10.1007/978-1-84882-919-0
4. Goel, R., Jain, A.: The implementation of image enhancement techniques on color n gray scale IMAGEs. In: 2018 5th PDGC, Himachal Pradesh, India, pp. 204–209 (2018)
5. Singh, K.B., Mahendra, T.V., Rao, C.V.: Image enhancement with the application of local and global enhancement methods for dark images. In: IESC, pp. 199–202 (2017)
6. Sawant, H.K., Deore, M.: A comprehensive review of image enhancement techniques. IJCTEE 1(2), 39–44 (2010)
7. Maini, R., Aggarwal, H.: A comprehensive review of image enhancement techniques. arXiv preprint arXiv:1003.4053 (2010)
8. Cao, G., Zhao, Y., Ni, R., Tian, H.: Anti-forensics of contrast enhancement in digital images. In: 12th MM&amp, Security 2010, pp. 25–34. ACM, New York (2010)
9. Prasad, S., Abi-Nahed, J.: Contrast enhancement in wavelet domain for graph-based segmentation in medical imaging. In: ICVGIP 2012. ACM, New York (2012)
10. Cheng, N., Zhao, T., Chen, Z., Fu, X.: Enhancement of underwater images by super-resolution generative adversarial networks. In: 10th ICIMCS 2018, pp. 1–4. ACM, New York (2018). Article 22
11. Ucuzal, H., Balikçi Çiçek, A.G.İ., Arslan, A.G.A.K., Çolak, C.: A web-based application for identifying objects in images: object recognition software. In: 2019 3rd ISMSIT, Ankara, Turkey, pp. 1–5 (2019)
12. Tehsin, S., et al.: Improved maximum average correlation height filter with adaptive log base selection for object recognition. In: Optical Pattern Recognition XXVII (2016)
13. Panchal, P., et al.: A review on object detection and tracking methods. Int. J. Res. Emerg. Sci. Technol. 2(1), 7–12 (2015)
14. Jain, A.K., Duin, R.P.W., Mao, J.: Statistical pattern recognition: a review. IEEE Trans. Pattern Anal. Mach. Int. 22(1), 4–37 (2000)

15. Anwar, M.W., Rashid, M., Azam, F., et al.: A model-driven framework for design and verification of embedded systems through SystemVerilog. Des. Autom. Embed. Syst. **23**, 179–223 (2019). https://doi.org/10.1007/s10617-019-09229-y
16. Rasheed, Y., et al.: A model-driven approach for creating storyboards of web based user interfaces. In: 7th ICCCM. ACM (2019)
17. Davies, J., et al.: Model-driven engineering of information systems: 10 years and 1000 versions. Sci. Comput. Program. **89**, 88–104 (2014)
18. Cuadrado, J.S., Izquierdo, J.L.C.: Applying model-driven engineering in small software enterprises. Sci. Comput. Program. **89**, 176–198 (2014)
19. Martínez, S., Gérard, S., Cabot, J.: On watermarking for collaborative model-driven engineering. IEEE Access **6**, 29715–29728 (2018)
20. Karasneh, B., Chaudron, M.R.V.: Img2UML: a system for extracting UML models from images. In: 2013 39th Euromicro Conference on Software Engineering and Advanced Applications, Santander, pp. 134–137 (2013)
21. Karasneh, B., Chaudron, M.R.V.: Extracting UML models from images. In: 2013 5th International Conference on Computer Science and Information Technology, Amman, pp. 169–178 (2013)
22. Ho-Quang, T., Chaudron, MR., Samúelsson, I., Osman, H.: Automatic classification of UML class diagrams from images. In: 2014 21st Asia-Pacific Software Engineering Conference, Jeju, pp. 399–406 (2014)
23. Ha, Y., Kim, B.: Shopping mall system with image retrieval based on UML. In: 2011 First ACIS International Symposium on Software and Network Engineering, Seoul, pp. 103–106 (2011)
24. Qasim, I., Anwar, M.W., Azam, F., Butt, W.H.: A model-driven mobile HMI framework (MMHF) for industrial control systems. J. IEEE Access **8**, 10827–10846 (2020)
25. Anwar, M.W., Rashid, M., Azam, F., Naeem, A., Kashif, M., Butt, W.H.: A unified model-based framework for the simplified execution of static and dynamic assertion-based verification. IEEE Access **8**, 104407–104431 (2020)
26. Rasheed, Y., Azam, F., Anwar, M.W.: A novel framework and tool for multi-purpose modeling of physical infrastructures. In: 12th ICCMS 2020, Brisbane, Australia (2020)
27. Gianni, D., Fuchs, J., De Simone, P., et al.: A modeling language to support the interoperability of global navigation satellite systems. GPS Solut. **17**, 175–198 (2013). https://doi.org/10.1007/s10291-012-0270-z
28. Object management group, unified architecture framework (UAF). https://www.omg.org/spec/UAF/About-UAF/. Accessed Feb 2020
29. MIEORF Archives. https://drive.google.com/drive/folders/1yc3-OhQbWG0KniMecr-xnT6GZmE5A_VZ?usp=sharing. Accessed Mar 2020
30. Simulink image processing toolbox, https://www.mathworks.com/products/image.html. Accessed Jun 2020
31. Eclipse ImageN. https://projects.eclipse.org/projects/technology.imagen. Accessed Jun 2020

Knowledge-Based Generation of the UML Dynamic Models from the Enterprise Model Illustrated by the Ticket Buying Process Example

Ilona Veitaite[1](✉) and Audrius Lopata[2]

[1] Institute of Applied Informatics, Kaunas Faculty, Vilnius University, Kaunas, Lithuania
`ilona.veitaite@knf.vu.lt`
[2] Faculty of Informatics, Kaunas University of Technology, Kaunas, Lithuania
`Audrius.Lopata@ktu.lt`

Abstract. The main scope of this paper is to introduce knowledge-based Enterprise model as sufficient data storage for different Unified Modelling Language (UML) models generation, by using all collected data. UML models can be generated from the Enterprise Model by using certain transformation algorithms presented in previous researches. Generation process from the Enterprise model is illustrated by a particular Ticket Buying example. Generated UML dynamic Use Case, Sequence, State and Activity models of the Ticket buying process demonstrate fullness of stored information in the Enterprise model.

Keywords: Knowledge-based · UML · Enterprise model · IS engineering

1 Introduction

Nowadays information system (IS) engineering process is quite challenging as for analysts, designers and as for any IS design process professionals. Enterprise modelling has become one of the most important elements in IS design process. Enterprise models applications are adapted in various ways and diverse types of models are created based on chosen Enterprise model [1, 2].

UML is a highly recognized and understood platform for IS design. It is a standard notation among professionals. UML can be used to model not just object-oriented IS engineering, but application structure, behavior, or/and business processes. UML models can generate code from the design, apply design patterns, perform impact and complexity analysis [1, 6, 8].

To ensure all these UML model applications is possible only then, when data used for UML models design is verified, validated and of enough quality. Enterprise model completely provides all necessary data and UML models generated from it by using transformation algorithms fully match this requirement [3, 5, 7, 9, 10].

Particular Enterprise meta-model and Enterprise model structure used as the background for this research are presented almost two decades ago. All previous researches

A. Lopata et al. (Eds.): ICIST 2020, CCIS 1283, pp. 26–38, 2020.
https://doi.org/10.1007/978-3-030-59506-7_3

are dedicated to prove that composition of these EMM and EM is enough for generation of different types of models in IS modelling process [10–12].

2 Knowledge-Based Enterprise Meta-model and Enterprise Model

EMM is formally defined EM structure, which consists of a formalized EM in line with the general principles of control theory. EM is the main source of the necessary knowledge of the particular business domain for IS engineering and IS re-engineering processes (Fig. 1) [3, 4].

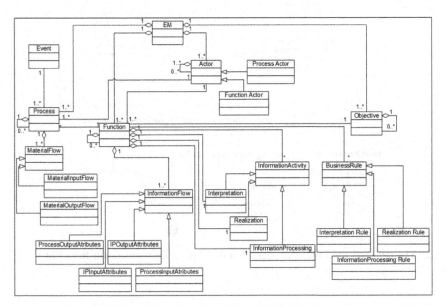

Fig. 1. Enterprise meta-model class diagram [3, 4, 10]

EM class model has twenty-three classes. Essential classes are Process, Function and Actor. Class Process, Function, Actor and Objective can have an internal hierarchical structure. These relationships are presented as aggregation relationships. Class Process is linked with the class MaterialFlow as aggregation relationship. Class MaterialFlow is linked with the classes MaterialInputFlow and MaterialOutputFlow as generalization relationship. Class Process is linked with Classes Function, Actor and Event as association relationship. Class Function is linked with classes InformationFlow, InformationActivity, Interpretation, InformationProcessing and Realization as aggregation relationship. These relationships define the internal composition of the Class Function. Class InformationFlow is linked with ProcessOutputAtributes, ProcessInputAtributes, IPInputAttributes and IPOutputAttributs as generalization relationship. Class InformationActivity is linked with Interpretation, InformationProcessing and Realization as generalization relationship. Class Function linked with classes Actor, Objective and Business Rule as association relationship. Class Business Rule is linked with Interpretation Rule, Realization Rule, InformationProcessing Rule as generalization relationship. Class Actor is linked with Function Actor and Process Actor as generalization relationship [3–5, 11].

Figure 2 presents the transformation algorithm of UML model generation from EM process and is described by the following steps [10, 11].

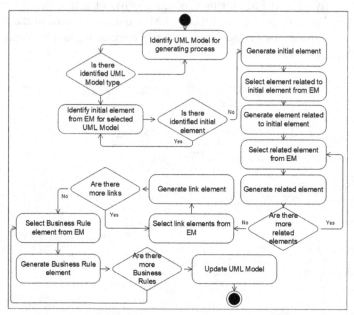

Fig. 2. The top level transformation algorithm of UML models generation from EM process [10–12]

- Step 1: Particular UML model for generation from the EM process is identified and selected.
- Step 2: If the particular UML model for generation from EM process is selected then algorithm process is continued, else the particular UML model for generation from EM process must be selected.
- Step 3: First element from EM is selected for UML model, identified previously, generation process.
- Step 4: If the selected EM element is an initial UML model element, then initial element is generated, else the other EM element must be selected (the selected element must be initial element).
- Step 5: The element related to the initial element is selected from the Enterprise model.
- Step 6: The element related to the initial element is generated as UML model element.
- Step 7: The element related to the previous element is selected from the Enterprise model.
- Step 8: The element related to the previous element is generated as UML model element.

- Step 9: If there are more related elements, then they are selected from EM and generated as UML model elements one by one, else the link element is selected from the Enterprise model.
- Step 10: The link element is generated as UML model element.
- Step 11: If there are more links, then they are selected from EM and generated as UML model elements one by one, else the Business Rule element is selected from the Enterprise model.
- Step 12: The Business Rule element is generated as a UML model element.
- Step 13: If there are more Business Rules, then they are selected from EM and generated as UML model elements one by one, else the generated UML model is updated with all elements, links and constraints.
- Step 14: Generation process is finished.

Table 1 presents part of Enterprise model elements and their descriptions in order to describe elements, which are necessary in this particular research.

Table 1. Description of knowledge stored in Enterprise model

Enterprise Model element	Description
Actor	In actor element can be stored information related with process or function executor. Actor element is responsible of information related with the process or function participant, it can be person, group of persons, subject such as an IS, subsystem, module and etc.
Process, Function	In process or function elements can be stored all information related with any user, entity, object, subject and its behavior. Process or function element is responsible of information related with any operation, activity, status change, movement which is implemented by any actor, entity, participant and etc.
Information Flow	In Information Flow element can be stored diverse information flow types, such as Information input and output attributes or/and process input and output attributes. Information Flow element is responsible of information related with each element input and output attributes, details which make impact on other elements, their state or status
Business Rule	In Business Rule element can be stored different rules such as interpretation, realization or/and information processing. Business rule element is responsible of information about how different elements in IS design phase are related; what restrictions and restraints are applied to these elements

3 Development of UML Models for Ticket Buying Process

This section deals with the detailed explanation of the Ticket buying process and how this process can be designed by using knowledge-based Enterprise model, where all knowledge related with the previously described example is stored. There is also explained, what knowledge is used for the generation particular UML models through certain transformation algorithms created for each UML model generation process [10, 12]. There are described UML Use Case, Sequence, State and Activity models generated form the Enterprise Model.

3.1 Ticket Buying Process Example and Its UML Models

The process of Ticket buying may seem very simple, but if this process would be analyzed from different perspectives in information systems design phase; if this process would be projected and designed for the fulfillment of its all possible functions it would take a lot of time and efforts of an analyst, designer and etc.

In IS lifecycle design phase all the details must be estimated. These details, this knowledge is stored in previously described Enterprise model and they are already verified and validated.

3.2 UML Use Case Model of Ticket Buying Process Example

A UML Use Case model is the primary form of system requirements for a new IS underdeveloped. Use cases specify the expected behavior – what?, and not the precise method of making it take place – how?. A key concept of use case modelling is that it assists to design a system from the end user's perspective. It is an powerful technique for communicating system behavior in the user's conditions by specifying all externally visible system behavior.

Table 2 presents UML Use Case model elements generated from the Enterprise model of Ticket buying example. In Enterprise Model all information related with actors, their functions and relationships between these functions is stored. There are three actors: Client, Manager and Ticket System. Ticket System as an actor is associated with all seven functions – use cases: Enquire ticket availability, Fill form, which includes use case of ticket booking or ticket cancelling, ticket booking includes ticket price payment and form printing, this includes ticket cancelling and this includes payment refunding. Client as an actor is associated with all functions except payment refunding, because it is Ticket system's function. Manager as an actor is associated only with two functions – uses cases: form printing and ticket canceling.

Figure 3 presents UML Use Case model of Ticket buying example generated step by step from the Enterprise Model through UML Use Case transformation algorithm.

Table 2. UML Use Case model elements generated from the Enterprise model of Ticket buying example [5, 7, 9]

Enterprise Model element	UML Use Case Model element	Ticket Buying example	Description
Actor	Actor	Client	There are three actors, each of them is behavioural classifier which defines a role played in particular example
		Manager	
		Ticket system	
Process, Function	Use Case	Enquire ticket availability	There are three use cases, each use case is a type of behavioural classifier that describes a unit of functionality performed by three actors
		Fill form	
		Book ticket	
		Pay ticket price	
		Print form	
		Refund payment	
		Cancel ticket	
Business Rule	Include	Six include elements	There are six include elements, each include is a directed relationship between two use cases which is used to demonstrate that behaviour of the included use case is inserted into the behaviour of the including use case

3.3 UML Sequence Model of Ticket Buying Process Example

UML Sequence model is an interaction model that detail how operations are implemented. This model captures the interaction between objects in the context of a collaboration. UML Sequence model is time focus and it shows the order of the interaction visually by using the vertical axis of the diagram to deliver time what messages are sent and when.

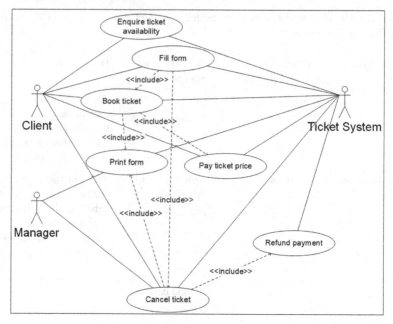

Fig. 3. UML use case model of ticket buying example

Table 3 presents UML Sequence model elements generated from the Enterprise model of Ticket buying example. In Enterprise Model all information related with actors and their collaboration is stored. There are three actors – process participants, which are called Lifelines in UML Sequence model: person – Client, subject – Ticket system, object – Ticket. Ticket has one execution specification, receives one message with details and sends one message of created ticket; Ticket system has three execution specifications, one is assigned for validation, after Client logs in, it returns result; second is assigned for form creation and third for ticket creation; all these are related with messages from Client. Client logs in, requests form, submits details, prints ticket – client sends four messages and receives two: validate login and acknowledgement of all requests of this particular process.

Figure 4 presents UML Sequence model of Ticket buying example generated step by step from the Enterprise Model through UML Sequence transformation algorithm [10].

3.4   UML State Model of Ticket Buying Process Example

UML State Model shows the different states of an entity. State model can also demonstrate how an entity responds to various events by changing from one state to another.

Table 4 presents UML State model elements generated from the Enterprise model of Ticket buying example. In Enterprise Model all information related with processes, functions and their state is stored. This model is from Client's perspective. There are

Table 3. UML Sequence model elements generated from the Enterprise model of Ticket buying example [5, 7, 9]

Enterprise Model element	UML Sequence Model element	Ticket Buying Example	Description
Actor	Lifeline	Client	There are three actors, in UML Sequence model three Lifelines, which are shown using a symbol that consists of a rectangle forming its "head" followed by a vertical line and these lines represent the lifetime of the actor – participant of the process
		Ticket system	
		Ticket	
Process, Function	Message	Login ()	There are eleven messages, related with actors and they define a communication between these actors
		Validate ()	
		Return ()	
		Request form ()	
		Create form ()	
		Submit details ()	
		Create ticket ()	
		Send details ()	
		Ticket created	
		Acknowledge	
		Take print ()	
Business Rules	Execution specification	Ten execution specifications	Each of ten executions specification element represents a period in the actor's lifetime

four information flows – composite states of a Client entity: validation, availability check, ticket booking and printing. All these composite states are conducted by particular behavioral state machine: Enter login details, Enter bus details, Enter self details, Booking successful, Logout.

Figure 5 presents UML State model of Ticket buying example generated step by step from the Enterprise Model through UML State transformation algorithm [10].

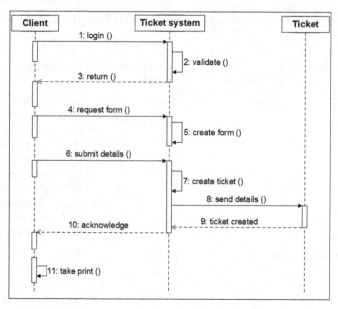

Fig. 4. UML sequence model of Ticket buying example

Table 4. UML State model elements generated from the Enterprise model of Ticket buying example [5, 7, 9]

Enterprise Model element	UML State Model element	Ticket Buying Example	Description
Process, Function	Behavioural state machine	Enter login details	Five states are used to specify discrete behaviour of a part of designed system through finite state transitions
		Enter bus details	
		Enter self details	
		Booking successful	
		Logout	
Information Flow	Composite state	Validation	Four states of an entity are defined as state that has substates
		Availability check	
		Booking Ticket	
		Printing	

3.5 UML Activity Model of Ticket Buying Process Example

UML Activity model describes how activities are coordinated to provide a service which can be at different levels of abstraction. Typically, an event needs to be gained by some operations, particularly where the operation is intended to gain a number of different

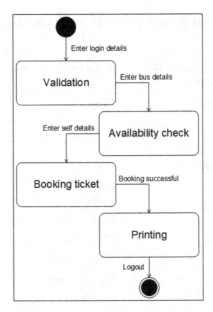

Fig. 5. UML state model of Ticket buying example

things that require coordination, or how the events in a single use case relate to one another, especially, use cases where activities may overlap and require coordination.

Table 5 presents UML Activity model elements generated from the Enterprise model of Ticket buying example. In Enterprise Model all information related with actors, their activities and relationships between these functions is stored. There is one business rule – control node, related with the process beginning, initial node. In this case, there is only one actor – one partition – Client. There are two Client activities before decision node: bus searching and checking tickets availability. In case, there is no available tickets, process finishes unsuccessful with one of final activity nodes. In other case, if there are available tickets, Client books tickets, fills details, submits details, makes payment and prints ticket. This process finishes as successful with second final activity node.

Figure 6 presents UML Activity model of Ticket buying example generated step by step from the Enterprise Model through UML Activity transformation algorithm [10].

Table 5. UML Activity model elements generated from the Enterprise model of Ticket buying example [5, 7, 9]

Enterprise Model element	UML Activity Model element	Ticket buying example	Description
Actor	Partition	Client	There is one partition and all activities are directly related with that actor
Function, Process	Activity	Search bus	There are eight activities directly related with one partition – Client. They represent a parameterized behaviour as coordinated flow of actions
		Check tickets availability	
		Book tickets	
		Fill details	
		Submit details	
		Make payment	
		Print ticket	
		Logout	
Business Rules	Control nodes	Initial node, two activity final nodes, decision node – are there available tickets	There are four control nodes: one node – Initial node in the beginning; one decision node, regarding which process finishes in success or otherwise; two activity final nodes one, in case of successful process, another, in case of unsuccessful process. Basically, control nodes are used to coordinate the flows between other nodes

All four UML dynamic models: Use case, Sequence, State and Activity of one Tickets buying process example are generated form Enterprise model, where sufficient, verified and validated data was stored. These four UML models define same example, but in diverse perspectives by showing different actors activities, states and use cases. Knowledge-based Enterprise model is sufficient storage of data, which is necessary for UML models generation by certain transformation algorithms of each UML model.

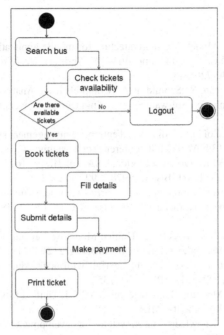

Fig. 6. UML activity model of Ticket buying example

4   Conclusions

The first part of the paper deals with the presentation of the knowledge-based Enterprise model, UML models generation form Enterprise model top level transformation algorithm, which is described step by step and also represents the idea of each UML model transformation algorithm. This part either presents some part of Enterprise model elements and describes their possible content necessary for further research.

The second part presents particular example, which data is stored in knowledge-based Enterprise model and it is used in generation process. There are presented four types of UML dynamic models for this particular example. Each mentioned UML model is generated through certain transformation algorithms.

Each subsection presents different UML dynamic model. All these UML models are generated from the Enterprise model. All information necessary for this generation process is stored in knowledge-based Enterprise model and all UML models elements of the analyzed example also described by their dependency to a certain elements stored in Enterprise model.

The presented example demonstrates that all knowledge stored in Enterprise model is enough for generation process; that Enterprise model elements are sufficient to convey all UML models element in different UML models perspectives. Every element of UML dynamic models can be generated from the Enterprise model and this can implement entire knowledge-based IS development cycle design phase.

References

1. Dunkel, J., Bruns, R.: Model-driven architecture for mobile applications. In: Abramowicz, W. (ed.) BIS 2007. LNCS, vol. 4439, pp. 464–477. Springer, Heidelberg (2007). https://doi.org/10.1007/978-3-540-72035-5_36
2. Eichelberger, H., Eldogan, Y., Schmid, K.A.: Comprehensive Analysis of UML Tools, their Capabilities and Compliance. Software Systems Engineering. Universität Hildesheim, version 2.0 (2011)
3. Gudas, S.: Architecture of knowledge-based enterprise management systems: a control view. In: Proceedings of the 13th World Multiconference on Systemics, Cybernetics and Informatics (WMSCI2009), 10–13 July, Orlando, Florida, USA, vol. III, pp. 161–266 (2009). ISBN - 10: 1-9934272-61-2 (Volume III). ISBN - 13: 978-1-9934272-61-9
4. Gudas, S.: Informacijos sistemų inžinerijos teorijos pagrindai/Fundamentals of information systems engineering theory (Lithuanian). Vilnius University (2012). ISBN 978-609-459-075-7
5. Jacobson, I., Rumbaugh, J., Booch, G.: Unified Modeling Language User Guide, 2nd edn. Addison-Wesley Professional, Boston (2005). ISBN: 0321267974
6. Jenney, J.: Modern methods of systems engineering: with an introduction to pattern and model based methods (2010). ISBN-13:978-1463777357
7. OMG UML: Unified Modeling Language version 2.5.1. Unified Modelling (2019). https://www.omg.org/spec/UML/About-UML/
8. Sajja, P.S., Akerkar, R.: Knowledge-Based systems for development. Adv. Knowl. Syst. Model Appl. Res. **1**, 1–11 (2010)
9. UML diagrams characteristic (2012). www.uml-diagrams.org
10. Veitaite, I., Lopata, A.: Transformation algorithms of knowledge based UML dynamic models generation. In: Abramowicz, W. (ed.) BIS 2017. LNBIP, vol. 303, pp. 59–68. Springer, Cham (2017). https://doi.org/10.1007/978-3-319-69023-0_6
11. Veitaite, I., Lopata, A.: Problem domain knowledge driven generation of uml models. In: Damaševičius, R., Vasiljevienė, G. (eds.) ICIST 2018. CCIS, vol. 920, pp. 178–186. Springer, Cham (2018). https://doi.org/10.1007/978-3-319-99972-2_14
12. Veitaite, I., Lopata, A.: Knowledge-based transformation algorithms of UML dynamic models generation from enterprise model. In: Dzemyda, G., Bernatavičienė, J., Kacprzyk, J. (eds.) Data Science: New Issues, Challenges and Applications. SCI, vol. 869, pp. 43–59. Springer, Cham (2020). https://doi.org/10.1007/978-3-030-39250-5_3

Standardised Questionnaires in Usability Evaluation. Applying Standardised Usability Questionnaires in Digital Products Evaluation

Oana Alexandra Rotaru[(✉)] [ID], Silviu Vert[ID], Radu Vasiu[ID], and Diana Andone[ID]

Politehnica University of Timişoara, 300006 Timişoara, Romania
oana.rotaru94@gmail.com, {silviu.vert,radu.vasiu,
diana.andone}@cm.upt.ro

Abstract. The usability evaluation plays a crucial role in the human-computer interaction. It is one of the basic elements used to verify the user interface quality and also, the quality of the system, as a whole. The goals of usability testing can vary by study, but usually they include: identifying problems in the design of a product or service, uncovering opportunities to improve, learning about the target user's behaviour and preferences. In this paper, we will present an analysis over the most commonly used standardised questionnaires. Also, based on a comparison between them, we will present the results of an analysis done by a group of students, who were asked to compare and decide which standardised questionnaire would be appropriate for their usability evaluation over a certain project. The students were split in teams, each team having a different project to analyse. Their activity is part of the "Interactivity and Usability" subject of Multimedia Technologies Master Degree Program of Politehnica University of Timişoara. We will also present a score of choosing some of the surveys and emphasise the pros and cons of the preferred questionnaires.

Keywords: Usability · Usability evaluation · Questionnaire · Usability methods · SUS · PSSUQ · SUMI · QUIS

1 Introduction

According to [1], usability is a web design (or an application design in general) approach, by which we decide how difficult for a user is learning and accessing an application. Developers should take into consideration that users are frequently familiar with some user interface patterns. Keeping this in mind, complicated designs and strange functionalities can be very confusing to the potential customers of any digital product [1].

Usability is defined by International Organization for Standardization (ISO) as "The extent to which a product can be used by specified users to achieve specific goals with effectiveness, efficiency, and satisfaction in a specified context of use" [1].

There are five main components which define usability, according to [1]:

© Springer Nature Switzerland AG 2020
A. Lopata et al. (Eds.): ICIST 2020, CCIS 1283, pp. 39–48, 2020.
https://doi.org/10.1007/978-3-030-59506-7_4

1. **Learnability** – How easy is to perform basic tasks for new users?
2. **Efficiency** – What time does it take for users to find what they came for?
3. **Memorability** – How hard is it for users to repeatedly perform their tasks?
4. **Error rate** – Errors made by users.
5. **Satisfaction** – The comfort users feel when using the design.

In this paper, we will present an analysis of the most commonly used standardised questionnaires for usability evaluation. Also, based on a comparison between them, we will statistically present the results of an analysis done by a group of students, who were asked to compare and decide which standardised questionnaire would be appropriate for their usability evaluation over a certain project. The students were split in teams, each team having a different project to analyse. Their activity is part of the "Interactivity and Usability" subject of Multimedia Technologies Master Degree Program of Politehnica University of Timişoara.

2   Standard Questionnaires Used in Usability Evaluation

The usability testing has a key importance in the human-computer interaction. It is one of the basic elements used to verify the user interface quality [2]. There are many definitions of usability. The actual definition of usability is based on the assumption that users are rational agents, who can interact with a system, being capable to use their knowledge and receiving information from the system's reactions to achieve their specific goals [3].

One of the popular applied methods in usability testing is the user observation, where participants are handed tasks on an product and their behaviour is observed and analysed by the people organising the usability testing.

Also, the questionnaire method is another good option when it comes to usability testing. It can briefly sum up the feedback of a possible user after navigating through an app, either mobile or web app.

As being mentioned in [4], people often think that a high level of usability can be accomplished just by adding a simple and clear interface. However, usability is much deeper than the superficial features of the user interface. The user interface features have an important impact on the usability of every product, yet an important role is played by the clear information which is presented to the user. So, a simple graphic user interface, with few and very easy-to-use elements, may not satisfy completely the user needs sometimes. An acceptable level of usability is reached when the design meets the user needs on a higher level [4].

However, in order to improve and also, somehow standardize the entire usability testing process, there were developed targeted questionnaires, based on the essential components of the usability itself: learnability, efficiency, memorability, error rate and user satisfaction.

Some well known surveys for post-study are System Usability Scale (SUS), Post Study System Usability Questionnaire (PSSUQ), Questionnaire for User Interaction Satisfaction (QUIS), and Software Usability Measurement Inventory (SUMI).

2.1 SUMI

According to [5], SUMI is a solution to the measurements of the user perception of the usability of a digital product. It offers the possibility to compare competing products and similar products, so it can give useful information for future updated on the software. It consists of a 50-item survey and it's intended to be managed by people with some previous experience using similar products. "The concept of usability as assessed by SUMI draws on the definition in ISO 9241 and relates to the European Directive on Health and Safety Standards for Workers with VDU Equipment" [5].

One important aspect of SUMI has been the development of a standardisation database, which consists of usability profiles of over 200 different kinds of applications such as: word processors, CAD and graphics packages, travel reservation systems, on-screen help systems.

According to [6], SUMI is especially used for evaluating product-against-product comparisons or for product against the standardisation database comparisons, in order to see how the product which is being rated compares against the average state-of-the-art market profile.

SUMI has also strengths and weaknesses. Some of its strengths are the following: it's a validated instrument, it is complex and it consists of a database with results available for comparison of own test results. The weaknesses can be: same drawbacks as with all subjective scales; focus mainly on software; scale mostly addresses classical usability issues, smaller part is about affect; the results are not highly informative for the future possibility of redesigning products. Also, SUMI is not free [7].

2.2 SUS

Another type of standardized questionnaire we will present is **SUS** (System Usability Scale), which is the most frequently used questionnaire to measure usability. It was created by John Brooke in 1986 [8]. In UX, SUS is always used in an online survey or after each usability testing session for users to fill in.

According to [8], SUS was not initially created for the websites usability testing measurements, it was developed at Digital Equipment Corporation in the UK in 1986 as a tool dedicated for electronic office systems usability engineering. While SUS is frequently used today to measure the usability of websites, its usage is not limited to websites. It can be used to measure any systems and applications, from digital products such as mobile apps, digital kiosks, laptops to machinery.

SUS is known as a simple, frequently used 10-statement questionnaire. The tool asks users to rate their perception of agreement or disagreement to the 10 statements—half worded positively, half negatively—about the software under review [8].

SUS has been proven as an efficient questionnaire and it is also a free tool.

2.3 PSSUQ

The **PSSUQ** (Post-Study System Usability Questionnaire) is a 16-item standardized questionnaire. It is frequently used to measure users perceived satisfaction of a website, software, system or product at the end of a study.

The items are seven-point graphic scales, anchored at the end points with the terms "Strongly agree" for 1 and "Strongly disagree" for 7 and a "Not applicable" point outside the scale. A group of usability evaluators selected the items on the basis of their comprehensive content regarding hypothesized constituents of usability. For example, the items assess such system characteristics as ease of use, ease of learning, simplicity, effectiveness, information and the user interface [9].

One of the advantages of using standardized usability questionnaires such as PSSUQ is its replicability. It can be easily replicated PSSUQ across the studies. Also, PSSUQ is free [10].

2.4 QUIS

According to [11], the Questionnaire for User Interaction Satisfaction(QUIS) is a usability testing tool created to measure the users subjective satisfaction with any computer interface. It contains a demographic questionnaire, a measure of general satisfaction over the entire product and also, it measures the users satisfaction on 4 certain threads, such as the screen factors, terminology and system feedback, learnability and system capabilities.

Also, the QUIS is commonly used in areas as commerce/industry, international education and research, domestic education and research users. Most of them use the QUIS in conjunction with a usability testing laboratory [11].

In the next chapter, we will present the case study applied on a group of students who had the task to choose between the presented surveys in order to customise and use them for their assigned projects usability evaluations.

3   Applied Case Study

A group of Multimedia Technologies master degree students were asked to compare all of these four types of questionnaire and they had to analyse which one is the most appropriate to use for their project. The students were split in 5 teams, each of the teams having assigned a certain mobile application or web platform.

3.1 Spotlight Heritage Timisoara Project

Team 1 had to realise a study on the Spotlight Heritage Timisoara mobile application and decide which standardised questionnaire would be the most appropriate option in order to use it for the questionnaire method applied in this case.

Spotlight Heritage Timișoara is a cultural project developed by the Politehnica University of Timișoara and the National Museum of Banat in collaboration with Timișoara 2021 European Capital of Culture Association.

The mobile app contains several stories about the city that highlights neighbourhoods and communities of the city. The first story is already implemented and it's called "Iosefin". In Fig. 1, there is a capture of a section from the mobile app.

The students decided to use the SUS questionnaire because it's fast and easy to use by the participants of the usability evaluation and also, for its rationale of the score calculation.

Fig. 1. Spotlight Heritage Timisoara mobile application (https://play.google.com/store/apps/details?id=eu.spotlighttimisoara&hl=en_US).

Fig. 2. OpenVMLH mobile application (https://play.google.com/store/apps/details?id=eu.openvirtualmobility.hub&hl=en_US).

The customized questions/statements of the SUS questionnaire applicable to the Spotlight Heritage Timișoara mobile app usability evaluation is presented as it follows:

1. I think I would frequently use this mobile app in Timișoara.
2. I think the app is easy to use.
3. The information in this app is useful.
4. The information regarding the Iosefin neighbourhood is really interesting.
5. There is a lot of useless information on this app.
6. I think the information on the app is quite incomplete.
7. This app won't help me in the future.
8. I can easily find the landmarks once selected as favourites.
9. This app is fast.
10. I'm comfortable with the design of this app.

3.2 Open Virtual Mobility Learning Hub Project

Team 2 was responsible for finding the appropriate type of survey for the Open Virtual Mobility Learning Hub mobile application[1] .

According to [12], The OpenVMLH (Virtual Mobility Learning Hub) is an innovative multilingual environment which was created as part of the Open Virtual Mobility, a

---

[1] (https://play.google.com/store/apps/details?id=eu.openvirtualmobility.hub&hl=en_US).

European-funded project, with the purpose to promote collaborative learning, social connectivism and networking as an instructional method, OERs as the main content and open digital credentials. In Fig. 2 presented above, there is a capture from the mobile application first page.

For this mobile app, the team decided to use the PSSUQ - Post-Study System Usability Questionnaire. The reasons for their choice are the following ones: its replicability, the PSSUQ is more complex than SUS and it would be helpful for finding precise results regarding the usability problems of the app and it's free.

As it follows, the students customised the questionnaire and the structure is presented below.

1. The login section was very easy and intuitive.
2. I find the app easy to use.
3. I didn't have many problems using the app.
4. I felt comfortable with the design of this app.
5. The menu is too complex.
6. The information on OpenVMLH app is useful.
7. I find the graphic interface easy to use.
8. The video tutorials on the app are useful and precise.
9. I enjoyed the entire design of the app.
10. The information on the app is well structured.
11. I didn't find on the app everything I searched for.
12. Communicating through this app is fast.
13. The OpenVMLH app sends suggestive error messages so I can easily understand what I should do.
14. I think this app helps you being productive.
15. The calendar sections on this app is easy to use.
16. I think this app will help me in the future.

3.3 E-Learning Center Website Project

Team 3 had to study the standardised questionnaires in order to decide which one would suit their own project usability evaluation regarding the E-learning Center website[2]. Also, in Fig. 3, there is a capture of the homepage of this website.

The students decided that SUS would be appropriate for their usability study over this website because the standard questions of the questionnaire are suitable for websites usability testing, so the major changes of the questions would be useless as long as it has been proven as a successful questionnaire in the past.

Also, the students customised the survey in such a way so it could be more specific on the E-learning Center website.

1. I think I could frequently use the E-learning Center website.
2. I think that this website is way too complex.
3. This website is easy to use.

---

[2] (https://elearning.upt.ro/ro/).

Fig. 3. E-learning Center website (https://ele arning.upt.ro/ro/).

Fig. 4. DigiCulture courses on UniCampus platform (https://unicampus.ro/).

4. I would need technical help in order to use this website.
5. The information on this website is well structured.
6. I think the menu of the website is too complicated.
7. The website is easy to learn to use.
8. I think that this website is way too difficult to use.
9. I felt comfortable using this website.
10. I think I have to improve my skills before using the E-learning Center website.

3.4 UniCampus Website Project

Team 4 had to realise a study on the UniCampus platform[3] in order to create their own questionnaire.

UniCampus is an initiative of the eLearning Center (CeL) of the Politehnica University of Timișoara, which aims to strengthen the recognition of the Romanian universities, the power of support and penetration in the social and educational life in Romania of quality, academic education, by promoting access to knowledge.

Its purpose is to create and develop the first MOOC (Massive Open Online Course) in Romania, as an online virtual platform for free, free courses, open to everyone [13].

In Fig. 4 presented above, there is a capture of the existing courses on UniCampus website.

The students concluded that using their customised version of the SUS questionnaire would be the best option. The reasons for their choice consists of the fact that it's a short questionnaire and it's easier to be filled by the participants, rather than a longer questionnaire which can be overwhelming for them. Also, they chose this standardised questionnaire for its balance between the positive and negative questions, which brings more objectiveness.

As it follows, this is the customised version of the SUS survey applicable for their project.

1. I would frequently use this website to improve my digital skills.
2. I think that the UniCampus website is too complex.
3. This website is easy to use.
4. I think that the video tutorials are really useful.
5. I think that the website is inconsistent.

---

[3] (https://unicampus.ro/).

6. I need technical support to use this website.
7. I think I learned this website very quickly.
8. I need more time to get used to this website.
9. I felt confident using the UniCampus website.
10. I need more technical background to use this website.

3.5 Virtual Museum of Politehnica University of Timisoara Project

The project assigned to Team 5 was a VR application developed for the Politehnica University of Timisoara Technical Museum. The application consists of a journey through the history of the university such as a virtual museum. Also, the application is not a final product yet. In Fig. 5, there is a capture from the application.

Fig. 5. Virtual museum application

The students from Team 5 concluded that the appropriate questionnaire for this application is the PSSUQ.

Through the reasons for their choice we noticed the number of questions which can cover the main possible usability problems of the application and also, choosing this type of survey rather than the SUS brings more specificity to the usability problems of the application.

The PSSUQ questionnaire proposal from Team 5 is presented below.

1. The application is complex and creative.
2. I didn't have problems at the selection of rooms in the application.
3. Navigating through this app is easy.
4. The historical content presented in the app was intelligible.
5. The objects descriptions from the app was easy to understand.
6. The sound implementation would be a real improvement.
7. The number of graphical elements was good enough.
8. All over, the objects recognition was easy without description.
9. The objects sorting by categories is well implemented.
10. The graphical elements were clear.
11. The information was clear and readable.

12. I didn't have problems with the interactions speed.
13. The level of interactions with the elements was enough.
14. The interaction with some elements was intuitive.
15. The entire graphical interface is friendly.
16. The text information is useful.

3.6 Discussion

As presented above, we can observe that 3 out of 5 teams tend to choose the SUS questionnaire for their usability evaluation of the projects so we can conclude that in our case, there is 60% predilection of using the SUS questionnaire and 40% predilection of using the PSSUQ.

Also, we could be able to previously predict the fact that after analysing all these four standardised questionnaires presented above, the students will tend to use these two types because both of them are free.

We can also observe that both of the teams which chose the PSSUQ have to test the VR application and the OpenVMLH mobile application, these products requiring more specific research for the possible usability problems.

Through the reasons mentioned by the students decided to use the SUS, we can notice that this standardised questionnaire offers fewer questions, it's an easy and objective type of questionnaire and also, being short encourages the participants to be honest and fast. Another reason for choosing the SUS is its replicability and the fact that it can be customised or not. An advantage of using the SUS is also the ease of the score calculation, demonstrating a logic rationale, with an equal number of positive and negative statements, with answers in a range between "Strongly Disagree" to "Strongly Agree". The interpretation of the obtained score can be found in [14].

Likewise, the students embracing the use of PSSUQ in their usability evaluations brought significant reasons for their analysis, such as the ease of use, the proper number of questions which is also an important aspect in the questionnaire method.

The PSSUQ offers 16 questions/statements that can be properly customisable so the survey is able to cover important aspects of the tested product. Contrarily, a longer questionnaire can be overwhelming for the participants, inducing thoughtless answers and subjectiveness.

Comparing the options of the teams participating in this case study, we can conclude that choosing one of the standardised questionnaires in usability evaluations depends on the complexity of any product, the stage of development. An example supporting these statements can be the decision to use the PSSUQ for the Virtual Museum VR application, which is not a final product and it's also a complex application.

Furthermore, choosing one of the questionnaires presented in this paper depends on the budget of the team organising the usability evaluation. As being said above, the students picked the free questionnaires-SUS, PSSUQ, instead of the paid ones - SUMI and QUIS.

An important point when it comes when picking the appropriate questionnaire is its complexity. As mentioned above, compared with a short questionnaire, a long survey can overwhelm the participants and induce thoughtless answers.

4 Conclusion and Future Work

As specified in the beginning of the paper, the goals of usability testing can vary by study, but usually they include: identifying problems in the design of a product or service, uncovering opportunities to improve, learning about the target user's behaviour and preferences.

Also, in this paper we researched and presented various types of commonly used standard questionnaires used in the user evaluation phase: SUS, PSSUQ, QUIS and SUMI.

Likewise, we presented a case study where five teams of master degree students had to choose between those four surveys in order to accomplish their usability evaluations work by the end of semester.

We obtained a score of 60% for using the SUS questionnaire and 40% for using the PSSUQ. We also emphasised above the pros and cons of using any of these two types of usability evaluation surveys.

As future work, the students will have to apply the questionnaires within the Interactivity and Usability subject at the Politehnica University of Timișoara and afterwards, we will analyse the impact of the chosen questionnaires over the assigned projects usability evaluations.

References

1. Krejcar, O.: Principles of usability in human-computer interaction. Journal **2**(5), 99–110 (2016). University of Hradec Kralove
2. Nielsen, J.: Usability engineering. In: The Computer Science and Engineering Handbook (1993)
3. Law, E., Jerman-Blažič, B.: Assessment of user rationality and adaptivity: a case study. In: Kinshuk, V., Sampson, D.G., Isaías, P. (ed.) Proceedings of the IADIS International Conference on Cognition and Exploratory Learning in Digital Age (CELDA 2004), Lisbon, Portugal, 15–17 December 2004, IADIS (2004)
4. Macleod, M.: Usability: practical methods for testing and improvement (1994)
5. Kirakowski, J., Corbett, M.: SUMI: the software usability measurement inventory. BJET **24**, 210–212 (1993)
6. Kulkarni, R., Padmanabham, P., Sagare, V., Maheshwari, V.: Usability evaluation of PS using SUMI (software usability measurement inventory). In: 2013 International Conference on Advances in Computing, Communications and Informatics (ICACCI), pp. 1270–1273 (2013)
7. SUMI. http://www.allaboutux.org/sumi. Accessed 28 Mar 2020
8. McLellan, S., Muddimer, A., Peres, S.C.: The effect of experience on system usability scale ratings. J. Usability Stud. **7**(2), 56–67 (2012)
9. Lewis, J.R.: Psychometric evaluation of the post-study system usability questionnaire: the PSSUQ (1992)
10. PSSUQ. https://uiuxtrend.com/pssuq-post-study-system-usability-questionnaire/. Accessed 2020
11. Harper, P.D., Norman, K.L.: Improving user satisfaction: the questionnaire for user interaction satisfaction version 5 (1993)
12. Andone, D., Vert, S., Mihaescu, V., Stoica, D., Ternauciuc, A.: Evaluation of the virtual mobility learning hub, Politehnica University of Timișoara (2016)
13. UniCampus. https://unicampus.ro/. Accessed 28 Mar 2020
14. SUS. https://uiuxtrend.com/measuring-system-usability-scale-sus/. Accessed 28 Mar 2020

Research of Semi-automated Database Development Using Data Model Patterns

Vytautas Volungevičius$^{(\boxtimes)}$ and Rita Butkienė

Kaunas University of Technology, Kaunas, Lithuania
{vytautas.volungevicius,rita.butkiene}@ktu.lt

Abstract. The paper focuses on the idea to semi-automate relational database development. Various approaches to ease, automate conceptual data modeling discussed. A chosen method to semi-automate conceptual data model development was pattern based-approach. This paper introduces a data model patterns library and a CASE tool to use it. Furthermore, an experiment was conducted to test the abilities of a CASE tool. The purpose of the experiment was to test the coverage and time aspects of an actual database schema reproduction using a CASE tool. Experiment results showed that patterns cover a large portion of a conceptual data model, and a new CASE tool reduces the time required to develop a conceptual data model by hand.

Keywords: Data model patterns · CASE tool · Database development · Conceptual data model · Semi-automated database development

1 Introduction

1.1 Database Development Process Steps

As software development has its core aspect subdivided into steps, each of which focuses on one aspect of development, the database development process can also be divided into steps. The most similar one of the software development life cycle to the database development cycle is the waterfall model. Graeme Simsion [1] offered a schema for the database development process from which three core aspects can be deduced:

1. From the established requirements and interaction with the Universe of Discourse, the conceptual data model is produced.
2. From a conceptual data model, the logical database schema can be produced using specific data definition language (DDL).
3. From the logical schema, SQL script should be created and executed in a DBMS to create a database with tables and constrains that where defined in the logical schema.

From the steps mentioned above, it is clear that the core of a database development process is a clear and precise conceptual data model [2].

© Springer Nature Switzerland AG 2020
A. Lopata et al. (Eds.): ICIST 2020, CCIS 1283, pp. 49–59, 2020.
https://doi.org/10.1007/978-3-030-59506-7_5

1.2   Problems that Occur While Creating a Conceptual Data Model

Even tho it is clear that the conceptual data is the core of the database, many problems still occur while creating a conceptual data model. Conceptual modeling requires a lot of attention and takes a lot of time. During this time, many novice designers face a lot of problems [3]. These problems were identified in many research papers, but further research shows that they remained unsolved [1]. One of such problems is a semantical mismatch. Most of the system requirements are written using natural language [4, 5], which might cause ambiguities as the same word in a different domain can mean a different thing [6].

Further expanding on semantic problems, not all relations that exist in the real world can be transferred and represented in a database [3]. Some relations are derived and only needed in a database model.

Another problem that a novice designer faces is a lack of experience [7]. Not only they lack experience in modeling, but they might also be unfamiliar with the domain area of which a conceptual data model is needed. The lack of knowledge of a specific domain is common among expert designers too. Both experts and novice designers struggle when it comes to finding entities that are necessary for the model to be correct [8].

There is a large number of other challenges that might be faced while designing a conceptual data model, but in this paper, we are not going to talk about them.

2   Related Works

As a result, to solve those challenges, there were many tries to automate or at least semi-automate a database creation process. Some of the methodologies that were suggested for semi-automated conceptual data modeling was:

- Linguistic-based approach – using natural language and creating entities processed from natural language requirements [9].
- Case-based approach – using cases repository to get a model to solve a specific problem at hand.
- Ontology-based approach [10] – using ontologies to create data models.
- Pattern-based approach – using existing data model patterns to create data models.

Comparing all these approaches by cost, usability, flexibility, and complexity, we would get the results like these (Table 1):

The linguistic-based approach would be most flexible if we could remove the limitations of natural language. Currently, it is difficult to apply this method in practice as it puts constraints on requirements language, that is why this method complexity is high and its usability is low. To develop a tool for natural language processing would require a substantial amount of money.

The case-based approach has the lowest complexity because if the case already exists in a repository, it might be ready to use. As for flexibility, if the existing model needs to change, all changes need to be done by hand. This approach is not used globally, as most repositories are private for every individual modeler. Creating and maintain a global use

Table 1. Existing methods comparison by cost, usability, flexibility, and complexity

Method	Cost	Usability	Flexibility	Complexity
Linguistic-based	High	Low	High	High
Case-based	High	Average	Low	Low
Ontology-based	High	Low	High	High
Pattern-based	Low	High	High	Average

case repository would cost a lot. That is why its cost is high and usability is average as most professional modelers have their private repositories.

Ontology-based approach, as with the linguistic-based approach, the data model would be easily changeable, but ontology models are very expensive. Large ontologies would generate a way to many entities that would not be needed in a data model. Currently, there are no user-friendly API to work with ontologies; that is why this method is rarely used to construct data models.

The pattern-based approach has the most advantages among the compared characteristics. It is not expensive as most patterns are already in books. Patterns are already often used unconsciously by modelers. Models created using patterns are easy to change. Sometimes it might be hard to choose the right pattern as there are various abstraction levels of patterns.

3   Data Model Patterns

3.1   Data Model Patterns and Their Benefits

A data model pattern is a set of entities and relationships between them organized a specific way to solve a particular problem. A pattern is an *accepted* solution to recurring problems, a beginner or an expert designer can use patterns in various scale database models.

3.2   Other Authors View on Data Model Patterns and Their Usage

Design patterns have been beneficial in software development. They not only speed up the development process but increase the quality of software systems. Tho integrating patterns in conceptual modeling might be challenging, but it is not impossible. Authors such as Hay [8], Fowler [11], Coad [12], created a library of proven modeling structures (patterns) and provided examples on how to adapt them.

Research already shows that experts reuse patterns, while novice designers do not [13]. Patterns may be a valid way to construct data models. However, to use them correctly, three steps need to be taken [14]:

1. First, the correct pattern must be chosen;
2. then it should be adapted to meet the current requirements;

3. It should be integrated into a model.

Only following these steps, a complete conceptual data pattern can be formed.

3.3 The Variety of Data Model Patterns and Their Abstraction Levels

As a concept of a data model pattern arose, the number of data model patterns increased as well. A pattern can be as small as containing only a single entity, and as large as a complete database schema for a specific domain. Not only that, but there are also various abstraction levels of patterns. For example, let us take Hay [8] proposed Parties data model pattern (Fig. 1).

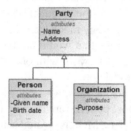

Fig. 1. "Party" pattern based on David C. Hay "Party" patterns

Only the core entities and attributes are in this pattern. If we take Len Silverston [15] suggested a more detailed version of this pattern (Fig. 2).

We can see a clear difference between abstraction levels in these patterns [16]. Differences in abstraction levels are one of the reasons why some modelers choose not to use patterns, as it might require a lot of changes to adapt it correctly [17].

3.4 The Need for a Tool to Use Data Model Patterns

It has been said that patterns could increase the quality and speed up the development of a conceptual data model. Most data model patterns are in books or articles. The libraries that contain data model patterns are also in textual format. Thus not allowing data model patterns to be used in CASE tools. The only way how modelers could use data model patterns is if they would redraw them by hand. Current technologies allow us to create a tool that would semi-automate pattern usage in the data modeling process.

4 Conceptual Data Model Creation Based on Data Model Patterns

4.1 Existing Data Model Patterns and Relationships Between Them

It has been established that there is a considerable amount of data model patterns. A few experts such as David C. Hay, Len Silverstone, Michael Blaha have proposed a set of data model patterns in their publications. In their books, they showed how a bigger data model could be made of small patterns. [8, 15, 18] Based on various research, there is a possibility to jump-start a database creation using patterns.

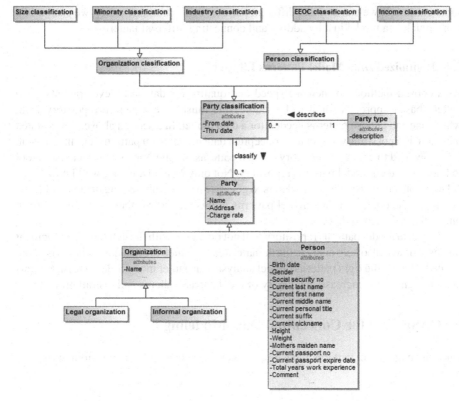

Fig. 2. "Party" pattern based on Len Silverston "Party" pattern

4.2 Domain Independent and Domain-Specific Data Model Patterns

As there is a huge amount of patterns, there was a need to categorize them. Data model patterns can be categorized into domain-independent and domain-specific patterns [16, 19]. Domain-independent patterns are made of generic entities that could be applied in any domain. For example, a domain-independent entity might be Party, Person, Organization. For a specific domain such as Heath care, there might be some domain-specific entities such as Patients, Diagnoses, Drugs, and so on.

Research shows that most database models can be covered by up to 50% using domain-independent patterns, and up to 75% using domain-specific patterns [19].

4.3 Data Model Development Using Data Model Patterns

An idea to create conceptual data models using patterns have been around for a few decades. As in many other areas of IT, patterns have already been adapted and used for a long time. For database creation processes until now, patterns were only used by experts who already know them. For that reason, there still is no semi-automatic way of using those patterns. Based on how patterns are constructed. Some of these patterns have the same entities. If we can connect different patterns using the same entity, we can build a conceptual data model just by adding and connecting different patterns.

4.4 Digitalized Data Model Patterns Library

As a chosen method, to increase speed and quality for database development was a pattern-based approach for it to be viable, one must have a pattern repository from which one can choose patterns needed for a data model. In a section above, it was stated that there is a possibility to create a conceptual data model from patterns. For that reason, it was decided to create a repository of such patterns. MagicDraw was selected as a tool to build such data model patterns repository. Not only MagicDraw use well know UML [4] notation, but it also allows modelers to generate a script for creating database objects. To ensure the quality of data model patterns in this repository, they were chosen from only a few selected authors.

This data model patterns repository will not only help with the database development process but will also help analyze the domain area for which the database schema is being created. Having the right patterns project analysts can gather more in-depth requirements and, in such a way, increase the quality of the database schema and overall project.

5   CASE Tool for Conceptual Data Modeling

Once the data model patterns repository was created, an idea to create a tool to use this repository arose.

5.1 The Idea and Purpose of a CASE Tool

The main goal of the CASE tool was too allow the user to copy a pattern into a data model diagram. As mentioned before, patterns sometimes contain the same entities and for that reason, while developing the CASE tool, the decision was made to use only one object of the same entity in all the patterns that it was used. The main focus of data model patterns is entities, not attributes. For that reason, most of the pattern entities contain only the most significant attributes. Users can modify the copied pattern entities based on their needs and still maintain a connection with the data model pattern repository, thus allowing the user to expand the data model with other patterns or entities from the repository.

5.2 CASE Tool Usage in the Database Development Process

Database schema development is a tedious process that requires a lot of repetitive work. Many databases can have the same entities; to draw them every time would be a waste of valuable time. This new CASE tool offers two new use cases for conceptual data modeling:

1. One of the ways this new tool could be used is to look for entities in the pattern repository and copy them into the data model diagram.

2. Another use case of this tool could be "exploratory" as the user could copy a few core entities from the pattern repository and build upon those further.

From the use cases mentioned above, it is clear that the tool can increase the speed of conceptual data model development, and in some cases, help to gather requirements or familiarize with unknown domain areas.

5.3   Data Modeling Tool Functions

A main data modeling function is showed in Fig. 3.

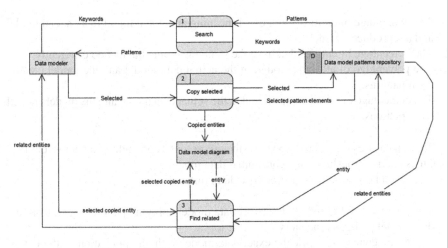

Fig. 3. CASE tool processes and data flow diagram

3. Data modeler can search entire data model patterns repository or search by a specific keywords.
4. From the search results, the data modeler can select entities that he wants to copy to the data model diagram.
5. From the data model diagram, the data modeler can select copied entity and search for its related elements.

Using these three processes, a conceptual data model can be build using a CASE tool and data model patterns.

6   Experiment

For a proof-of-concept that the use of data model patterns is a rational method to create a database model, an experiment was conducted. In this experiment, an exemplary open source database model was selected and tried to reproduce it applying data model patterns chosen from developed CASE tool repository. It is highly unlikely that the usage of patterns can ensure 100% reproduction of any large or medium database model. In addition, the time it takes to create a model is an important feature when choosing a model development method. Therefore, to measure the success of the CASE tool developed and a patterns library 2 main criteria were chosen:

1) Coverage of the original model by the reproduced model;
2) The ration of the time required to redraw the exact data model using the method proposed to the time needed to redraw the same model without method application.

The first criterion is measured by calculating such measures:

1. The percentage of entities[1] with exact meaning and name found in an actual model and a reproduced model.
2. The percentage of entities that have the same meaning[2] but named differently.
3. The percentage of attributes found in the actual data model and the model created from patterns.
4. The percentage of relationships found in the actual data model and the model created from patterns.

These measures were chosen because they represent a core individual items (entities, attributes and relationships) of a conceptual data model.

The second criterion is measured by calculating:

5. The time required to redraw the exact data model applying patterns taken from the data model patterns repository of CASE tool;
6. The time needed to redraw the exact data model without application of the CASE tool data model patterns repository.

It is important to mention that the chosen original data model was modified a bit as it contained history tables and memory address, timestamp attributes - these attributes and tables where not included in coverage measures calculation.

6.1   Experiment Flow and the Chosen Database Model

A database schema chosen for an experiment was Microsoft exemplary database AdventureWorks Rev 10.00.0009. The reason behind this choice was that there are not many open source database schemas available, and it was complex enough to show the possibilities that the usage of patterns brings. The experiment was divided into steps:

1. As the AdventureWorks database does not have a conceptual data model, the first step of the experiment was to make reverse engineering of the database schema and get

---

[1] Exact entities – entities that have same identical name in the examplary database and in data model patterns for example "Person", "Employee".

[2] Entities with the same semantic value – entities that are named the same or use synonyms or more generic names for example "Store" and "Organization" or "Customer" and "Party".

a conceptual data model[3]. All unnecessary attributes such as FK, PK, *rowguid,* and *ModifiedDate* provided in the original schema model were removed. Entities that constitutes a many-to-many relationship and do not have any additional attributes were also removed from the conceptual data model. During the transformation from the database schema to a conceptual data model, a time required to redraw the model was measured.

2. The aim of the next step was to reproduce the same model[4] using only a CASE tool.

   a. Firstly as there were entities that were in AdventureWorks database schema and patterns library using a search function, such entities were found. Once they were found, they have been copied from patterns library into a data model diagram
   b. Secondly, using a second use case provided by a CASE tool to look for related library elements, the rest of the model entities were added. Related elements from the library were selected based on their semantic value.

Once there were no more entities in a pattern library that could cover entities or attributes in a conceptual data model of the AdventureWorks database, an experiment was finished. A time that took to reproduce the original model applying data model patterns was measured, and coverage of the model was calculated.

6.2 Experiment Results

The results of the experiment were presented in Fig. 4.
   Results show:

1. The exact coverage of the entities in the original data model by the data model that was developed using data model patterns was only 14%. It is because the entities in the patterns are named using more generic names, and in an actual data model, most modelers prefer entity names that clearly represent the objects types of the domain area.
2. The coverage of entities that have the same meaning but can differ in name forms was 76%. This number supports previous researcher's results. As it was stated that there is a possibility to cover 75% [19].
3. For the coverage of attributes, the result was 47%. As expected, it is challenging to cover attributes with patterns entities, as they tightly coupled with the domain area and a specific business logic and data that the business needs.
4. For the coverage of relationships, the result was 58%. As the original database model contained entities that were not covered based on the semantic aspect, the relationships that those entities contained were not covered too. That is why the coverage of the relationship is lower than entities.
5. While testing time consumption to draw the test model by hand, it took 75:29 min, and to draw the same model using a library and tool created, it took 29:01 min.

---

[3] Adventure works conceptual data model - https://github.com/vytautas101/Data-modelling/blob/master/adventure%20works/adventure%20works.png.

[4] Reproduced conceptual data model - https://github.com/vytautas101/Data-modelling/blob/master/adventure%20works/reproduced%20model.png.

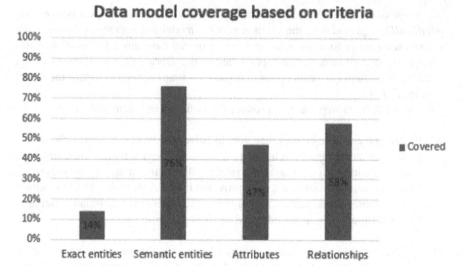

Fig. 4. Experiment results

The overall results of the experiment show that the new tool and data model patterns have merit, and expanding the data model patterns library and improving the CASE tool, the results could be even better. Of course, some might argue that the data models created using patterns lack clarity, but they are more flexible. To increase the clarity of the model entities copied from the patterns library can be renamed, thus increasing the readability of the data model.

References

1. Simsion, G.: Data Modeling Theory and Practice. Technics Publications, LLC, New York (2007)
2. Simsion, G., Witt, G.: Data Modelling Essentials. Morgan Kaufmann, San Francisco (2004)
3. Batra, D.: Cognitive complexity in data modeling: causes and recommendations. Requirements Eng. 12(4), 231–244 (2007). https://doi.org/10.1007/s00766-006-0040-y
4. Mich, L., Franch, M., Inverardi, P.: Market research for requirements analysis using linguistic tools. Requirements Eng. 9(1), 40–56 (2004). https://doi.org/10.1007/s00766-003-0179-8
5. Neill, C.J., Laplante, P.A.: Requirement engineering: the state of the practice. IEEE Softw. 20(6), 40–45 (2003)
6. Song, I.-Y., Trujillo, J., Yano, K., Lujan-Mora, S.: A taxonomic class modeling methodology for object-oriented analysis. In: Information Modelling Methods and Methodologies. Advanced Topics in Databases Series, pp. 216–240. Idea Group Publishing, Hershey (2004)
7. Namgyu, K., Sangwon, L., Songchun, M.: Formalized entity extraction methodology for changeable business requirements. J. Inf. Sci. Eng. 24, 649–671 (2008)
8. Hay, D.C.: Data Model Patterns: Conventions of Though. Dorset House Publishing, New York (1996)
9. Chen, P.P.-S.: English sentence structure and entity-relationship diagram. Inf. Sci. 29(2–3), 127–149 (1983)

10. Embley, D.W.: Toward semantic understanding: an approach based on information extraction. In: Proceedings of the 15th Australasian Database Conference, vol. 27, pp. 3–12 (2004)

11. Fowler, M.: Analysis Patterns: Reusable Object Models. Addison Wesley, Menlo Park (1997)

12. Coad, P., North, D., Mayfield, M.: Object Models: Strategies, Patterns, Applications. Yourdan Press, New Jersey (1995)

13. Shanks, G.: Conceptual data modeling process: a study of novice and expert. In: Proceedings of the 1st International Conference on Object-Role Modeling (1994)

14. Solomon, A., Vidya, M.: Data modeling patterns: a method and evaluation. In: Proceedings of the Fifteenth Americas Conference on Information Systems, San Francisco, California (2009)

15. Silverston, L.: The Data Model Resource Book, Volume 1: A library of Universal Data Models for All Enterprises. Wiley, Hoboken (2001)

16. Hay, D.C.: Enterprise Model Patterns: Describing the World (UML Version). Technics Publications, New Jersey (2011)

17. Hay, D.C.: Data Model Patterns: A Metadata Map (The Morgan Kaufmann Series in Data Management Systems). Morgan Kaufmann, San Francisco (2006)

18. Blaha, M.: Patterns of Data Modeling. CRC Press, Cambridge (2010)

19. Giles, J.: The Nimble Elephant: Agile Delivery of Data Models Using a Pattern-Based Approach. Technics Publications, New Jersey (2012)

Decision-Making Model at the Management of Hybrid Power Grid

Sergii Tymchuk[1] ⓘ, Sergii Shendryk[2(✉)] ⓘ, Vira Shendryk[2] ⓘ, Anton Panov[1] ⓘ,
Anastasia Kazlauskaite[2] ⓘ, and Tetiana Levytska[3] ⓘ

[1] Kharkiv Petro Vasylenko National Technical University of Agriculture, 19 Rizdviana Street,
Kharkiv 61052, Ukraine
stym@i.ua
[2] Sumy State University, 2 Rymskogo-Korsakova Street, Sumy 40007, Ukraine
{s.shendryk,v.shendryk}@cs.sumdu.edu.ua,
kazlauskayte15@gmail.com
[3] Pryazovskyi State Technical University, 7 Universytets'ka Street, Mariupol 87555, Ukraine
tlevitiisys@gmail.com

Abstract. This paper is devoted to developing a model of decision-making regarding the optimal control of the Hybrid Grid mode parameters, considering the forecast of changes in the parameters of generation and electricity consumption in the Microgrid. The decision-making problem at the management of Hybrid Power Grids is formed in the conditions of uncertainty and incompleteness of the input information. It cannot be considered as an optimization problem but should be evaluated as a multidimensional and multiscale problem. In this research the information support components, arrays of alternative possible regimes have been formed, based on expert evaluation, the decision selection criteria have been defined, fuzzy production rules have been formulated, which consider the operational logic of the hybrid grid. The developed system of fuzzy production rules allows in the functioning process of the Hybrid Power Consumption System to make changes in the mode of operation in order to increase energy savings, resource components of the power consumption system and electricity quality.

Keywords: Decision-making model · Hybrid Power Grid · Subscriber point

1 Introduction

The decision-making problem at the management of Hybrid Power Grids is formed in the conditions of uncertainty and incompleteness of the input information, which makes it impossible to formalize it as the exact mathematical model [1]. Various scales of measurement with varying degrees of detail are used to evaluate the parameters affecting the functioning, consequently the decision-making task of determining the effective mode of a Hybrid Grid operation cannot be considered as an optimization problem but should be evaluated as a multidimensional and multiscale problem.

Meanwhile, by many authors, this task is regarded as a task of operational control based on the current status of the mode parameters. A detailed analysis of this approach

A. Lopata et al. (Eds.): ICIST 2020, CCIS 1283, pp. 60–71, 2020.
https://doi.org/10.1007/978-3-030-59506-7_6

is given in [2]. This approach is implemented in existing Hybrid Power Supply Systems with the possibility of connection to a Centralized Power System, for example described in [1, 3]. The problem with Hybrid Power Systems is that they do not account for possible changes in power and power generation modes in the nearest future.

This work's purpose is to develop a model of decision-making regarding the optimal control of the Hybrid Grid mode parameters, taking into account the forecast of changes in the parameters of generation and electricity consumption in the Microgrid.

This paper is dedicated to the method of the choosing the possible existing state of the Hybrid Power Grid that allows to strike a balance between generation and consumption of electricity with sufficient the generated electricity quality. The issues of the choice of effective state based on the operational logic of the Power Grid operation will be considered, the effective decision-making methods based on fuzzy logic will be described, as well as the management decisions issues using additional current information about an established mode and predictive information about electricity generation and consumption will be explored, the change Hybrid Power Grid structure by switching changes will be carried out.

2 Problem Statement

From the possible existing states of the Hybrid Power Grid, one should be chosen that allows to strike a balance between generation and consumption of electricity with sufficient the generated electricity quality. The solution choice should also be based on the operational logic of the Power Grid operation. Therefore, in this case for effective decision-making should use of decision-making methods based on fuzzy logic.

A Microgrid is a System of Subscribers, each of them has owning renewable energy sources. Accordingly, the decision-making system for managing the Microgrid modes should be multilevel. The lower level corresponds to the Subscriber Point level, which is the one considered in this research.

An important feature of the subscriber point management system is that they are set up to maintain the current balance of consumption - electricity generation. Therefore, almost the only way to influence with the operation of the Electrical Modes Control System of the Subscriber Point is to promptly change its structure due to switching changes. It is proposed to monitor the control process by monitoring the electricity quality, as well as the total capacity of its production from various renewable energy sources or different combinations thereof. Management decisions are suggested to be made using additional current information on the established mode, as well as predictive information obtained on the mathematical models' basis.

3 Configuration of Subscriber Point

The Subscriber Point is connected to the Hybrid Microgrid by means of the B1 switch (Fig. 1). Renewable Energy Sources (RES) are connected by means of switches B2–B5. Non-critical and balance load is connected by means of switches B6, B7. Critical load cannot be disconnected from the Power Grid. Renewable Energy Sources have convectors (K1–K3) convert the DC voltage current of the source into AC voltage current of Power Grid. These processes are controlled by autonomous device Controllers. Their task is to maintain either a constant voltage or the required load capacity of a Subscriber Point. Such regulation possibilities are limited because as a rule, they do not consider the qualitative indicators of electricity, the integrated electricity consumption and power generation characteristics, the forecast environment characteristics and the influence of other Subscriber Points.

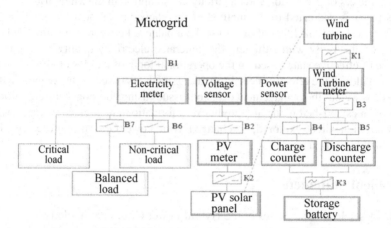

Fig. 1. The structure of the Hybrid Grid Subscriber Point

The effective operation mode of the Subscriber Point is ensured by connecting Renewable Energy Sources or various separate combinations thereof, together with the possible connection of batteries in charge or discharge mode (if necessary), as well as connecting to the Microgrid (if necessary). The solution choice comes from possible alternatives considering the Hybrid Grid operating logic.

4 Decision-Making Model

4.1 Decision-Making Criteria

As the first type of decision-making criterion is proposed to accept the electricity quality indicator in a fuzzy form.

Grid voltage sensors provide up-to-date information on phase voltages U_A, U_B, U_C, as well as interfacial voltages U_{AB}, U_{AC}, U_{BC}. This gives the ability to control the electricity quality indicators related to the voltage.

Firstly, it is an indicator of the voltage deviation, which is established δUy. A fuzzy estimate of this indicator is given in [4]. For operational control, it is more convenient to use fuzzed data from voltage sensors, as it is showed on Fig. 2.

Let U_H be the nominal value of the corresponding voltage deviation; $\mu_{\delta U_{yn}}$, $\mu_{\delta U_{yL}}$, $\mu_{\delta U_{yh}}$ are the corresponding membership functions to the normal, low, and high voltage index, which is established.

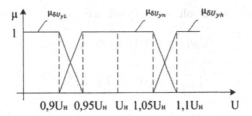

Fig. 2. Fuzzification of an indicator δUy

The membership function to the term "normal" voltage $\mu_{\delta U_{yn}}$ is formed on the basis of the fazzed quality norms given in [4].

$\mu_{\delta U_{yL}}$, $\mu_{\delta U_{yh}}$ reflect the deviation degree from the regulatory documents requirements.

Formally defined membership functions are as follows:

$$\mu_{\delta U_{yL}} = max\left\{0, min\left\{1, \frac{0,95U_H - U}{0,05U_H}\right\}\right\}$$

$$\mu_{\delta U_{yh}} = max\left\{0, min\left\{1, \frac{U - 0,9U_H}{0,05U_H}, \frac{1,1U_H - U}{0,05U_H}\right\}\right\}$$

$$\mu_{\delta U_{yh}} = max\left\{0, min\left\{1, \frac{U - 1,05U_H}{0,05U_H}\right\}\right\} \tag{1}$$

Fuzzing is carried out in two voltage types: phase and interphase. Phase and interphase voltages are considered to be a fuzzy value with the terms: low (L), normal (n) and high (h): U_{AL}, U_{An}, U_{Ah}, U_{BL}, U_{Bn}, U_{Bh}, U_{CL}, U_{Cn}, U_{Ch}; U_{ABL}, U_{ABN}, U_{ABh}, U_{ACL}, U_{ACn}, U_{ACh}, U_{BCL}, U_{BCn}, U_{BCh}.

Secondly, it is the voltage asymmetry coefficient of the reverse sequence K2U and the voltage asymmetry coefficient of the zero sequence K0U.

Measurement and calculation method K_{2U}, K_{0U} are determined by the state standard for electricity quality

$$K_{2U} = \frac{U_{2(1)}}{U_{HM}} \cdot 100,$$

where the current voltage value of the reverse sequence

$$U_{2(1)} = 0,62\left(U_{M_{max}} - U_{M_{min}}\right),$$

$$U_{M_{max}} = max(U_{AB}, U_{AC}, U_{BC}),$$

$$U_{M_{min}} = min(U_{AB}, U_{AC}, U_{BC}).$$

The U_{HM} is the nominal interfacial voltage value.

$$K_{0U} = \frac{U_{6(1)}}{U_{nf}} \cdot 100,$$

where the current value of the voltage zero sequence

$$U_{0(1)} = 0,62\left(U_{fmax} - U_{fmin}\right),$$

$$U_{fmax} = \max(U_A, U_B, U_C),$$

$$U_{fmin} = \min(U_A, U_B, U_C).$$

In these expressions, U_{nf} is the nominal phase voltage value.

For fuzzing the asymmetry coefficients, we introduce two terms: normal (n) and high (h). Accordingly, the fuzzy sets corresponding to these terms are K_{2Un}, K_{2Uh}, K_{0Un}, and K_{0Uh}. In Fig. 3 shows their graphical and then formal appearance.

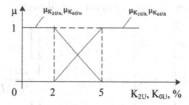

Fig. 3. Fuzzification of asymmetry coefficients

The term membership functions are formed on the basis of the fuzzed quality standards given in [4].

$$\mu_{K_{2Un}, K_{0Un}} = max\left\{0, min\left\{1, \frac{5-K}{3}\right\}\right\},$$

$$\mu_{K_{2Uh}, K_{0Uh}} = max\left\{0, min\left\{1, \frac{K-2}{3}\right\}\right\}. \tag{2}$$

Only two of these Quality Indicators can be modified in the Microgrid.

As the second decision-making criterion type, it is proposed to select the electric capacity received by the Subscriber Point from the Microgrid. This criterion is minimizing. It shows how much a Subscriber Point is able to function autonomously.

4.2   Current's Mode Parameters of the Subscriber Point Power Supply System

Power sensors provide information on the current state of electricity generation and consumption.

Firstly, it is the solar panel power P_{sb}. It is proposed to fuzzy the parameter P_{sb} by introducing three terms: low (L), normal (n) and high (h). The term membership functions are as follows:

$$\mu_{P_{sbL}} = max\left\{0, min\left\{1, \frac{P_{sbmod} - P_{sb}}{P_{sbmod} - P_{sbmin}}\right\}\right\},$$

$$\mu_{P_{sbn}} = max\left\{0, min\left\{1, \frac{P_{sb} - P_{sbmin}}{P_{sbmod} - P_{sbmin}}, \frac{P_{sbmod} - P_{sb}}{P_{sbmax} - P_{sbmod}}\right\}\right\},$$

$$\mu_{P_{sbh}} = max\left\{0, min\left\{1, \frac{P_{sb} - P_{sbmod}}{P_{sbmax} - P_{sbmod}}\right\}\right\}. \tag{3}$$

The characteristic parameters of expressions (3) are obtained from the forecast dependences given in [5, 6], but for different periods of the year. P_{sbmin} - for December 22; P_{sbmax} - for June 22; P_{sbmod} - for March 21 or September 21.

Secondly, it is the wind turbine power P_W. It is proposed to fuzzy the parameter P_W by introducing three terms: low (L), normal (n) and high (h). The terms membership functions are as follows:

$$\mu_{P_{WL}} = max\left\{0, min\left\{1, \frac{P_{wmin} - P_W}{P_{wmod} - P_{wmin}}\right\}\right\},$$

$$\mu_{P_{Wn}} = max\left\{0, min\left\{1, \frac{P_W - P_{wmin}}{P_{wmod} - P_{wmin}}, \frac{P_{wmod} - P_W}{P_{wmax} - P_{wmod}}\right\}\right\},$$

$$\mu_{P_{Wh}} = max\left\{0, min\left\{1, \frac{P_W - P_{wmod}}{P_{wmax} - P_{wmod}}\right\}\right\}. \tag{4}$$

The characteristic parameters of expressions (4) are obtained from the predicted dependencies, P_{wmin} - for the minimum parameter values; P_{wmax} - for maximum parameter values, P_{wmod} - for modal parameter values.

Thirdly, it is the battery capacity PB. It is proposed to fuzzy the P_B parameter by introducing two terms: low (L) and high (h). The term membership functions are as follows:

$$\mu_{P_{BL}} = max\left\{0, min\left\{1, \frac{0,75P_{Bmax} - P_B}{0,5P_{Bmax}}\right\}\right\},$$

$$\mu_{P_{Bh}} = max\left\{0, min\left\{1, \frac{P_B - 0,25P_{Bmax}}{0,5P_{Bmax}}\right\}\right\}. \tag{5}$$

In expressions (5) P_{Bmax} is the maximum battery capacity, which is determined by the technical passport.

Fourthly, it is the current power consumption W. The parameter W is proposed to be fuzzed by introducing three terms: low (L), normal (n) and high (h). The term membership functions are as follows:

$$\mu_{W_L} = max\left\{0, min\left\{1, \frac{W_{mod} - W}{W_{mod} - W_{min}}\right\}\right\},$$

$$\mu_{W_n} = max\left\{0, min\left\{1, \frac{W - W_{min}}{W_{mod} - W_{min}}, \frac{W_{mod} - W}{W_{max} - W_{mod}}\right\}\right\},$$

$$\mu_{W_h} = max\left\{0, min\left\{1, \frac{W - W_{mod}}{W_{max} - W_{mod}}\right\}\right\}. \tag{6}$$

The characteristic parameters of expressions (6) are obtained based on the analysis of statistical data, which are used in the development of forecast dependencies [7].

4.3 Predictive Values of Mode's Parameters

The mathematical models given in [5–7] allow estimating the predictive data for electricity generation and consumption in a Hybrid Grid every three hours during the 24 h.

Firstly, it is the solar panel power P_{IIsb}, which is calculated when the environmental parameters are changed according to the weather forecast after three hours. It is proposed to fuzzy the parameter P_{IIsb} by introducing three terms: low (L), normal (n) and high (h). The term membership functions are analogous (3).

Secondly, it is the wind turbine power P_{IIW}, which is calculated when the environmental parameters are changed according to the three-hour weather forecast. It is proposed to fuzzy the parameter P_{IIW} by introducing three terms: low (L), normal (n) and high (h). The term membership functions are analogous (4).

Thirdly, it is the power consumption W_{II}, which is calculated according to the short-term forecast model for a period of three hours. It is proposed to fuzzy the parameter W_{II} by introducing three terms: low (L), normal (n) and high (h). The functions of term membership are similar (6).

4.4 Output Parameters

The output parameters of decision-making model are the control commands of the B1, B5–B7 switches (Fig. 1).

Switches B2, B3, B4 are always switched on when operating the mains. They turned off only in cases of dismantling, repair or individual maintenance.

The B1 switch connects the Subscriber Point to the Hybrid Microgrid, the B5 switch connects the Storage Battery for discharge to the Subscriber Grid, the B6 switch connects non-critical load to the Subscriber Point Grid, the B7 switch connects the balance load to the Subscriber Grid.

Non-critical load is one that can be switched off without damage if necessary. Balancing load helps to consume a small excess of electricity, which is more profitable to use at a Subscriber Point than to give to the Microgrid.

Let the fuzzy value $B1 = <B1_{on}, B1_{off}>$.

Membership function B1 value terms are as follows:

$$\mu_{B1_{off}} = max\left\{0, min\left\{1, \frac{1 - B1}{1}\right\}\right\},$$

$$\mu_{B1_{on}} = max\left\{0, min\left\{1, \frac{B1}{1}\right\}\right\}. \tag{7}$$

Similarly, $B5 = <B5_{on}, B5_{off}>$, $B6 = <B6_{on}, B6_{off}>$, $B7 = <B7_{on}, B7_{off}>$. The membership functions B5–B7 value terms have the form similar to (7).

4.5 Formation of Fuzzy Production Rules for Managing the Hybrid Grid Operation Modes

When we have the current values terms of fuzzy operational parameters (1)–(6) and predictive parameters, it is possible to form a Fuzzy Inference System regarding the choice of Hybrid Power Grid operation mode.

The fuzzy reasoning for B1 control consists of two rules:

$$If((((U_{AL} \text{ and } U_{BL} \text{ and } U_{CL}) \text{ or } (U_{ABL} \text{ and } U_{ACL} \text{ and } U_{BCL}) \text{ or } (K_{2Uh} \text{ and } K_{0Uh})) \text{ and }$$
$$P_{SBL} \text{ and } P_{WL} \text{ and } P_{BL} \text{ and } P_{nSBL} \text{ and } P_{nWL} \text{ and not } W_{nL}) \text{ or } (((U_{Ah} \text{ and } U_{Bh} \text{ and } U_{Ch})$$
$$\text{or } (U_{ABh} \text{ and } U_{ACh} \text{ and } U_{BCh})) \text{ and } P_{SBh} \text{ and } P_{Wh} \text{ and } P_{Bh} \text{ and } P_{nSBh} \text{ and } P_n W_h \text{ and }$$
$$\text{not } W_{nh}) \text{ then } B1_{on} \tag{8}$$

$$If(((U_{An} \text{ or } U_{Ah} \text{ and } U_{Bn} \text{ or } U_{Bh} \text{ and } U_{Cn} \text{ or } U_{Ch}) \text{ or } (U_{ABn} \text{ or } U_{ABh} \text{ and } U_{ACn} \text{ or } U_{ACh}$$
$$\text{and } U_{BCn} \text{ or } U_{BCh})) \text{ and } (P_{SBn} \text{ or } P_{SBh} \text{ and } P_{Wn} \text{ or } P_{Wh}) \text{ then } B1_{off}. \tag{9}$$

The first rule consists of two parts. The first part means that when all phase voltages are low or all interphase voltages are low or both coefficients of asymmetry are large, and at the same time there is a low level of electricity generation, a low Battery, the generation is not expected to increase and the load is not expected to increase, there is no other way out than to connect a Subscriber Point to a Hybrid Microgrid. The second part of the rule means that when all phase or interphase voltages are large and the energy generation is large with a high Battery level, and no significant reduction in generation and load is expected, there is an excess of electricity that can be released into the Microgrid.

The second rule means that when all phase or interphase voltages have a normal or high level and the generation of electricity is at a normal or high level, then the Subscriber Point is able to provide autonomous power from alternative sources and can be disconnected from the Microgrid.

$$If((P_{SBL} \text{ or } P_{SBn}) \text{ and } (P_{WL} \text{ or } P_{Wn}) \text{ and } P_{Bh} \text{ and } P_{nSBL} \text{ and } P_{nWL} \text{ and } (W_{nh} \text{ or } W_{nn}))$$
$$\text{then } B5_{on}. \tag{10}$$

$$If((P_{SBh} \text{ or } P_{SBn}) \text{ and } (P_{Wh} \text{ or } P_{Wn}) \text{ and } P_{Bh} \text{ and } (P_{nSBL} \text{ or } P_{nSBn}) \text{ and } (P_{nWL}P_{nWn}) \text{ and } W_{nh})$$
$$\text{then } B5_{off}. \tag{11}$$

The third rule means that the battery connects to the discharge in low or normal generation at high charge, with a predicted decrease in generation to a low level and a predicted average or high load level.

The fourth rule means that at a high or normal level of generation, a large level of charge, with a predicted decrease in generation and increase in load, it is necessary to keep the charge until the expected voltage mode of power consumption. If the predictive conditions of generation are fulfilled, then the third rule will work and the battery will turn on for discharge.

This predictive discharge mode is not provided by the standard automatic charge-discharge control algorithm. However, due to this interference with the information system, it is possible to extend the mode of autonomous electricity consumption to a Subscriber Point.

$$If((U_{AL} \text{ or } U_{BL} \text{ or } U_{CL}) \text{ and } (U_{ABL} \text{ or } U_{ACL} \text{ or } U_{BCL}) \text{ and } W_h \text{ and } W_{nh}) \text{ then } B6_{off}. \tag{12}$$

$$If((U_{An} \text{ and } U_{Bn} \text{ and } U_{Cn} \text{ and } U_{ABn} \text{ and } U_{ACn} \text{ and } U_{BCn} \text{ and } W_n \text{ and } (W_{nn} \text{ or } W_{nL}))$$
$$\text{then } B6_{on}. \tag{13}$$

The fuzzy reasoning for B7 also has two rules:

$If((U_{An}or\ U_{AL})$ and $(U_{Bn}or\ U_{BL})$ and $(U_{Cn}or\ U_{CL})$ and $(U_{ABn}or\ U_{ABL})$ and $(U_{ACn}or$

$U_{ACL})$ and $(U_{BCn}or\ U_{BCL})$ and K_{2Un} and K_{0Un} then $B7_{off}.$ (14)

$If((U_{An}or\ U_{Ah})$ and $(U_{Bn}or\ U_{Bh})$ and $(U_{Cn}or\ U_{Ch})$ and $(U_{ABn}or\ U_{ABh})$ and $(U_{ACn}or$
$U_{ACh})$ and $(U_{BCn}or\ U_{BCh})$ and K_{2Un} and $K_{0Un})$ then $B7_{on}.$ (15)

The method of defuzzification is offered - according to the maximum actuation force, namely:

if $\mu_{B1_{off}} > \mu_{B1_{on}}$ *– switch off the switch B1,*
if $\mu_{B1_{off}} < \mu_{B1_{on}}$ *– switch on the switch B1.*
Similarly, for B5–B7 switches.

Checking the decision-making model adequacy was performed on the Power System of a particular Subscriber Point.

Testing of the fuzzy production decision-making rules system was performed in the Matlab Fuzzy Logic Toolbox software extension package (Fig. 4).

Testing was carried out for the Hybrid Power Grid, which included the Amerisolar AS-6P30 solar panel with a total area of 20 m^2, the FLAMINGO AERO wind units, and the Pulsar HTL12-300 battery [1]. Electricity consumption data throughout the year were used to estimate the consumption pattern. The proposed decision-making model testing was performed at three-hour intervals during the day.

The implementation of the fuzzy inference of the decision-making model was carried out using the Mamdani algorithm. For defuzzification, the method of the rule maximum actuation force was triggered.

Fuzzification was performed for each of the input and output variables.

For a fuzzy inference system, further input parameters are conveniently to present not in ab-solute but in relative form. This approach generalizes the methodology because it will not be tied to the specific parameters of the hybrid power system. This requires a slight correction of expressions (3)–(6).

Solar power in relative form is accepted as P_{sb}/P_{sbmod}. Similarly, wind power is P_w/P_{wmod}. Accordingly, the predictive values of these parameters will be taken as P_{nsb}/P_{sbmod}, P_{nw}/P_{wmod}.

For the rechargeable battery, entered the relative parameter P_b/P_{bmax}, and for more accurate and predictive loading respectively W/W_{mod} and W_n/W_{mod}.

The decision to enable or disable switches B1, B5–B7 in clear logic is shown by clear commands - 0, 1, in a fuzzy form, this decision depends on the evaluation of the command execution degree to switch on or off switches in the range 0–1. Therefore, the terms membership functions of the output variables have the form as shown in Fig. 5.

After the input parameters were fuzzed, a system of Mamdani fuzzy logic rules was developed. The complex rules of logical inference (8–15) have been broken down into a number of simple production rules. Total of such rules 31.

Examples of characteristic surfaces for the rule base for switchs B1, B5–B7 are shown in Figs. 6, 7, 8 and 9.

Figures 6, 7, 8 and 9 clearly illustrates the correctness of fuzzy logic inference system construction, its compliance with the tasks.

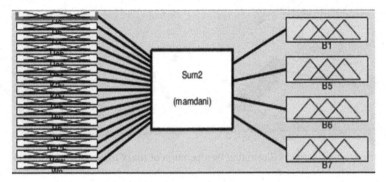

Fig. 4. Logic inputs and outputs formation

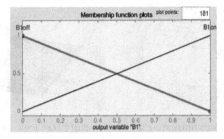

Fig. 5. The term membership function of the output variable B1

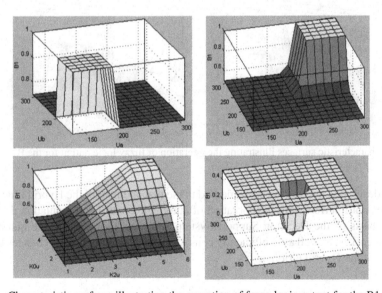

Fig. 6. Characteristic surfaces illustrating the operation of fuzzy logic output for the B1 switch

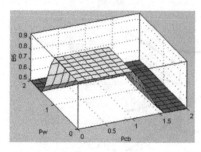 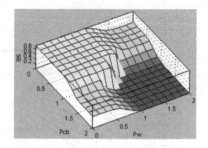

Fig. 7. Characteristic surfaces illustrating the operation of fuzzy logic output for the B5 switch

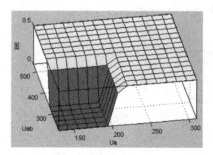 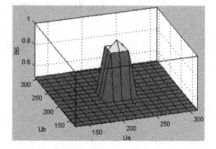

Fig. 8. Characteristic surfaces illustrating the operation of fuzzy logic output for the B6 switch

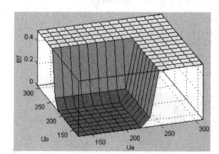 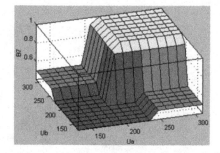

Fig. 9. Characteristic surfaces illustrating the operation of fuzzy logic output for the B7 switch

The developed decision-making method in the management of the Hybrid Electrical Grid does not interfere with the operation of automatic control and regulation devices. It is the basis of the Decision Support System and aims to normalize the quality of electrical energy, as well as to efficiently consume it by promptly making changes to the structure of the Hybrid Grid itself.

5 Conclusions

The decision-making problem in the management of the Hybrid Power Grid is considered. The information support components for decision support in the management of the Hybrid Grid have been determined.

Arrays of alternative possible regimes have been formed, based on expert evaluation, the decision selection criteria have been defined, fuzzy production rules have been formulated, which take into account the operational logic of the hybrid grid.

Thus, the developed system of fuzzy production rules allows in the functioning process of the Hybrid Power Consumption System to make changes in the mode of operation in order to increase energy savings, resource components of the power consumption system and electricity quality. The fuzzy rules system, formed on the basis of expert judgment and mathematical models for predicting the level of generation and consumption, takes into account the operational logic of the hybrid electricity network operation with a sufficient level of electricity quality and is part of the knowledge base.

References

1. Arcos-Aviles, D., Pascual, J., Marroyo, L., Sanchis, P., Guinjoan, F.: Fuzzy logic-based energy management system design for residential grid-connected microgrids. IEEE Trans. Smart Grid, 530–543 (2016). https://doi.org/10.1109/TSG.2016.2555245
2. Shahid Laiq, M., Ahmed, S., Khan, Z.A., Irfan Khattak, M., Sadaf, A.: A comparison of fuzzy control schemes to enhance sustainability in microgrid. In: Barolli, L., Xhafa, F., Conesa, J. (eds.) BWCCA 2017. LNDECT, vol. 12, pp. 516–532. Springer, Cham (2018). https://doi.org/10.1007/978-3-319-69811-3_47
3. Teo1, T.T., Logenthiran, T., Woo1, W.L., Abidi, K.: Advanced control strategy for an energy storage system in a grid-connected microgrid with renewable energy generation. IET Smart Grid 1(3), 96–103 (2018). https://doi.org/10.1049/iet-stg.2018.0024
4. Tymchuk, S.A., Miroshnyk, A.A.: Assess electricity quality by means of fuzzy generalized index. East Eur. J. Adv. Technol. 3/4(75), 26–31 (2015). https://doi.org/10.15587/1729-4061.2015.42484
5. Tymchuk, S., Shendryk, S.: Mathematical model of solar battery for balance calculations in hybrid electrical grids. In: International Conference on Modern Electrical and Energy Systems (MEES 2017), Kremenchuk, Ukraine, pp. 204–207 (2017). https://doi.org/10.1109/MEES.2017.8248890
6. Tymchuk, S., Shendryk, S., Shendryk, V., Piskarov, O., Kazlauskayte, A.: Fuzzy predictive model of solar panel for decision support system in the management of hybrid grid. In: Damaševičius, R., Vasiljevienė, G. (eds.) ICIST 2019. CCIS, vol. 1078, pp. 416–427. Springer, Cham (2019). https://doi.org/10.1007/978-3-030-30275-7_32
7. Tymchuk, S., Katiukha, I.: Development of regression coefficient selection quality criterion in power consumption forecasting problems. East. Eur. J. Enterp. Technol. 8(71), 16–20 (2014). https://doi.org/10.15587/1729-4061.2014.27664

Mining Data with Many Missing Attribute Values Using Global and Saturated Probabilistic Approximations Based on Characteristic Sets

Patrick G. Clark[1], Jerzy W. Grzymala-Busse[1,2(✉)], Teresa Mroczek[2], and Rafal Niemiec[2]

[1] Department of Electrical Engineering and Computer Science, University of Kansas, Lawrence, KS 66045, USA
patrick.g.clark@gmail.com, jerzy@ku.edu
[2] Department of Artificial Intelligence, University of Information Technology and Management, 35-225 Rzeszow, Poland
{tmroczek,rniemiec}@wsiz.rzeszow.pl

Abstract. In this paper, incomplete data sets have missing attribute values of two types: lost values and "do not care" conditions. Our algorithm of data mining, based on rule induction, uses two types of probabilistic approximations, called global and saturated. Thus, we use four different ways of rule induction, applying two types of missing attribute values with two types of probabilistic approximations. We used ten-fold cross validation to estimate an error rate. Previous results, with data sets with 35% of missing attribute values, show that there is no universally best way of rule induction. Therefore, in our current experiments, we use data sets with many missing attribute values. As follows from our new results, the best way of data mining should be selected by running experiments taking into account all four possibilities.

Keywords: Incomplete data mining · Characteristic sets · Rough set theory · Probabilistic approximations

1 Introduction

In this paper, incomplete data sets have missing attribute values of two types: lost values and "do not care" conditions. Lost values mean that the original values were deleted, so we are going to use only existing attribute values for rule induction. A lost value is denoted by "?". "Do not care" conditions indicate that a missing attribute value may be replaced by any existing attribute value. A "do not care" condition is denoted by "*".

Our algorithm of data mining, based on rule induction, uses two types of probabilistic approximations, called global and saturated. A probabilistic approximation is a generalization of the idea of lower and upper approximations known in rough set theory. A probabilistic approximation is defined by a

ⓒ Springer Nature Switzerland AG 2020
A. Lopata et al. (Eds.): ICIST 2020, CCIS 1283, pp. 72–83, 2020.
https://doi.org/10.1007/978-3-030-59506-7_7

probability α, if $\alpha = 1$, a probabilistic approximation is reduced to the lower approximation; if α is a small positive number, e.g., 0.001, the probabilistic approximation becomes the upper approximation. Usually, probabilistic approximations are applied to completely specified data sets [13–21]. Such approximations were generalized to incomplete data sets in [9].

Characteristic sets for incomplete data sets with any interpretation of missing attribute values were introduced in [8]. A global probabilistic approximation was introduced in [1]. Recently, a new idea of probabilistic approximation, called a saturated probabilistic approximation was introduced in [4]. Our main objective is to compare both probabilistic approximations in terms of an error rate, evaluated by ten-fold cross validation. The Modified Learning from Examples Module, version 2 (MLEM2) [3] was used for rule induction.

Previous results, with data sets with 35% of missing attribute values, show that there is no universally best way of rule induction [4]. Therefore, in our current experiments we use data sets with many missing attribute values. In our experiments, four ways for mining incomplete data sets were used, since we combined two options of probabilistic approximations: global and saturated with two interpretations of missing attribute values: lost and "do not care" conditions. Our new results show the best way of data mining should be selected by running experiments taking into account all four possibilities.

2 Incomplete Data

Our main ideas are illustrated using a small data set presented in Table 1. Rows of this table represent cases, while columns are labeled by variables. The set of all cases will be denoted by U. In Table 1, $U = \{1, 2, 3, 4, 5, 6, 7, 8\}$. Independent variables are called attributes and a dependent variable is called a decision and is denoted by d. The set of all attributes will be denoted by A. In Table 1, $A = \{Temperature, Wind, Humidity\}$. The value for a case x and an attribute a is denoted by $a(x)$. For example, $Temperature(1) = medium$.

Table 1. A Decision Table

	Attributes			Decision
Case	Temperature	Wind	Humidity	Trip
1	Medium	Medium	Low	Yes
2	High	?	*	Yes
3	*	Low	Medium	Yes
4	?	*	Medium	Yes
5	High	High	?	No
6	Low	High	*	No
7	*	?	High	No
8	Medium	*	High	No

The set X of all cases defined by the same value of the decision d is called a *concept*. In Table 1, a concept associated with the value *yes* of the decision *Trip* is the set $\{1, 2, 3, 4\}$.

For a variable a and its value v, a *block* of the variable-value pair (a, v), denoted by $[(a, v)]$, is the set $\{x \in U \mid a(x) = v\}$ [5]. For incomplete decision tables, the definition of a block of an attribute-value pair is modified in the following way:

- if for an attribute a and a case x we have $a(x) = ?$, the case x should not be included in any blocks $[(a, v)]$ for all values v of attribute a;
- if for an attribute a and a case x we have $a(x) = *$, the case x should be included in blocks $[(a, v)]$ for all specified values v of attribute a.

For the data set from Table 1, the blocks of attribute-value pairs are:
[(Temperature, low)] = $\{3, 6, 7\}$,
[(Temperature, medium)] = $\{1, 3, 7, 8\}$,
[(Temperature, high)] = $\{2, 3, 5, 7\}$,
[(Wind, low)] = $\{3, 4, 8\}$,
[(Wind, medium)] = $\{1, 4, 8\}$,
[(Wind, high)] = $\{4, 5, 6, 8\}$,
[(Humidity, low)] = $\{1, 2, 6\}$,
[(Humidity, medium)] = $\{2, 3, 4, 6\}$, and
[(Humidity, high)] = $\{2, 6, 7, 8\}$.

For a case $x \in U$ and $B \subseteq A$, a *characteristic set* $K_B(x)$ is defined as the intersection of the sets $K(x, a)$, for all $a \in B$, where the set $K(x, a)$ is defined in the following way:

- if $a(x)$ is specified, then $K(x, a)$ is the block $[(a, a(x))]$ of attribute a and its value $a(x)$;
- if $a(x) = ?$ or $a(x) = *$, then $K(x, a) = U$.

For example, for Table 1 and $B = A$,
$K_A(1) = \{1\}$,
$K_A(2) = \{2, 3, 5, 7\}$,
$K_A(3) = \{3, 4\}$,
$K_A(4) = \{2, 3, 4, 6\}$,
$K_A(5) = \{5\}$,
$K_A(6) = \{6\}$,
$K_A(7) = \{2, 6, 7, 8\}$, and
$K_A(8) = \{7, 8\}$.

3   Probabilistic Approximations

In this section, we discuss two types of probabilistic approximations: global and saturated.

3.1 Global Probabilistic Approximations

An idea of the global probabilistic approximation, restricted to lower and upper approximations, was introduced in [11,12], and presented in a general form in [1]. Let X be a concept, $X \subseteq U$. A *B-global probabilistic approximation* of the concept X, based on characteristic sets, with the parameter α and denoted by $appr_{\alpha,B}^{global}(X)$ is defined as the following set

$$\bigcup \{K_B(x) \mid \exists\, Y \subseteq U \;\forall\, x \in Y,\; Pr(X|K_B(x)) \geq \alpha\}. \tag{1}$$

Obviously, for some sets B and X and the parameter α, there exist many B-global probabilistic approximations of X. In addition, the algorithm for computing B-global probabilistic approximations is of exponential computational complexity. Therefore, in our experiments we used a heuristic version of the definition of B-global probabilistic approximation, called a MLEM2 B-global probabilistic approximation of the concept X, associated with a parameter α and denoted by $appr_{\alpha,B}^{mlem2}(X)$, [1]. This definition is based on the rule induction algorithm MLEM2 [7]. The MLEM2 algorithm is used in the Learning from Examples using Rough Sets (LERS) data mining system [2,6,7]. The approximation $appr_{\alpha,B}^{mlem2}(X)$ is constructed from characteristic sets $K_B(y)$, the most relevant to the concept X, i.e., with $|X \cap K_B(y)|$ as large as possible and $Pr(X|K_B(y)) \geq \alpha$, where $y \in U$. If more than one characteristic set $K_B(y)$ satisfies both conditions, we pick the characteristic set $K_B(y)$ with the largest $Pr(X|K_B(y))$. If this criterion ends up with a tie, a characteristic set is picked up heuristically, as the first on the list [1].

In this paper, we study MLEM2 B-global probabilistic approximations based on characteristic sets, with $B = A$, and calling them, for simplicity, *global probabilistic approximations* associated with the parameter α, denoted by $appr_{\alpha}^{mlem2}(X)$. Similarly, for $B = A$, the characteristic set $K_B(X)$ is denoted by $K(x)$.

Let $E_\alpha(X)$ be the set of all eligible characteristic sets defined as follows

$$\{K(x) \mid x \in U, Pr(X|K(x)) \geq \alpha\}. \tag{2}$$

A heuristic version of the MLEM2 global probabilistic approximation is presented below.

MLEM2 global probabilistic approximation algorithm
input: a set X (a concept), a set $E_\alpha(X)$,
output: a set T ($appr_{\alpha}^{mlem2}(X)$)
begin
    $G := X$;
    $T := \emptyset$;
    $Y := E_\alpha(X)$;
    while $G \neq \emptyset$ **and** $Y \neq \emptyset$
        begin
            select a characteristic set $K(x) \in Y$

such that $|K(x) \cap X|$ is maximum;
if a tie occurs, select $K(x) \in Y$
with the smallest cardinality;
if another tie occurs, select the first $K(x)$;
$T := T \cup K(x)$;
$G := G - T$;
$Y := Y - K(x)$
  end
end

For Table 1, all distinct MLEM2 global probabilistic approximations are
$appr_1^{mlem2}(\{1, 2, 3, 4\}) = \{1, 3, 4\}$,

$appr_{0.75}^{mlem2}(\{1, 2, 3, 4\}) = \{1, 2, 3, 4, 6\}$,

$appr_{0.5}^{mlem2}(\{1, 2, 3, 4\}) = \{1, 2, 3, 4, 5, 6, 7\}$,

$appr_1^{mlem2}(\{5, 6, 7, 8\}) = \{5, 6, 7, 8\}$,

$appr_{0.75}^{mlem2}(\{5, 6, 7, 8\}) = \{2, 5, 6, 7, 8\}$ and

$appr_{0.5}^{mlem2}(\{5, 6, 7, 8\}) = \{2, 3, 5, 6, 7, 8\}$.

3.2 Saturated Probabilistic Approximations

Another heuristic version of the probabilistic approximation is based on selection
of characteristic sets while giving higher priority to characteristic sets with larger
conditional probability $Pr(X|K(x))$. Additionally, if the approximation covers
all cases from the concept X, we stop adding characteristic sets.

Let X be a concept and let $x \in U$. Let us compute all conditional probabilities
$Pr(X|K(x))$. Then, we sort the set

$$\{Pr(X|K(x)) \mid x \in U\}. \tag{3}$$

Let us denote the sorted list of such conditional probabilities by $\alpha_1, \alpha_2,...,$
α_n, where α_1 is the largest. For any $i = 1, 2,..., n$, the set $E_i(x)$ is defined as
follows

$$\{K(x) \mid x \in U, Pr(X|K(x)) = \alpha_i\}. \tag{4}$$

If we want to compute a saturated probabilistic approximation, denoted by
$appr_\alpha^{saturated}(X)$, for some α, $0 < \alpha \leq 1$, we need to identify the index m such
that

$$\alpha_m \geq \alpha > \alpha_{m+1}, \tag{5}$$

where $m \in \{1, 2, ..., n\}$ and $\alpha_{n+1} = 0$. Then, the saturated probabilistic approximation $appr_{\alpha_m}^{saturated}(X)$ is computed using the following algorithm.

Saturated probabilistic approximation algorithm
input: a set X (a concept), a set $E_i(x)$ for
$i = 1, 2, ..., n$ and $x \in U$, index m
output: a set T $(appr_{\alpha_m}^{saturated}(X))$
begin
$\qquad T := \emptyset;$
$\qquad Y_i(x) := E_i(x)$ for all $i = 1, 2, ..., m$ and $x \in U$;
$\qquad$ **for** $j = 1, 2, ..., m$ **do**
$\qquad\qquad$ **while** $Y_j(x) \neq \emptyset$
$\qquad\qquad\qquad$ **begin**
$\qquad\qquad\qquad\qquad$ select a characteristic set $K(x) \in Y_j(x)$
$\qquad\qquad\qquad\qquad$ such that $|K(x) \cap X|$ is maximum;
$\qquad\qquad\qquad\qquad$ if a tie occurs, select the first $K(x)$;
$\qquad\qquad\qquad\qquad Y_j(x) := Y_j(x) - K(x);$
$\qquad\qquad\qquad\qquad$ **if** $(K(x) - T) \cap X \neq \emptyset$
$\qquad\qquad\qquad\qquad\qquad$ **then** $T := T \cup K(x);$
$\qquad\qquad\qquad\qquad$ **if** $X \subseteq T$ **then exit**
$\qquad\qquad\qquad$ **end**
end

For Table 1, all distinct saturated probabilistic approximations are
$appr_1^{saturated}(\{1, 2, 3, 4\}) = \{1, 3, 4\},$

$appr_{0.75}^{saturated}(\{1, 2, 3, 4\}) = \{1, 2, 3, 4, 6\},$ and

$appr_1^{saturated}(\{5, 6, 7, 8\}) = \{5, 6, 7, 8\}.$

Note that $appr_{0.5}^{mlem2}(\{1, 2, 3, 4\})$ covers the cases 5 and 7 in spite of the fact that these cases are not members of the concept $\{1, 2, 3, 4\}$. The set $\{1, 2, 3, 4, 5, 6, 7\}$ is not listed among saturated probabilistic approximations of the concept $\{1, 2, 3, 4\}$.

3.3 Rule Induction

For given global and saturated probabilistic approximations associated with a parameter α, rule sets are induced using the rule induction algorithm based on another parameter, also interpreted as a probability, and denoted by β. This algorithm also uses MLEM2 principles [10]. This algorithm was presented, e.g., in [1].

For example, for Table 1 and $\alpha = \beta = 0.5$, using the saturated probabilistic approximations, the MLEM2 rule induction algorithm induces the following set of rules:

(Humidity, medium) → (Trip, yes),
(Humidity, low) → (Trip, yes),
(Wind, high) & (Humidity, high) → (Trip, no),
(Temperature, high) & (Wind, high) → (Trip, no), and
(Temperature, low) & (Humidity, high) → (Trip, no).

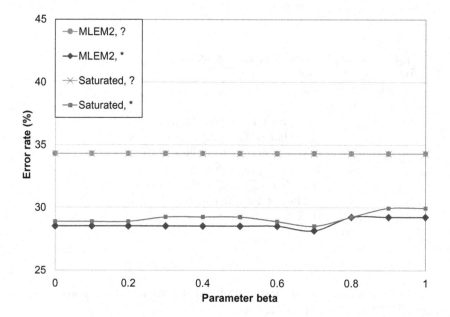

Fig. 1. Error rate for the *Breast cancer* data set with 45% missing attribute values

4   Experiments

Our objective was to find the best way among four ways of rule induction. In our experiments we utilized data sets stored at the University of California at Irvine *Machine Learning Repository*. For every data set, a template was created. Such a template was formed by replacing randomly existing specified attribute values by *lost values*. The same templates were used for constructing data sets with "do not care" conditions, by replacing "?"s with "*"s. The maximum percentage of missing attribute values was determined by the requirement that no row of the data set should contain only missing attribute values.

In our experiments, we used the MLEM2 rule induction algorithm. In all experiments, the parameter α was equal to 0.5. Results of our experiments are presented in Figures 1, 2, 3, 4, 5, 6, where "MLEM2" denotes a MLEM2 global probabilistic approximation, "Saturated" denotes a saturated probabilistic approximation, "?" denotes lost values and "*" denotes "do not care" conditions. In our experiments, four ways for mining incomplete data sets were used,

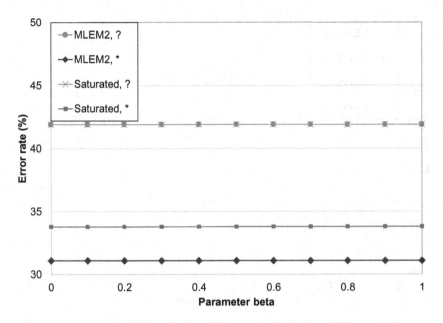

Fig. 2. Error rate for the *Echocardiogram* data set with 40% missing attribute values

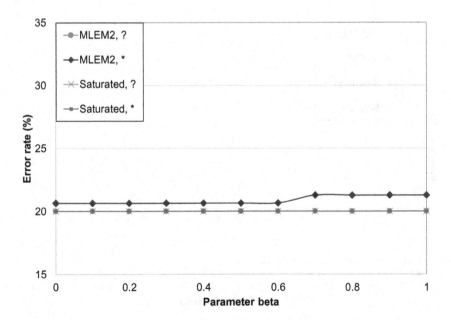

Fig. 3. Error rate for the *Hepatitis* data set with 60% missing attribute values

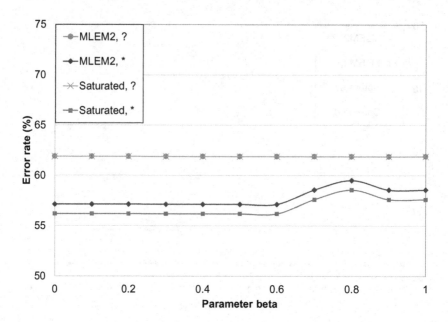

Fig. 4. Error rate for the *Image segment* data set with 50% missing attribute values

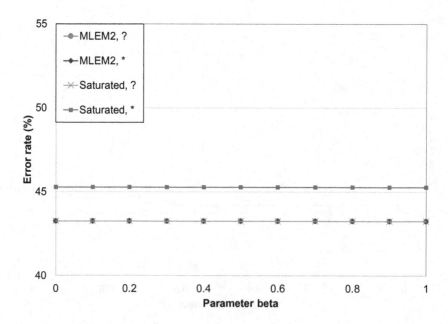

Fig. 5. Error rate for the *Lymphography* data set with 55% missing attribute values

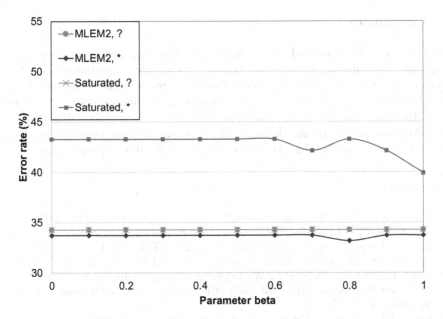

Fig. 6. Error rate for the *Wine recognition* data set with 65% missing attribute values

Table 2. Results of statistical analysis

Data set	Friedman test results (5% significance level)
Breast cancer	(MLEM2, *) & (Sat., *) are better than (MLEM2, ?) & (Sat., ?)
	(MLEM2, *) is better than (Saturated, *)
Echocardiogram	(MLEM2, *) is better than (Saturated, *)
	(Saturated, *) is better than (MLEM2, ?) & (Saturated, ?)
Hepatitis	(MLEM2, ?) & (Sat., *) & (Sat, ?) are better than (MLEM2., *)
Image segment	(Saturated, *) is better than (MLEM2, *)
	(MLEM2, *) is better than (MLEM2, ?) & (Saturated, ?)
Lymphography	(MLEM2, *) & (MLEM2, ?) & (Sat., ?) are better than (Sat., *)
Wine recognition	(MLEM2, *) is better than (MLEM2, ?) & (Saturated, ?)
	(MLEM2, ?) & (Saturated, ?) are better than (Saturated, *)

since we combined two options of probabilistic approximations: global and saturated with two interpretations of missing attribute values: lost and "do not care" conditions.

Results of our experiments on four ways of rule induction were compared by the Friedman rank sum test with the post-hoc multiple comparisons (a 5% level of significance). A summary of experimental results is presented in Table 2.

5   Conclusions

In this paper, we compared four ways of rule induction, applying two types of missing attribute values with two types of probabilistic approximations. For every data set, we computed an error rate using ten-fold cross validation. As follows from our experiments, there were significant differences between the four ways. However, the best way, associated with the smallest error rate, depends on a data set. For a specific data set, the best way to data mining should be selected by running experiments, taking into account all four possibilities.

References

1. Clark, P.G., Gao, C., Grzymala-Busse, J.W., Mroczek, T., Niemiec, R.: A comparison of concept and global probabilistic approximations based on mining incomplete data. In: Damaševičius, R., Vasiljevienė, G. (eds.) ICIST 2018. CCIS, vol. 920, pp. 324–335. Springer, Cham (2018). https://doi.org/10.1007/978-3-319-99972-2_26
2. Clark, P.G., Grzymala-Busse, J.W.: Experiments on probabilistic approximations. In: Proceedings of the 2011 IEEE International Conference on Granular Computing, pp. 144–149 (2011)
3. Clark, P.G., Grzymala-Busse, J.W.: Experiments on rule induction from incomplete data using three probabilistic approximations. In: Proceedings of the 2012 IEEE International Conference on Granular Computing, pp. 90–95 (2012)
4. Clark, P.G., Grzymala-Busse, J.W., Mroczek, T., Niemiec, R.: A comparison of global and saturated probabilistic approximations using characteristic sets in mining incomplete data. In: Proceedings of the Eight International Conference on Intelligent Systems and Applications, pp. 10–15 (2019)
5. Grzymala-Busse, J.W.: LERS–a system for learning from examples based on rough sets. In: Slowinski, R. (ed.) Intelligent Decision Support. Handbook of Applications and Advances of the Rough Set Theory, pp. 3–18. Kluwer Academic Publishers, Dordrecht (1992)
6. Grzymala-Busse, J.W.: A new version of the rule induction system LERS. Fundamenta Informaticae **31**, 27–39 (1997)
7. Grzymala-Busse, J.W.: MLEM2: a new algorithm for rule induction from imperfect data. In: Proceedings of the 9th International Conference on Information Processing and Management of Uncertainty in Knowledge-Based Systems, pp. 243–250 (2002)
8. Grzymala-Busse, J.W.: Rough set strategies to data with missing attribute values. In: Notes of the Workshop on Foundations and New Directions of Data Mining, in conjunction with the Third International Conference on Data Mining, pp. 56–63 (2003)
9. Grzymala-Busse, J.W.: Generalized parameterized approximations. In: Proceedings of the 6-th International Conference on Rough Sets and Knowledge Technology, pp. 136–145 (2011)
10. Grzymala-Busse, J.W., Clark, P.G., Kuehnhausen, M.: Generalized probabilistic approximations of incomplete data. Int. J. Approximate Reasoning **132**, 180–196 (2014)
11. Grzymala-Busse, J.W., Rzasa, W.: Local and global approximations for incomplete data. In: Proceedings of the Fifth International Conference on Rough Sets and Current Trends in Computing, pp. 244–253 (2006)

12. Grzymala-Busse, J.W., Rzasa, W.: Local and global approximations for incomplete data. Trans. Rough Sets **8**, 21–34 (2008)
13. Grzymala-Busse, J.W., Ziarko, W.: Data mining based on rough sets. In: Wang, J. (ed.) Data Mining: Opportunities and Challenges, pp. 142–173. Idea Group Publ, Hershey (2003)
14. Pawlak, Z., Skowron, A.: Rough sets: some extensions. Inf. Sci. **177**, 28–40 (2007)
15. Pawlak, Z., Wong, S.K.M., Ziarko, W.: Rough sets: probabilistic versus deterministic approach. Int. J. Man Mach. Stud. **29**, 81–95 (1988)
16. Ślęzak, D., Ziarko, W.: The investigation of the bayesian rough set model. Int. J. Approximate Reasoning **40**, 81–91 (2005)
17. Wong, S.K.M., Ziarko, W.: INFER–an adaptive decision support system based on the probabilistic approximate classification. In: Proceedings of the 6-th International Workshop on Expert Systems and their Applications, pp. 713–726 (1986)
18. Yao, Y.Y.: Probabilistic rough set approximations. Int. J. Approximate Reasoning **49**, 255–271 (2008)
19. Yao, Y.Y., Wong, S.K.M.: A decision theoretic framework for approximate concepts. Int. J. Man Mach. Stud. **37**, 793–809 (1992)
20. Ziarko, W.: Variable precision rough set model. J. Comput. Syst. Sci. **46**(1), 39–59 (1993)
21. Ziarko, W.: Probabilistic approach to rough sets. Int. J. Approx. Reason. **49**, 272–284 (2008)

Analytical Model of Design Workflows Organization in the Automated Design of Complex Technical Products

Nikolay Voit[✉], Sergey Kirillov, Semen Bochkov, and Irina Ionova

Computing Technique Department, Ulyanovsk State Technical University, Ulyanovsk, Russia
n.voit@ulstu.ru, kirillovsyu@gmail.com, bochkovsi@ido.ulstu.ru,
epira@mail.ru

Abstract. Authors have developed a new analytical model for organizing design workflows, including orchestration and choreography compositions of hybrid dynamic diagrammatic models of design workflows in computer-aided systems (CAD) and computer-aided systems of production preparation (CAPP). Their analysis, control, synthesis, transformation and interpretation in different graphic language bases, designed to increase the hybrid dynamic diagrammatic design workflows models interoperability degree in CAD and CAPP on the basis of the ensemble principle. The model differs from analogues in that it provides the system functions and communication protocol definition, which increases their interconnection.

1 Introduction

The relevance of research is determined by the fact that it is aimed at solving a fundamental problem of increasing the diagrammatic automated systems workflows models processing efficiency in order to reduce the time spent on their development, increasing the diagrammatic models workflows processing success (fulfilling the requirements for resource constraints, including functionality, financial component and deadlines), as well as improving the diagrammatic models quality (semantic error control). These problems have great practical importance [33].

Automated systems are defined in GOST 34.601-90 as an organizational and technical system that provides solutions based on automation of information processes in various fields of activity (management, design, production, etc.) or their combinations, as well as in IEEE 1471 International Standard as complex systems intensively using software. In the business process management theory, theoretical computer science, and design automation theory, the stages of creating such systems are represented by design workflows of designers who intensively use software (computer) development tools. The processing of such workflows (business processes) in the paradigm of end-to-end digital design contains key design procedures: analysis and synthesis, which are one of the newest areas of research and significantly affect the result and success of design. At the same time, the problem of the success of design decisions in these theories has been dealt with for more than 30 years, such attention to the problem is caused by a

A. Lopata et al. (Eds.): ICIST 2020, CCIS 1283, pp. 84–101, 2020.
https://doi.org/10.1007/978-3-030-59506-7_8

high degree of development (project solutions) going beyond the planned time, financial and functional parameters. In the existing theory, the reasons are identified and recommendations are made to increase the complex computer-aided systems design success, however, according to the Standish Group engaged in research in the field of successful development of automated systems, only 40% of developments are currently being completed successfully.

The work has the following structure. In "Related works" section there is an overview of modern researches in workflows theory, grammars and data flows. In the third section choreography and orchestration models are described, axioms and operational semantics rules of the choreographic model are given. The fourth section shows application of the choreography conceptual model on the example of large enterprise provided with diagrammatical view.

2   Related Works

The Common Workflow Language (CWL) workflows descriptors are researched in [1], which allow analyzing data in various computing environments (Docker containers virtualization). The authors developed CWL-metrics, a utility tool for cwltool (a reference implementation of CWL), for collecting Docker container runtime metrics and workflow metadata for analyzing resource requirements. To demonstrate the use of this tool, the authors analyzed 7 workflows on 6 types of instances. Analysis results show that choosing the type of instance allows to reduce financial costs and execution time using the required amount of computing resources. However, in the CWL-metrics implementation proposed by the authors, there are no functions for collecting metric data from parallel tasks in workflows.

[2] is devoted to the dynamic access control approach for business processes development. Authors offer a context-oriented and trust-oriented work environment. The proposed approach focuses on inter-component relationships, where steps are performed online or offline to avoid performance bottlenecks. It should be noted that the presented context-oriented access structure is applicable only for solving problems related to business processes in service-oriented computing.

[3] described a new approach to the systematic support of engineers using model-driven system architectures for process design and plant automation. The authors investigated a new aspect the virtual intelligent objects design in enterprise data models, which represents the life cycle of an object. A methodology is described that enables users to define the life cycle for classes of objects depending on the context and goals of the projects. The authors performed workflows research and analysis to form a library of production processes for certain objects classes. However, the dynamic distributed workflows analysis and control methods are not considered.

The [4] describes a new effort assessment model based on use cases reuse, called use case reusability (UCR), designed for projects that reuse artifacts previously developed in past projects with a similar scope. The basis for the new model for assessing efforts is the use case model. The UCR model introduces a new classification of use cases based on their reuse, and includes only those technical factors that, according to experts, have a significant impact on the efforts for targeted projects. It is worth noting that the classification of precedents in terms of the possibility of reuse occurs manually, which takes a lot of time. Also, when testing the UCR model, mainly small design solutions were used, and therefore certain deviations in the assessment of efforts for complex technical solutions and automated systems can be expected.

The [5] presents a methodology for exchanging specialized CAx data between the design and modeling department, in particular, between CAD and other modeling tools. General steps, such as filtering, aggregation, and preprocessing, as well as selecting and using appropriate interfaces, result in flexible and reusable workflows. The identification and use of such workflows speed up the modeling phase, ensures transparency of the development process, and allows to reuse and refine the process steps and intermediate results. The approach proposed by the authors can simplify the binding of design tools, but cannot completely solve this problem.

In [6], an ontology is proposed for collecting, presenting, and documenting knowledge related to hierarchical workflows of decision-making in the meta-design of complex engineering systems. An approach to creating a process template procedure is presented to simplify the reuse of filled template instances in a future project. However, the paper does not show how decisions are made regarding the management of distributed information and how the ontology proposed by the authors is regulated to collect relevant knowledge about design decisions.

In [7], the authors presented an environment for integrating all stages of the life cycle (design, configuration, implementation, analysis and evaluation) of business process management, in which types of business processes and their instances can be modeled, visualized, controlled and automatically synchronized using general presentation of models and code.

In [8], the authors developed the SciPipe workflow programming library, implemented in the Go programming language, for managing complex and dynamic pipelines in bioinformatics, chemoinformatics, and other fields. SciPipe is based on the principles of streaming programming to support the flexible development of workflows based on a library of stand-alone, reusable components. The tool proposed by the authors is specialized and is not intended for very complex workflows, such as working with nested loops, dynamic scheduling and parameterization, which is often found in complex automated systems.

In [8], an approach to the selection of services for modeling business processes is proposed. At the first stage, the function similarity method is used to select services from the service repository to create a set of candidate services that checks the description of functions to find suitable services, especially a service can publish one or more functions through several interfaces. At the second stage, a method based on the probabilistic model verification, which includes the composition of services and calculation of stochastic behavior in accordance with the workflow structures, is used to quantitatively verify process instances. Next, experiments are carried out to demonstrate the efficiency and effectiveness of the proposed method compared to traditional methods.

In [10], an improved two-stage approach of exact query based on the graph structure is proposed. At the filtering stage, a composite task index, which consists of a label, a connection attribute and a task attribute, is used to obtain candidate models, which can significantly reduce the number of process models that need to be tested at a specific time

- the verification algorithm. At the verification stage, a new subgraph isomorphism test based on the task code is proposed to clarify the set of candidate models. The experiments are conducted on six synthetic model kits and two real model kits. However, the algorithm has polynomial computational complexity.

In [11], success and failure factors for the implementation of business process management technologies in organizations were investigated.

Workflow mining in highly changing areas is researched in [12], focusing on creating models of process instances (in the form of instance graphs) from simple event logs.

The [13] shows how to combine the advantages of BPMS with the advantages of the blockchain platform. The article presents a blockchain-based BPMN execution engine called Caterpillar.

In the [14], according to the author, the most solid foundation in the theory of workflows at present is Petri nets. In the analysis, the author identifies the following errors: blocked tasks, deadlock - "freezing", active deadlock (endless loop), performing tasks after reaching the end point, the presence of chips in the network after the network is shut down, and others. He also claims that most modern workflow modeling languages (BPMN, EPCs, FileNet, etc.) are built on WF networks, a subclass of Petri nets. However, taking into account the very wide distribution of tools for working with BPMN- and similar diagrams, for applying the author's methods there is a need for initial translation of the original diagrams into the Petri net, which leads to unnecessary costs.

In [15], the authors extend the generalized LR algorithm to the case of "grammars with a left context", which supplement context-free grammars with special operators for referencing the left context of the current substring, as well as a join operator (as in conjunctive grammars) to combine syntactic conditions. All the usual components of the LR algorithm, such as a parsing table, shift and reduce actions, etc., are extended to handle context statements. The resulting algorithm is applicable to any grammar with a left context, but it has the same performance in cubic time for the worst case.

The work of science school led by prof. Yarushkina N.G. [16] is the closest to the set problem. The article presents the selection and justification of the notation of design diagrams for the description of technological processes using the example of a fragment of the model for the description of the technological process "Assembly of the door frame" at the CJSC Aviastar-SP. A description of the approach to the transformation of UML – OWL and the search for a similar software project from the repository by the severity of common design patterns using ontological engineering methods is given. However, the work does not address the issues of semantic analysis of diagrammatic workflows based on the linguistic approach.

In [17], authors use ontologies in the process of "multisite" software development. A semantic notation in the source code is proposed for understanding the code by the machine in accordance with the user ontology of the project, but there is no connection with grammars.

The [18] presents mathematical models of granularity and graduality. The author offers an improved method of fuzzy granulation. The practical application of fuzzy granulation in the tourism sector is considered, however, there is no connection with grammars in the work.

The problem of error neutralization and its solution is well reflected in classical works on compilers [19]. An error neutralization method for RV grammars has also been proposed [20]. However, they did not solve the issues of neutralization for diagrammatic models of dynamic distributed work flows.

Translation of visual language models into another target language based on RV-grammars is solved in [21]. However, the task of translating several interconnected diagrammatic models of workflows presented in different languages into the target language is not considered.

In [22], an algorithm for the synthesis of context-free grammars based on input examples is presented. An algorithm structure consisting of two phases is proposed. Phase 1 contains the following steps: synthesis of regular expressions, selection, sorting, verification of structures and calculation of the complexity of the algorithm. Phase 2 contains the following steps: studying the recursive properties of a language, translating regular expressions into a context-free grammar, sorting grammars, checking constructs, computing algorithm complexity. However, the synthesized grammar is not temporal (temporary).

The [23] developed the AZee framework, which allows synthesizing the grammar of sign language. Gestures are presented in the form of diagrams that display the state of body parts in accordance with gestures. The synthesized grammar is not temporal temporal).

The [24] considers the problem of storage and dissemination of knowledge about the organization's activities, presented as a set of business process models. An approach is proposed to build a repository that allows you to analyze business process models and formulate recommendations for their improvement, determine the semantic similarity between business process models in order to reuse them when designing new or improving existing organization business processes. The main drawback of the proposed approach is the lack of analysis of workflows for semantic and structural errors.

The [25] is devoted to the problem of finding frequent and similar fragments in work processes using graph analysis methods. The authors examine various representations that can be used to encode workflows before evaluating their similarity, taking into account the efficiency and effectiveness of the data mining algorithm. However, the issue of building a library or repository of such workflows for reuse is not addressed.

WorkflowHunt, a hybrid architecture for searching and discovering workflows for universal repositories, which combines keyword search and semantic search, allowing finding relevant workflows using various search methods, is presented in [26]. The work presents a search engine design for scientific repositories of workflows, however, the WorkflowHunt system allows you to only extract workflows, but does not check them automatically for compliance with a request, an expert is required for this.

3   Design Workflows Organization Analytical Model

The choreography and orchestration model's composition focused on a large project and production enterprises is represented by the analytical model CM which has the following form [27, 28]:

$$CM = \{(Organization_n, Orchestration_n), Choreography, Ensemble\},$$

where $(Organization_i, Orchestration_i)$ pair define internal organization design workflows, $i \in N$. Label link n provides an unambiguous connection of the organization with its orchestration. Choreography is globally defined on entire pairs set $(Organization_n, Orchestration_n)$ i.e. it is available at any $Organization_i$ and $Orchestration_i$. $Organization_i = \{id, name\}$ is a set containing the serial number of the organization id and its name $name$, where each design and industrial organization is identified by id, and $id \in N$.

Let $AllName$ be the set of all the names of organizations, therefore, $name \in AllName$. Let $Variable$ is an x, y, z variables set. Mark $x_1, x_2, \ldots, x_n$ as a tuple $\tilde{x}$. Let $Command_{name}$ be the commands names set. $Command_{direction} = \{ow, rr\}$ is a commands types set, where ow means one-way exchange whereas rr means query-answer exchange. A command itself is described by name and type:

$$command = \{(title, direction)|title \in Command_{name}, direction \in Command_{direction}\},$$

and each command has the unique name.

The transition system states of the composition, choreography and orchestration conceptual model are determined by the variables values and calculated by the exchange function $Function_{rel} : Variable \rightarrow Value$. The value range of this function is calculated by the formula ψ and equals $v \in Value \cup \{\emptyset\}$. $Function_s(x) = \emptyset$ means that x is undefined. $S[v/x]$ means that the system in the state S has variable x with the value v (we can also state that $S[\tilde{v}/\tilde{x}]$ means that tuple $x_1, x_2, \ldots, x_n$ has values $v_1, v_2, \ldots, v_n$, respectively):

$$S[v/x] = S',$$

$$S'(x') = \begin{cases} v & \text{if } x' = x \\ S(x') & \text{else} \end{cases}$$

Variables can have a limited set of values. Backus-Naur logical conditions form for describing variables restrictions allows set the initial system state:

$$\phi ::= x \leq expression | expression \leq x | \neg \phi | \phi \wedge \phi,$$

where $expression$ is an expression which can have variables and means v in S state. $expression_S \rightarrow v$ means that $expression$ has calculated value v in S state. As a rule, in order to mark that ϕ is performed in S state, $S \vdash \phi$ notation is used. Rules for ϕ are the following:

$$S(x) = \emptyset \Rightarrow S \vdash (x \nleq \emptyset \wedge \emptyset \nleq x)$$
$$expression_S \rightarrow v, S(x) \nleq v \Rightarrow S \vdash x \nleq expression$$
$$expression_S \rightarrow v, v \nleq S(x) \Rightarrow S \vdash expression \nleq x$$
$$S \vdash \phi' \wedge S \vdash \phi'' \Rightarrow S \vdash \phi' \wedge \phi''$$
$$= \neg (S \vdash \phi) \Rightarrow S \vdash \neg \phi$$

Choreography and orchestration interexchange is formally defined as follows:

$$Interaction ::= 0|\theta|Interactioin; Interactioni|$$
$$::= Interaction\|Interaction \left|\sum_{i\in N}^{+} \theta_i; Interaction_i\right|$$
$$::= \sum_{i\in N}^{\oplus} \phi_i?\theta_i; Interaction_i$$
$$\theta ::= (Choreography ::= \rho_A, Orchestaration_i ::= \left\{(workflow, state)_{id_i}\right\}, operation, \tilde{x}, \tilde{y},$$
$$direction)|x ::= expression,$$

where N is natural series of numbers, θ is a design workflow successor. ::= $\left(\rho_A, (workflow, state)_{id_i}, title, \tilde{x}, \tilde{y}, direction\right)$ means that exchange between ρ_A choreographer and $(workflow, state)_{id_i}$ orchestrator successfully completed. *title* means exchange command name $(title, direction) \in Command$. Tuples $\tilde{x}, \tilde{y}$ are necessary during sending and receiving of exchange design workflows, respectively. *direction* sets sending ($\uparrow$) and receiving ($\downarrow$) of design workflows. $x ::= expression$ means that *expression* is assigned to x.

Exchange design workflows can have a zero (0) value, basic operator θ value, sequence $(I; I)$ view, parallelism $(I\|I)$ view, unconditional (unrestricted) choice $\sum_{i\in N}^{+} \theta_i; I_i$, conditional (restricted) choice $\sum_{i\in N}^{\oplus} \phi_i?\theta_i; I_i$. Unconditional choice is performed regardless of the system state CM, described by the ϕ condition.

Assume actions during design workflows exchange as *exchange* and view at as follows:

$$exchange_I = \left\{\lambda|\lambda = \left(\rho_A, (workflow, state)_{id_i}, title, \tilde{v}, direction\right)\right\} \cup \{time_{clock}\}$$

where λ is exchange parameter, $time_{clock}$ is time. $(I, S) \xrightarrow{exchange} (I', S')$ means occurrence of *exchange* provided with exchange and the system CM changed its state from (I, S) to (I', S').

Let Θ be set of all possible states of CM. Operational semantics can be viewed as $\rightarrow \Theta \times exchange \times \Theta$. Table 1 contains possible exchanges in choreography and orchestration composition model CM, where $\delta \subseteq command$.

Structural congruence defines the exchange equivalents $0; I$ which are moniods where 0 means empty set and, in addition, end of exchange, after that next exchange can start. Exchanges 1 and 2 describe the interaction, which is a request or response depending on the value of *direction*. When executing the query $(direction = \uparrow)$ the information contained in the tuple $\tilde{x}$ oft he sender *choreography*, is transmitted by the *command* to the tuple $\tilde{y}$ of the receiver $(workflow, state)_{id_i}$. When a response is received $(direction = \downarrow)$ the information contained in the tuple $\tilde{y}$ of the receiver $(workflow, state)_{id_i}$, is transmitted by the *command* to the tuple $\tilde{x}$ of the sender *choreography*. Exchange 3 provides the assignment of the result of *expression* to the variable x calculated in state S updating the state of the choreography. The rules of sequence, parallelism and congruence determine the exchange order and equivalence, respectively. The unconditional selection rule provides the disjunction of the exchange $(\theta_i; I_i, S) \xrightarrow{\upsilon} (\theta_i', S')$. The conditional selection rule deals with the condition ϕ_i according to which a strict disjunction exchange $(\theta_i; S) \xrightarrow{\upsilon} (0, S')$ is fulfilled.

Ensemble is an interoperability scheme (ensemble) of hybrid dynamic diagrammatic models of design workflows that defines the choreography and orchestration exchange

Table 1. Description of axioms and operational semantics rules in the *CM* model

Axioms

Exchange 1 – Sending

$$[(choreography, (workflow, state)_{id_i}, command, \tilde{x}, \tilde{y}, \uparrow), S] \xrightarrow{\lambda} ($$
$$, \lambda = (choreography, (workflow, state)_{id_i}, command, \tilde{\delta}, \uparrow),$$
$$\tilde{\delta} = S(\tilde{x})$$

Exchange 2 – Receiving

$$[(choreography, (workflow, state)_{id_i}, command, \tilde{x}, \tilde{y}, \downarrow), S] \xrightarrow{\lambda} ($$
$$, \lambda = (choreography, (workflow, state)_{id_i}, command, \tilde{\delta}, \downarrow),$$
$$\tilde{\delta} = S(\tilde{y})$$

Rules

Exchange 3 – Assignment
$$\frac{expression_S \rightarrow \upsilon}{(x ::= expression, S) \xrightarrow{\tau} (0, S[\upsilon \, / \, x])}$$

Exchange 4 – Sequence
$$\frac{(I, S) \xrightarrow{\upsilon} (I', St')}{(I; D, S) \xrightarrow{\upsilon} (I'; D, S')}$$

Exchange 5 – Parallelism
$$\frac{(I, S) \xrightarrow{\upsilon} (I', S')}{(I \parallel D, S) \xrightarrow{\upsilon} (I' \parallel D, S')}$$

Exchange 6 – Congruence
$$\frac{I \equiv I', (I, S) \xrightarrow{\upsilon} (D, S'), D \equiv D'}{(I', S) \xrightarrow{\upsilon} (D', S')}$$

Exchange 7 – Unconditional choice
$$\frac{(\theta_i; I_i, S) \xrightarrow{\upsilon} (I'_i, S'), i \in N}{(\sum_{i \in N}^{+} \theta_i ; I_i, S) \xrightarrow{\upsilon} (I'_i, S')}$$

Exchange 8 – Conditional choice
$$\frac{S \vdash \phi_i, (\theta_i; St) \xrightarrow{\upsilon} (0, S'), S \nvdash \phi_j, j \in N, j < i}{(\sum_{i \in N}^{\oplus} \phi_i? \, \theta_i ; I_i, S) \xrightarrow{\upsilon} (I_i, S')}$$

Structural congruence
$$0; I \equiv I$$
$$I \parallel \mathbf{0} \equiv I$$
$$I \parallel D \equiv D \parallel I$$
$$(I \parallel D) \parallel F \equiv I \parallel (D \parallel F)$$

functions set *Function$_{rel}$*. In this case *Ensemble* = {*Interaction* → *Map*} determines when which orchestrators and choreographers (roles) will be involved in the design workflows. The interaction scenario between choreographers and orchestrators is set in *Map* by a tuple of call names of the corresponding exchange commands $Map = (title_1, \tau_1), (title_2, \tau_2), \ldots, (title_n, \tau_n)$ ranked by time τ.

4 Instances of the Analytical Model for Organizing Design Workflows

We will develop a copy of the *CM* conceptual model for coordination of design documentation when designing complex automated systems for a typical large design and production enterprise. Let an instance of a conceptual model have the following roles:

- Chief, or $\rho_{department\,manager}$,
- Executives, or $\rho_{the\,junior\,executives}$,
- Head of topic, or $\rho_{Head\,of\,a\,topic}$,
- Chief of a sector, or $\rho_{chief\,of\,a\,sector}$.

For each role, define design workflows set as follows:

$$\delta_{departmentmanager} = \{(problem\,definition\,Control\,Center, ow),$$
$$(Approval, rr), (OSN, rr), (The\,End\,of\,Agreed\,upn\,documents, ow),$$
$$(departmental\,manager\,Checking, rr)\},$$

where *problem definition Control Center* is statement of the problem by the chief, *Approval* is design documentation approval by the chief, *OSN* is transfer of documentation for rationing materials and labor, *The End of Aggredd upn documents* is the design documentation approval stage completion, *department manager Checking* is control of *OVK*, *OPZM*, *OMO* (see meanings below).

$$\delta_{thejuniorexecutives} == \{(development, rr), (quire, rr), (checking, rr), (route, rr),$$
$$(remarks, rr), (rework, rr)\},$$

where *development* is design documentation development, *quire* is requirements analysis and executives definition, *checking* is design documentation control, *route* is manufacturing route selection, *remarks* is – drafting of remarks to the design documentation, *reworks* design documentation modification.

$$\delta_{Headofatopic} == \delta_{thejuniorexecutives} \cup \cup$$
$$\{(NKS, rr), (checking, rr), (TControl, rr), (OVK, rr),$$
$$(OPZM, rr), (Head\,of\,a\,topic\,Checking, rr),$$
$$(Technical\,sector, rr), (OMO, rr)\},$$

where *NKS* is drawing up a statement of purchased products of the regulatory design sector, *checking* is the statement control, *TControl* is process control defining whether it is possible on the enterprise, *OVK* is making purchases in the external equipment department, *OPZM* is materials purchasing (wire, rubber etc.), *Head of a topic Checking* is checking by the head of topic *NKS*, *TControl*, *OVK*, *OPZM*, *Technical sector* is obtaining permission to use parts in the reliability department (for example, to use electro-radio products), *OMO* performance of metrological measurements in the metrological support department.

$$\delta_{chief\ of\ a\ sector} = \{(agree, rr), (Design\ and\ Laboratory\ Return, rr),$$
$$(Select\ a\ document\ type,\ rr),$$
$$(Design\ \&\ Laboratory\ Checking, rr),$$
$$(Exit\ from\ a\ Route\ Checking, rr),$$
$$(Desgin\ and\ Laboratory\ Exit, ow),$$

$$(Head\ of\ a\ sector, rr)\}$$

where *agree* is request for the design documentation approval by the head of topic, *Design and Laboratory Return* – design documentation coordination with the head of topic, *Select a document type* – documentation type definition (for designers, for circuit designers), *Design & Laboratory Checking* design documentation control by the head of the topic, *Exit from a Route Checking* is decision making according to the control results, *Desgin and Laboratory Exit* is design documentation forming completion by the head of topic, *Head of a sector* is *NKS*, *TControl*, *OVK*, *OPZM* control by the head of topic for the designers [29–31].

For each role define variables set.

$$\widetilde{Variable}_{departmentmanager} = issue, dse ::= \{3DModels, specifications, schemes\},$$

where *issue* is technical task, *dse* is assembly parts set, consisting of 3D-models set *3DModels*, specifications set *specifications*, drawings set *schemes*.

$$\widetilde{Variable}_{Headofatopi} \equiv \widetilde{Variable}_{departmentmanager} \equiv \widetilde{Variable}_{chiefofasector} \text{ means that}$$
head of topic, chief and chief of a sector variables sets are equal when design documentation coordination, i.e. technical task, assembly parts, 3D-models, specifications, drawings and schemes are available for them.

Next we define exchanges, or design workflows.

$$ProblemDefinition ::= wf\ 1 = \{(\rho_{department\ manager}, \rho_{the\ junior\ executives},$$
$$(problem\ definition\ Control\ Center, ow), issue, \downarrow)\}$$

One-way design workflow means setting the task by the chief to the executives.

$$DevelopmentReq1 ::= wf\ 2; wf\ 3 == \{(\rho_{department\ manager}, \rho_{the\ junior\ executives},$$
$$(development, rr), dse, \uparrow);$$
$$(\rho_{the\ junior\ executives}, \rho_{department\ manager},$$
$$(development, rr), dse, \downarrow)\}$$

This hybrid dynamic design workflow of the request-response type occurs between the chief and executives, including the head of the topic, in which there is a request from the chief to the executives for the technical task analysis. The head of the topic, in turn, forms a documentation set (parts and assembly units, 3D-models, specifications, assembly drawings, etc.).

$$DevelopmentReq2 ::= wf\,16;\ wf\,3 ==$$

$$\{(\rho_{Head\ of\ a\ topic},\ \rho_{chief\ of\ a\ sector},$$

$$(development,\ rr),\ dse,\ \uparrow)$$

$$(\rho_{Head\ of\ a\ topic},\ \rho_{the\ junior\ executives},$$

$$(development,\ rr),\ dse,\ \downarrow)\}$$

The hybrid dynamic design workflow *DevelopmentReq2* means that the revision is completed and it is necessary to form a new set of documents taking into account the revision (parts andassembly units, 3D-models, specifications, assembly drawings, etc.).

$$QuireReq ::= wf\,4;\ wf\,5 ==$$

$$\left\{\left(\rho_{the\ junior\ executives},\ \rho_{Head\ of\ a\ topic},\ (quire,\ rr),\ dse,\ \uparrow\right);\ \left(\rho_{Head\ of\ a\ topic},\ \rho_{the\ junior\ executives},\ (quire,\ rr),\ dse,\ \downarrow\right)\right\}$$

The design workflows *QuireReq* of request-response type determines the performers, terms, requirements for the product, development tools, selection and purchase of materials, items and standard solutions, the documents set formation.

$$CheckingReq ::= wf\,6;\ wf\,7 == \{(\rho_{the\ junior\ executives},\ \rho_{Head\ of\ a\ topic},\ (checking,\ rr),\ dse,\ \uparrow);$$

$$(\rho_{Head\ of\ a\ topic},\ \rho_{the\ junior\ executives},\ (checking,\ rr),\ dse,\ \downarrow)\}$$

The hybrid dynamic design workflow *CheckingReg* means documentation set forming control.

$$RouteReq1 ::= wf\,8;\ wf\,9 == \{\left(\rho_{Head\ of\ a\ topic},\ \rho_{the\ junior\ executives},\ (route,\ rr),\ dse,\ \uparrow\right);$$

$$\left(\rho_{Head\ of\ a\ topic},\ \rho_{chief\ of\ a\ sector},\ (route,\ rr),\ dse,\ \downarrow\right)\}$$

The hybrid dynamic design workflow *RouteReg1* means documentation set transfer to the chief of a sector.

$$RouteReq2 ::= wf\,8;\ wf\,10 == \{\left(\rho_{Head\ of\ a\ topic},\ \rho_{the\ junior\ executives},\ (route,\ rr),\ dse,\ \uparrow\right);$$

$$\left(\rho_{Head\ of\ a\ topic},\ \rho_{the\ junior\ executives},\ (route,\ rr),\ dse,\ \downarrow\right)\}$$

The hybrid dynamic design workflow *RouteReq2* means documentation set transfer to the revision.

$$AgreeReq1 ::= wf\,12;\ wf\,18 == \{\left(\rho_{Headofatopic},\ \rho_{chiefofasector},\ (agree,\ rr),\ dse,\ \uparrow\right);$$

$$\left(\rho_{Headofatopic},\ \rho_{thejuniorexecutives},\ (agree,\ rr),\ dse,\ \downarrow\right)\}$$

The hybrid dynamic design workflow *AgreeReq1* means documentation set coordination with the chief of a sector and transferring it to the revision.

$$AgreeReq2 ::= wf\,12;\ wf\,17 == \{\left(\rho_{Headofatopic},\ \rho_{chiefofasector},\ (agree,\ rr),\ dse,\ \uparrow\right);$$

$$\left(\rho_{chiefofasector},\ \rho_{thejuniorexecutives},\ (agree,\ rr),\ dse,\ \downarrow\right)\}$$

The hybrid dynamic design workflow *AgreeReq2* means documentation set coordination with the chief of a sector and transferring it to the further coordination with designers and circuit designers.

$$DesignandLaboratoryReturnReq1 ::= wf\,67;\ wf\,70 ==$$

$$\{(\rho_{Headofatopic},\ \rho_{chiefofasector},$$
$$(DesignandLaboratoryReturn, rr), dse, \uparrow);$$
$$(\rho_{Headofatopic},\ \rho_{chiefofasector},$$
$$(DesignandLaboratoryReturn, rr), dse, \downarrow)\}$$

The hybrid dynamic design workflow *DesignandLaboratoryReturnReq1* means documentation set preparing by chief of a sector to the head of topic.

$$DesignandLaboratoryReturnReq2 ::= wf\,67;\ wf\,71 ==$$

$$\{(\rho_{thejuniorexecutives},\ \rho_{chiefofasector},$$
$$(DesignandLaboratoryReturn, rr), dse, \uparrow);\ (\rho_{chiefofasector},\ \rho_{thejuniorexecutives},$$
$$(DesignandLaboratoryReturn, rr), dse, \downarrow)\}$$

The hybrid dynamic design workflow *DesignandLaboratoryReturnReq2* means documentation set preparing by chief of a sector to the executives for revision.

$$RemarksReq1 ::= wf\,72;\ wf\,13 ==$$
$$\{(\rho_{departmentmanager}, \rho_{Headofatopic}, (remarks, rr), dse, \uparrow);$$
$$(\rho_{Headofatopic},\ \rho_{thejuniorexecutives}, (remarks, rr), dse, \downarrow)\}$$

The hybrid dynamic design workflow *RemarksReq1* means that documentation set control by chief is failed and the set if send to the executives for revision.

$$RemarksReq2 ::= wf\,19;\ wf\,13 ==$$
$$\{(\rho_{chiefofasector}, \rho_{Headofatopic}, (remarks, rr), dse, \uparrow);$$
$$(\rho_{Headofatopic},\ \rho_{thejuniorexecutives}, (remarks, rr), dse, \downarrow)\}$$

The hybrid dynamic design workflow *RemarksReq2* means that documentation set control by head of topic is failed and the set if send to the executives for revision.

$$RemarksReq3 ::= wf\,11;\ wf\,13 ==$$
$$\{(\rho_{chiefofasector}, \rho_{Headofatopic}, (remarks, rr), dse, \uparrow);$$
$$(\rho_{chiefofasector},\ \rho_{thejuniorexecutives}, (remarks, rr), dse, \downarrow)\}$$

The hybrid dynamic design workflow *RemarksReq3* means that documentation set control by chief of a sector is failed and the set if send to the executives for revision.

$$RemarksReq4 ::= wf\,76;\ wf\,13 ==$$
$$\{(\rho_{Headofatopic}, \rho_{chiefofasector}, (remarks, rr), dse, \uparrow);$$
$$(\rho_{chiefofasector},\ \rho_{thejuniorexecutives}, (remarks, rr), dse, \downarrow)\}$$

The hybrid dynamic design workflow *RemarksReq4* means that documentation set control by chief is failed and the set if send to the executives for revision.

$$RemarksReq5 ::= wf\, 80;\, wf\, 13 ==$$
$$\{(\rho_{departmentmanger},\, \rho_{Headofatopic},\, (remarks,\, rr),\, dse,\, \uparrow);$$
$$(\rho_{Headofatopic},\, \rho_{thejuniorexecutives},\, (remarks,\, rr),\, dse,\, \downarrow)\}$$

The hybrid dynamic design workflow *RemarksReq4* means that documentation set control is failed on the formatting standards and the set if send to the executives for revision.

$$ReworkReq ::= wf\, 14;\, wf\, 15 ==$$
$$\{(\rho_{Headofatopic},\, \rho_{chiefofasector},\, (rework,\, rr),\, dse,\, \uparrow);$$
$$(\rho_{chiefofasector},\, \rho_{thejuniorexecutives},\, (rework,\, rr),\, dse,\, \downarrow)\}$$

The hybrid dynamic design workflow *ReworkReq* means that documentation set revision is completed and transferred to the head of topic.

$$ApprovalReq1 ::= wf\, 73;\, wf\, 74 ==$$
$$\{(\rho_{Head\ of\ a\ topic},\, \rho_{department\ manager},\, (Approval,\, rr),\, dse,\, \uparrow);$$
$$(\rho_{department\ manager},\, \rho_{Head\ of\ a\ topic}(Approval,\, rr),\, dse,\, \downarrow)\}$$

The hybrid dynamic design workflow *pprovalReq1* means that documentation set is formed, checked, approved by the chief and transferred to the department of standardization and normative control.

$$ApprovalReq2 ::= wf\, 73;\, wf\, 75 ==$$
$$\{(\rho_{Head\ of\ a\ topic},\, \rho_{department\ manager},\, (Approval,\, rr),\, dse,\, \uparrow);$$
$$(\rho_{Head\ of\ a\ topic},\, \rho_{the\ junior\ executives},\, (Approval,\, rr),\, dse,\, \downarrow)\}$$

The hybrid dynamic design workflow *ApprovalReq2* means that chief control of the design documentation set is failed and the set is transferred to the executives for revision.

$$OSNReq1 ::= wf\, 77;\, wf\, 78 ==$$
$$\{(\rho_{department\ manager},\, \rho_{the\ junior\ executives},\, (OSN,\, rr),\, dse,\, \uparrow);$$
$$(\rho_{the\ junior\ executives},\, \rho_{Head\ of\ a\ topic}(OSN,\, rr),\, dse,\, \downarrow)\}$$

The hybrid dynamic design workflow *OSNReq*1 means that standards control of documentation set is successful.

$$OSNReq2 ::= wf\,77; wf\,79 ==$$
$$\{(\rho_{department\,manager}, \rho_{Head\,of\,a\,topic}, (OSN, rr), dse, \uparrow);$$
$$(\rho_{Head\,of\,a\,topic}, \rho_{the\,junior\,executives}, (OSN, rr), dse, \downarrow)\}$$

The hybrid dynamic design workflow *OSNReq*2 means that standards control of documentation set is failed and the set is transferred to the executives for revision.

$$The\,End\,of\,Aggreed\,upn\,documents ::= wf\,105 = \left\{\left(\rho_{Head\,of\,a\,topic}, \rho_{department\,manager}, dse, \downarrow\right)\right\}$$

The hybrid dynamic design workflow *The End of Aggreed upn documents* means that approved documentation set is transferred from the head of topic to the chief.

Ensemble [32] of the *CM* conceptual model is defined with the compositional model given on the Fig. 1 in a diagrammatical view.

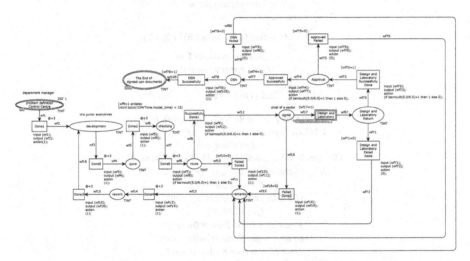

Fig. 1. The hybrid dynamic design workflows of workflows organization analytical model on the example of project procedure of design documentation coordination

$$Ensemble ==$$

$$(Done1,3),(Done5,3),(Done2,3),$$

$$\left(\sum_{i=0}^{1}(Done6,3)?\uparrow 1;\uparrow 0\right),$$

$$\downarrow 0(Failed\ Done1,0),$$

$$(Done4,3),(Done3,3),$$

$$\downarrow 1\left(\sum_{i=1}^{1}(Succsessfully\ Done1,0)?\uparrow 1;\uparrow 0\right),$$

$$\downarrow 0(Filed\ Done2,0),\downarrow w(Done4,3),(Done3,3)\blacksquare\downarrow 1$$

$$\left(\ \left(\sum_{i=0}^{1}(Design\ and\ Laboratory,0)?\uparrow 1;\uparrow 0\right),\ \right)$$

$$\downarrow 0(Design\ and\ Laboratory\ Failed\ Done,0),\uparrow w,$$

$$\downarrow 1(\sum_{i=0}^{1}\quad\begin{array}{c}(Design\ and\ Laboratory\ Successfully\ Done,0)?\\ \uparrow 1;\\ \uparrow 0)\end{array}\quad,$$

$$\downarrow 0(Approved\ Failed,0)\uparrow w,$$

$$\downarrow 1(\sum_{i=0}^{1}(Approved\ Successfully,0)?\uparrow 1;\uparrow 0),$$

$$\downarrow 0(OSN\ Failed,0)\uparrow w,$$

$$(OSN\ Successfully,0)\ \blacksquare$$

$$Design\ and\ Laboratory =$$

$$(\sum_{i=0}^{1}(Successfully\ Done2,0)?\uparrow 2;\uparrow 1),$$

$$\downarrow 2(Design\ Done,0)\uparrow w,$$

$$\downarrow 1(Laboratory\ Done,0),$$

$$= \langle\quad\quad\quad\quad\quad\quad\quad\quad\quad\quad\quad\quad\quad\quad\rangle$$

$$\downarrow w(\sum_{i=0}^{1}(Exit\ from\ a\ Route,0)?\uparrow 1;\uparrow 0),$$

$$\downarrow 0(Exit\ from\ a\ Route\ Failed\ Done,0)\blacksquare,$$

$$\downarrow 1(Exit\ from\ a\ Route\ Successfully\ Done)\blacksquare$$

$$Design\ Done ==$$

$$(Design\ Done,3),(NKS\ Done,3),(Failed\ Done,0),$$

$$(NKS\ Successfully\ Done,0),(Fork\ 'AND',),$$

$$(T.Control\ Done,0),$$

$$(OVK\ Done,0),(OPZM\ Done,0),$$

$$\langle\quad\quad(Join\ 'AND'),\quad\quad\rangle$$

$$(Head\ of\ a\ topic\ Failed\ Done,0),$$

$$(Head\ of\ a\ topic\ Successfully\ Done,0),$$

$$(Head\ of\ a\ sector\ Failed\ Done,0),$$

$$(Head\ of\ a\ sector\ Successfully\ Done,0)$$

$$Laboratory\ Done ==$$

$$(Laboratory\ Done,5),$$

$$(Technical\ sector\ Done,0),$$

$$(Fork\ 'AND',0),(Laboratory\ OVK\ Done,0),$$

$$(Laboratory\ OMO\ Done,0),$$

$$(Join\ 'AND'),(OVK\ OPZM\ OMO\ Failed\ Done,0),$$

$$\langle\quad\quad(for\ Remarks,0),\quad\quad\rangle$$

$$(OVK\ OPZM\ OMO\ Successfully\ Done,0),$$

$$(DM\ Failed\ Done,0),$$

$$\begin{pmatrix}Department\ manager\ Checking\ Successfully\ Done,\\ 0\end{pmatrix},$$

$$(head\ of\ a\ topic\ Failed\ Done,0),$$

$$(Head\ of\ a\ topic\ Successfully\ Done,0)$$

Initial values of variables in CM have the following values.

$$X =< problem\ definition\ Control\ Centre ::= 200'1 >$$

Initial values of variables in *CM* have the following values.

$$X = \langle problem\ definition\ Control\ Centre ::= 200'1 \rangle$$

5 Conclusion

Authors have developed an analytical model for organizing hybrid (different graphic language bases) dynamic diagrammatic models of design workflows in CAD and CAPP with the purpose of increasing the interoperability of hybrid dynamic diagrammatic design workflow models, including a composition of orchestration and choreography of workflows based on the principle of ensemble. The analytical model developed by the authors was successfully implemented in the program code and introduced into the production of a large design organization and allowed to obtain an economic effect of 3% when coordinating the documentation.

Future works researches are related to the interpretation of diagrammatic models of design work flows.

Acknowledgments. The reported research was funded by Russian Foundation for Basic Research and the government of the region of the Russian Federation, grant № 18-47-730032.

References

1. Ohta, T., Tanjo, T., Ogasawara, O.: Accumulating computational resource usage of genomic data analysis workflow to optimize cloud computing instance selection. GigaScience 8(4), 1–11 (2019). https://doi.org/10.1093/gigascience/giz052
2. Bhattasali, T., Chaki, N., Chaki, R., Saeed, K.: Context and trust aware workflow-oriented access framework. In: Proceedings of the International Conference on Software Engineering and Knowledge Engineering, SEKE-2016, http://ksiresearchorg.ipage.com/seke/seke16 paper/seke16paper_179.pdf. Accessed 29 Feb 2020
3. Bigvand, G., Fay, A.: A workflow support system for the process and automation engineering of production plants. In: 2017 IEEE International Conference on Industrial Technology (ICIT), pp. 1118–1123 (2017). https://doi.org/10.1109/ICIT.2017.7915519
4. Rak, K, Car, Ž., Lovrek, I.: Effort estimation model for software development projects based on use case reuse. J. Softw. Evol. Process, 31 (2019). https://doi.org/10.1002/smr.2119
5. Weingartner, L., Sadlauer, A., Hehenberger, P., Boschert, S.: Workflows for the exchange of specialized CAx data. Comput. Aided Des. Appl. 13(4), 440–448 (2016). https://doi.org/10.1080/16864360.2015.1131532
6. Wang, R., et al.: Ontology-based representation of meta-design in designing decision workflows. J. Comput. Inf. Sci. Eng. 19(1) (2019). https://doi.org/10.1115/1.4041474
7. Goldstein, A., Johanndeiter, T., Frank, U.: Business process runtime models: towards bridging the gap between design, enactment, and evaluation of business processes. IseB 17(1), 27–64 (2018). https://doi.org/10.1007/s10257-018-0374-2
8. Lampa, S., Dahlö, M., Alvarsson, J., Spjuth, O.: SciPipe: a workflow library for agile development of complex and dynamic bioinformatics pipelines. GigaScience, 8(5) (2019). DOI:https://doi.org/10.1093/gigascience/giz044

9. Gao, H., Chu, D., Duan, Y., Yin, Y.: Probabilistic model checking-based service selection method for business process modeling. Int. J. Software Eng. Knowl. Eng. **6**(27), 897–923 (2017). https://doi.org/10.1142/s0218194017500334

10. Huang, H., Peng, R., Feng, Z.: Efficient and exact query of large process model repositories in cloud workflow systems. IEEE Trans. Serv. Comput. **11**(5), 821–832 (2018). https://doi.org/10.1109/TSC.2015.2481409

11. Reijers, H.A., Vanderfeesten, I., van der Aalst, W.M.P.: The effectiveness of workflow management systems: a longitudinal study. Int. J. Inf. Manage. **36**(1), 126–141 (2016). https://doi.org/10.1016/j.ijinfomgt.2015.08.003

12. Diamantini, C., Genga, L., Potena, D., van der Aalst, W.M.P.: Building instance graphs for highly variable processes. Expert Syst. Appl. **59**, 101–118 (2016). https://doi.org/10.1016/j.eswa.2016.04.021

13. López-Pintado, O., García-Bañuelos, L., Dumas, M., Weber, I., Ponomarev, A.: Caterpillar: a business process execution engine on the Ethereum blockchain. Softw. Pract. Exper. **49**, 1162–1193 (2019). https://doi.org/10.1002/spe.2702

14. Aalst, W.M.P.: Everything you always wanted to know about petri nets, but were afraid to ask. In: Hildebrandt, T., van Dongen, B.F., Röglinger, M., Mendling, J. (eds.) BPM 2019. LNCS, vol. 11675, pp. 3–9. Springer, Cham (2019). https://doi.org/10.1007/978-3-030-26619-6_1

15. Barash, M., Okhotin, A.: Generalized LR parsing algorithm for grammars with one-sided contexts. Theory Comput. Syst. **61**(2), 581–605 (2016). https://doi.org/10.1007/s00224-016-9683-3

16. Yarushkina, N.G., Afanasyeva, T.V., Negoda, V.N., Samohvalov, M.K., Namestnikov, A.M., Guskov, GYu., Romanov, A.A.: Integration of project diagrams and ontologies in the aircraft manufacturing enterprise capacity balancing task. Autom. Remote. Control Process. **4**(50), 85–93 (2017)

17. Wongthongtham, P., Pakdeetrakulwong, U., Marzooq, S.H.: Ontology annotation for software engineering project management in multisite distributed software development environments. Softw. Project Manag. Distrib. Comput., pp. 315–343. Springer, Cham (2017)

18. Lisi, F.A., Mencar, C.: A system for fuzzy granulation of OWL ontologies. In: Petrosino, A., Loia, V., Pedrycz, W. (eds.) WILF 2016. LNCS (LNAI), vol. 10147, pp. 126–135. Springer, Cham (2017). https://doi.org/10.1007/978-3-319-52962-2_11

19. Aho, A., Sethi, R., Ullman, J., Lam, M.: Compilers: Principles, Techniques, and Tools, 2nd edn. Addison-Wesley, Boston (2006)

20. Sharov, O.G., Afanas'ev, A.N.: Neutralization of syntax errors in graphic languages. Program. Comput. Softw. **1**(34), 61–66 (2008)

21. Sharov, O.G., Afanasev, A.N.: Methods and tools for translation of graphical diagrams. Program. Comput. Softw. **3**(37), 171–179 (2011)

22. Bastani, O., Sharma, R., Aiken, A., Liang, P.: Synthesizing program input grammars. ACM SIGPLAN Notices **6**(52), 5–110 (2017)

23. Filhol, M., McDonald, J., Wolfe, R.: Synthesizing sign language by connecting linguistically structured descriptions to a multi-track animation system. In: Antona, M., Stephanidis, C. (eds.) UAHCI 2017. LNCS, vol. 10278, pp. 27–40. Springer, Cham (2017). https://doi.org/10.1007/978-3-319-58703-5_3

24. Kopp, A., Orlovskyi, D.: An approach to business process models repository development. Inf. Process. Syst. **2**(153), 60–68 (2018)

25. Harmassi, M., Grigori, D., Belhajjame, K.: Mining workflow repositories for improving fragments reuse. In: Cardoso, J., Guerra, F., Houben, G.-J., Pinto, A.M., Velegrakis, Y. (eds.) KEYSTONE 2015. LNCS, vol. 9398, pp. 76–87. Springer, Cham (2015). https://doi.org/10.1007/978-3-319-27932-9_7

26. Diaz, J.S.B., Medeiros, C.B.: WorkflowHunt: combining keyword and semantic search in scientific workflow repositories. In: 2017 IEEE 13th International Conference on e-Science (e-Science), pp. 138–147 (2017) IEEE

27. Afanasyev, A., Voit, N., Timofeeva, O., Epifanov, V.: Analysis and control of hybrid diagrammatical workflows. In: Abraham, A., Kovalev, S., Tarassov, V., Snasel, V., Vasileva, M., Sukhanov, A. (eds.) IITI 2017. AISC, vol. 679, pp. 124–133. Springer, Cham (2018). https://doi.org/10.1007/978-3-319-68321-8_13

28. Voit, N., Kirillov, S., Kanev, D.: Automation of workflow design in an industrial enterprise. In: Misra, S., Gervasi, O., Murgante, B., Stankova, E., Korkhov, V., Torre, C., Rocha, A.M.A.C., Taniar, D., Apduhan, B.O., Tarantino, E. (eds.) ICCSA 2019. LNCS, vol. 11623, pp. 551–561. Springer, Cham (2019). https://doi.org/10.1007/978-3-030-24308-1_44

29. Afanasyev, A., Voit, N., Ukhanova, M., Ionova, I.: Analysis of design-technology workflows in the conditions of large enterprise. In: Abraham, A., Kovalev, S., Tarassov, V., Snasel, V., Vasileva, M., Sukhanov, A. (eds.) IITI 2017. AISC, vol. 679, pp. 134–140. Springer, Cham (2018). https://doi.org/10.1007/978-3-319-68321-8_14

30. Afanasyev, A., Ukhanova, M., Ionova, I., Voit, N.: Processing of design and manufacturing workflows in a large enterprise. In: Gervasi, O., Murgante, B., Misra, S., Stankova, E., Torre, C.M., Rocha, A.M.A.C., Taniar, D., Apduhan, B.O., Tarantino, E., Ryu, Y. (eds.) ICCSA 2018. LNCS, vol. 10963, pp. 565–576. Springer, Cham (2018). https://doi.org/10.1007/978-3-319-95171-3_44

31. Voit, N., Ukhanova, M., Kirillov, S., Bochkov, S.: Method to create the library of workflows. In: Sosnin, P., Maklaev, V., Sosnina, E. (eds.) Proceedings of the IS-2019 Conference, Ulyanovsk, Russia, 24–27 September 2019 (2019). http://ceur-ws.org/Vol-2475/paper8.pdf

32. Kovalchuk, S., Boukhanovsky, A.: Towards ensemble simulation of complex systems. Proc. Comput. Sci. 51(2015), 532–541 (2015). https://doi.org/10.1016/j.procs.2015.05.280

33. WhiteStein Technology. https://www.whitestein.com/

A Model-Driven Framework for Optimum Application Placement in Fog Computing Using a Machine Learning Based Approach

Madeha Arif$^{(\boxtimes)}$, Farooque Azam, Muhammad Waseem Anwar, and Yawar Rasheed

Department of Computer and Software Engineering, College of E&ME, National University of Sciences and Technology (NUST), H-12, Islamabad, Pakistan
{marif.cse19ceme,yawar.rasheed18}@ce.ceme.edu.pk,
{farooq,waseemanwar}@ceme.nust.edu.pk

Abstract. The pervasiveness of ubiquitously connected smart devices are the main factors in shaping the computing. With the advent of Internet of things (IoTs), massive amount of data is being generated from different sources. The centralized architecture of cloud has become inefficient for the services provision to IoT enabled applications. For better support and services, fog layer is introduced in order to manage the IoT applications demands like latency, responsiveness, deadlines, resource availability and access time etc. of the fog nodes. However, there are some issues related to resource management and fog nodes allocation to the requesting application based on user expectations in the fog layer that need to be addressed. In this paper, we have proposed a Framework, based on Model Driven Software Engineering (MDSE) that practices Machine Learning algorithms and places fog enabled IoT applications at a most suitable fog node. MDSE is meant to develop software by exploiting the problem at domain model level. It is the abstract representation of knowledge that enhances productivity by maximization of compatibility between the systems. The proposed framework is a meta-model that prioritizes the placement requests of applications based on their required expectations and calculates the abilities of the fog nodes for different application placement requests. Rules based machine learning methods are used to create rules based on user's requirements metrics and then results are optimized to get requesting device placement in the fog layer. At the end, a case study is conducted that uses fuzzy logic for application mapping and shows how the actual application placement will be done by the framework. The proposed meta-model reduces complexity and provides flexibility to make further enhancements according to the user's requirement to use any of the Machine Learning approaches.

Keywords: Fog computing · Meta-modeling · Cloud computing · Model driven · Fog computing nodes · Internet of Things · Application placement · Model driven software engineering · Machine learning · Fuzzy logic

1 Introduction

Internet of things is the most vibrant topic in the rising technology currently. Through Big data and cloud computing, the communication among people has gone closer and

© Springer Nature Switzerland AG 2020
A. Lopata et al. (Eds.): ICIST 2020, CCIS 1283, pp. 102–112, 2020.
https://doi.org/10.1007/978-3-030-59506-7_9

closer. There is obvious shortcoming of this growing data on cloud. It has become challenge to manage this data and provide resources to huge number of connected IoTs. There are various problems associated to cloud computing including response time, low responsiveness, high latency, low throughput etc. The devised solution suggested for problems related to cloud computing was to introduce some distributed system that can handle the resources allocation more appropriately. This concept is named as fog computing. The aim of fog computing architecture is to fully utilize the benefits of distributed computing and address the problems of cloud computing. Cisco introduced the idea of fog computing in 2012 [24]. The basic idea was not to replace the cloud but to supplement fog computing. Fog computing contains various edge networks with many IoT devices, sensors etc. that are linked by these edge networks called Fog Nodes. [25]. Some characteristics of fog computing technology are described as: 1) Fog computing has dense and extensive geographic distribution. 2) Fog nodes provide a fast-wireless access to mobile nodes. 3) Due to closeness of the edge to the customer, the latency is very low. 4) Fog computing creates the environment of large number of network nodes that helps in environment monitoring. 5) Fog also supports real time computation and analysis. 6) Low energy is required as it is distributed system. 7) Fog environment supports various hardware and software device due to heterogeneity.

The contribution of this paper is a meta-model for application placement on fog nodes using machine learning algorithms. The Proposed meta-model takes user's preferences and places the request on the node with most optimized features that fulfill the user's expectations. It reduces the complexity and provides the flexibility to enhance the model according to the user's requirements as per the true essence of Model Driven Software Engineering [18, 26].

2 Literature Review

Internet of Things (IoT) will increase by additional 26 billion devices installed by the year 2020 [1]. These IOT devices generate a huge amount of data that is needed to be processed and analyzed in the real time [2]. For carrying out computations of IOTs a large scaled data centers called 'clouds' are installed. However, there are some shortcomings like high broadcast cost, congestion, mobility, location awareness and latency in services provision. For overcoming these limitations of cloud computing, Cisco introduced the idea of fog for enhancing the cloud computing paradigm [3, 4]. Following are the Fog computing approaches that use machine learning algorithms.

2.1 Related Work

Baoling et al. [5] proposed a design and application of Fog Computing Model that is based on big data. Fog computing model is a multi-layered model in which fog layer is composed of structurally heterogeneous nodes. These nodes are scattered, and they collect device data from the edge of the network and analyse it quickly. This fog computing model alleviates the pressure of cloud computing on computing, communication and storage of big data. Wag et al. [6] proposed a fog-based framework and a model based on programming for IoT applications found in the smart grid. The proposed architecture is comprised of three layers. First layer the terminal layer contains smart devices that send data to the upper layer. They also proposed a distributed coordination dataflow programming model for the fog-based architecture. They used electrical vehicle intelligent services to simulate and evaluate their fog architecture and programming model. Dang et al. [7] has proposed a model to solve the security issue of fog-based architecture. They call it data protection model for fog computing. This model ads new features to the fog-based model. They have added a region-based trust component to resolve the newly connected devices, FPRBAC is for verification and authorization for dealing with the mobility management issue. Boqi et al. [8] proposed a Resource Allocation Strategy called as Double-Matching strategy for a Fog Computing Networks focusing on cost efficiency. Author had investigated that there is resource allocation problem in all the three layers of the fog networks. Based on cost efficiency, a double matching policy was developed based on deferred acceptance algorithm (DA-DMS). Nader et al. [9] proposed a UAVFog: A UAV-Based Fog Computing for the Internet of Things. There are some IoT applications that are available in the far away and remote areas that are far from reach like deserts, forests, places underwater or mountains. The model is based on the basic principles of fog computing with additional advantage of having the UAV mobility that can take fog to the remotely located places where they are needed most.

2.2 Fog Node Allocation Algorithms

Heuristic Based. Yao et al. [10] used heuristic-based algorithm for resource allocation and application placement in fog layer. Performance evaluation metric used was the deployment cost. Advantages of the approach was that there was low complexity in computation, heterogeneous cloudlets and user's mobility patterns were considered. Major limitation was that they lacked proper algorithm evaluation. Similarly, Minh et al. [11] also used heuristic based method to evaluate performance of their model based on Energy utilization, Latency and Network usage. Advantages include context-aware information support, low latency, network usage and energy utilization. Their limitations include resource cost not considered, increased computational complexity and overhead of the approach has not been calculated. Again, Kabirzadeh et al. [15] used Hyperheuristic based approach for addressing Energy consumption, Network usage, Execution time and Cost in Fog networks. Their work reduced energy consumption, cost and time as well. Simulation was performed in iFogSim. The proposed model unfortunately had low support for scalability.

Genetic Algorithm. Skarlet et al. [13] has used genetic algorithm for performance evaluation based on Execution delay, Service placement rate and Execution cost. They used iFogSim for evaluation of the model. Advantages involved handling of service placement problem and considered heterogeneous applications and resources. Major limitations were that the resource cost was not considered, and the proposed framework was platform dependent.

Bees Life Algorithm. Bitam et al. [14] used Bees Life Algorithm for memory management and to reduce execution time of CPU. The algorithm was evaluated with Simulation done in C++. Performance metrics were CPI execution time and the memory allocated.

Limitations were that they used static idea of scheduling and there was low scalability support.

Adaptive Based. An adaptive based approach was used by Cardellini et al. [17] for improving Node utilization, applications latency and inter-node traffic. Prototype method was used for evaluation of the model. The approach resulted into increased runtime scheduling reduced latency and reduced execution time. Low availability, scalability and Centralized topology were the major drawbacks in this model.

Reinforcement Learning Based. Xu et al. [27] used Reinforcement learning-based method to improve the convergence speed, run time performance, higher harvesting efficiency, support for renewable-powered systems. Limitations include less support for scalability and the simulation was not performed for the model evaluation.

Game Theory. Game Theory was used by Khan et al. [19] for improving Cache Hit rate. Prototype (Apache Storm) method was used for evaluation of the model. The approach resulted into Self-organizing and improved cache hits ratio. The major drawback was they never considered content and node profile in this model. Simulation was done in OMNeT++.

Threshold Based. Li et al. [20] has used genetic algorithm for performance evaluation based on Resource utilization, Execution time. They used iFogSim for evaluation of the model. Advantages involved minimum overhead, more scalability, dynamic tuning of proper load thresholds. Major limitations were that no investigation of energy consumption and throughput bottleneck.

Social Network Analysis (SNA) Based. Sood et al. [29] used social network analysis-based method to reduce the number of deadlocks detected, energy consumption, resource utilization and latency. Limitations were that they did not analyze bandwidth and time. Simulation was performed in CloudSim.

Game Theory. Game Theory was used by He et al. [21] for improving number of moving nodes and running time. Prototype (Apache Storm) method was used for evaluation of the model. The approach resulted into reduced computational complexity and minimum service latency. The major drawback was that the proposed algorithm has not been assessed in a real case study.

Approximate Algorithm. Anglanoet et al. [23] used Approximate Algorithm for maximization of profit. The algorithm was evaluated with Simulation done in C++. Performance metrics were maximization profit and low delay. Limitations include lack of a suitable simulation and workload forecast has not been considered.

After a detailed literature review, it has been observed that there is a huge challenge of application placement and resource allocation in the fog layer. To fulfill the user's need and expectations, it is required to propose a simple and scalable framework for application placement on fog nodes. Since Model Driven Software Engineering reduces complexity through abstraction [22, 28], therefore the proposed framework based on model driven approach fulfills the requirement of a simple and scalable framework for application placement on fog nodes.

3   Proposed Framework

The proposed framework is a meta-model for placement of IoT enabled device on Fog node. Assigned fog node is the node that provides optimum user expectation satisfaction in terms of access rate, processing time, turnaround time etc. Fog is an intermediate computing paradigm between cloud and the IoT devices. Nodes are organized in a hierarchical order in Fog layer. Fog nodes are divided into two categories [12]. The top layer of nodes is called Fog Computational Nodes. They provide resources to the fog enabled applications for data analysis and processing. The lowest located fog nodes are the nodes closest to the users. These are called the Fog Gateway Nodes. IoT devices with fog enabled applications subscribe to the Fog environment through FGN to get monitored, executed and placed in the Fog environment.

Last layer is of IoT enabled user's devices. This layer contains multiple devices which are using IoT apps installed on them and send signals to the Fog layer. Placement of these requests signals is the main challenge being addressed here. The placement is done based on the user's expectation requirements.

3.1   The Meta-Model

The proposed Framework is a meta-model shown in Fig. 1. This model contains two main submodules:

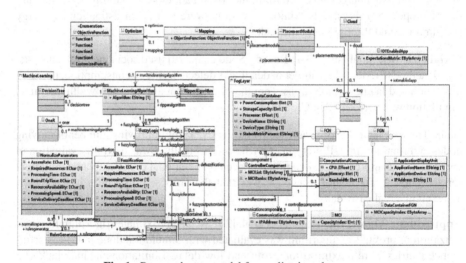

Fig. 1. Proposed meta-model for application placement

Fog Layer. Fog module is composed of Fog Computational Node and Fog Gateway Node. Fog Computational Node further consists of communication, controller and computational component. Fog layer can have multiple fog computing nodes. Each IoT device can be connected to a limited number of nodes. Computational components contain multiple Micro Computing Instances (MCI) where application executions are assigned. Communication components perform networking tasks like packet forwarding, routing etc. Controller component is there to monitor and control the functions of communication and computational component. Fog gateway node contains application display unit and a data container.

Machine Learning Layer. The most important layer where the actual placement logic is performed is the machine learning layer. This layer provides a machine learning algorithm selector. Rules based algorithms can be selected among four of these: Fuzzy logic, OneR, Rippers Algorithm and Decision Tree.

3.2 Application Placement with Proposed Meta-Model

Application Initiation. Initiation unit initiates the client's application through the Fog Gateway Node in the fog layer. It allows users to convey their expectations. The capacity index from Micro Computing Instances MCI are stored in data containers.

Placement Module. Then comes the placement module. Here, there is the main idea of the research. Placement module performs the actual application placement based on the optimum satisfaction of the user expectations related to quality of services.

Machine Learning Module. This model is a generic model that provides various machine learning rule-based methods to the users to select and get the optimum application placement in the fog layer. The reason for using rule-based methods is the variety of input that can vary from user to user and can be enhanced or reduced as per the user's requirements. User expectations metrics include: Access rate, required resources, Processing time, Round trip time, Resource availability, Processing speed and Service Delivery Deadline. In meta-model these parameters are interpreted as 1(Slow), 2(Normal), 3(Fast) based on their degree respectively. These values are then normalized within a specific range. After normalization, rules are generated. These rules are stored in another class called rules container. This process is called fuzzification. The next step is Fuzzy Inference. Here, the associated outputs are combined to produce a single degree value. In de-fuzzification, exact value of maximum rating of user's expectation is calculated.

Application Mapping. The objective function in the mapping module then optimizes the rating value and the application is placed in a respective node in the Fog layer. Objective function can vary according to the user's preference and can be customized as well.

4 Case Study

The proposed model is applied on a real time scenario. Consider an application that is IoT enabled and installed on user's device. Application sends signals to the fog layer through Fog Gateway Node. The Fog gateway node initiates the application and displays it on the user's IoT device. It collects expectation matrix from the IoT app provided by the user and save it in data container. Expectation metrics is given in Table 1.

The system will perform placement based on these metrics.

Table 1. Expectation parameters

Metrics	Values
Access rate	0
Required resources	1
Processing time	0
Round trip time	2
Resource availability	0
Processing speed	1
Service Delivery Deadline	2

4.1 Fuzzy Logic

Fuzzy logic is applied here for the two reasons: firstly, such systems get stable results quickly and secondly, it is scalable as well. User's Expectation parameters are normalized first and then converted to fuzzy dimensions using membership function. Hence a membership degree of each expectation parameter is obtained through this function. Set of fuzzy rules are then generated. Using the rules membership degree of the fuzzy output is determined. For each fuzzy output there is a singleton value as a result of de-fuzzification.

4.2 Optimization

This value will then be used by the optimizer to place application on a fog computing node. Optimizer will solve the optimization problem and application placement will be done based on some objective function. Proposed instance model is shown in Fig. 2. This model provides optimum placement of all the requesting applications.

5 Discussion

The proposed meta-model is a generic approach to model the problem of application placement in the fog layer, at the abstract level. Modeling provides a compact and flexible way of providing a solution. This meta-model is for fog enabled application placement in the fog layer. There are various approaches being proposed in the past studies that has addressed the same issue. Our proposed method is a much better method for application placement as compared to the rest due to the following reasons: 1) It has reduced the complexity of the placement system by providing the lower level implementation baseline in an abstract form. 2) The model is reusable and can be modified as required with more user expectation metrics for similar systems. 3) The optimum placement of application can be achieved through this model. 4) The model is flexible and can be enhanced for additional machine learning algorithms. 5) The model can generate an organized code (after model to text transformation) in python with various modules of the model as functions. Python is well known language for implementing machine

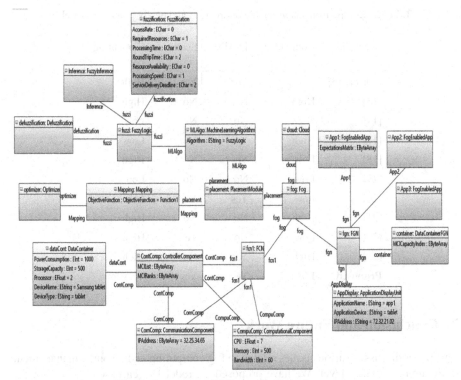

Fig. 2. Instance model for application placement

learning algorithms and many built in packages are available, so implementation of rule generation algorithms will be a simpler task in python. 6) This model can be used as a source model for model to model or model to text transformation.

The model has been validated with some realistic parameters of user expectations. Validation shows that the proposed technique is capable enough to address the problem systematically and efficiently. The model has some generic approach that needs to be converted to concrete implementation after code generation. User can define many things including objective function and optimization algorithm.

6 Model Evaluation

Evaluation criteria for model has been defined based on certain parameters i.e. **(1) Complexity:** How much the proposed algorithm is complex from computational point of view, iterations and execution and resources? **(2) Flexibility:** How much an algorithm is vulnerable to adopt modifications in future? **(3) Scalability:** How much a system can be enhanced for more functionality and features? **(4) Computational Cost:** Cost of running an algorithm based on time, resources utilization and efficiency (Table 2).

There are certain limitations of the proposed model. Model cannot be directly translated to required language. There is always a platform and location dependency. Moreover, user is required to provide implementation details in the code.

Table 2. Comparison analysis table of previous and newly proposed model.

Algorithm	Complexity	Flexible	Scalable	Computing cost
[10, 11, 15]	Low	Yes	Yes	High
[13]	High	No	No	High
[14]	High	No	No	Low
[17]	High	Yes	Yes	Low
[18]	Low	Yes	No	High
[19]	Low	No	No	Low
[20]	Low	Yes	Yes	Low
[21]	High	No	No	High
[22]	Low	No	Yes	High
[23]	High	Yes	No	High
Proposed	**Low**	**Yes**	**Yes**	**Very low**

7   Conclusion and Future Work

This paper discusses various issues related to fog computing and resource management in the context of fog layer. We have proposed a Model Driven based framework for placement of IoT applications on Fog nodes in Fog computing environment. It uses machine learning approach to allocate fog node. The framework has provided flexibility for adding more user expectations in terms of metrics and creates more rules using machine learning algorithms. Output of model will be a python code. Model is validated through an application placement case study using fuzzy logic algorithm. The framework has provided flexibility for adding more user expectations in terms of metrics and creates more rules using machine learning algorithms. This model is a generic solution to the problem of application placement in fog environment which is flexible to be enhanced and transformed into a well-formed code. For future work, this model can be further simulated and can be used for real time scenarios. It can be automated and thereafter used for various customized scenarios of fog applications as well.

References

1. Al-Fuqaha, A., Guizani, M., Mohammadi, M., Aledhari, M., Ayyash, M.: Internet of Things: a survey on enabling technologies, protocols, and applications. IEEE Commun. Surveys Tuts. **17**(4), 2347–2376 (2015)
2. Lin, J., et al.: A survey on Internet of Things: architecture, enabling technologies, security and privacy, and applications. IEEE Internet Things J. **4**(5), 1125–1142 (2017)
3. Bonomi, F., Milito, R., Zhu, J., Addepalli, S.: Fog computing and its role in the internet of things. In: Proceedings of the First Edition of the MCC Workshop on Mobile Cloud Computing, pp. 13–16. ACM (2012)

4. Stojmenovic, I., Wen, S.: The fog computing paradigm: scenarios and security issues. In: FedCSIS. IEEE (2014)
5. Qin, B., et al.: Design and application of fog computing model based on big data. In: 2019 IEEE 2nd International Conference on Information and Computer Technologies (ICICT), pp. 93–97. IEEE, March 2019
6. Wang, P., Liu, S., Ye, F. and Chen, X.: A fog-based architecture and programming model for iot applications in the smart grid (2018). arXiv preprint arXiv:1804.01239
7. Dang, T.D., Hoang, D.: A data protection model for fog computing. In: 2017 Second International Conference on Fog and Mobile Edge Computing (FMEC), pp. 32–38. IEEE, May 2017
8. Jia, B., Hu, H., Zeng, Y., Xu, T., Yang, Y.: Double-matching resource allocation strategy in fog computing networks based on cost efficiency. J. Commun. Networks **20**(3), 237–246 (2018)
9. Mohamed, N., Al-Jaroodi, J., Jawhar, I., Noura, H., Mahmoud, S.: UAVFog: a UAV-based fog computing for Internet of Things. In: 2017 IEEE SmartWorld, Ubiquitous Intelligence & Computing, Advanced & Trusted Computed, Scalable Computing & Communications, Cloud & Big Data Computing, Internet of People and Smart City Innovation (SmartWorld/SCALCOM/UIC/ATC/CBDCom/IOP/SCI), pp. 1–8. IEEE, August 2017
10. Yao, H., Bai, C., Xiong, M., Zeng, D., Fu, Z.: Heterogeneous cloudlet deployment and user-cloudlet association toward cost effective fog computing. Concurr. Comput. Pract. Experience (CCPE) **29**(16), e3975 (2017)
11. Minh, Q.T., et al.: Toward service placement on fog computing landscape. In: 2017 4th NAFOSTED Conference on Information and Computer Science. IEEE (2017)
12. Mahmud, R., Srirama, S.N., Ramamohanarao, K., Buyya, R.: Quality of experience (QoE)-aware placement of applications in fog computing environments. J. Parallel Distrib. Comput. **132**, 190–203 (2019)
13. Skarlat, O., Nardelli, M., Schulte, S., Borkowski, M., Leitner, P.: Optimized IoT service placement in the fog. SOCA **11**(4), 427–443 (2017). https://doi.org/10.1007/s11761-017-0219-8
14. Bitam, S., Zeadally, S., Mellouk, A.: Fog computing job scheduling optimization based on bees swarm. Enterp. Inf. Syst. (EIS) **12**(4), 373–397 (2017)
15. Kabirzadeh, S., Rahbari, D., Nickray, M.: A hyper heuristic algorithm for scheduling of fog networks. Algorithms **19**, 20 (2017)
16. Sun, Y., Lin, F., Xu, H.: Multi-objective optimization of resource scheduling in fog computing using an improved NSGA-II. Wirel. Pers. Commun. **102**(2), 1369–1385 (2018)
17. Cardellini, V., et al.: On QoS-aware scheduling of data stream applications over fog computing infrastructures. In: 2015 IEEE Symposium on Computers and Communication (ISCC). IEEE (2015)
18. Rasheed, Y., et al.: A model-driven approach for creating storyboards of web based user interfaces. In: Proceedings of the 2019 7th International Conference on Computer and Communications Management. ACM (2019)
19. Khan, J.A., Westphal, C., Ghamri-Doudane, Y.: Offloading content with self-organizing mobile fogs. In: 2017 29th International Teletraffic Congress (ITC 29). IEEE (2017)
20. Li, C., Zhuang, H., Wang, Q., Zhou, X.: SSLB: selfsimilarity-based load balancing for large-scale fog computing. Arab. J. Sci. Eng. **43**(12), 7487–7498 (2018)
21. He, X., Ren, Z., Shi, C., Fang, J.: A novel load balancing strategy of software-defined cloud/fog networking in the internet of vehicles. China Commun. (Chinacom) **13**(2), 140–149 (2016)
22. Rasheed, Y., Azam, F., Anwar, M.W.: A novel framework and tool for multi-purpose modeling of physical infrastructures. In: 12th (ICCMS 2020), Brisbane Australia (2020)
23. Anglano, C., Canonico, M., Guazzone, M.: Profit-aware resource management for edge computing systems. In: Proceedings of the 1st International Workshop on Edge Systems, Analytics and Networking. ACM (2018)

24. Bonomi, F., Milito, R., Zhu, J., et al.: Fog computing and its role in the Internet of Things. In: Edition of the MCC Workshop on Mobile Cloud Computing, pp. 13–16. ACM (2012)
25. Yin, Y.: Research and implementation of embedded intelligent gateway based on Internet of Things. Beijing University of Technology (2013)
26. Anwar, M.W., Rashid, M., Azam, F., Kashif, M., Butt, W.H.: A model-driven framework for design and verification of embedded systems through System Verilog. Des. Autom. Embed. Syst. 4, 179–223 (2019). https://doi.org/10.1007/s10617-019-09229-y
27. Xu, J., Ren, S.: Online learning for offloading and auto scaling in renewable-powered mobile edge computing. In: Global Communications Conference (GLOBECOM), IEEE. IEEE (2016)
28. Anwar, M.W., Rashid, M., Azam, F., Naeem, A., Kashif, M., Butt, W.H.: A unified model-based framework for the simplified execution of static and dynamic assertion-based verification. IEEE Access 8, 104407–104431 (2020)
29. Sood, S.K., Singh, K.D.: SNA based resource optimization in optical network using fog and cloud computing. Opt. Switch Netw. 33(3), 114–121 (2017)

Diffusion of Knowledge in the Supply Chain over Thirty Years - Thematic Areas and Sources of Publications

Anna Maryniak[ID], Yuliia Bulhakova[ID], Włodzimierz Lewoniewski[ID], and Monika Bal[(✉)][ID]

Poznań University of Economics and Business, al. Niepodległości 10, 61-875 Poznań, Poland
{anna.maryniak,yuliia.bulhakova,wlodzimierz.lewoniewski, monika.bal}@ue.poznan.pl

Abstract. The subject of consideration is the diffusion of knowledge about supply chain management analyzed through the prism of countries, journals, scientific carriers of knowledge and detailed analysis of keywords.

The research aims to diagnose which thematic areas of the supply chain have dominated in the last three decades, i.e. since 2019, and therefore in which direction the diffusion of knowledge has developed.

In total, almost 80,000 literary items were generated from SCOPUS. The author's program was used for some research stages.

As a result of the research, it was found, among other things, that in the initial stage of development of management sciences most of the works were published in the field of inventory management, with time the focus was on the costs of supply chain management, and nowadays the topics related to the sustainable supply chain are dominant. At the same time, the topics that are constantly in the spotlight have been identified as well as topics where knowledge diffusion is growing rapidly.

In the future, by adopting a very short analysis time series, it is possible to identify likely new dynamic research foci such as supply chain 4.0

Keywords: Supply chain · Knowledge diffusion · Industry 4.0

1 Development of Scientific Knowledge in the Field of Supply Chains - the Inclusion of Bibliometric

So far, the development of knowledge in the field of supply chain management has been examined through the prism of its horizontal flow between the links constituting the chain. Among others, research gaps have been pointed out concerning knowledge management processes such as knowledge: creation, storage, transfer, sharing, application in relation to such areas as: "factors affecting knowledge management", "knowledge management systems", "barriers", "performance" [6].

© Springer Nature Switzerland AG 2020
A. Lopata et al. (Eds.): ICIST 2020, CCIS 1283, pp. 113–126, 2020.
https://doi.org/10.1007/978-3-030-59506-7_10

Research gaps were sought in such areas as "organizational context", "interpersonal and team characteristics", "cultural characteristics", "individual characteristics", "motivational factors" [36] and such areas as outsourcing, new product development, decision support, risk management and construction [24]. Diffusions of knowledge in a narrow subject area, such as the closed supply chain loop, were also studied [26].

This study focuses on the diffusion of scientific knowledge, i.e. at levels other than those mentioned above. The research aimed to identify the dominant theoretical and empirical thematic areas which have been undertaken in the last thirty years, i.e. since 2019.

The research was inspired by publications in which the diffusion of knowledge was considered through the prism of journalistic carriers [27].

Establishing directions for the development of knowledge on supply chains (SC) can be a signpost for supply chain decision-makers. It is therefore essential to take up this thread.

The research was conducted in several stages (Fig. 1). Because in the fourth and fifth stages the themes were combined, the author's program was used in these stages.

At the beginning of the research the carriers of knowledge in supply chain management were identified. Countries, authors and publishing positions were adopted as the carriers.

It is presented in which countries the authors who were most productive came from (Fig. 2) and who specifically is the most active creator in the supply chain management sciences (Table 1).

In the first decade analyzed, countries such as the United States, the United Kingdom, and Canada dominated the dissemination of supply chain knowledge. In the supply chain management sciences, countries such as Germany, India and the United Kingdom, the United States and China have been at the forefront of productivity-oriented research. It can, therefore, be concluded that the development of science has significantly expanded to include Asian countries.

Table 1. Authors who published the most in the field of SC at individual time intervals. Source: own elaboration based on the Scopus.

Years	Authors
1990–1994	Towill D.R., Ellram L.M., Cooper M.C., Berry D., Bessant J.
1995–1999	Towill D.R., Anon, Naim M.M., Van Hoek R.I., Holmström J.
2000–2004	Tinham B., Towill D.R., Navas D., Anon, Chai Y.
2005–2009	Zhao L., Chan F.T.S., Deshmukh S.G., Puigjaner L., Disney S.M.
2010–2014	Sarkis J., Govindan K., Chan F.T.S., Choi T.M., Huang G.Q.
2015–2019	Govindan K., Gunasekaran A., Sarkis J., Choi T.M., Jermsittiparsert K

This is probably due to the rapidly growing economic level in these countries, the growing number of science centres and the attractiveness of Asian markets for locating supply chain links there. Among the authors who have been most

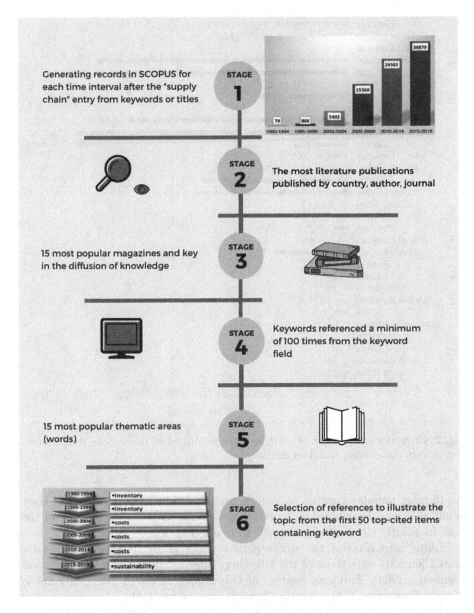

Fig. 1. Research stages.

productive at least for a decade, there are such scientists as Towill D.R., Chan F.T.S., Sarkis J., Govindan K., Choi T.M.

In the next research stage, it was determined which journals are of key importance for the SC knowledge fusion, i.e. how the role of these journals has changed over the ten-year period. For this purpose, out of most frequently cited items,

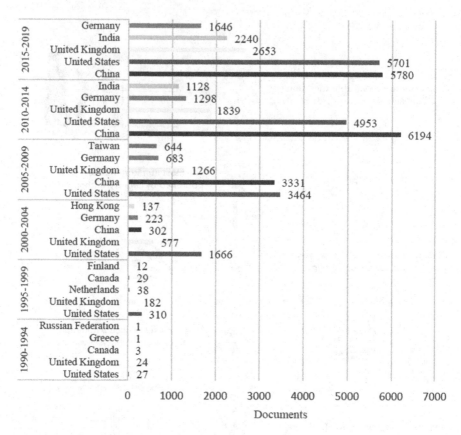

Fig. 2. Countries where most SC articles were published in the various time frames. Source: own elaboration based on the Scopus.

the 15 most popular journals in a given period of time were selected and their significance was determined as a percentage, taking as 100% the number of the most frequently cited articles from all 15 items (Fig. 3).

Taking into account the whole period under study, the most frequently quoted journals were those of the following: *Internatinal Journal of Production Economics* (764), *European Journal of Operational Research* (453), *Journal of Cleaner Production* (381), *Supply Chain Management* (353).

Over the years studied, there are two carriers of knowledge, which runs through over the last sixty years and stand at the same time highly ranked among the sources containing the most frequently quoted items. These are, respectively, the International Journal of Production Economics and the *International Journal of Physical Distribution and Logistics Management*. Since the mid-1990s, the magazine *Supply Chain Management* has also played a very important role.

Recently, the journal *Journal of Cleaner Production* has become particularly important.

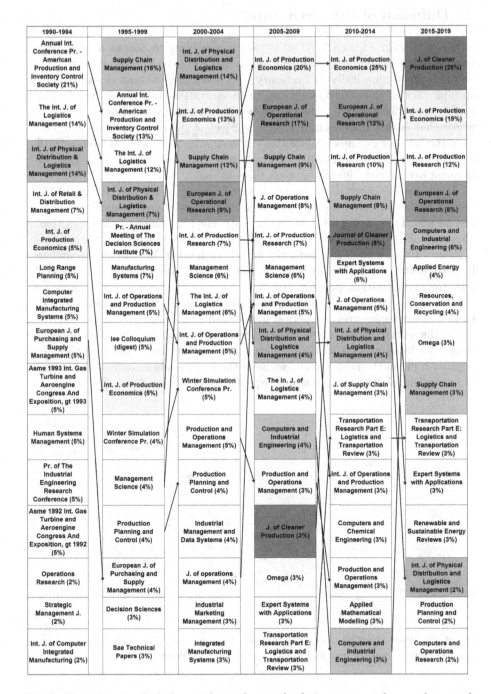

Fig. 3. Magazines in which the articles in the supply chain were most frequently quoted in selected time series. Source: own elaboration based on the Scopus.

2   Diffusion of Research Topics

In the next stage of the study, all keywords according to Scopus nomenclature were separated. Next, the words that were cited 100 or more times were analyzed and grouped thematically (if necessary). For example, the cost slogan included such phrases as "cost" into one group: "transportation cost", "cost-benefit analysis", "cost-effectiveness", "cost reduction", "cost analysis". In the next step, words that do not directly indicate the subject of the research were eliminated from the list. For example, "algorithms", "heuristics methods", "China", "problem solving". The resulting list of words was arranged according to the most frequent occurrence - fifteen for each time series.

Based on the analysis of source data (Table 2), it can be concluded that the popularity of some topics has increased particularly dynamically over the last decade. These are "sustainability", "life cycle", "commerce", "competition", "human" and "coordination", "risk analysis", "sales", "ecology". There is also a group of topics that is constantly at a high level of interest of researchers. It is connected with such slogans as: cost analysis, information management, inventory, competition, product design.

Due to the extensive list of generated data, Table 2 presents a ranking of the most popular topics over the period under study.

In the initial period of knowledge development on supply chain management, the focus was on stock management (1990–2004). Costs were the most popular topic in the next decade, while in the last decade examined the interest of researchers shifted to sustainable aspects of the supply chain (Fig. 4).

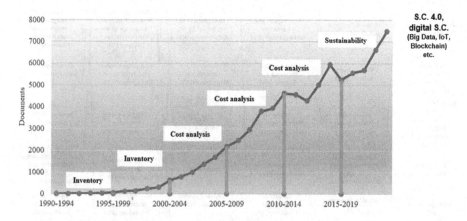

Fig. 4. Number of articles on SC published in each time slot, indicating the most popular topics. Source: own elaboration based on the Scopus.

Based on the analysis of the latest literature (keywords) from 2019–2020, it can be assumed that in the next decade 2020–2024 the focus will be on Industry

Table 2. The most common thematic words in the series temporary - diffusion of research topics.

Name	1990 -1994	1995 -1999	2000 -2004	2005 -2009	2010 -2014	2015 -2019
			Ranking position			
Sustainability					5	1
Cost analysis	3	3	1	1	1	2
Risk analysis				7	8	3
Sales			14	5	2	4
Ecology					11	5
Information management			11	4	3	6
Inventory	1	1	2	2	6	7
Life cycle						8
Commerce					9	9
Competition		5	12	3	7	10
Human						11
Green supply chain					15	12
Coordination				14	10	13
closed-loop supply chain						14
Product design		10	7	9	13	15
Quality control	9					
Radio frequency identification (rfid)					12	
Production control	4	7	14	15		
Marketing	2	4	6	10		
Electronic commerce			5	6		
Customer satisfaction		12	3	8		
Strategic planning	5	2	4	11		
Information technology		9	8	12	14	
Industry				13	4	
Societies and institutions	10	11	12			
Enterprise resource planning			9			
Purchasing	13	6				
Resource allocation		8				
Distribution of goods	6	13				
Electronic data interchange	8					
Personnel	12					
Just in time production	7	15				
Control systems	11					
Just in time production		14				
Raw materials	14					
Total quality management	15					

4.0 related topics in the context of supply chains, including in particular technologies such as: IoT, Big Data, Cloud Computing, Block chain, CPS, Cyber security, M2M, Layered Production of Products (Additive Manufacturing, 3D Printing), Augmented Reality, Autonomous Robots, Autonomous Vehicles, Technology of Systems Locating Moving Objects in Real-Time.

Selected, most popular topics (inventory: 1990–1994 and 1995–1999, cost: 2000–2004, 2005–2009 and 2010–2014, sustainable supply chain: 2015–2019) were analyzed in terms of their content. Within their framework, sample issues were presented.

A comprehensive discussion of these issues and an extension of the analysis to the remaining identified topics in Table 2 may be the basis for future deliberations, the publication of which (due to the volume of the generated data) would require a book character.

2.1   Time Interval 1990–1994

In the period under study, the focus of scientists was primarily on aspects of stock management.

The publications analyzed in the period under review show that knowledge about basic, optional stock management strategies that can be implemented is necessary to make the right decisions [38]. It is a starting point for deeper analyses. It is noted that stock levels in supply chains can be optimized by reducing the scope of disruptions and changing the structure of the supply chain system [21] and by introducing various concepts and tools such as layout, pull system, JiT, EDI [29]. However, the most effective way to optimize stock levels results from sharing information in the supply chain with a clear separation of real demand from demand related to the need to maintain stock [38]. It is important to consider stocks in the context of decentralizing control of goods flows in the supply chain (where centralization is not impossible for organizational reasons and information flow problems). Creating optimization models for this flow is very necessary for economic life [17]. As a rule, models take into account many important factors, which complement each other. For example, the introduction of stock management in the JIT system should go hand in hand with a free flow of information in the supply chain [33].

2.2   Time Interval 1995–1999

In the second separated period, the scientific world also focused on the aspects of stock management. The studies stress the importance of knowing the reasons for the appearance of the so-called bullwhip effect. It is believed that demand signal processing, rationing game, order batching, and price variations are the primary sources of flow level distortions and there are indicated ways of leveling them, which primarily are based on the proper flow of information [18]. The importance of the bullwhip effect to a firm differs greatly depending on the specific business environment.

Given appropriate conditions, however, eliminating the bullwhip effect can increase product profitability by 10–30% [25]. However, there are situations when it is impossible to definitely predict the demand and the seller is exposed to the risk of predetermined rise volumes that were not sold. In such a situation, it is possible to set such a price level for the producer purchasing its goods that it is beneficial for both parties [10]. From the works from this period, it can be concluded that sharing information and greater cooperation leads to better stock management. Therefore, the following can be concluded. It is recommended to introduce EDI type tools [12] and other solutions. However, there are also opposing opinions. It has been proved that competition rather than cooperation results in decreasing inventory level [4].

2.3   Time Interval 2000–2004

In the next period, supply chain studies continued to focus on costs. Opportunities for cost reduction were seen in the integration of partners in the supply chain. Among other things, the benefits of using the VMI concept [19] as well as an online platform that is more accessible to smaller players than EDI [11] are pointed out. This contributes to reducing inequalities in the benefit-sharing chain. This is important because, as it is emphasized, the phenomenon of shifting activities and costs of supply chain management systems to contractors is common [31]. Empirical research has shown that in chains where information exchange is full, costs are on average more than 2.0% lower than in those where information is exchanged only in the traditional form of orders. However, the use of IT technology to improve the flow of goods in the chain results in a much greater cost reduction (on average by about 20%) than using it to exchange information [3].

Another issue raised during this period was the development of so-called Key Performance Indicators of supply chains. The research has shown that one of the KPIs traditionally used in the business is logistics costs, which in practice are measured in companies regardless of the measurement of quality, delivery performance or time. Modern methods, on the other hand, are based on value measurement, however, the financial result is still the most frequently used KPI (in 38%), so cost analysis remains crucial [14].

2.4   Time Interval 2005–2009

In the subsequent period under examination, costs were still the most frequently dis-cussed issue in supply chain management publications. The cost criterion is indicated in the studies as one of the most important criteria in the process of selecting a global supplier, apart from the quality, service efficiency, supplier profile and risk [7].

Among other things, it is indicated that transactional costs in the supply chain include both direct costs of relationship management and the costs of potential bad management decisions. According to the theory of transactional costs, it is assumed that the contractors in our chain are opportunistic and it is necessary to control and monitor their actions in a costly manner. On the other hand, limited rationality caused by communication disruptions forces to mistrust and burdensome conclusion of detailed contracts [5].

Particularly in the second half of the period under consideration, cost, sustainability, and green supply chain issues were often combined in studies. Companies expect that the implementation of green activities will result in the reduction of costs incurred due to the waste of resources and pollution, which in turn will contribute to increased competitiveness [28,35]. Moreover, it has been proven that respecting employee rights and safety rules in a sustainable supply chain reduces labor costs [5].

At the same time, it is emphasized that the conviction of high implementation costs of such initiatives is one of the most important internal barriers in the transformation of the supply chain to a more sustainable one [5,28,35]. One of the ways to reduce them is to implement them is to use lean management at the same time [28].

The analysis crystallizes three basic research topics: stocks (first and second time frames), costs (third, fourth and fifth-time frames) and sustainable activities in the supply chain (sixth-time frames). Given that the number of publications has been growing dynamically over the years (and that other attractive topic have there-fore emerged), it can be assumed that the importance of the established, most popular topic is increasing as time progresses.

2.5   Time Interval 2010–2014

In the next period, costs were still among the most common topics in the context of supply chain management. During this time, among other things, modeling shows that the competitiveness of a product moving along the supply chain is highly dependent on optimizing the entire supply chain over the entire planning horizon. Thus, this cost is not only influenced by, for example, the price of the raw material obtained, but also, to a large extent, by economies of scale or proximity to sales markets [16]. It is also stressed that it is not appropriate to adopt the cost criterion when selecting contractors in supply chains [15].

The cost issue is also related to the greening of economic life. For example, it is indicated that profits in the supply chain due to its "greening" increase in the situation of integration of its participants. This can be ensured by means of a formal mechanism, such as the construction of a contract for the producer's wholesale price [32]. Empirical research also concludes that by designing environmentally friendly products and recovering products and packaging, organizations reduce costs for the organization [9].

2.6   Time Interval 2015–2019

In the sixth period, the issue of "sustainability" from the perspective of supply chain management was the most popular interest of the authors. Among other things, it has been shown that social risks are perceived as "slightly lower risk" than economic or environmental ones, even though social problems are more visible in the media [13]. An interesting discovery is also a negative correlation be-tween the financial crisis and energy consumption and pollution. This indicates a temporary, positive environmental impact resulting from the economic downturn.

The studies also prove that focusing on green technologies in production, storage, and logistics processes increase customer demand and save costs, which ultimately increases the economic stability of companies and their profitability [23]. The scientific literature also emphasizes that for the green supply chain, the operational risk (machine, equipment or facility failures, shortage of skilled labor, level of green technology, etc.) takes priority over other risk categories. The financial risk category comes second and plays a key role in the adoption of the green supply chain management concept [8]. With regard to building operational processes, attention is also paid to the methodology of choosing green suppliers. It is illustrated how AHP and VIKOR tools can be useful in this process [22].

3   Proposals for Future Research

As a result of the work undertaken on the content of the most frequently quoted items, it can be concluded that there is a need to increase research on the relations between the selected key topics, especially in a holistic approach, covering all participants in a given undertaking.

The creation of sustainable chains should primarily aim to optimize the stock management, as there is a huge potential for savings, not yet fully exploited, in the efficient stock management, the reduction of CO_2 emissions and the reduction of waste (which are associated with the movement and storage of goods).

The implementation of sustainability principles into supply chains can lead to optimization of stock levels among all participants. It is important to examine the direction and strength of this correlation. Therefore, there is a need for evidence:

H1: The implementation of the idea of a sustainable supply chain has a positive impact on stock management in social, environmental, and economic terms.

Determining the extent of this impact and the results of this can motivate sustainable action and bring new knowledge in the area of management and quality sciences (Fig. 5).

There is also a need to explore the links between the implementation of sustainable activities in the supply chain and business costs.

Studies to date indicate reductions in energy consumption, waste, etc., but there is little concrete calculation of the savings generated.

It is therefore provisionally assumed that:

H2: The implementation of sustainable chains has a positive and measurable impact on the financial sphere of the whole supply chain (Fig. 5).

Previous review studies of the supply chain focus, for example, on current trends (concerning sustainability [34], individual 4.0 technologies such as IoT, Blockchain [2,37]), defining the supply chain [20] or designing the supply chain in uncertain conditions [30].

The authors made qualitative and quantitative analyses mainly through the prism of thematic areas, theoretical models, detailed technologies, innovative solutions in the context of one or more industries [1,39].

Based on the obtained research results it is not possible to make a benchmarking about already existing items of the review work, because none of the items adopted the same time sequence and the same research methodology.

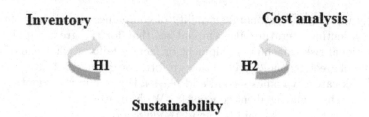

Fig. 5. Research scheme - the relationship between key topics undertaken in the SC. Source: [own elaboration based on the Scopus]

Furthermore, by using a dedicated search algorithm, the work was based on a much larger record base than traditional search work (using keywords or themes, or abstracts) and was not concentrated on specific themes or industries, so it adopted a holistic approach.

4   Conclusions

As a result of the work carried out, it was found that the most dynamic development of SC knowledge in countries such as the United States and China, and its most popular scientific medium, taking into account all the years studied, was the International Journal of Production Economics, whereas for the last five years it was the Journal of Cleaner Production.

Over the past thirty years, it has emerged that the science of supply chain management and quality is still based on inventory management and cost analysis, while in recent years, issues relating to the implementation of sustainable activities in supply chains have become increasingly important. Also, in the period under study, topics related to such slogans as: risk analysis, sales, chain greening, information management, product life cycle, human, commerce, coordination, competition, product design were popular. Over the past thirty years, it has emerged that the science of sup-ply chain management and qualities continues to be based on inventory management and cost analysis, while in recent years issues relating to the implementation of sustainable activities in supply chains, risk, sales, green chains, information management, and product life cycle assessment have gained particular importance.

It has also been concluded that there is a need for research to capture the links be-tween the main identified themes in the supply chain management sciences over the years. Given that current scientific studies are generating a dynamic diffusion of economic knowledge 4.0, it is likely that this will be the fourth fundamental research topic.

References

1. Backs, S., Jahnke, H., Lüpke, L., Stuecken, M., Stummer, C.: Supply chain strategies of the apparel industry in research: a literature review. Jobs Announc. **21**, 1–18 (2020)
2. Ben-Daya, M., Hassini, E., Bahroun, Z.: Internet of things and supply chain management: a literature review. Int. J. Prod. Res. **57**(15–16), 4719–4742 (2019)
3. Cachon, G.P., Fisher, M.: Supply chain inventory management and the value of shared information. Manage. Sci. **46**(8), 1032–1048 (2000)
4. Cachon, G.P., Zipkin, P.H.: Competitive and cooperative inventory policies in a two-stage supply chain. Manage. Sci. **45**(7), 936–953 (1999)
5. Carter, C.R., Rogers, D.S.: A framework of sustainable supply chain management: moving toward new theory. Int. J. Phys. Distrib. Logistics Manag. **38**(5), 360–387 (2008)
6. Cerchione, R., Esposito, E.: A systematic review of supply chain knowledge management research: state of the art and research opportunities. Int. J. Prod. Econ. **182**, 276–292 (2016)
7. Chan, F.T., Kumar, N.: Global supplier development considering risk factors using fuzzy extended AHP-based approach. Omega **35**(4), 417–431 (2007)
8. Dubey, R., Gunasekaran, A., Papadopoulos, T., Childe, S.J., Shibin, K., Wamba, S.F.: Sustainable supply chain management: framework and further research directions. J. Clean. Prod. **142**, 1119–1130 (2017)
9. Eltayeb, T.K., Zailani, S., Ramayah, T.: Green supply chain initiatives among certified companies in malaysia and environmental sustainability: investigating the outcomes. Resour. Conserv. Recycl. **55**(5), 495–506 (2011)
10. Emmons, H., Gilbert, S.M.: Note the role of returns policies in pricing and inventory decisions for catalogue goods. Manage. Sci. **44**(2), 276–283 (1998)
11. Frohlich, M.T., Westbrook, R.: Arcs of integration: an international study of supply chain strategies. J. Oper. Manag. **19**(2), 185–200 (2001)
12. Gavirneni, S., Kapuscinski, R., Tayur, S.: Value of information in capacitated supply chains. Manage. Sci. **45**(1), 16–24 (1999)
13. Giannakis, M., Papadopoulos, T.: Supply chain sustainability: a risk management approach. Int. J. Prod. Econ. **171**, 455–470 (2016)
14. Gunasekaran, A., Patel, C., Tirtiroglu, E.: Performance measures and metrics in a supply chain environment. Int. J. Oper. Prod. Manag. **21**(1–2), 71–87 (2001)
15. Ho, W., Xu, X., Dey, P.K.: Multi-criteria decision making approaches for supplier evaluation and selection: a literature review. Eur. J. Oper. Res. **202**(1), 16–24 (2010)
16. Huang, Y., Chen, C.W., Fan, Y.: Multistage optimization of the supply chains of biofuels. Transp. Res. Part E Log. Transp. Rev. **46**(6), 820–830 (2010)
17. Lee, H.L., Billington, C.: Material management in decentralized supply chains. Oper. Res. **41**(5), 835–847 (1993)
18. Lee, H.L., Padmanabhan, V., Whang, S.: Information distortion in a supply chain: the bullwhip effect. Manage. Sci. **50**(12), 1875–1886 (2004)
19. Lee, H.L., So, K.C., Tang, C.S.: The value of information sharing in a two-level supply chain. Manage. Sci. **46**(5), 626–643 (2000)
20. LeMay, S., Helms, M.M., Kimball, B., McMahon, D.: Supply chain management: the elusive concept and definition. Int. J. Log. Manag. **28**(4), 1425–1453 (2017)
21. Levy, D.: Chaos theory and strategy: theory, application, and managerial implications. Strateg. Manag. J. **15**(S2), 167–178 (1994)

22. Luthra, S., Govindan, K., Kannan, D., Mangla, S.K., Garg, C.P.: An integrated framework for sustainable supplier selection and evaluation in supply chains. J. Clean. Prod. **140**, 1686–1698 (2017)
23. Mangla, S.K., Kumar, P., Barua, M.K.: Risk analysis in green supply chain using fuzzy ahp approach: a case study. Resour. Conserv. Recycl. **104**, 375–390 (2015)
24. Marra, M., Ho, W., Edwards, J.S.: Supply chain knowledge management: a literature review. Expert Syst. Appl. **39**(5), 6103–6110 (2012)
25. Metters, R.: Quantifying the bullwhip effect in supply chains. J. Oper. Manag. **15**(2), 89–100 (1997)
26. Peng, H., Shen, N., Liao, H., Xue, H., Wang, Q.: Uncertainty factors, methods, and solutions of closed-loop supply chain–a review for current situation and future prospects. J. Clean. Prod. **254**, 120032 (2020)
27. Pilkington, A., Meredith, J.R.: The diffusion network of research knowledge in operations management. Int. J. Oper. Prod. Manag. **38**(2), 333–349 (2018)
28. Rao, P., Holt, D.: Do green supply chains lead to competitiveness and economic performance? Int. J. Oper. Prod. Manag. **25**(9), 898–916 (2005)
29. Scott, C., Westbrook, R.: New strategic tools for supply chain management. Int. J. Phys. Distrib. Logist. Manag. **21**(1), 23–33 (1991)
30. Stock, J.R., Boyer, S.L.: Developing a consensus definition of supply chain management: a qualitative study. Int. Phys. Distrib. Logist. Manag. **39**(8), 690–711 (2009)
31. Subramani, M.: How do suppliers benefit from information technology use in supply chain relationships? MIS Q. Manag. Inf. Syst. **28**(1), 45–73 (2004)
32. Swami, S., Shah, J.: Channel coordination in green supply chain management. J. Oper. Res. Soc. **64**(3), 336–351 (2013)
33. Towill, D.R., Naim, M.M., Wikner, J.: Industrial dynamics simulation models in the design of supply chains. Int. J. Phys. Distrib. Logist. Manag. **22**(5), 3–13 (1992)
34. Tseng, M.L., Islam, M.S., Karia, N., Fauzi, F.A., Afrin, S.: A literature review on green supply chain management: trends and future challenges. Resour. Conserv. Recycl. **141**, 145–162 (2019)
35. Walker, H., Di Sisto, L., McBain, D.: Drivers and barriers to environmental supply chain management practices: lessons from the public and private sectors. J. Purchas. Supply Manag. **14**(1), 69–85 (2008)
36. Wang, S., Noe, R.A.: Knowledge sharing: a review and directions for future research. Hum. Resource Manag. Review **20**(2), 115–131 (2010)
37. Wang, Y., Han, J.H., Beynon-Davies, P.: Understanding blockchain technology for future supply chains: a systematic literature review and research agenda. Supply Chain Manag. Int. J. **24**(1), 62–84 (2019)
38. Wikner, J., Towill, D.R., Naim, M.: Smoothing supply chain dynamics. Int. J. Prod. Econ. **22**(3), 231–248 (1991)
39. Wong, D.T., Ngai, E.W.: Critical review of supply chain innovation research (1999–2016). Ind. Mark. Manage. **82**, 158–187 (2019)

Software Engineering - Special Session on Intelligent Systems and Software Engineering Advances

Genetic Optimization Approach to Construct Schedule for Service Staff

Dalia Čalnerytė[✉] [iD], Andrius Kriščiūnas, and Rimantas Barauskas

Kaunas University of Technology, Studentu Street 50-407, 51368 Kaunas, Lithuania
{dalia.calneryte,andrius.krisciunas,rimantas.barauskas}@ktu.lt

Abstract. Rostering is a complex problem widely analyzed in the optimization area in order to create proper solutions in acceptable duration. After examination of the existing solutions, genetic optimization with greedy approach for schedule construction was proposed for the real-life staff timetable-scheduling problem. The algorithm consists of two steps. In the first step, the greedy approach is used to create an initial in polynomial time depending on the numbers of workers and tasks. In the second step, the genetic optimization is performed with respect to the schedules created initially. Using the proposed approach, it is possible to consider hard and soft requirements, such as staff overtime, preferable but optional tasks, free-time periods etc., as a weighted combination of them by defining weights in the evaluation function next to the proper parameter. The cascaded task assignments enable to consider hard constraints such as workers' holidays or short non-working periods, minimum break requirements, obligatory working periods and other constraints which appear in real life. The dataset of more than 2000 tasks and 50 flight service staff has been used for testing. The analysis showed that the proposed algorithm can be easily parallelized and adopted to big datasets.

Keywords: Combinatorial optimization · Staff rostering · Genetic algorithm

1 Introduction

Schedule construction for the service staff is a complex problem, especially if the task distribution is not uniform in the scheduled time and there are special requirements on task performance. For example, in case the schedule is constructed for the flight customer service staff, there may be requirements to have a certificate to maintain a flight. Obviously, the staff timetable directly depends on the flight schedule. The set of requirements combined with state labor laws and preferences of timetable make scheduling a challenging problem. Such construction of the schedule is based on the tasks rostered for workers.

In this article, an algorithm for the problem of scheduling customer service staff group was proposed. The algorithm was designed to fulfill the needs of the airport with approximately 50 ground staff members and 1000 flights per month. With respect to the requirements of the company, 2 or 3 staff members handle each flight. On the contrary to most of the algorithms proposed in the earlier research, the limited availability of

© Springer Nature Switzerland AG 2020
A. Lopata et al. (Eds.): ICIST 2020, CCIS 1283, pp. 129–139, 2020.
https://doi.org/10.1007/978-3-030-59506-7_11

workers due to the planned holidays or obligatory training sessions is considered in this research.

The proposed algorithm combines the genetic optimization to find the best set of tasks for each worker and greedy approach to construct a schedule. Firstly, greedy approach was employed to construct an initial schedule. Secondly, genetic optimization was performed to obtain a new set of tasks suggested for workers. Finally, after the main steps of genetic algorithm, a schedule was again constructed using the greedy approach. The proposed algorithm ensures that the hard constraints are not violated after an optimization step. On the contrary to the obligatory constraints defined by the country labor laws, the requests may not be satisfied. They are usually related to the convenience of the timetable.

2 Literature Review

The algorithms for the rostering problem have been an object of research for decades. Recent computational capabilities and application of parallel computing allow to improve the existing solutions or create the new ones which satisfy the real-life demands. One of the mostly analyzed rostering problems is the nurse rostering [1, 2] which is a part of the home health care rostering system [3]. Although the nurse rostering problem is highly dependent on the constraints, instances and requirements [4], it generalizes the rostering problem applied in various areas. Rostering and scheduling problems are also met in other areas such as the driver rostering in public bus transport [5] and the aircraft crew rostering [6]. They all can be generalized to the personnel scheduling problem [7–9].

Main modules, application areas and solution methods of the rostering process, were discussed in [10]. The main principles for schedule construction were presented in [11] with the guidelines how to formulate the objective function and constraints. Various techniques or their combinations were applied to minimize the objective function which defines the goodness of the schedule. The heuristic decomposition approaches were applied for the personnel rostering problem in [12]. Mathematical programming formulation for the scheduling problem with hierarchical approach to plan the workforce for check-in counters was provided in [13]. A staff rostering system with heuristic algorithm based on simulated annealing was described in [14]. Despite the different approaches proposed to solve the problem, it is stated that the genetic algorithm with the composite chromosome is still an effective and efficient method to use in the shift assignment process [15].

Various procedures of the genetic optimization were applied for the rostering problem. For example, two types of mutation steps were applied to solve the airline crew recovery problem [16]. In this article, the population was constructed of the two-dimensional chromosomes which represented the flights assigned to workers at the given period. In [17], the genetic optimization approach for crew-pairing was proposed for the real life dataset and the objective function minimization was performed by the multi-point crossover operation.

The comprehensive review of the existing approaches was provided in [18]. The existing staffing and scheduling solutions were classified by the performance metrics, approach and application area. Unfortunately, it was concluded that although the research field grows rapidly, most of the solutions lack the implementation for the real-life problems and even real-life solutions are limited to relatively simple stationary approximations.

Although the constraints used in the scheduling problem usually are defined by the country laws, their formulations are similar in all countries and the respective research. The main difference between the solution proposed in this article and other research is the flexibility of the shifts. For example, usually just few types of shifts such as morning, afternoon and night are considered in the nurse rostering problem [4] as it is stated that flexibility of the shift patterns complicates the scheduling problem. In this article the algorithm to form the shifts dynamically based on the tasks assigned to worker is suggested. This allows to combine different tasks in one shift according to the individual worker's certificates and constraints.

3   Problem Definition and Formulation

The nomenclature used in the article is summarized in the Table 1.

Table 1. Nomenclature.

Notation	Description
E	Set of tasks
W	Set of workers
C	Set of hard constraints
S	Set of task types
Parameters of task, $e \in E$	
e_s	Task start time
e_e	Task end time
e_t	Task type, $e_t \in S$
Worker's parameters, $w \in W$	
w_{mwt}	Maximum working time per month
w_{mo}	Maximum overtime per month
w_{mwds}, w_{mns}	Maximum consecutive working days/nights
w_{pwds}	Preferred consecutive working days
w_{mfds}	Minimum consecutive free days
w_{pfds}	Preferred consecutive free days
$\{w_{s_1}, \ldots, w_{s_K}\} \in w_s$	Types of tasks w is certified to perform
$\{w_{wp_L}, \ldots, w_{wp_K}\} \in w_{wp}$	Obligatory working periods
$\{w_{nwp_1}, \ldots, w_{nwp_K}\} \in w_{nwp}$	Non-working periods

The rostering problem is classified as an optimization problem with constraints. The constraints include service resources, worker preferences, laws determined by country, etc. The constraints are categorized to hard and soft. The examples of hard constraints $c_k^w \in C$ are timetable rules defined by the country labor laws, set of tasks a worker is certified to perform, ability to perform only one task at a time. The constructed schedule is defined as valid if it does not violate any hard constraints. Soft constraints correspond to worker's requests to construct a schedule which satisfies the specific requirements. Although due to the shortage of workers or other reasons soft constraints can be violated, this results in the increased value of the objective function. The aim is to minimize the penalty generated by the violation of the soft constraints and unassigned tasks. The problem can be formulated as:

$$\min(\Phi_1 + \Phi_2), c_k^w = 1, \forall c_k^w \in C, \forall w \in W \tag{1}$$

$$\Phi_1 = \sum_{e \in E_u} (a_e * (e_e - e_s)) \tag{2}$$

$$\Phi_2 = \sum_{w \in W} \left(a_o * f_o(X^w) + a_l * f_l(X^w) + a_d * f_d(X^w) + a_v * f_v(X^w)\right) \tag{3}$$

here E_u is the set of unassigned tasks, $(e_e - e_s)$ is the task duration and a_e is a coefficient, which defines the importance of each task. X^w is a schedule constructed for the specific worker w. In the proposed approach, worker's schedule X^w is an array for the scheduling period discretized to intervals. The functions f_o, f_l, f_d, f_v evaluate the goodness of this worker's schedule, where f_o is the overtime, f_l returns the idle time (the total working time without tasks assigned), f_d corresponds to the summed absolute differences between the preferred and planned in the schedule consecutive free days $\left(|w_{mfds} - w_{pfds}|\right)$ and f_v returns the number of short working periods. The coefficients a_o, a_l, a_d, a_v next to the terms allow to control the impact of each parameter to the penalty value.

4   Algorithm

The minimization of the objective function (1) is based on the genetic optimization. The schedule construction process is provided in Fig. 1.

The algorithm consists of three main stages. The first stage is the preparation of the data structures for the later stages. The initial set of solutions is created in the second stage. The obtained solutions are improved in the third stage which is dedicated for the optimization.

In the first stage the scheduled period is discretized to short periods (for example, 15 min). The templates $\{X_1, \ldots, X_{|W|}\} \in X$ of the timetable with the periods possible to work are formatted for each worker. The template X_i consists of array, where each element can obtain values -1, 0 or 1. The value -1 means that the worker cannot work at that period because of the hard constraints. The value 1 defines that the period is assumed as a working period and the obligatory tasks are assigned to the worker at that time. The value 0 is used as a default value in the template and means that the working period can be formed in the corresponding period. The template of worker's schedule is filled according to the information provided in w_{wp} and w_{nwp}. Usage of the initial templates enables to ensure that the hard constraints are not violated in the later stages. At the second stage, N initial individuals in the form of task-worker distributions are created. Each individual is represented by an independent schedule $I = (X, E_w, E_u)$ which consists of a timetable X for all workers, lists E_w of tasks assigned to each worker and a list E_u of unassigned tasks. After this step, all schedules are valid and meet all hard constraints.

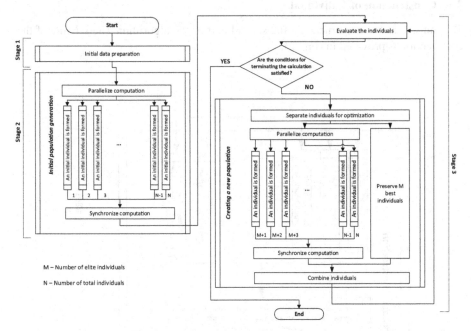

Fig. 1. Scheme of the schedule construction.

At the third stage, the genetic optimization is performed. The task-worker distributions after the initial construction of valid schedules are used as a current population. As the schedules are dependent on the task-worker distribution, they are newly created at each iteration. The individuals are sorted according to the goodness of the schedules respective to the task-worker distribution. The optimization is performed by preserving M elite schedules. The remaining part $(N - M)$ of schedules are regenerated in parallel using mutation and permutation of the current stage individuals. The parent individuals are chosen by tournament from K random individuals for each mutation. The optimization loop is terminated if one of the following conditions is satisfied:

- value of the objective function is equal to zero;
- value of the objective function does not change for the determined number of iterations;
- optimization process lasts longer than specified.

In practice, optimization loop should be terminated due to the second condition. This means that it is the best solution found under the given limitations. The first condition means that the solution was found, but the better solution may exist by the means of convenience with respect to the working time. The third condition indicates that the convergence of the solution is too slow and worker constraints, genetic optimization parameters N, M or computational resources should be revised to obtain result in the desired time.

4.1 Construction of Individual

The individual I is constructed at the second part of the algorithm. The scheme of the construction is provided in (Fig. 2).

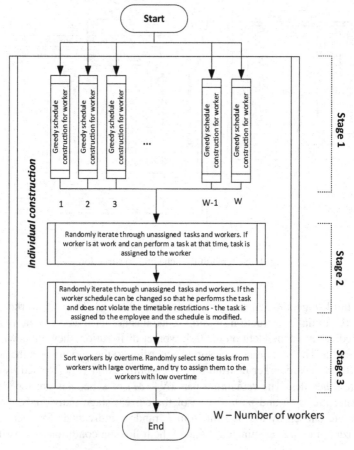

Fig. 2. Scheme for construction of an individual

If worker does not have any obligatory working periods, the construction of an individual begins with the greedy algorithm. The tasks assigned to the worker are sorted with respect to the start time and consecutively added to the schedule in case that addition does not violate the hard constraints provided. This solution is heuristic and skipping some tasks even though all the constraints are met could result in a better global solution. The optimal solution leads to two possibilities for each assignment such as to add the task to the schedule or to skip the task. Unfortunately, two choices lead to exponential complexity on the contrary to the proposed solution which can be implemented with linear complexity for one worker and the total complexity for all workers resulting in $O(|W| \times |E|)$. If worker has the obligatory working periods, the initial schedule is formed in the data preparation stage. The additional tasks must be included with the consideration of the previous and next periods in order not to violate the hard constraints. Valid schedules are generated for the workers in this step and X is filled with respect to the working/non-working periods.

After the first stage, the set of unassigned tasks E_u consists of the tasks which cannot be performed by the worker they were assigned initially. However, they can still be performed by the other workers. In the second stage, the attempts to assign the unassigned tasks to other random certified workers are made under the following conditions:

1. if the task can be performed by the worker during idle time without violating timetable restrictions, the task is assigned to the worker;
2. if the schedule can be changed so that it does not violate the timetable restrictions, the task is assigned to the worker and the schedule is modified.

Because of the consecutive filling of the timetable in the first stage, the worker can have long working periods with no tasks assigned. Condition 1 means that the timetable does not change but such idle periods are filled with tasks as much as possible. Condition 2 means that the initial schedule of the worker is changed by extending the existing working periods or adding new periods with considering the working time constraints. The implementation of 1 is less expensive by the means of computational resources, because it is enough to check only the break time constraints before assigning the tasks to the worker with the idle working period. In order to modify the schedule under the condition 2, it is necessary to check all worker's constraints such as consecutive working days and nights, overtime, etc. This constraint check can be performed locally, and asymptotical complexity of the second stage remains $O(|W| \times |E|)$.

The third stage is designed to balance the working time of all workers by redistributing tasks between them. Due to the different set of task types which can be performed by a worker, the tendency is that the workers with a wide set have large overtime and the working time of others may be even less than the maximum working time without overtime. The perfect balance would lead to the huge computational resources as the balance ratios of the workers change after each step. Thereafter, the second stage could be invoked after the change or a set of changes. That is why only a limited number of attempts to redistribute tasks is performed. The attempt consists of selecting random tasks assigned to the workers with the highest overtime and trying to assign them to the workers with the smallest overtime. The complexity of this procedure depends on the number of attempts but the upper bound of the schedule construction remains $O(|W| \times |E|)$.

4.2 Genetic Optimization Stage

Two approaches to create task-worker distributions were implemented in order to obtain various combinations and preserve the achieved tolerable solutions.

The first approach is designed to slightly modify the obtained results. This approach is applied with the probability μ. After selecting two parents from the previous population, they are modified so that the unassigned tasks are assigned to random worker who is certified to perform such task. Although the main part of task-worker distribution remains the same, the schedules or the number of unassigned tasks can change crucially. For example, if the newly assigned tasks are performed earlier, the schedule is created based on them instead of the previous tasks due to the greedy approach used in the construction. The modification results in the large changes if the solution in the previous population was bad and small changes if the solution was close to optimal. After all tasks are assigned to workers, two schedules for the modified task-worker distributions are constructed and the one with the lower objective function value is selected as an individual for the new population.

The second approach is based on the traditional two-point crossover of two individuals and is designed to create distributions significantly different from the previous population. Firstly, two random indices $P1$ and $P2$ ($P1 < P2$) are generated. The child individual is formed by assigning the tasks with indices $[0; P1 - 1]$ and $[P2 + 1; |E| - 1]$ according to the first parent and tasks with indices $[P1; P2]$ according to the second parent. If the task is unassigned in the parental distribution, it is assigned to the random worker who can perform this task type. In order to maintain almost even influence of the both parents, the difference ($P2 - P1$) is equal to at least 40% and at most 60% of the number of tasks. Secondly, the mutation is performed by assigning a small number of random tasks to possible random workers. Finally, the schedule is constructed for the created task-worker distribution.

5 Analysis of Results

The worker set consists of 52 workers who work either full or part time. There are 23 full-time workers who can perform tasks for 176 h in the analyzed month, 8 part-time workers with 132 expected working hours and 21 half-time workers with 88 working hours. The working hours of the month can vary because of vacation, working arrangements, etc. The maximum number of consecutive working days is 5, minimum number of free days is 2, the possible overtime which does not exceed 20 h for each worker.

The main aim of the optimization is to minimize the number of the unassigned tasks and construct a valid schedule. The coefficients in the objective function are $a_e = 1000$, $a_o = 10, a_l = 1, a_d = 10, a_v = 1$ and were the same for all cases. These values were set after consultation with the client and reflects to the client's preferences. Additional high penalty coefficient (1 000 000) for working only one day between the free periods enables to create a convenient schedule for workers. The unassigned tasks have a major influence in the objective function. They are evaluated by taking into account the duration of the unassigned tasks multiplied by parameter a_e as it is easier to assign shorter tasks, but longer tasks form the main structure of the schedule. In order to guarantee that a flight is serviced by at least one worker, the tasks in the group related to the same flight also have coefficients which define priorities. Other coefficients (a_l, a_v, a_d) have weak influence in the final value of the objective function because they represent the workers' preferences to work longer shifts instead of several short periods, to have a defined number of free days and to have shorter idle time.

The same dataset of worker and tasks, hard and soft constraints was used in all numerical examples. The tournament size equal to 5 was used to select the parent individuals in all cases. The numerical experiments were conducted using population size of 30 individuals and number of the elite individuals equal to 15. The high value of the objective function is obtained because of the several predefined non-working periods which bound one possible working day.

It should be noted that the optimization process can last differently due to randomness. In addition, the results can differ although all the parameters are the same. However, the provided results demonstrate the main tendency of the convergence with different parameters of the genetic optimization.

The influence of the steps in the 2nd and the 3rd stages (Fig. 2) is considered. The results were compared with a standard two-point crossover genetic algorithm with no additional steps to improve the result. All tests were carried out on an Intel Core processor 3.2 GHz and 24 GB RAM and they were conducted considering 5 independent runs.

The changes of the objective function values in calculation time for the algorithm with no or several additional stages after the genetic optimization are given in Fig. 3 and μ value equal to 0.3. The label A represents the results obtained with all three stages included in the optimization. The label B denotes the results if only the two stages are performed excluding the redistribution of the tasks. The results generated for the algorithm with the additional step of assigning the tasks during the idle time without schedule modification are labeled C. Label D represents the results obtained if only the first stage of the individual construction is used in the algorithm. The label GA represents the values obtained using a standard crossover genetic algorithm with no additional steps. Although all tests were terminated due to the exceeded number of maximum iterations with the same best solution, for the tests GA, C and D the calculation time up to termination was significantly shorter than for the cases A and B. The results of standard genetic algorithm (GA) are slightly improved by the combination of two crossover approaches (D). The first step of the second stage (C) gives another improvement of the results. However, the biggest step towards the acceptable solution is made by adding the second step of the second stage when the tasks are assigned by modifying the constructed schedule (B). The third stage of task redistribution (A) gives another slight improvement which results is a fairer and more convenient schedule for the workers.

In this article we provide a fragment of the schedule formatted using all three stages of the algorithm (Fig. 4). These workers are employed either full time (ID9, ID34) or part time (ID3, ID45). Grey areas define non-working periods given as hard constraints. Dashed border represents days with obligatory working periods. If obligatory working period is short, other tasks may be performed that day by extending the working period.

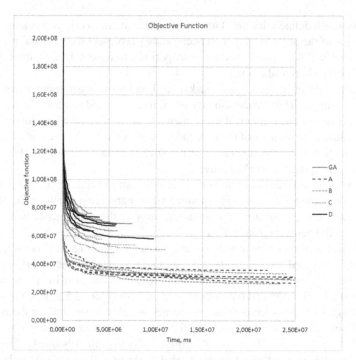

Fig. 3. Changes of the objective function values in calculation time for the standard genetic algorithm (GA), all stages included (A), 1st and 2nd (both steps) stages included (B), 1st and 2nd (1st step) stages included (C), 1st stage included (D).algorithm (GA), all stages included (A), 1st and 2nd (both steps) stages included (B), 1st and 2nd (1st step) stages included (C), 1st stage included (D).

															Day																	
	1	2	3	4	5	6	7	8	9	10	11	12	13	14	15	16	17	18	19	20	21	22	23	24	25	26	27	28	29	30	31
ID3	03:15 05:45	07:30 19:30	19:30 07:30			04:00 06:30	17:30 20:00			02:15 18:00			03:00 05:30	03:30 06:00	04:30 07:00	03:00 05:30	09:15 12:00			17:30 20:00	11:30 18:00	05:00 07:30			07:30 19:30 07:30 19:30	19:30 07:30 19:30 07:30					03:00 05:30
ID9	03:15 17:00	04:30 19:00				02:45 18:45			04:30 21:00			03:00 16:00			04:00 19:00			05:00 18:00	08:45 23:45			03:15 16:00	04:30 21:00		03:30 12:00	02:15 19:00				01:30 16:45	03:00 18:30
ID34		00:15 13:45	02:30 19:15				03:15 14:00	04:00 16:30			03:30 16:30	03:30 16:45	07:30 19:00			04:00 13:45	04:00 19:45			04:00 15:30	04:00 19:00			11:45 19:45	10:45 13:30	03:15 19:45			03:15 16:45	04:00 16:30	08:30 19:45
ID45	04:00 13:00	04:00 06:30	03:00 05:45	11:00 13:30			03:30 06:00	03:15 14:00	04:00 13:15	11:30 10:45			03:15 05:45	12:30 19:45	19:15 21:45	20:45 05:00	17:15 19:45			02:00 04:30	03:30 06:00	04:00 19:45			04:00 13:30			11:30 20:30	11:30 14:00	11:30 14:15	04:00 06:30

Fig. 4. Fragments of the schedule with the lowest value of the objective function.

6   Conclusions

The application of genetic optimization to construct a schedule for the workers of the flight service staff in the combination of the greedy approach to construct a schedule for the individual worker was presented in this article. The testing was performed by analyzing the real-life situations. This also enabled to adjust the algorithm to various demands such as obligatory working periods and flexible shifts generated in the rostering process which usually are not considered in research.

It has been shown that the algorithm can be applied to construct a main core of the schedule by assigning most of the tasks to workers. The algorithm consists of three main stages such as individual construction and schedule improvement. The improvement stages enable to reduce the value of the objective function significantly. Although the objective in a schedule construction process is to satisfy all the constraints, usually in practice it is not possible because of the lack of workers, complex flight schedule or other reasons. The goodness of the schedule is a value judgment and the importance of the criteria can be controlled by varying the coefficient values next to the respective criterion in the objective function.

References

1. Abdennadher, S., Schlenker, H.: Nurse scheduling using constraint logic programming. In: Sixth National Conference on Artificial Intelligence, AAAI, pp. 838–843 (1999)
2. Zheng, Z., Liu, X., Gong, X.: A simple randomized variable neighbourhood search for nurse rostering. Comput. Ind. Eng. **110**, 165–174 (2017)
3. Lin, C.C., Hung, L.P., Liu, W.Y., Tsai, M.C.: Jointly rostering, routing, and rerostering for home health care services: a harmony search approach with genetic, saturation, inheritance, and immigrant schemes. Comput. Ind. Eng. **2018**, 151–166 (2017)
4. Ayob, M., Hadwan, M., Nazri, M.Z.A., Ahmad, Z.: Enhanced harmony search algorithm for nurse rostering problems. J Appl Sci. **13**(6), 846–853 (2013)
5. Xie, L., Kliewer, N., Suhl, L.: Integrated driver rostering problem in public bus transit. Procedia Soc. Behav. Sci. **54**, 656–665 (2012)
6. Doi, T., Nishi, T., Voß, S.: Two-level decomposition-based matheuristic for airline crew rostering problems with fair working time. Eur. J. Oper. Res. **267**, 428–438 (2017)
7. Brucker, P., Qu, R., Burke, E.: Personnel scheduling: models and complexity. Eur. J. Oper. Res. **210**(3), 467–473 (2011)
8. Lin, S.W., Ying, K.C.: Minimizing shifts for personnel task scheduling problems: a three-phase algorithm. Eur. J. Oper. Res. **237**(1), 323–334 (2014)
9. Smet, P., Brucker, P., De Causmaecker, P., Vanden, B.G.: Polynomially solvable personnel rostering problems. Eur. J. Oper. Res. **249**(1), 67–75 (2016)
10. Ernst, A., Jiang, H., Krishnamoorthy, M., Sier, D.: Staff scheduling and rostering: a review of applications, methods and models. Eur. J. Oper. Res. **153**(1), 3–27 (2004)
11. Blöchliger, I.: Modeling staff scheduling problems. A tutorial. Eur. J. Oper. Res. **158**(3), 533–542 (2004)
12. Smet, P., Ernst, A.T., Vanden, B.G.: Heuristic decomposition approaches for an integrated task scheduling and personnel rostering problem. Comput. Oper. Res. **76**, 60–72 (2016)
13. Stolletz, R.: Operational workforce planning for check-in counters at airports. Transp. Res. Part E Logist. Transp. Rev. **46**(3), 414–425 (2010)
14. Dowling, D., Krishnamoorthy, M., Macketizie, H., Sier, D.: Staff rostering at a large international airport. Ann. Oper. Res. **72**(1–4), 125–147 (1997)
15. Xue, N., Landa-Silva, D., Triguero, I., Figueredo, G.P.: A genetic algorithm with composite chromosome for shift assignment of part-time employees. In: 2018 IEEE Congress on Evolutionary Computation CEC 2018 – Proceedings, pp. 1–8 (2018)
16. Guo, Y., Suhl, L., Thiel, M.P.: Solving the airline crew recovery problem by a genetic algorithm with local improvement. Oper. Res. **5**(2), 241–259 (2005)
17. Souai, N., Teghem, J.: Genetic algorithm based approach for the integrated airline crew-pairing and rostering problem. Eur. J. Oper. Res. **199**(3), 674–683 (2009)
18. Defraeye, M., Van Nieuwenhuyse, I.: Staffing and scheduling under nonstationary demand for service: a literature review. Omega **58**, 4–25 (2016)

Sigma Key Agreement Protocol for e-Banking System

Donatas Bartkus[1], Ausrys Kilciauskas[2], and Eligijus Sakalauskas[3(✉)]

[1] NFQ Technologies, Brastos g. 15, Kaunas, Lithuania
donatas.bartkus@nfq.lt
[2] Department of Applied Informatics, Vytautas Magnus University,
K. Donelaicio g. 58, Kaunas, Lithuania
ausrys.kilciausk@gmail.com
[3] Department of Applied Mathematics, Kaunas University of Technology,
K. Donelaicio St. 73, 44249 Kaunas, Lithuania
eligijus.sakalauskas@ktu.lt

Abstract. In this paper the solution of preventing active adversary attack, namely Man-in-the-Middle (MiM) attack in e-Banking system is presented. The vulnerable part of communications between user and Bank is the poor authentication level at the user's side. Therefore, it is a challenge to provide users by the modern means of authentication using e.g. smart phones.

The conjunction of Diffie-hellman key agreement protocol and Schnorr identification protocol is presented by transforming Schnorr identification protocol to Sigma protocol.

It is proved that proposed protocol is secure against active adversary attack, namely against MiM attack under the discrete logarithm assumption.

Keywords: Cryptography · Identification · Key agreement protocol · Sigma protocol

1 Introduction

Diffie-Hellman (DH) key agreement protocol (KAP) is a very important part to provide secure communications. It is a main part of HTTPS protocol. But nevertheless it is vulnerable to well known Man-in-the-Middle (MiM) attack [1] that is an active adversary attack.

MiM attack is an active adversary attack when the adversary uses the interaction between legal parties to try and learn something that will let him impersonate Alice to Bank and Bank to Alice. Suppose Alice runs an identification protocol with Bank over the internet. An active adversary controls the channel and can block or inject messages at will. The adversary waits for Alice to run the identification protocol with Bank and relays all protocol messages from one side to the other. Once the identification protocol completes successfully, the adversary sends requests to the bank that appear to be originating from Alice. The bank honors these requests, thinking that they came from Alice. In effect, the

A. Lopata et al. (Eds.): ICIST 2020, CCIS 1283, pp. 140–146, 2020.
https://doi.org/10.1007/978-3-030-59506-7_12

adversary uses Alice to authenticate to the bank and then "hijacks" the session to send his own messages to the Bank. As a consequence of these attacks adversary can decrypt secret messages exchanged between parties or compromise their secret keys.

HTTPS protocol is widely used in e-banking systems. But nevertheless, so far there is a very poor authentication level on the user's side. Every bank can authenticate himself using public key – PuK and its certificate which is recognizable by user's browser, while users are using passwords or random number generators supplied by bank. In 2019 the new authentication method appeared named as Smart-Id. It is more secure than password based methods but nevertheless Smart-Id does not exploits all opportunities that can provide recent cryptography.

The solution for MiM attack prevention is a realization of authenticated key agreement protocol (AKAP) using public key infrastructure (PKI) methods.

The radical solution can be the cryptographic chip implemented in user's smart phone or in his credit card. This cryptographic chip could be supplied by bank to user with public key cryptosystem (PKC) parameters and supporting software. This software can be used to more secure authentication and communication session creation using AKAP. Moreover, AKAP can be combined together with biometric identification methods which popularity is growing nowadays but not so rapid as desirable.

But nevertheless PKI is quite complicated system and it has small popularity among the users so far.

In general, the main principle to realize AKAP is to sign the data exchanged in DH KAP or equivalently to use a certain identification protocol.

So far, the security of these identification protocols are based on a stronger security assumption, namely on the decisional Diffie-Hellman assumption (DDH) [2]. It would be preferable to use weaker assumption, namely well known discrete logarithm assumption [2].

It is desirable also that the identification protocol be compatible with the DH KAP to reduce the computation resources in the user's side. The most suitable in this case is Schnorr identification protocol [2]. According to [2] so far there are no results confirming or denying the resistance of Schnorr identification protocol against active adversary.

In this paper we propose AKAP protocol based on combination of Diffie-Hellman key agreement protocol (DH-KAP) and Schnorr identification protocol modified to sigma Schnorr identification (SS-Id) protocol. The theorem proving a security of this protocol against active adversary under the discrete logarithm assumption is formulated.

We will consider e-banking system with two legal parties communication with each other, namely user Alice and Bank and adversary as an illegal party. We assume that in all cases adversary has public keys of both parties and system parameters (SP) of used cryptographic system.

2 Preliminaries

We are dealing with a cyclic group G_q of prime order q being a subgroup of cyclic multiplicative group of integers $Z_p^* = \{1, 2, \ldots, p - 1\}$ where multiplication is performed modulo p. Then q is a prime factor of $p - 1$. Let g is a generator g of G_q. Then according to Lagrange's theorem and its consequences all elements of G_q except 1 are generators. The explanations of these notions can be found in [2].

Let x be an integer $1 \leq x \leq q - 1$, then dexp() in G_q is defined as follows:

$$\text{dexp}_g(x) = g^x \mod p = a, a \in G_q. \tag{2.1}$$

The inverse function to dexp() is a discrete logarithm function $\text{dlog}_g(a)$ and is defined as follows

$$\text{dlog}_g(a) = x \mod (q - 1), \tag{2.2}$$

where generator g is a base of discrete logarithm function.

If g is a generator in G_q then function dexp() is one-to-one and performs the following mapping

$$\text{dexp}: Z_{q-1} \rightarrow G_q, \tag{2.3}$$

where $Z_{q-1} = \{0, 1, 2, \ldots, q - 1\}$ is a ring of integers with addition and multiplication operation modulo q.

The necessary but not sufficient security assumption for protocols based on discrete exponent function is discrete logarithm problem (DLP) and associated discrete logarithm assumption.

Definition 2.1. Discrete Logarithm Problem – DLP is to find x in (2.1) when g, p and a are given.

Definition 2.2. Discrete logarithm assumption. We say that the discrete logarithm (DL) assumption holds for G_q if the probability to find x in (2.1) when g, p and a are given is negligible.

For example, when p and q are sufficiently large and suitably chosen primes the discrete logarithm problem in the group G_q is believed to be hard to compute. Prime p should be at least 2048-bits, and q should be at least 256-bits.

To generate random and uniformly distributed parameters for cryptographic protocols we use the special notation. For example, if we choose uniformly a random element r from the set S then we write

$$r = \text{rand}(S). \tag{2.4}$$

We will need a notion of one-way function (OWF) which we define in the following non-formal way.

Definition 2.3. Let $F: A \rightarrow B$ be a function. Function F is said to be one-way if: 1) for given $x \in A$, it is computationally easy to compute $y = F(x)$, which corresponds to the direct F value computation; 2) for given $y \in B$, it is computationally hard to compute (at least single) $x \in A$ such that $F(x) = y$, which corresponds to the inverse F value computation.

Conjecture 2.4. Discrete exponent function defined in (2.1) is a candidate OWF.

Indeed, the computation of $g^x \mod p$ can be done efficiently even for large numbers commonly referred to as square-and-multiply algorithms. But its inverse value computation corresponds to DLP and is reckoned as hard using classical (non-quantum) computers. But nevertheless, due to [3] DLP can be solved in polynomial-time using quantum algorithms running on quantum computers.

Sigma KAP there presented is using the system parameters $SP = (p, g)$, namely large (secure) prime number p and generator g of group G_q. We assume that SP are generated by Bank. Then Bank randomly generates his private key $PrK_B = y$, where

$$y = \text{rand}(Z_q), y \in Z_q, 1 < y < q, \tag{2.5}$$

and corresponding public key $PuK_B = b$

$$b = g^y \bmod p, b \in G_q. \tag{2.6}$$

System parameters $SP = (p, g)$ and Bank's $PuK = b$ are openly distributed among all Bank's customers including Alice.

When user Alice opens her account in the Bank, then during registration phase she receives $SP = (p, g)$, Bank's $PuK_B = b$ and certified software for Sigma KAP realization.

In addition, there are two opportunities for Alice to complete registration operation.

Either she receives Bank generated public and private key pair $PrK_A = x$, $PuK_A = a$, for her where

$$x = \text{rand}(Z_q), x \in Z_q, 1 < x < q, \tag{2.7}$$

$$a = g^x \bmod p, \tag{2.8}$$

or she generates this key pair by herself using special certified application software supplied by Bank. In the latter case Alice keeps secret its $PrK_A = x$ from anyone (including Bank).

In both cases all parameters mentioned above are kept in certain storage device (e.g. USB token, SIM card, Smart phone apps, etc.) together with certified application program. So every user including Alice has system parameters $SP = (p, g)$, Bank's $PuK_B = b$, her $PuK_A = a$ and her $PrK_A = x$. All parties including adversary shares the common information, namely system parameters $SP = (p, g)$ and Bank's $PuK_B = b$. In addition we assume also that adversary knows also public keys of users.

3 Sigma KAP

Sigma KAP is realized by three communications between Alice and Bank. This protocol is a conjunction of Diffie-Hellman [4] key agreement protocol and Schnorr identification protocol [5] by transforming Schnorr identification protocol to Sigma protocol [2].

We assume that Bank is the trusted party and therefore he can prove his identity to users by his signature and PuK_B certificate realized in the lower level protocols such as SSL/TLS. In this connection we assume that Alice is a prover P and she uses protocol $P(x, a)$ with input parameters (x, a) and Bank is a verifier using the verification protocol $V(a)$ with input parameter a respectively.

Sigma KAP realization is the following.

1. Alice chooses at random number $u = \mathrm{rand}(Z_q)$ and computes **commitment** t in the following way

$$t = g^u \bmod p, \; tl \in G_q. \tag{3.1}$$

Alice sends (t, a) to the Bank.

2. Bank after receiving (t, a) verifies if user with his/her public key a is included in his customers database and belongs to Alice. If it is ok, then Bank seeks Alice to prove that she knows corresponding her private key x. Bank chooses at random number $v = \mathrm{rand}(Z_q)$ and computes **challenge** h in the following way

$$h = g^v \bmod p, \; h \in G_q. \tag{3.2}$$

Bank sends (h) to Alice.

3. Alice computes secret session key k_{AB} according to Diffie-Hellman key agreement protocol

$$k_{AB} = h^u \bmod p. \tag{3.4}$$

Alice having her secrets u and x computes the following **response**

$$r = u + xh + a \bmod (p - 1). \tag{3.5}$$

Alice sends (r) to the Bank.

At this stage protocol communications are finished.

Bank after receiving r verifies if Alice knows her private key x corresponding to her public key a, which is registered in Bank's database. The verification equation is the following

$$g^r = ta^h g^a \bmod p. \tag{3.6}$$

If the last equation is valid, then identification procedure is passed successfully.

Bank computes the common session secret key k_{BA} according to Diffie-Hellman key agreement protocol

$$k_{BA} = t^v \bmod p. \tag{3.7}$$

Obviously at this moment parties agreed on their common session key $k = k_{AB} = k_{BA}$ and they can continue communication using created secure channel with agreed secret key k.

In this protocol commitment t and challenge h serves also as open key agreement parameters in DH-KAP. Due to this duplication protocol has effective realization in the user's side. The most consuming operations are exponentiation operations modulo p. They require approximately $\log_2(q)$ multiplication modulo p operations. If q is 256 bits length, then the total number of exponentiations is bounded by $2 * 256 = 512$ performed modulo p, where p is of 2048 bits length. If user's computation device has 64 bits central processor unit, then protocol realization can be performed within 2–3 s.

The difference between convenient Schnorr identification protocol and Sigma KAP is that Alice being a prover P is using two parameters (x, a) in her proof computations and hence it complies with the definition of Sigma protocol. As a consequence, there is also an additional variable g^a in a verification Eq. (3.6). The realization of Sigma protocol is required for security proof presented in the next section.

4 Sigma KAP Security Analysis

For security considerations we accept the most powerful active adversary model. In this model adversary is being able to arrange active attack where he controls the communication channel and can block or inject messages at will. The adversary waits for Alice to run the identification protocol with Bank and relays all protocol messages from one side to the other. Once the identification protocol completes successfully, the adversary sends requests to the bank that appear to be originating from Alice. The bank honors these requests, thinking that they came from Alice. In effect, the adversary uses Alice to authenticate to the bank and then "hijacks" the session to send his own messages to the Bank. As a consequence of these attacks adversary can decrypt secret messages exchanged between parties or compromise their secret keys.

One of the very "popular" kind of this attack is Man-in-the-Middle (MiM) attack. The HTTPS protocol is vulnerable to this kind of attack [1] due to the lack of authentication from the user's side.

To prove the security of Sigma KAP we accept the following assumptions.

1. Since Bank's identification can be performed on the HTTPS level and is based on Schnorr identification protocol we assume that presented identification protocol corresponds to the Honest Verifier Zero Knowledge (HVZK) protocol with respect to the Bank as a verifier.
2. Sigma KAP provides knowledge soundness.
3. Challenge space is sufficiently large to prevent its total scan and brute force attack, i.e. it is of cardinality 2^q for sufficiently large $q = 256$.
4. Under the DL assumption dexp() function is conjectured one-way function.

The following theorem we formulate without proof.

Theorem 4.1. If assumptions 1–4 holds, then Sigma KAP here presented is secure against active adversary attacks.

The complete proof is presented in our recent publication [6].

5 Conclusions

In this paper the solution of preventing Man-in-the-Middle (MiM) attack in e-Banking system is presented.

This protocol is resistant against the active adversary attack, i.e. Man-in-the-Middle attack under the effectively realizable assumptions formulated in the paper.

Proposed protocol has effective realization in the user's side. The total number of exponentiations is bounded to $2 * 256 = 512$ performed modulo p of 2048 bits length. If user's computation device has 64 bits central processor unit, then protocol realization can be performed within 2–3 s.

References

1. Callegati, F., Cerroni, W., Ramilli, M.: Man-in-the-middle attack to the HTTPS protocol. IEEE Secur. Priv. Mag. **7**, 78–81 (2009)

2. Boneh, D., Shoup, V.: A graduate course in applied cryptography (2017). https://crypto.sta nford.edu/~dabo/cryptobook/
3. Shor, P.W.: Polynomial-time algorithms for prime factorization and discrete logarithms on a quantum computer. SIAM J. Comput. **26**, 1484–1509 (1997)
4. Diffie, W., Hellman, M.: New directions in cryptography. IEEE Trans. Inf. Theory **22**(6), 644–654 (1976)
5. Schnorr, C.P.: Efficient identification and signatures for smart cards. In: Brassard, Gilles (ed.) CRYPTO 1989. LNCS, vol. 435, pp. 239–252. Springer, New York (1990). https://doi.org/10. 1007/0-387-34805-0_22
6. Kilciauskas, A., Butkus, G., Sakalauskas, E.: Authenticated key agreement protocol based on provable secure cryptographic functions. Informatica **31**(2), 277–298 (2020)

Table Header Correction Algorithm Based on Heuristics for Improving Spreadsheet Data Extraction

Viacheslav Paramonov[1,2]([✉]) [iD], Alexey Shigarov[1,2] [iD], and Varvara Vetrova[3] [iD]

[1] Matrosov Institute for System Dynamics and Control Theory of Siberian Branch,
Russian Academy of Sciences, Irkutsk, Russia
{slv,shigarov}@icc.ru
[2] Institute of Mathematics and Information Technologies, Irkutsk State University,
Irkutsk, Russia
[3] School of Mathematics and Statistics, University of Canterbury,
Christchurch, New Zealand
varvara.vetrova@canterbury.ac.nz

Abstract. A spreadsheet is one of the most commonly used forms of representation for datasets of similar type. Spreadsheets provide considerable flexibility for data structure organisation. As a result of this flexibility, tables with very complex data structures could be created. In turn, such complexity makes automatic table processing and data extraction a challenging task. Therefore, table preproccessing step is often required in the data extraction pipeline. This paper proposes a heuristic algorithm for the correction of a table header in a spreadsheet. The aim of the proposed algorithm is to transform a machine-readable structure of the table header into its visual representation. The algorithm achieves this aim by iterating through table header cells and merging some of them according to proposed heuristics. The transformed structure, in turn, allows to improve quality of spreadsheet understanding and data extraction further in the pipeline. The proposed algorithm was implemented in the TabbyXL toolset.

Keywords: Data transformation · Table extraction · Table analysis · Spreadsheet · Table header · Heuristics

1 Introduction

Data analysis needs structured data. However, data often are available only in a weakly structured form, such as arbitrary spreadsheet tables. For example, there is a large volume of tabular data presented in statistical reports, financial statements, safety data sheets, or business credit assessments. Many applications of data science and business intelligence potentially could use such datasets.

This work was supported by the Russian Science Foundation, grant number 18-71-10001.

A. Lopata et al. (Eds.): ICIST 2020, CCIS 1283, pp. 147–158, 2020.
https://doi.org/10.1007/978-3-030-59506-7_13

Spreadsheet is a type of software program or a document that allow to organise, store, and analyse data in tabular form. Tables are one of the most convenient and common forms for presentation of information of the same type such as enumeration of quantities, schedules, etc. One of the most popular formats of spreadsheets is Excel. This data format first appeared in the 1980s and made a revolution in tabular data preparation and processing [7]. Currently, it has a widespread use [9,12]. Many spreadsheets that contain valuable information such as statistical and financial reports, digests etc. are available on the Internet. Extraction data from these spreadsheets is one of the key tasks of business intelligence.

Active usage by a large number of diverse users in various domains led to the increasing complexity of tables presented in the Excel format [1]. The complexity of the tabular structure often could lead to numerous errors in data organisation. This issue could be traced back to the 1980s and it is still relevant today [11, 12]. Data preparation (cleansing, recovering cells and their relationships etc.) improves quality of table extraction and understanding.

Automated data extraction from spreadsheets and web-tables can be a time–consuming process. Therefore, it is highly desirable to reduce manual processing as much as possible when large volumes of arbitrary tables need to be processed. In recent years, this challenge attracted attention of the scientific community in the areas of document understanding, data management, and information retrieval. However, few efforts of the community were devoted to developing methods and tools for cleansing messy tabular data [13,16].

One example of a cleansing challenge lies in the difference between a machine-readable organisation (physical layer) and a human-readable representation (visual layer) of spreadsheet cells. In other words, visually we may determine a cell but in fact, this cell might consists of several other cells in the physical layer. Such discrepancy between physical and visual layers is demonstrated in the Fig. 1.

In this paper, we define a visual layer of the table as its representation in a human-readable form. It this form, it is possible to visually determine borders of the cells even when they are not explicitly indicated, for example, by lines. Such characteristic of tabular structure leads to complication of its analysis, especially in the case of automatic processing in tasks of data extraction. Automated identification and extraction of tables in spreadsheets presents a significant challenge [2,8].

This paper presents an approach for automatic correction of machine-readable form of table header in Excel documents to its human-readable form. The aim of this correction is to match physical representation of cells with the visual one. This is achieved here by transforming (merging) cells. The proposed heuristic approach allows to further improve quality of spreadsheet data extraction. We implementated the proposed algorithm as a package for TabbyXL[1] [14] tool for extraction and canonicalisation of tabular documents.

---

[1] https://github.com/tabbydoc/tabbyxl.

	A	B	C	D
1				
2	Items	Total		
3		1990	1995	2000

a. Physical presentation
of table structure

	A	B	C	D
1				
2	Items	Total		
3		1990	1995	2000

b. Visual presentation
of table structure

Fig. 1. Example of a table structure. Dashed lines indicate the physical boundaries of the cells. Continuous lines are visible lines defined by the table author. As can be seen in the Fig. (a), only cells B3, C3, D3 match with their visual representation, Fig. (b). Physical and visual layer presentation doesn't match for all other cells. Thus, one could easily recognise visually (b) that a cell A1:A3 is, in fact, one cell. However, it is represented by three separate cells: A1, A2, and A3, in the physical layer. The cell in the range B1:D2 is a union of cells B1, C1, D1 and merged range B2:D2.

2   Motivation

In practice, many available spreadsheet tables are hand-coded. The tables can originally be produced by some reporting systems from databases but after that end-users modify them manually, including their layout, style formatting, and content. As a result, end-users can roughly split or merge cells when it does not affect table interpretation by other people (but not machines). However, often such modifications can cause errors in processing by software applications. Whereas end-users use logical cells represented implicitly, programs can typically read physical ones represented explicitly only. For example, when one logical cell is split physically then the parts of its textual content can be placed in different physical cells. In this case, the textual content of one logical cell can remain understandable by humans as a whole data item but it can become unreadable by programs.

The automatic table understanding requires cleansing of cell structure before analysis and interpretation of the content. As a result of the table cleansing, its logical cells should correspond to its physical cells one-to-one.

3   Related Work

There are several studies dealing with spreadsheet table structure analysis. Thus, the paper [4] is devoted to challenges in detecting tables and understanding their elements. Authors suggested an approach for detecting tables in spreadsheets and identification of their components such as header, labels, data, etc. They proposed to analyse cells content, fonts and visual styles in order to detect tables in spreadsheets and their elements, such as header, labels, data. Approach proposed in our paper could be utilised in the method suggested by [4] as data preparation step in order to improve tabular element detection.

Usefulness of correct semantic structure also shown in [3]. They noted that some empty cells may be used as separators for header elements whereas others might be a part of another cell on the visual level. This, in turn, influences on table structure understanding. The authors in [6] also noted that correct detection of cells' structure is important for table understanding and element classification.

4   Algorithm of Table Header Correction

4.1   Definitions and Assumptions

Tables generated by different creators may have significantly different schemes of data organisation. However, several regions [10] can be distinguished in each table, such as:

- **Header** – cells that represents the label(s) of a column(s). Its structure could be flat or hierarchical;
- **Attributes** – cells that might be found in the left-most or right-most columns of a table.
- **Metadata** – cells that provide additional information regarding the worksheet as a whole or its specific sections.
- **Data** – cells that form the actual content of the table.
- **Derived** – cells that may be presented in the Data block. They contain derived values of other cells. However, derived cells can have a different structure from the core data cells, therefore we need to treat them separately.

A table header represents the top part of a table and serves to simplify the understanding of table contents. The structure of a header might be very diverse (with one of the multiple levels, flat or hierarchical). There exists few methods to determine position of the header in the table [5]. In this paper, we utilise heuristics to identify bottom line of the header based on cell position and styles.

We will call a cell *non-empty* if it contains information (text, numbers, formulas, etc.). When a cell does not contain any data we will call it *empty*. We assume here that all cells in the header of the visual layer are non-empty. The only exception of this assumption is an empty cell that is surrounded by visible borders. In other cases, each empty cell is merged with a non-empty cell. Merging of an empty cell with empty cells and a non-empty cell with non-empty cells depends on cell positions and border styles.

The following subsection describes an algorithm for restoring the physical structure of table header cells in order to match with their visual presentation. Firstly, the following definitions and assumptions about the features of the table header structure and its analysis were made:

- A *visual border* is a visible line of any style that bounding the cell;
- *Cell width* is a number of merged cells in horizontal direction;
- *Cell height* is a number of merged cells in vertical direction;
- A single (non-merged) cell height and width is 1;
- Header width equals with table width;
- The upper cells are no wider than lower cells;

– Each cell in the visual layer of the header is non-empty;
– Cells of top levels have vertical borders that coincide with vertical borders of lower level cells as it shown by bold lines in the Fig. 2a. Figure 2b shows an incorrect case with no coinciding borders of cells in upper and lower positions.

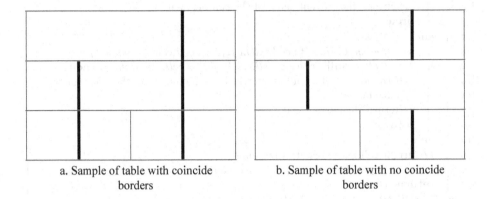

a. Sample of table with coincide   b. Sample of table with no coincide
         borders   borders

Fig. 2. Example of a table structure (physical layer)

4.2   Algorithm of Table Header Correction

The analysis and recovery of the table header structure starts with the top-left cell. We use operation *getCell(left, top)* to find a cell in the table by its left and top coordinates. If this cell does not exist (either coordinates are incorrect or this cell is inside a merged area), the operation returns **null**, otherwise a cell object will be returned. We use *merge(cellA, cellB)* operation to merge cells in the area between *cellA* and *cellB*. The result of this operation is a merged cell. If merging is impossible then the operation returns *cellA*. Border style of merged cell forms from the styles of borders of the top-left *cellA* and the bottom-right *cellB* cells. All data in merged non-empty cells are converted to text and concatenated by a space symbol. Text style in a merged cell will have a centre alignment.

The main idea of the header correction approach is to iterate sequentially through all cells of the header and make a decision about the need for their transformation. Our approach is divided into 4 blocks. They are shown as pseudocode in Algorithms 1–4. Two Algorithms 1 and 2 are responsible for cell extension in horizontal and vertical directions respectively. Algorithms 3 and 4 are used for iteration through cells and call Algorithms 1 and 2.

Firstly, each cell is analysed for the possibility of expansion in the vertical direction (Algorithm 1). In essence, cells are merged in the vertical direction if the cells below the current cell have the same left and right coordinates, and there are no visual horizontal borders between them.

The Algorithm 2 illustrates the method of cell expansion in the horizontal direction. The deque data structure is used to check the border of cells for

Data: cell, bottomBorder
Result: cell
```
1   //Expand cell vertically
2   do
3       if cell = null or cell.BottomBorderStyle ≠ null then
4           //There are no cells below the current cell or there is a visual border
5           //between the current cell and the cell below it
6           break
7       end
8       lowerCell ← getCell(left : cell.cellLeft, top : cell.cellBottom + 1)
9       if lowerCell = null or lowerCell.cellRight! = cell.cellRight )) then
10          //If the lower cell is null or its width is different from the width of the
11          // current cell
12          //Return the current cell
13          return cell
14      end
15      //Current cell is the result of merging
16      cell ← merge(cellA : cell, cellB : lowerCell)
17      return cell
18  while cell.BottomBorder < bottomBorder;
```

Algorithm 1: Vertical expansion of a cell

merging. This implementation allows to decide which cells on the right-hand side of the current cell needs to be merged with it. The algorithm initialised with the following information: the right-hand side cell, which should be checked for the possibility of expanding and merging with the current cell; the bottom border of the current cell; the possible right border of the extension.

Firstly, the current cell expands vertically by the Algorithm 1 if possible. After that, the possibility of expansion in the horizontal direction is checked. Cells could be merged in the horizontal direction in the following cases (Fig. 3):

- heights of the cells are equal;
- both the current and right-hand side cells are empty (cells A1 and B1 in the Fig. 3a);
- the current cell is empty, but the right-hand side cell is non-empty (cells A1 and B1 in the Fig. 3b);
- the current cell is non-empty and all cells further on the right are empty if they exist (cells A1:C1 in the Fig. 3c)

The expansion in horizontal direction of a cell is impossible if:

- the visual border exists (cells C1:D1 in the Fig. 3c);
- both current and right cells are non-empty (cells B1:C1 in the Fig. 3d).

The case of cell expansion when the current cell is empty, but the right-hand side cell is non-empty is of the greatest interest. In this case, the algorithm analyses the right-hand side cells and makes a decision which of them should be

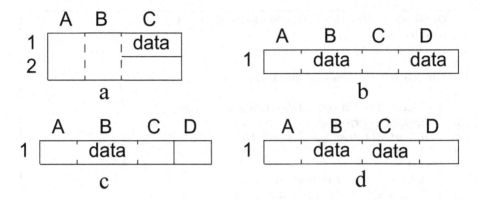

Fig. 3. Cases of tabular structure for horizontal extension. (a) The cell A1:A2 should be merged with the cell B1:B2. However, the B1:B2 could not be merged with the C1 because their heights are different. The vertical extension of the C1 is impossible due to the horizontal border. Fig(b): The A1 should be merged with the B1 but not with the C1. The reason is that the D1 cell is non-empty. The C1 should be merged with the D1. (c) Cells A1, B1, C1 should be merged. The correction process should be stopped because there is a border between the C1 and D1 cells. (d) The A1 and B1 cells should be merged. Further merging is impossible due to non-empty cell C1.

merged based on the following rules. Cells are sequentially checked for possibility of merging until the right border of the header or a visual vertical border are reached. If the new current cell is empty and all other cells on the right-hand side are empty as well, then all cells are merged. If one of the right-hand side cells is non-empty, then the cells are merged until the first cell with data is found.

A *deque* data structure is used to process the case described above when there is an alternation of empty and non-empty cells as shown in the Fig. 3b. Cells are added to the back of the *deque* sequentially. If a second non-empty cell is found then all empty cells are sequentially removed from the back of the *deque* until a non-empty cell is found. The front and back elements of the *deque* determine the boundaries of the merging area.

Algorithm 3 analyses cells of the top level of the header and expands them if needed. Vertical borders of the transformed cells of the top level define the borders of all lower cells and make up a *block*. The purpose of this algorithm is to simplify further analysis of the header.

Further Algorithm 4 iterates through a block of cells and transforms them, if necessary. The data structure *stack* is used for sequential processing of cells. Within the borders of the current block, the top cell is added as the first element of the *stack*. Then, the algorithm moves to the lower cell, extends it if possible and adds it to the *stack*. After the lower border of the header is reached, the algorithm removes the cell object from the *stack*, takes the cell to the right of the current one and adds it to the *stack*. The block processing method finishes when there are no elements left in the stack.

```
Data: cell, rightBorder, bottomBorder, leftCellText
Result: cell
1  f ← false
2  newCell ← cell
3  //Iterate cells in horizontal direction
4  do
5  │   //Expand cell in vertical direction if acceptable
6  │   newCell ← expHeight(cell : newCell)
7  │   if newCell.bottom ≠ cell.bottom then
8  │   │   break
9  │   end
10 │   if leftCellText = true then
11 │   │   if newCell.rawText ≠ null then
12 │   │   │   deque.add(newCell)
13 │   │   end
14 │   else
15 │   │   break
16 │   end
17 │   end
18 │   else
19 │   │   if newCell.rawText ≠ null then
20 │   │   │   leftCellText = true
21 │   │   │   if f = false then
22 │   │   │   │   f = true
23 │   │   │   end
24 │   │   end
25 │   │   deque.add(newCell)
26 │   end
27 │   newCell ← getCell(left : newCell.right + 1, top : cell.top)
28 while newCell ≠ null and newCell.rightBorder ≤ rightBorder;
29 //There is second non-empty cell in the deque
30 if f = true and deque.size > 1 and deque.peekLeast().rawText ≠ null then
31 │   deque.pollLast()
32 │   //Remove objects from deque until first non-empty cell will be found
33 │   while deque.peekLast().rawText = null do
34 │   │   deque.pollLast()
35 │   end
36 end
37 //Get new cell as merged cell
38 cell ← mergeCells(cellA : deque.peekFirst, cellB : deque.peekLast)
```

Algorithm 2: Check cells for expansion possibility

In summary, the Algorithm 4 allows to sequentially iterate through cells in the table header and recover their structure. As a result of this algorithm, all cells in the block will have a structure that matches with its visual representation.

```
Data:  table, headerRightBorder, headerBottomBorder
Result:  table (with transformed structure)
1  //Start analyse the header with left cell leftPosition equal 1
2  //Run top level cells to define borders for lower cells
3  do
4  |    //Analyse cells on top level only
5  |    topLevelCell ← table.getCell(left : leftPosition, top : 1)
6  |    if topLevelCell = null then
7  |    |    //Unable to get the cell to the right. Exit form the cycle
8  |    |    break
9  |    end
10 |    //Expand the cell vertically and horisontally, if permissible
11 |    topLevelCell ← expandCell(topLevelCell)
12 |    if topLevelCell.cellBottom < HeaderBottomBorder then
13 |    |    //If cell height less than height of the header, all below cells should be
               alnalysed
14 |    |    buildBlock(topLevelCell)
15 |    end
16 |    leftPosition ← topLevelCell.cellRight + 1
17 while topLevelCell.RightBorder < HeaderRightBorder;
```

Algorithm 3: Getting blocks of header

5   Testing and Evaluation

The following testing procedure was carried out in order to evaluate the correctness of the algorithm. We used Troy_200 dataset[2] (subset of SAUS dataset[3]) collected by George Nagy for the experimental evaluation. This dataset contains data from different statistical reports presented in the Microsoft Excel format. All tables were marked by the **$START** and **$END** tags for identification of tables in an Excel worksheet.

In order to estimate the accuracy of the proposed header transformation and correction algorithm, each table from the Troy_200 dataset was firstly manually processed. The manual processing consisted of an expert adjusting the header cells in such a way that their physical and visual structures were matched. During the manual correction, an expert only merged cells and no cell splitting operations were performed. As a result, we obtained a new dataset of statistical tables where machine-readable structure of the table header is equivalent to its visual structure. It is worth to note that the manual correction is not always unique.

The accuracy of the algorithm was estimated in the following way. The three datasets are considered: Troy_200 dataset (a), the dataset corrected automatically by our algorithm (b), and the dataset obtained by the expert correction (c). For each of the datasets, the total number of cells in all headers was counted.

---

[2] http://tc11.cvc.uab.es/datasets/Troy_200_1.

[3] https://catalog.data.gov/dataset/statistical-abstract-of-the-united-states.

Data: topCell
1 $seekHeight \leftarrow$ **true**
2 //Push the cell to the stack data structure
3 $stack.push(topCell)$
4 **while** $stack.size() > 0$ **do**
5   $\quad cell \leftarrow stack.peek()$
6   $\quad$ **if** $cell.bottom = bottomBorder$ **and** $seekHieght =$ **true then**
7    $\quad\quad \mid seekHeight \leftarrow false$
8   $\quad$ **end**
9   $\quad$ **if** $seekHeight =$ **true then**
10   $\quad\quad newCell \leftarrow getCell(left : cell.leftBorder, top : cell.bottomBorder + 1)$
     $\quad\quad$ //Get lower cell
11   $\quad\quad newCell \leftarrow expandCell(cell : cell, rightBorder :$
     $\quad\quad topCell.rightBorder, bottomBorder : bottomBorder)$ //And expand it
12   $\quad\quad stack.push(newCell)$ //Push object to the stack
13   $\quad$ **end**
14   $\quad$ **else**
15   $\quad\quad newCell \leftarrow stack.pop()$
16   $\quad\quad$ **if** $stack.size() = 0$ **then**
17    $\quad\quad\quad \mid$ **break**
18   $\quad\quad$ **end**
19   $\quad\quad$ **if** $newCell.rightBorder < cell.rightBorder$ **then**
20    $\quad\quad\quad newCell \leftarrow getCell(left : cell.rightBorder + 1, top : cell.topBorder)$
21    $\quad\quad\quad$ **if** $newCell =$ **null then**
22     $\quad\quad\quad\quad \mid$ **break**
23    $\quad\quad\quad$ **end**
24    $\quad\quad\quad$ //Try to expand cell
25    $\quad\quad\quad newCell \leftarrow expandCell(cell : newCell, rightBorder :$
      $\quad\quad\quad topCell.rightBorder, bottomBorder : bottomBorder)$
26    $\quad\quad\quad$ **if** $newCell.rightBorder = topCell.rightBorder$ **and**
      $\quad\quad\quad newCell.bottomBorder = bottomBroder$ **then**
27     $\quad\quad\quad\quad \mid$ **break**
28    $\quad\quad\quad$ **end**
29    $\quad\quad\quad stack.push(newCell)$
30   $\quad\quad$ **end**
31   $\quad$ **end**
32 **end**

Algorithm 4: Block structure analysis

In addition, correctly identified cells were counted by finding all identical cells in the headers of datasets (b) and (c). We define here identical cells as cells with the same position in the header and the same dimensions (width and height). The resulting number of cells in the headers of the three datasets is as follows:

– **8108** – dataset (a);
– **3800** – dataset (b);
– **3846** – dataset (c);

- **3730** – number of identical cells in the datasets (b) and (c).

Finally, evaluation of the results of the proposed algorithm for header correction is expressed by the following values:

- accuracy = **0.095** – the ratio between the total number of cells correctly identified by the algorithm and summation count of cells correctly identified by the algorithm, incorrectly identified cells by the algorithm, and cells identified by the expert that are not identified by the algorithm;
- recall = **0.969** – the ratio between the number of correctly identified cells by the algorithm and their total number;
- precision = **0.981** – the ratio between the number of correctly identified cells by the algorithm and the number of cells identified by the expert.

6   Conclusions

We have demonstrated in this paper a heuristic approach for structure correction of table header which serves to improve automatic table analysis and understanding. The aim of the proposed algorithm is to match physical cell structures to their visual representation. This correction allows to uniquely link the table header with the data. The proposed heuristic approach demonstrates good results for automatic table cells correction. However, we envisage that the results might be improved if the features of the text and cell style were also taken into account.

The proposed algorithm provides new possibilities for cleansing a table header where cells in a visual layer are improperly split into physical ones. It can be used in software development for spreadsheet data extraction and transformation. Particularly, we implemented this algorithm in TabbyXL [14,15], a toolset for rule-based software development for spreadsheet data canonicalization [15]. The algorithm is incorporated as an optional pre-processing step in the pipeline of converting data from arbitrary spreadsheet to a structured form. We believe that the implemented pipeline can facilitate data extraction from hand–coded tables represented in spreadsheets and web-pages.

In summary, we have demonstrated a heuristic approach for structure correction of table header in order to further improve automatic table analysis and understanding.

References

1. Calimeri, F., Hamlen, K., Leone, N. (eds.): Practical Aspects of Declarative Languages. 20th International Symposium, PADL 2018, Los Angeles, CA, USA, January 8–9, 2018, Proceedings, 1st edn. Springer, Cham (2018). https://doi.org/10.1007/978-3-319-73305-0
2. Chen, Z., Dadiomov, S., Wesley, R., Xiao, G., Cory, D., Cafarella, M., Mackinlay, J.: Spreadsheet property detection with rule-assisted active learning. In: Proceedings of the 2017 ACM on Conference on Information and Knowledge Management - CIKM 2017. ACM Press (2017). https://doi.org/10.1145/3132847.3132882

3. Dong, H., Liu, S., Fu, Z., Han, S., Zhang, D.: Semantic structure extraction for spreadsheet tables with a multi-task learning architecture. In: Workshop on Document Intelligence (DI 2019) at NeurIPS 2019, December 2019. https://www.microsoft.com/en-us/research/publication/semantic-structure-extraction-for-spreadsheet-tables-with-a-multi-task-learning-architecture/

4. Doush, I.A., Pontelli, E.: Detecting and recognizing tables in spreadsheets. In: Doermann, D.S., Govindaraju, V., Lopresti, D.P., Natarajan, P. (eds.) The Ninth IAPR International Workshop on Document Analysis Systems, DAS 2010, Boston, Massachusetts, USA, 9–11 June 2010. ACM International Conference Proceeding Series, pp. 471–478. ACM (2010). https://doi.org/10.1145/1815330.1815391

5. Fang, J., Mitra, P., Tang, Z., Giles, C.L.: Table header detection and classification. In: AAAI (2012)

6. Gonsior, J., Rehak, J., Thiele, M., Koci, E., Günther, M., Lehner, W.: Active learning for spreadsheet cell classification. In: Workshop Proceedings of the EDBT/ICTDT 2020 Joint Conference, March 2020. https://sea-data.ml/

7. Guerrero, H.: Excel Data Analysis. Modeling and Simulation, 2nd edn. Springer, Cham (2019). https://doi.org/10.1007/978-3-030-01279-3

8. Koci, E., et al.: XLIndy. In: Proceedings of the ACM Symposium on Document Engineering 2019 - DocEng 2019. ACM Press (2019). https://doi.org/10.1145/3342558.3345409

9. Koci, E., Thiele, M., Romero, O., Lehner, W.: Table identification and reconstruction in spreadsheets. In: Dubois, E., Pohl, K. (eds.) CAiSE 2017. LNCS, vol. 10253, pp. 527–541. Springer, Cham (2017). https://doi.org/10.1007/978-3-319-59536-8_33

10. Paramonov, V., Shigarov, A., Vetrova, V., Mikhailov, A.: Heuristic algorithm for recovering a physical structure of spreadsheet header. In: Borzemski, L., Świątek, J., Wilimowska, Z. (eds.) ISAT 2019. AISC, vol. 1050, pp. 140–149. Springer, Cham (2020). https://doi.org/10.1007/978-3-030-30440-9_14

11. Raković, L., Sakal, M., Vuković, V.: Improvement of spreadsheet quality through reduction of end-user overconfidence: case study. Periodica Polytech. Soc. Manag. Sci. **27**(2), 119–130 (2019). https://doi.org/10.3311/ppso.12392

12. Ronen, B., Palley, M.A., Lucas, H.C.: Spreadsheet analysis and design. Commun. ACM **32**(1), 84–93 (1989). https://doi.org/10.1145/63238.63244

13. Shigarov, A., Khristyuk, V., Mikhailov, A.: TabbyXL: software platform for rule-based spreadsheet data extraction and transformation. SoftwareX **10**, 100270 (2019). https://doi.org/10.1016/j.softx.2019.100270

14. Shigarov, A.O., Mikhailov, A.A.: Rule-based spreadsheet data transformation from arbitrary to relational tables. Inf. Syst. **71**, 123–136 (2017). https://doi.org/10.1016/j.is.2017.08.004

15. Shigarov, A.O., Paramonov, V.V., Belykh, P.V., Bondarev, A.I.: Rule-based canonicalization of arbitrary tables in spreadsheets. In: Dregvaite, G., Damasevicius, R. (eds.) ICIST 2016. CCIS, vol. 639, pp. 78–91. Springer, Cham (2016). https://doi.org/10.1007/978-3-319-46254-7_7

16. Song, J., Koutra, D., Mani, M., Jagadish, H.V.: GeoFlux. In: Proceedings of the 2018 International Conference on Management of Data - SIGMOD 2018. ACM Press (2018). https://doi.org/10.1145/3183713.3193546

A Review of Self-balancing Robot Reinforcement Learning Algorithms

Aistis Raudys$^{(\boxtimes)}$ ⓘ and Aušra Šubonienė$^{(\boxtimes)}$

Institute of Computer Science, Vilnius University, 47 Didlaukio,
08303 Vilnius, Lithuania
{aistis.raudys,ausra.suboniene}@mif.vu.lt
https://mif.vu.lt/lt3/en/about/structure/institute-of-computer-science/

Abstract. We analyse reinforcement learning algorithms for self balancing robot problem. This is the inverted pendulum principle of balancing robots. Various algorithms and their training methods are briefly described and a virtual robot is created in the simulation environment. The simulation-generated robot seeks to maintain the balance using a variety of incentive training methods that use *non-model-based* algorithms. The goal is for the robot to learn the balancing strategies itself and successfully maintain its balance in a controlled position. We discuss how different algorithms learn to balance the robot, how the results depend on the learning strategy and the number of steps. We conclude that different algorithms result in different performance and different strategies of keeping the robot balanced. The results also depend on the model training policy. Some of the balancing methods can be difficult to implement in real world.

Keywords: Self-balancing robot · Reinforcement learning · Neural networks

1 Introduction

We analyse two-wheeled robot balancing problem. The movement of such a robot is modelled using an inverted pendulum model as the robot's centre of mass is above the pivot point. This model is inherently unstable, and must be actively balanced in order to remain upright. Various sensors and state measurements can be used, but the most common are wheel encoders and IMU sensors, using a combination of accelerometers and gyroscopes. Sensors directly measure robot's velocity, angular velocity of wheels as well as robot's angle.

These measurements are then used by the controller to provide commands to actuators in order to achieve the desired behaviour of a robot. The controller creates low power signals, which are passed through the amplifier and then sent to the actuators, which create robot forces and torques. The movement and forces of a robot are measured using sensors, which feed the measurements back to the controller. Because of such feedback, the process is called closed loop

© Springer Nature Switzerland AG 2020
A. Lopata et al. (Eds.): ICIST 2020, CCIS 1283, pp. 159–170, 2020.
https://doi.org/10.1007/978-3-030-59506-7_14

control. Power disturbances and sensor errors are often included in the model control cycle.

Majority of such algorithms are human coded and do not pay attention to real world factors such as slipping, load, wear-and-tear and so on. The analysis is often simplified making an assumption that amplifiers and actuators are perfect at generating control forces and angular moments which are required by the controller. It is also assumed that the sensors measure the performance of the robot perfectly. The model is also simplified by ignoring the fact that the controller is typically implemented at a finite frequency. Instead, it is assumed that control rules operate in continuous time. Then the control scheme of the robot can be simplified into a control loop of a controller feeding required forces to the actuators. They change the state of a robot which is measured by the sensors and then used again by the controller to make the next step.

Traditionally control loop mechanisms such as proportional–integral–derivative controller (PID), linear–quadratic regulator (LQR) or fuzzy logic controllers or their variations were widely used in robotics control systems. PID and its variants are some of the most common controllers in balance control [4,5]. Even though smaller balancing errors can be achieved using LQR instead of PID controller [1], the mathematical model is needed in order to achieve better results. Also, settling times using LQR can be longer than using PID controller [4]. Fuzzy logic controllers are also used to solve the balance problem. Although both PID and fuzzy logic controller can achieve extremely small steady state errors [6], fuzzy logic controller can be more stable than conventional PID controller [6,7]. In addition to this, fuzzy logic controllers are also combined with neural networks, which results in improved stability and adaptability of the robot [15,17].

In addition to controllers mentioned above, neural networks are also proven to provide good control mechanisms. Either using simple neural networks alone [4], or using recurrent neural networks [8,12,19], improved adaptability to the changes in terrain or mass can be achieved. Even though various solutions provide good results in solving the balancing problem, it is often very difficult to compare different controllers, especially the ones using various neural networks algorithms due to different models of the robot that is used for testing, different experimental conditions and varying parameters of the system. All these possible changes complicate the analysis of different algorithms for balance control. The analysis and comparison of different reinforcement learning algorithms for the balancing problem will result in comparable results for any future work. Several different algorithms will be analysed using a controlled and fully reproducible environment, which allows for direct comparison between different reinforcement learning algorithms which are either mentioned here or created later.

2   Control Algorithms Without Reinforcement Learning

2.1   Proportional–Integral–Derivative Controller (PID)

The usual closed-loop controller in robotics is the PID (proportion-integral-derivative) controller. The three separate controllers (P, I and D) are connected to generate a control signal. The PID controller tries to maintain the output such that there is zero error between the process variable and the desired behavior.

The proportional, or P-controller, produces an output that is proportional to the current error. As long as there is an error (process variable at a non-desired point), Controller I will continuously increase or decrease the controller output value, thus reducing the error. If the error is high, integral mode will increase or decrease the controller output quickly. D controller's output depends on the error rate variation over time multiplied by the derivative constant which allows the system react faster when needed. By combining P, I and D controllers, a PID controller is obtained which is able to control the system so that the robot remains in a balanced position. To control not only the balance but also the displacement of the robot, i.e. to move in a plane, two PID controllers are used one for speed and one for tilt.

2.2   Linear–Quadratic Regulator (LQR)

Linear Quadratic Regulator (LQR) – is an algorithm which is concerned with operating a dynamic system at minimum cost. It can be considered as an automatic way of finding an appropriate state-feedback controller and is a controller that can be optimal in two aspects- balancing and lost cost. Having the system model expressed as $\dot{x} = Ax + Bu$, the feedback control rule minimizing the price value is $u = -Kx$, where K is found by $K = R^{-1}B^T P(t)$ and P is found by solving Riccatti's differential equation.

Then u is selected as an input to achieve the system control objective and obtain a closed loop system dynamics rule $\dot{x} = Ax + Bu$.

3   Reinforcement Learning Algorithms

3.1   LTSM and MLP Policies in Reinforcement Learning Algorithms

The policy defines robot's way of behaving at a given time. Algorithm must find such policy with maximum expected return. In this work two policies were studied with several reinforcement learning algorithms: multilayer perceptron (MLP) and long short-term memory (LSTM). MLP policy is often used in control applications where linear function is not sufficient. Neural network inputs are angles between individual parts of the robot or robot and the environment, and the speed at which those angles change. LSTM policy adds complexity to the robot's behaviour as it uses information learned at previous steps in order to make a decision on a certain action. Information is processed using write, read and keep gates as well as an information cell. The results not only return the output value, but also update the internal state. This way knowledge gained in previous states influence future decisions.

3.2 DeepQ Learning

DeepQ learning algorithm is based on the idea of Q-learning [16], which is a model-free reinforcement learning algorithm for solving Markov decision process. Q-learning finds the policy which maximises the expected value of total reward by iteratively computing the values for the action-value function. Q-learning was later combined with deep learning by DeepMind [10] into DeepQ learning algorithm as a way to approximate Q-values. Instead of updating individual Q-values, using DeepQ learning the updates are performed to the parameters of the network.

DeepQ learning also uses the experience replay which allows for greater data efficiency, behaviour distribution is averaged over many previous states, and randomizing batches breaks correlations between samples. Also, DeepQ learning derives Q-values in one forward pass where Q-values for are predicted for each action for a given state as opposed to Q-learning, where state and action are needed to be given as inputs resulting in Q-value for that particular state and action. In the robotics environment, DeepQ learning produces better results for robot balance compared to usual controllers such as LQR or PID, although PID could sometimes lead to more stable results [11].

3.3 Trust Region Policy Optimisation (TRPO)

TRPO is an on-policy algorithm, which updates policies not by keeping old and new policies close in parameter space, but by taking the largest possible step to improve performance within the bound of constraint [14]. This determines how close the new and old policies are allowed to be. As a result, TRPO avoids situations where small differences in parameter space could have very large differences in performance improving the balance quickly and monotonically.

TRPO uses single path procedures in order to collect state-action pairs, together with Monte Carlo estimates for Q-values. It then creates the predicted goals and constraints by averaging samples. Finally, the strategy parameter vector is updated using conjugate gradient algorithm, followed by line search.

Although TRPO performs well for certain applications, it is computationally expensive, as it calculates H matrix for each iteration of the algorithm. It is unable to scale to big networks and also suffers from sample inefficiency.

3.4 Advantage Actor-Critic (A2C)

Advantage Actor-Critic method [9] is a variant of more general actor-critic algorithms which combine value-based methods and policy based methods. In actor-critic methods both value function and policy function are learned. Q-value is learned by parametrising Q-function using neural network. Critic updates the parameters of value function, which could be action value or state value, depending on the algorithm. Actor then updates policy parameters in the direction suggested by the critic.

In A2C algorithm Q-values can be expressed by combining the state value function V(s) and the advantage value $A(s_t, a_t) = r_{t+1} + \gamma V_v(s_{t+1}) - V_v(s_t)$, which is used to determine how better one action is compared to the other action at a given state, as opposed to the value function, which captures only how rewarding the current state is. Then the update equation becomes:

$$\nabla_\theta J(\theta) \sim \sum_{t=0}^{T-1} \nabla_\theta log \pi_\theta(a_t, s_t)(r_{t+1} + \gamma V_v(s_{t+1}) - V_v(s_t)) \tag{1}$$

Then instead of the critic learning the Q-values, it learns the advantage values, which is possible using only one neural network for the state-value function V(s). In this way the action is evaluated not only on the basis of how good it is, but also how much it can be improved. The advantage function in A2C makes the model more stable and reduces the high variance of the policy network.

3.5 Sample Efficient Actor-Critic with Experience Replay (ACER)

ACER uses a combination of ideas used in several other algorithms, some of which are discussed above. ACER uses multiple worker threads like A2C, a replication buffer, RETRACE algorithm and trust region optimisation. On the other hand ACER introduces several new approaches, such as truncated importance sampling with bias correction, stochastic dueling network architectures, and a new trust region policy optimization method [18].

Policy network is used to estimate the probabilities of actions. During a learning phase data sample is taken from categorical action distribution, related to these probabilities. During a testing phase the actions related to the highest probabilities are used.

During every policy update these steps are performed: the state values are found, then Q-retrace is calculated, followed by collecting gradients and calculating policy gradients, also the trust region is updated, which is used to minimise the difference between the updated policy and mean policy to ensure the stability of the algorithm [18].

3.6 Proximal Policy Optimization (PPO)

Instead of trying to limit or optimise the size of the strategy update step as in TRPO or ACER algorithms, which lead to difficult implementation or issues in practical use for algorithms which have shared parameters for policy and value functions, PPO uses clipped probability rations. It creates a pessimistic policy evaluation (the lower threshold). In order to optimise the policy, data selection and sample creation using policy are constantly changed through multi-epoch optimisation of data samples.

PPO [13] uses fixed-length trajectory segments. During each iteration, each of the N actors acting in parallel runs the policy in the environment for a fixed number of steps T and collects data from those steps. Then the advantage estimates are computed. After this has been done for every actor, the surrogate loss function is constructed and optimised, and the network parameters are updated.

In the neural network architecture, where strategy and value function share common parameters, the loss function uses a policy substitute and a value function error element. Also, the objective function is supplemented by adding an entropy element to ensure sufficient exploration.

4   Robot Model and Environment

The model of the robot was created in OpenAI Gym environment [2]. The model consists of one rectangular parallelepiped of size $20\,cm \times 5\,cm \times 40\,cm$, imitating the body of the robot. The mass of the body is $0.8\,kg$, and the center of mass is at the center of the body. Two cylindrical wheels were attached to the body, with a diameter of $10\,cm$ and width of $2\,cm$. Each wheel weighs $0.1\,kg$. The robot starts each simulation from a slight angle in order to start balancing (Fig. 1).

Fig. 1. Visualisation of robot in OpenAI environment

The simulation environment for the robot was created using OpenAI Gym [2] toolkit together with PyBullet physics engine [3]. A plane was created through x and z axis, and standard acceleration of free fall set as $10\ m/s^2$. In order to learn, the robot was able to choose from 9 different discrete actions which allow the robot to increase or decrease current angular velocity of wheels by 0, 0.1, 0.2, 0.5 or 1 rad/s. This allowed the robot to fine tune small oscillations in order to maintain the balanced position as well as sharply increase the angular velocity or even change the direction of movement if needed.

The state of the environment consists of the tilt angle of the robot, the angular velocity of the robot and the angular velocity of the wheels. Angular velocity of each wheel is not used in order to avoid cheating. This would allow the robot to learn undesirable balancing strategies, such as using angular velocity of the same amplitude but different direction for each wheel, which would result in the robot maintaining the balance by spinning around its axis.

The reward of for each state at time t is calculated using the formula:

$$r_t = 1 - |\alpha| \cdot 0.1 - |v_c - v_d| \cdot 0.01 \tag{2}$$

where α - tilt angle of the robot (rad), v_c - current angular velocity of wheels (rad/s), v_d - desired velocity of wheels (rad/s). In order to achieve a balanced position with no movement back and forth (as opposed to moving in one direction in a stable position) desired velocity $v_d = 0$ is used. Such reward was chosen in order to keep the cumulative reward in a relatively low order and to deduct points for deviating from desired angle of 0 rad more heavily than deviating from desired velocity. This means that the primary goal of the robot should become maintaining a tilt close to 0 rad. As long as the robot maintains a reasonably upright position, it should have little concern about the velocity used.

5   Results

The robot was trained using five different reinforcement learning algorithms: DeepQ learning, TRPO, A2C, ACER and PPO. The simulation was stopped and started again when the robot was falling i.e. position of center of the robot's body was below 15 cm (approximately 1.4 rad tilt) or relatively stable position was maintained for 1500 steps. Simulation data was read at the rate of 100 steps per second in the simulation environment. Figure 2 shows the results of balancing the robot using different reinforcement learning algorithms and MLP policy. A2C, ACER, PPO and TRPO algorithms did not learn to balance the robot during given time frame of 30,000 total steps. While testing these algorithms and running the simulation with models learned, the robot lost its balance and fell within the first 2 s. DeepQ algorithm achieved good results within the given time frame and was successful in balancing the robot within 0.5 rad angle range. Other algorithms were not successful. However, increasing the learning limit to 50000 total steps PPO algorithm (Fig. 2, PPO 2) was successful in learning to maintain the balance. However increasing the time for learning not necessarily results in successfully maintaining the balance. The same experiment of increasing learning time to 50000 steps was tried with ACER algorithm, which did not produce good results compared with PPO algorithm, and the robot still fell during the first few seconds.

The two algorithms that were successful in maintaining the balance after learning using MLP policy resulted in different strategies to accomplish the task. DeepQ algorithm balanced the robot using within much smaller angle range than PPO algorithm (DeepQ - about 0.179 rad, PPO - 1.6376 rad). Also, PPO algorithm used much greater angular velocity of the wheels than DeepQ algorithm, which was in general more stable (Fig. 3). While PPO algorithm used greater angular velocity constantly, DeepQ algorithm generally used quite small velocities, except for periodical angle adjustments using greater velocities than usual, but still usually smaller than biggest velocities using PPO algorithm.

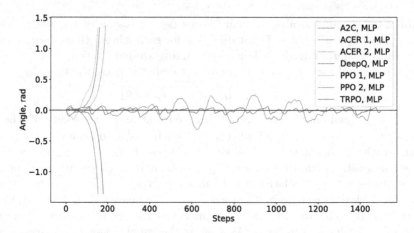

Fig. 2. Changes in tilt angle after learning with MLP policy

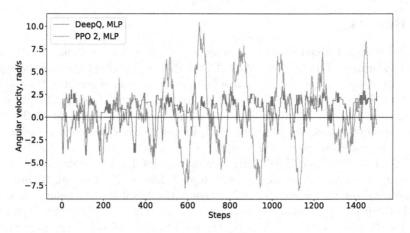

Fig. 3. Changes in angular velocity of wheels after learning with MLP policy

LSTM policy was tried with three algorithms: A2C, ACER and DeepQ, all of which learned to successfully balance the robot within the given time frame of 30000 steps. As it can be seen in Fig. 4, A2C algorithm was visibly worse than ACER and DeepQ algorithms in maintaining a steady balanced position. A2C balanced the robot within 0.5023 rad range, while ACER - 0.1336, and DeepQ - 0.1828 rad range. Besides balancing the robot in the smallest angle range, ACER algorithm also required the smallest range of angular velocity of wheels to maintain the balance (about 5.57 rad/s amplitude). While DeepQ algorithm used almost twice as big velocity range as ACER (10.29 rad/s velocity range), the full range was never used within short time intervals. As shown in Fig. 5, the velocity that was used followed the angle of robot's tilt closely, and changed from peak to peak during intervals of about 2.5 s, while A2C oscillated between

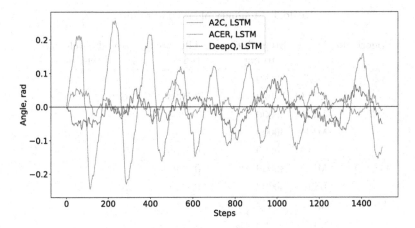

Fig. 4. Changes in tilt angle after learning with LSTM policy

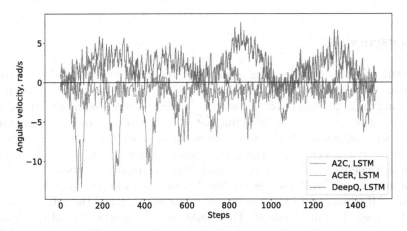

Fig. 5. Changes in angular velocity of wheels after learning with LSTM policy

highest velocities in one direction and highest velocities in different one about every 0.5 s. This makes A2C performance less stable compared with the other two algorithms used.

Detailed results are shown in Table 1. ACER and DeepQ algorithms learned to balance the robot within a smaller tilt range than A2C and PPO algorithms. ACER and DeepQ algorithms also needed a smaller range of angular velocity than A2C or PPO to keep the balance. ACER together with LSTM policy learned the most stable way to keep the balance using smallest tilt and angular velocity range, while both DeepQ MLP and DeepQ LSTM were comparably close. A2C, ACER, TRPO and PPO algorithms combined with MLP policy was unsuccessful in learning the task, although results can be improved in some cases either by changing to LSTM policy, or by increasing the learning steps allowed although this does not guarantee successful balance of the robot.

Table 1. Summary of training results.

Algorithm	Policy	Steps during learning	Tilt range, rad	Angular velocity of wheels, rad/s
A2C	MLP	30000	–	–
	LSTM	30000	0.5023	17.98
ACER	MLP	30000	–	–
	MLP	50000	–	–
	LSTM	30000	0.1336	5.57
DeepQ	MLP	30000	0.179	8.76
	LSTM	30000	0.1828	10.29
TRPO	MLP	30000	–	
PPO	MLP	30000	–	–
	MLP	50000	0.565	18.54

6   Discussion

Different reinforcement learning algorithms require different number of steps to learn to maintain a balanced position. Algorithms that were successful in balancing the robot do so in different ways - trying to keep the tilt angle as low as possible, allowing the tilt angle to fluctuate within a certain radian range, using very sharp changes in wheel rotation to balance, or maintaining the changes in wheels' motion as small as possible, only occasionally adjusting the position with sharp movements to bring the robot back into the upright position.

In most cases, MLP policies produced poor results in comparison to LSTM policies. MLP policies resulted in less sustainable balance of the robot, or at all failed to keep the robot upright. This could be explained by LSTM monitoring the state and evaluating results in the context of past actions, whereas MLP policy only evaluates the current situation, or a buffer of previous situations consisting of single-case observations. This facilitates the LSTM policy in the balancing task by analysing what lead to the current state, paying more attention to the connection between past actions and the current state. It appears that monitoring historical actions are beneficial in robot's stability.

The results were obtained by performing experiments in a simulation, and were not tested with the real life robot. To obtain similar results using a real robot, many unsuccessful attempts to balance would be carried out. In the simulation environment up to 271 falls were necessary for an algorithm to learn to balance the robot. This could result in hardware damage or measurement errors during the impact or introduce measurement noise for subsequent tries. However, even with a maximum protection of robot's hardware the learned ways of keeping the robot in a balanced position would not be feasible. No constraints were enforced on the change of direction of wheels' rotation. The agent could have chosen to go as far as rotating the wheels at any speed to one direction, then in 10 ms reduce the speed by 1 rad/s. This could also result in the constant change in the direction of wheels' rotation every 10 ms, which is hardly sustainable for typical motors used in the models of two-wheeled robots. As a result, not all of the trained models that were obtained in simulation could be implemented using the real robot.

For future research we plan two directions. One: to make our learning methods more sophisticated and penalize for excessive energy consumption, excessive swinging and other undesirable behavior, to train the robot to use different loads, go uphill/downhill and ride uneven terrain. The other direction is to apply these models on real world two-wheeled robots and continue to train from real life data.

References

1. Bature, A.A., et al.: A comparison of controllers for balancing two wheeled inverted pendulum robot. Int. J. Mech. Mechatron. Eng. **14**(3), 62–68 (2014)
2. Brockman, G., et al.: Openai gym. arXiv preprint arXiv:1606.01540 (2016)
3. Coumans, E., Bai., Y.: PyBullet, a Python module for physics simulation in robotics, games and machine learning (2017)
4. Glushchenko, A.I., Petrov, V.A., Lastochkin, K.A.: On development of neural network controller with online training to control two-wheeled balancing robot. In: International Russian Automation Conference (RusAutoCon), IEEE 2018, pp. 1–6 (2018)
5. Imtiaz, M.A., et al.: Control system design, analysis & implementation of two wheeled self balancing robot (TWSBR). In: 2018 IEEE 9th Annual Information Technology, Electronics and Mobile Communication Conference (IEMCON), pp. 431–437 (2018)
6. Kharola, A., et al.: A comparison study for control and stabilisation of inverted pendulum on inclined surface (IPIS) using PID and fuzzy controllers. Perspect. Sci. **8**, 187–190 (2016)
7. Kim, H.-W., Jung, S.: Fuzzy logic application to a two-wheel mobile robot for balancing control performance. Int. J. Fuzzy Logic Intell. Syst. **12**(2), 154–161 (2012)
8. Liang, S., Gan, F.: Balance control of two-wheeled robot based on reinforcement learning. In: Proceedings of 2011 International Conference on Electronic & Mechanical Engineering and Information Technology, IEEE 2011, vol. 6, pp. 3254–3257 (2011)
9. Mnih, V., et al.: Asynchronous methods for deep reinforcement learning. In: International Conference on Machine Learning, pp. 1928–1937 (2016)
10. Mnih, V., et al.: Playing Atari with deep reinforcement learning. arXiv preprint arXiv:1312.5602 (2013)
11. Rahman, M.D.M., Rashid, S.M.H., Hossain, M.M.: Implementation of Q learning and deep Q network for controlling a self balancing robot model. Robot. Biomimetics **5**(1), 1–6 (2018). https://doi.org/10.1186/s40638-018-0091-9
12. Ren, H., Ruan, X.: Bionic self-learning of two-wheeled robot based on skinner's operant conditioning. In: 2009 International Conference on Computational Intelligence and Natural Computing, IEEE 2009, vol. 1, pp. 389–392 (2009)
13. Schulman, J., et al.: Proximal policy optimization algorithms. arXiv preprint arXiv:1707.06347 (2017)

14. Schulman, J., et al.: Trust region policy optimization. In: International Conference on Machine Learning, pp. 1889–1897 (2015)
15. Kuo-Ho, S., Chen, Y.-Y., Shun-Feng, S.: Design of neural-fuzzy-based controller for two autonomously driven wheeled robot. Neurocomputing **73**(13–15), 2478–2488 (2010)
16. Sutton, R.S., Barto, A.G.: Reinforcement Learning: An Introduction. MIT Press, Cambridge (2018)
17. Tatikonda, R.C., Battula, V.P., Kumar, V.: Control of inverted pendulum using adaptive neuro fuzzy inference structure (ANFIS). In: Proceedings of 2010 IEEE International Symposium on Circuits and Systems, IEEE 2010, pp. 1348–1351 (2010)
18. Wang, Z., et al.: Sample efficient actor-critic with experience replay. arXiv preprint arXiv:1611.01224 (2016)
19. Xia, P., Li, Y.: The control of two-wheeled self-balancing vehicle based on reinforcement learning in a continuous domain. In: 32nd Youth Academic Annual Conference of Chinese Association of Automation (YAC), IEEE 2017, pp. 1084–1089 (2017)

Exploring Web Service QoS Estimation
for Web Service Composition

Guillermo Rodríguez[1]([⊠]), Cristian Mateos[1], and Sanjay Misra[2]

[1] ISISTAN-UNICEN-CONICET, Tandil, Argentina
{guillermo.rodriguez,cristian.mateos}@isistan.unicen.edu.ar
[2] Covenant University, Ota, Nigeria
ssopam@gmail.com

Abstract. Web development, machine ubiquity, and the availability of communication networks impacted device design, replacing the idea of an isolated personal computer with one of distributed and connected computers. A web service is a component of software which provides a specific functionality that can be accessed over the Internet. Software development through the assembly of independent services follows the Service-Oriented Computing (SOC) paradigm. One key in the SOC model is that third parties provide resources by presenting only external access interfaces. In this context, the analysis of issues related to the quality of service (QoS) becomes crucial for several development activities related to web services, spanning the discovery of services, their selection, composition and their adaptation in client systems. As far as we know, little has been done in terms of estimation of unknown quality attribute levels when those attributes have high priority in client systems. In this study, a linear regression-based statistical approach is explored to evaluate the relationship between the quality attributes provided by Web services and the metrics related to their interfaces defined in WSDL. This issue is a cornerstone in web service composition for verifying and ascertaining the levels of quality attributes provided by candidate services when QoS data is missing. Finally, we illustrate the approach by performing experiments with public QoS web service datasets and service interface metrics, explore its limitations, and delineate future steps.

Keywords: Web service · Quality of service · Software metrics · Web service composition · Linear regression

1 Introduction

Modern software systems are especially distinguished by their increasing complexity and scale. The Service Oriented Computing (SOC) model has slowly gained ground within the tech industry. The composition of the services with SOC drives the software development. Such services can be offered by third parties, which only show external access interfaces [1]. Particularly, web services are

© Springer Nature Switzerland AG 2020
A. Lopata et al. (Eds.): ICIST 2020, CCIS 1283, pp. 171–184, 2020.
https://doi.org/10.1007/978-3-030-59506-7_15

software components that can be almost seamlessly integrated into more complex distributed applications [2]. Such distributed web-based applications, generally known as service-based systems, depend on certain third parties to ensure that their services meet the necessary or approved quality of service (QoS). An Internet application can invoke multiple services (for example, a web service for trading acts can invoke a payment service which may then invoke an authentication service for validation). Such a scenario is called Web service composition, and the data/invocation flow may be statically or dynamically defined [3].

The analysis of questions related to QoS becomes crucial for several related activities with web services, from the discovery of the services, the selection of them, their composition and their adaptation in client systems. Therefore, QoS is currently a subject of research of significant importance in the field of Web services [4]. In this sense, various types of proposals and approaches have emerged with the definition and analysis of quality of service in Web services for different related activities. An important question, for example, is: What requirements can make a service have "good" quality? The response to this question requires that a shared framework of understanding be developed in which multiple actors are involved in quality assessment. Definitions of these structures are the quality models, and they are called technological objects introduced to organize and standardize the principles and meanings of quality factors in web services. However, as in many other areas of Engineering, there is no single model for quality agreed by the community, but there are several proposals. These proposals can differ in several aspects, being size, structure, terminology, underlying principles some examples. Any web service has the characteristic of presenting clear interfaces that define its functionality; the interface of a web service serves not only as a means of communication between the client and server, but as a specification of such functionality. Historically, software engineers have used the catalogs of metrics as an important tool to estimate the quality of their artifacts of software. In addition, the definitions of a web service interface have several dimensions, such as complexity and consistency, which can be evaluated [5].

The importance of service interfaces and more specifically their non-functional attributes has been highlighted by previous research. In particular, the work of [6] identifies common bad practices that are found in the interfaces of public services, which affect the comprehensibility and discoverability of the services described. In this context, comprehensibility is the ability of a service interface description to be self-explanatory, that is, a software engineer can reason effectively about a service's functionality only by looking at its interface description. Discoverability, on the other hand, refers to a service 's ability to be retrieved conveniently from a registry or archive based on a partial summary of its features, that is, a question. Around the same time, the author defines a series of metrics in [5] for measuring the complexity and efficiency of the service interfaces. At present there are no works that allow estimating the quality of web services from the perspective of complexity, size or quality of its interface. It should be noted that in the context of this work it is crucial to estimate the quality levels of the attributes of the candidates web services to compose based on the interfaces of these services, since as the composition can be carried out in different ways, that is, combining different services, Choosing the services to compose that have the best quality, implies a better performance as a result of the composition. These improvements range from obtaining results in a shorter period of time, achieving higher reliability of the system, to increasing service availability.

In this work, we explore a preliminary approach that allows software developers to predict values of quality attributes, with a certain level of confidence that should satisfy the web services candidates to be part of a service composition. As it is not always possible to determine the levels of quality attributes or to verify that candidate services meet the quality attributes they exhibit, the approach explored in this paper would assist developers to estimate these quality levels based on the values of the metrics of interfaces proposed in the well-known Sneed's catalog. The idea behind this work is based on the use of these metrics as early indicators to warn software developers of quality of services that take part in a process of service composition. To solve the problem of estimating levels of quality, we explore multivariate linear regression, where the dependent variable is the level of a quality attribute and the independent variables are each of the metrics proposed in the Sneed's catalog. In conclusion, experiments carried out with the QWS Dataset[1] have revealed fruitful insights in the context of quality assessment in service composition.

The remainder of this paper was arranged as follows. The background is described in Sect. 2. The related work is discussed in Sect. 3. The proposed approach is set out in Sect. 4. Our empirical evaluation is described in Sect. 5, and summarized. Lastly, the findings and possible study lines are set out in Sect. 6.

2   Background

Nowadays, with the aim to address the needs of the Industry, software development processes have increased their confidence in software reuse [7]. Service Oriented Computing (SOC) is a prominent paradigm of utmost utility for the development of distributed applications, which promotes the uncoupled reuse of software [8]. This model aims to provide support in heterogeneous environments when designing distributed applications. In addition, SOC encourages the cost- and time-effective production and delivery of an application. Online services are used as the building blocks to allow for versatile composition of applications [9].

A web service is a part of software that can be exposed and invoked using standard Web protocols. The language used to specify web services is called WSDL and it is based on XML. A web service can thus be defined in terms of the functionality it provides (its public interface), the description of the operations it provides, the outgoing messages associated with each operation, as well as the data types used as parameters. These operations and messages are defined in the abstract, and then linked to a particular transportation protocol such as SOAP

---

[1] The QWS Dataset, https://zenodo.org/record/3557008#.Xk1fxWhKjI.

or HTTP. The discovery of potentially relevant services, which meet the needs of the developer, is a process that involves the search for these in discovery entities materialized in registries [10].

The specifications of quality attributes, including those related to performance, protection, modificability, reliability and usability, have a major impact on a system's software architecture [11]. Much of a software architecture's life is spent designing software systems to meet a collection of specifications for software quality attributes, typically including scalability, security, performance, and reliability. These are often informally called "-ilities" of an application (although, of course, some of them -e.g. performance- do not fit properly under this lexical specification). The specifications for quality attributes are part of an application's non-functional requirements which capture multiple aspects of how an application's functional requirements are achieved. Both applications may have non-functional specifications which can be expressed in terms of specifications for the quality attributes.

In this context, the analysis of issues related to QoS is of vital importance in the field of web services composition, since knowing the quality of services guarantees that a better new application can be obtained at the time of composing. Linear regression analysis is especially a statistical technique used to research the relationship between variables that adapts to a wide variety of situations [13]. The regression model is used in social science to forecast a wide variety of phenomena, from economic indicators to various aspects of human behaviour. Within the context of market research, it may be used to determine in which of the different media to invest more effectively; or to predict the number of sales of a given product [12,13]. Although there are works that have used linear regression to calculate the efficiency of [14] web services, the study of web service interface metrics and quality attributes seems to be an unexplored area of research.

3   Related Work

Sneed in [5] focused on metrics from a practical point of view, analyzing interfaces for web services. This consists of various types of metrics to calculate the sophistication and efficiency of web services, ranging from specific metrics such as the number of lines of code and number of declarations. All the metrics described can be found in the interface of a web service. Finally, Sneed proposes the SoftAudit tool, which after receiving as input a list of WSDL files, allows for assessing the quality of the interface of a web service. From a non-functional standpoint, Gambhir et al. [14] created a linear regression model for evaluating the quality of web services using the tool WEKA. From a dataset that contains information about quality attributes, the authors built a multivariate linear regression model to predict the quality of some attributes in the absence of others.

The authors analyzed quality of service (QoS) in Web services composition in [18]. Their research is focused on the premise that they have different QoS, criteria and costs for each task in a collection of web services with similar functionalities, so when choosing web services for each task this leads to an optimization problem. As a solution, they proposed a heuristic that allows for obtaining 99% of the optimal solution, taking less than 2% of the time of the exact standard algorithm. The authors proposed to implement genetic algorithms in [19] to improve the quality of service (QoS) in order to obtain better response time or total cost. Given low efficiency, genetic algorithms are a more scalable alternative, and the generic QoS attributes are more accessible to handle.

In [20], the service composition model based analysis is provided, with a emphasis on quality attribute evaluation, that is, efficiency and reliability. They created a tool called ATOP, which automatically transforms a model of service composition design into a model of analysis, which in turn feeds a probabilistic model for predicting quality. Along this line, the authors proposed to formulate a web services configuration through Petri networks by analyzing the graphical structure and algebraic properties in [21]. The result is then used to formulate multiple QoS attribute optimization. In summary, they have obtained that the architecture provides a programming model for the development and assembly of business systems using a service-oriented architecture through the composition of services.

A QoS-based approach to Web service selection is suggested in [22]. The approach presents an equitable and simple algorithm for evaluating multiple metrics based on quality. Researchers use Web Services Modeling Ontology (WSMO) for service annotation definitions with QoS data to define a service quality ontology and its vocabulary. The authors present a complex method of selection, using an optimal algorithm of normalization. Several contemporary approaches are proposed in [23] which use AI to explore alternative solutions when making a composition of web services. IIn this way, compositions of the versatile and adaptable web service can be created, thus achieving better interoperability between distributed and heterogeneous applications.

There is little work to the best of our knowledge on the exploration of relationships between web service interfaces and the consistency of such services from a web service composition perspective. For this reason, our work explores the relationship between the metrics of the Sneed catalog and the QoS-metrics defined by Al-Masri to obtain unknown values of a metric given the values of correlated metrics.

4   Our Approach

In this research work, we delineate an approach that allows software developers to predict quality attribute levels, with a certain confidence level, which the candidate web services must satisfy in order to be part of a service composition. Figure 1 depicts our approach, which is divided into 5 stages. First, there is a WSDL file dataset that contains values of the quality attributes proposed by Al-Masri (1). This set of files is pre-processed to be used later by the SoftAudit tool provided by Sneed and thus obtain a dataset with the interface metrics of

the WSDL files (2) [5]. Once both datasets are prepared with their respective
metrics separately, the KNIME tool[2] is used to merge the dataset into one that
combines the information from both sources (3). In this stage, the Infostat tool[3]
(4) is used to assess statistical assumptions previously to build linear regression
models. Finally, linear regression models are built by considering Sneed's catalog
metrics as independent variables and Al-Masri quality attributes as dependent
variables (5). Hence, we can state our research question as follows:

RQ: *With respect to the composition of web service, is it possible to complete
missing information on either web service interface metrics or web service quality
attribute levels, and what is the effectiveness given the public QoS-datasets?*

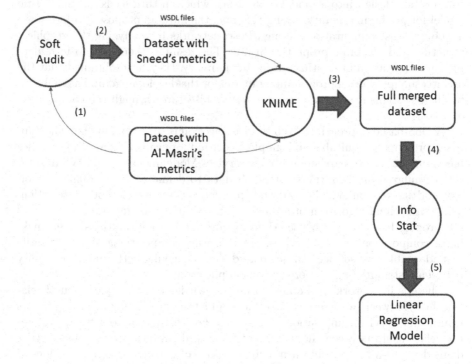

Fig. 1. Schema of our proposed approach.

In order to build linear regression models, we used the following methodology:

1. Perform correlation analysis (matrix) for all independent variables by using
   Pearson correlation (r).
2. For each independent variable, verify
   (a) Sample normality (Shapiro-Wilk test)
   (b) Homoscedasticity with the dependent variable

---

[2] https://www.knime.com/.
[3] https://www.infostat.com.ar/.

(c) If assumptions are verified
    i. Run the regression model
    ii. Check adjusted squared-R coefficient
    iii. Check Fisher statistic F
    iv. Check p-value probability of independent variable coefficients
3. Assemble the Linear Regression equation

Next we step into our proposed approach. Firstly, the correlation matrix allows us to select variables with a considerable correlation (positive or negative) higher than 0.5. For example, let us assume we select two variables from our experimental dataset, namely Interface Modularity and Number of Object-Points ($r = 0.56$), and then we check the sample normality as depicted in Fig. 2.

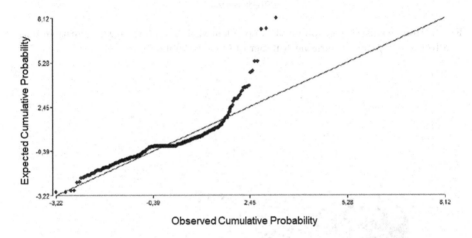

Fig. 2. Normality graph for the Interface Modularity dependent variable in relation to the independent variable Number of Object-Points.

By observing the variability of the dependent variable Interface Modularity at each level of the independent variable Number of Object-Points and not finding any pattern where the variability grows as the values of Number of Object-Points grow, we can affirm that the homocedasticity criterion is achieved as shown in Fig. 3.

Thirdly, we should run the linear regression algorithm and obtain the model as illustrated by Fig. 4. Then, we checked the quality metrics of a linear regression model, namely adjusted squared-R factor (0.32), p-value (<0.0001) and F-test (F $= 342.34$, $p < 0.05$). As a result, the metrics show a weak linear regression model; the resulting equation could infer values of the Interface Modularity metric but with a low level of confidence.

$$Interface Modularity = 0.14 + 1.0e - 04 * Number of Object Points + error$$

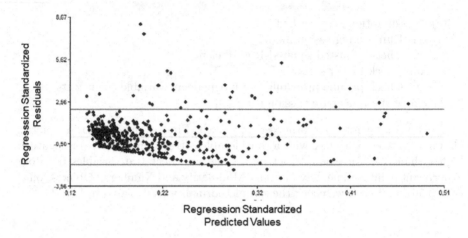

Fig. 3. Homocedasticity graph for the dependent variable Interface Modularity in relation to the independent variable Number of Object-Points.

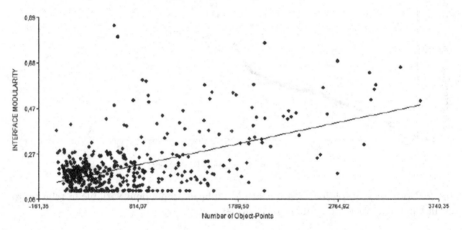

Fig. 4. Linear regression graph for the dependent variable Interface Modularity in relation to the independent variable Number of Object-Points.

5   Experimental Evaluation

To evaluate our approach, we used a publicly available Quality of Web Service (QWS) dataset[4]. The dataset have been utilized by related studies [15, 16] and consists of a set of QoS measurements for 2507 real web service implementations. The web services were collected using the Web Service Crawler Engine (WSCE) [15] and quality measurements were obtained using the Quality of Web Service Manager (QWSMan) [16]. Each web service calculation consists of nine QoS parameters

---

[4] The QWS Dataset, https://zenodo.org/record/3557008#.Xk1fxWhKjIU.

which are calculated using benchmark software for commercial web service. Table 1 shows description of the QoS parameters and their measuring units.

Table 1. QoS parameters and units from Al-Masri dataset.

Parameter name	Description	Units
Response time	Time taken to send a request and receive a response	ms
Availability	Number of successful invocations/Total invocations	%
Throughput	Total Number of invocations for a given period of time	Invokes/Second
Successability	Number of response/number of request messages	%
Reliability	Ratio of the number of error messages to total messages	%
Compliance	The extent to which a WSDL document follows WSDL specification	%
Best practices	The extent to which a Web service follows WS-I Basic Profile	%
Latency	Time taken for the server to process a given request	%
Documentation	Measure of documentation (i.e. description tags) in WSDL	%
WsRF	Web Service Relevancy Function: a rank for Web Service Quality	%
Service classification	Levels representing service offering qualities (1 through 4)	Classifier
Service name	Name of the Web service	None
WSDL address	Location of the Web Service Definition Language (WSDL) file on the Web	None

The quality and complexity of the web services were calculated using Soft-Audit [5]. This tool performs a static analysis on the service interface to measure its quality and complexity. The full list of measures and their descriptions are listed in Table 3. In order to obtain interfaces listed in the QWS dataset, we retrieved the WSDL documents using URLs provided on the dataset. A total of 1162 (46.35%) WSDL documents were successfully retrieved when the experiment was carried out. Out of the 1345 (53.64%) WSDL documents that were unavailable on the Internet, we retrieved 374 WSDL documents from the QWS-WSDL dataset [17]. Finally, we were able to calculate the quality and complexity of 1536 (61.26%) web services. Table 2 and 3 shows the descriptive statistical analysis of quality and complexity measurements, respectively.

Table 2. Descriptive statistics of QoS of services from Al-Masri's dataset.

	Mean	Std dev	Min	Max
Response time (ms)	356.28	456.32	38.00	4651.00
Availability (%)	82.95	17.45	7.00	100.00
Throughput (invokes/second)	8.30	7.27	0.20	41.20
Successability (%)	85.94	18.60	8.00	100.00
Reliability (%)	69.25	9.05	33.00	89.00
Compliance (%)	88.92	10.06	50.00	100.00
Best practices (%)	79.44	7.87	54.00	95.00
Latency (ms)	54.73	186.03	0.33	3881.25
Documentation (%)	31.11	30.19	1.00	97.00

Table 3. Descriptive statistics of the Sneed's metrics from the dataset.

	Mean	Std dev	Min	Max
Number of Function-Points	50.68	99.86	1.00	1013.00
Number of Data-Points	396.77	397.73	0.00	2763.00
Number of Object-Points	463.68	495.98	2.00	3562.00
Number of Results/Output Variables	16.90	33.90	0.00	359.00
Number of Arguments/Input Variables	31.80	52.19	0.00	894.00
Interface Data Complexity	0.80	0.15	0.10	0.90
Interface Relation Complexity	0.81	0.18	0.10	0.90
Interface Format Complexity	0.31	0.23	0.10	0.90
Language Complexity (Halstead Metric)	0.20	0.11	0.16	0.88
Interface Structure Complexity	0.17	0.14	0.10	0.90
Data Flow Complexity (Elshof Metric)	0.31	0.23	0.10	0.90
Interface Modularity	0.24	0.18	0.10	0.85
Interface Reusability	0.67	0.19	0.29	0.90
Interface Testability	0.40	0.36	0.10	0.90
Interface Conformity	0.62	0.38	0.00	1.00

The experiments were divided in two phases. On the one hand, linear regression equations were found for the relationships between the metrics proposed by Sneed, and on the other hand, the linear regression equations for the relationships between the metrics proposed by Al-Masri. In order to perform the tests, each dataset was divided into two groups: 75% for "training" and 25% for "testing". The 75% of WSDL documents were used to find the linear regression equations, whereas the remaining 25% were used to calculate the estimation error using the least-squares technique.

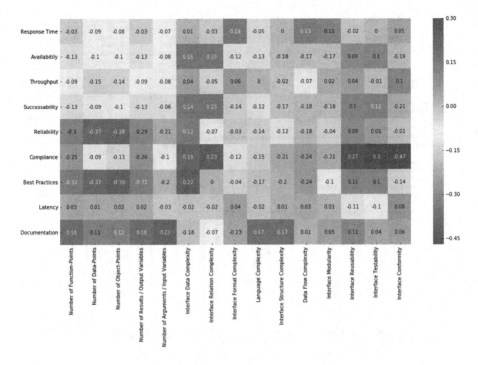

Fig. 5. Correlation matrix between Sneed's and Al-Masri's metrics

In order to study the correlation between Sneed's metrics and Al-Masri's metrics, we calculated the Pearson correlation as shown in Fig. 5. The matrix is a heatmap that shows the correlation strength between variables. Regarding our aforementioned research question (RQ), we observed that there was no considerable correlation between the metrics proposed by Sneed (web service interface metrics) and the ones proposed by Al-Masri (web service quality attribute levels). In principle, whether Sneed's metrics are good QoS predictors should be evaluated in light of a higher amount of service descriptions. So, we decided to study each group of metrics separately because we found stronger correlations as shown in Fig. 6.

In his catalog, Sneed classifies the metrics into three groups, namely Service Interface Size, Service Interface Complexity, and Service Interface Quality. Thus, we propose to predict metrics belonging to the Service Interface Quality group from the metrics belonging to the Service Interface Size and Service Interface Complexity groups.

We found that Interface Modularity is the metric that showed the highest values of correlations with the rest of the variables, but when analyzing the adjusted squared-R factor, we observed a lower value in comparison with the Interface Reusability metric. Despite having less correlation with the rest of the variables, it showed higher adjusted squared-R factors close to 1. Another finding related to the Interface Modularity metric is the higher precision in the

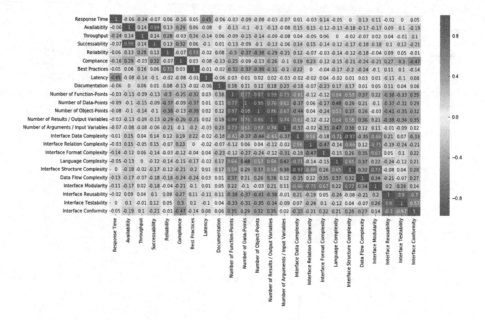

Fig. 6. Correlation matrix from full merged dataset.

linear regression models related to metrics belonging to the Service Interface Complexity in comparison with the ones belonging to the Service Interface Size group. To sum up, the best linear regression models found were the following:

$$InterfaceModularity = 0.08 + 0.63 * InterfaceStructureModularity + 0.00264$$

Additionally, we found a multivariate linear regression model, where the dependent variable Interface Modularity depends on 4 independent variables:

$$InterfaceModularity = -0.25 + 0.11 * IDC + 1.13 * ISC + 0.02 * DFC - 0.13 * LC + 0.102$$

where IDC is Interface Data Complexity, ISC is Interface Structure Complexity, DFC is Data Flow Complexity, LC is Language Complexity. Finally, as for the equations defined for the Al-Masri model, the best equation found according to linear regression quality metrics was:

$$Availability = 3.21 + 0.92 * Successability + 9.222$$

6   Conclusions

In this work, a series of linear regression models were presented, which allow users, from a set of metrics, to predict others from the same set. That is, in the absence of certain metrics, these can be obtained by just applying an equation. Providing metrics to quantify web services is still a maturing area, and thus reducing the number of individual metrics employed by users to test web service quality might alleviate the burden of web service QoS assessment upon composing existing services. In the beginning, we have taken into account the dataset provided by Al-Masri, which in turn contained information on the Quality attributes that each WSDL file (i.e. web service). This dataset was pre-processed to obtain the interface metrics of each web service that Sneed proposes in his catalog through the use of the SoftAudit tool. Then, our approach aimed to predict the metrics of the quality attributes that each WSDL file met from analyzing its interface. As it was not possible to find a relationship between both datasets because there was no correlation between the variables defined in each group, we studied the datasets separately.

According to the experimental results carried out with a dataset of 2500 Web services, several linear regression models were found that allow predicting service interface metrics based on their size and complexity metrics. Likewise, it was possible to find models that allow software practitioners to infer quality attributes from known attributes. In practical terms, linear regression models were developed to detect patterns, forecast performance, and draw conclusions backed by an input dataset, either a QoS-dataset or a Sneed catalog metric dataset.

As future work, we are working on several issues. Firstly, we are planning to explore AI techniques such as association rules, neural networks, and clustering, among others. Secondly, we will normalize the dataset provided by Al-Masri, to study the correlation between the variables and corroborate whether the lack of normalization impacts on the study. Thirdly, we plan to collect information from various databases containing quality information from WSDL files to see whether a correlation analysis relationship can be identified using the SoftAudit tool.

Acknowledgment. We thank M. J. Silva and E. Scott who helped us with the development of the approach and the experiments. Also, we thank to Covenat University, especially to the Center for Research, Innovation and Discovery, for its invaluable support.

References

1. Coscia, J.L.O., Crasso, M., Mateos, C., Zunino, A., Misra, S.: Predicting web service maintainability via object-oriented metrics: a statistics-based approach. In: Murgante, B., et al. (eds.) ICCSA 2012. LNCS, vol. 7336, pp. 29–39. Springer, Heidelberg (2012). https://doi.org/10.1007/978-3-642-31128-4_3
2. Alonso, G., Casati, F., Kuno, H., Machiraju, V.: Web services. In: Web Services, pp. 123–149. Springer, Heidelberg (2004). https://doi.org/10.1007/978-3-662-10876-5_5
3. Menasce, D.A.: Composing web services: a QoS view. IEEE Internet Comput. **8**(6), 88–90 (2004)
4. Wei, Y., Blake, M.B.: Service-oriented computing and cloud computing: challenges and opportunities. IEEE Internet Comput. **14**(6), 72–75 (2010)

5. Sneed, H.M.: Measuring web service interfaces. In: 2010 12th IEEE International Symposium on Web Systems Evolution (WSE), pp. 111–115. IEEE, September 2010

6. Rodriguez, J.M., Crasso, M., Zunino, A., Campo, M.: Improving Web Service descriptions for effective service discovery. Sci. Comput. Program. **75**(11), 1001–1021 (2010)

7. Wang, Y., Stroulia, E.: Flexible interface matching for web-service discovery. In: Proceedings of the Fourth International Conference on Web Information Systems Engineering, WISE 2003, pp. 147–156. IEEE, December 2003

8. Huhns, M.N., Singh, M.P.: Service-oriented computing: key concepts and principles. IEEE Internet Comput. **9**(1), 75–81 (2005)

9. Ezenwoke, A., Misra, S., Adigun, M.O.: An approach for e-commerce on-demand service-oriented product line development. Acta Polytechnica Hungarica **10**(2), 69–87 (2013)

10. Hanzhang, W., Kessentini, M.: Refactoring Web Services Interface Using Many-Objective Search (2019)

11. Rodríguez, G., Díaz-Pace, J.A., Soria, Á.: A case-based reasoning approach to reuse quality-driven designs in service-oriented architectures. Inf. Syst. **77**, 167–189 (2018)

12. Agresti, A.: An Introduction to Categorical Data Analysis. Wiley, Hoboken (2018)

13. Stockburger, D.W.: Multivariate Statistics: Concepts, Models, and Applications. David W. Stockburger (1998)

14. Gambhir, S., Arora, P., Gambhir, J.: Regression model for Quality of Web Services dataset with WEKA. Int. J. Electron. Comput. Sci. Eng. **2**, 927–932 (2013)

15. Al-Masri, E., Mahmoud, Q.H.: WSCE: a crawler engine for large-scale discovery of web services. In: IEEE International Conference on Web Services (ICWS 2007), pp. 1104–1111. IEEE, July 2007

16. Al-Masri, E., Mahmoud, Q.H.: QoS-based discovery and ranking of web services. In: 2007 16th International Conference on Computer Communications and Networks, pp. 529–534. IEEE, August 2007

17. Al-Masri, E., Mahmoud, Q.H.: Discovering the best web service: a neural network-based solution. In: 2009 IEEE International Conference on Systems, Man and Cybernetics, pp. 4250–4255. IEEE, October 2009

18. Berbner, R., Spahn, M., Repp, N., Heckmann, O., Steinmetz, R.: Heuristics for QoS-aware web service composition. In: 2006 IEEE International Conference on Web Services (ICWS 2006), pp. 72–82. IEEE, September 2006

19. Canfora, G., Di Penta, M., Esposito, R., Villani, M.L.: An approach for QoS-aware service composition based on genetic algorithms. In: Proceedings of the 7th Annual Conference on Genetic and Evolutionary Computation, pp. 1069–1075, June 2005

20. Gallotti, S., Ghezzi, C., Mirandola, R., Tamburrelli, G.: Quality prediction of service compositions through probabilistic model checking. In: Becker, S., Plasil, F., Reussner, R. (eds.) QoSA 2008. LNCS, vol. 5281, pp. 119–134. Springer, Heidelberg (2008). https://doi.org/10.1007/978-3-540-87879-7_8

21. Xiong, P., Fan, Y., Zhou, M.: Web service configuration under multiple quality-of-service attributes. IEEE Trans. Autom. Sci. Eng. **6**(2), 311–321 (2009)

22. Wang, X., Vitvar, T., Kerrigan, M., Toma, I.: A QoS-aware selection model for semantic web services. In: Dan, A., Lamersdorf, W. (eds.) ICSOC 2006. LNCS, vol. 4294, pp. 390–401. Springer, Heidelberg (2006). https://doi.org/10.1007/11948148_32

23. Rodríguez, G., Soria, Á., Campo, M.: AI-based web service composition: a review. IETE Tech. Rev. **33**(4), 378–385 (2016)

Random Forests and Homogeneous Granulation

Krzysztof Ropiak[⊠] and Piotr Artiemjew

Faculty of Mathematics and Computer Science,
University of Warmia and Mazury in Olsztyn, Olsztyn, Poland
{kropiak,artem}@matman.uwm.edu.pl

Abstract. The work is a continuation of our research on the application of the newly discovered homogeneous granulation technique. The method gives the possibility to reduce the size of decision-making systems while maintaining their classification efficiency without the need to estimate the optimal approximation radii. The level of system approximation depends on the level of homogeneity of decision classes. That is, the tolerance of modification of objects with their preservation in a given class. Being motivated by effectiveness of our recently developed Ensemble model of Random Granular Reflections - where the homogeneous granulation technique was used to select objects for individual learning iterations - we have checked the effectiveness of the Random Forest in the context of boosting the classification on granular data. In the applied technique, an appropriate subset of attributes and objects is used in individual learning iterations. This means that training data is reduced in two ways. The results of experiments carried out on selected data from the UCI repository show reasonable efficiency on significantly reduced training systems.

Keywords: Homogeneous granulation · Random Forest · Rough sets · Decision Systems · Classification

1 Introduction

The Random Forest technique used to boost classification is one of the most significant discoveries in the family of data mining techniques. It is at the top of methods for improving multi-label classification. In our work we checked the effectiveness of this technique with data reduced by homogeneous granulation - see [3,4] and [5]. The homogeneous granulation method applies the approximation scheme proposed by Polkowski [8]. The detailed theoretical introduction is in the works [8,10] and later in [11]. Naturally, we provide the necessary theories to make things clear.

It is worth adding that, the new technique has been recently applied to a very promising ensemble model - the ensemble of granular reflections - [6] and that is the main motivation for testing homogeneous granulation in the random forests model.

© Springer Nature Switzerland AG 2020
A. Lopata et al. (Eds.): ICIST 2020, CCIS 1283, pp. 185–195, 2020.
https://doi.org/10.1007/978-3-030-59506-7_16

The rest of the paper contains the following content. In Sect. 2 we have a theoretical introduction to basic granulation scheme - see [8]. In Sect. 3 we introduce homogeneous granulation with toy example. In Sect. 4 we present the reference random forest model. In Sect. 5 we present the experimental session and summarize the work in Sect. 6.

Let's start by describing the basic scheme of granulation technique we used.

2   The Granulation Techniques - Basic Scheme

Theoretical background of rough inclusions can be found in Polkowski [9,10,12, 13], a detailed discussion may be found in Polkowski [14].

The standard rough inclusion μ is defined as

$$\mu(v, u, r) \Leftrightarrow \frac{|IND(u, v)|}{|A|} \geq r \tag{1}$$

where

$$IND(u, v) = \{a \in A : a(u) = a(v)\}, \tag{2}$$

The parameter r is the *granulation radius* from the set $\{\frac{0}{|A|}, \frac{1}{|A|}, ..., \frac{|A|}{|A|}\}$.

2.1   The Process of Training System Covering

In the process of covering - the objects of training system are covered based on chosen strategy. We use simple random choice because it is the most effective method among studied ones - see [11]).

The last step of the granulation process is as shown in the next section.

2.2   Granular Reflections

In this step we formed the granular reflections of the original training system based on the granules from the found coverage. Each granule $g \in COV(U, \mu, r)$ from the coverage is finally represented by a single object formed using the Majority Voting (MV) strategy.

$$\{MV(\{a(u) : u \in g\}) : a \in A \cup \{d\}\} \tag{3}$$

The granular reflection of the decision system $D = (U, A, d)$ is the decision system $(COV(U, \mu, r)$, the set of objects formed from granules.

$$v \in g_r^{cd}(u) \text{ if and only if } \mu(v, u, r) \text{ and } (d(u) = d(v)) \tag{4}$$

for a given rough (weak) inclusion μ.

Detailed information about our new method of granulation is presented in the next section.

3   Homogeneous Granulation

The granules are formed as follows,

$$g_{r_u}^{homogeneous} = \{v \in U : |g_{r_u}^{cd}| - |g_{r_u}| == 0, \; for \; minimal \; r_u \; fulfills \; the \; equation\}$$

where

$$g_{r_u}^{cd} = \{v \in U : \frac{|IND(u,v)|}{|A|} \le r_u \; AND \; d(u) == d(v)\}$$

and

$$g_{r_u} = \{v \in U : \frac{|IND(u,v)|}{|A|} \le r_u\}$$

$$r_u \in \{\frac{0}{|A|}, \frac{1}{|A|}, ..., \frac{|A|}{|A|}\}$$

3.1   Toy Example of Homogeneous Granulation

Considering training decision system from Table 1.

Homogeneous granules for all training objects:

$$g_{0.385}(u_1) = (u_1, u_6, u_{10}, u_{11}, u_{12}, u_{18}, u_{20}),$$
$$g_{0.462}(u_2) = (u_2, u_3, u_4, u_5, u_9, u_{23}),$$
$$g_{0.539}(u_3) = (u_2, u_3, u_5),$$
$$g_{0.615}(u_4) = (u_4),$$
$$g_{0.539}(u_5) = (u_3, u_5, u_{21}, u_{23}),$$
$$g_{0.462}(u_6) = (u_4, u_6, u_{16}, u_{20}, u_{21}),$$
$$g_{0.539}(u_7) = (u_7, u_{15}, u_{17}),$$
$$g_{0.462}(u_8) = (u_7, u_8, u_{13}),$$
$$g_{0.462}(u_9) = (u_2, u_4, u_9),$$
$$g_{0.615}(u_{10}) = (u_{10}),$$
$$g_{0.385}(u_{11}) = (u_1, u_6, u_{11}, u_{12}, u_{20}),$$
$$g_{0.385}(u_{12}) = (u_1, u_{11}, u_{12}, u_{18}, u_{20}),$$
$$g_{0.615}(u_{13}) = (u_{13}),$$
$$g_{0.385}(u_{14}) = (u_{14}, u_{15}, u_{24}),$$
$$g_{0.615}(u_{15}) = (u_{15}),$$
$$g_{0.539}(u_{16}) = (u_{16}),$$
$$g_{0.539}(u_{17}) = (u_7, u_{15}, u_{17}),$$
$$g_{0.389}(u_{18}) = (u_1, u_2, u_6, u_{10}, u_{12}, u_{18}, u_{20}, u_{21}, u_{23}),$$
$$g_{0.615}(u_{19}) = (u_{19}),$$
$$g_{0.462}(u_{20}) = (u_1, u_6, u_{11}, u_{12}, u_{18}, u_{20}),$$
$$g_{0.462}(u_{21}) = (u_3, u_5, u_6, u_{21}, u_{23}),$$
$$g_{0.615}(u_{22}) = (u_{22}),$$
$$g_{0.462}(u_{23}) = (u_2, u_3, u_5, u_{21}, u_{23}),$$
$$g_{0.462}(u_{24}) = (u_7, u_{15}, u_{24}),$$

Table 1. Training data system (U_{trn}, A, d), (a sample from heart disease data set)

	a_1	a_2	a_3	a_4	a_5	a_6	a_7	a_8	a_9	a_{10}	a_{11}	a_{12}	a_{13}	d
u_1	74.0	0.0	2.0	120.0	269.0	0.0	2.0	121.0	1.0	0.2	1.0	1.0	3.0	1
u_2	65.0	1.0	4.0	120.0	177.0	0.0	0.0	140.0	0.0	0.4	1.0	0.0	7.0	1
u_3	59.0	1.0	4.0	135.0	234.0	0.0	0.0	161.0	0.0	0.5	2.0	0.0	7.0	1
u_4	53.0	1.0	4.0	142.0	226.0	0.0	2.0	111.0	1.0	0.0	1.0	0.0	7.0	1
u_5	43.0	1.0	4.0	115.0	303.0	0.0	0.0	181.0	0.0	1.2	2.0	0.0	3.0	1
u_6	46.0	0.0	4.0	138.0	243.0	0.0	2.0	152.0	1.0	0.0	2.0	0.0	3.0	1
u_7	60.0	1.0	4.0	140.0	293.0	0.0	2.0	170.0	0.0	1.2	2.0	2.0	7.0	2
u_8	63.0	0.0	4.0	150.0	407.0	0.0	2.0	154.0	0.0	4.0	2.0	3.0	7.0	2
u_9	40.0	1.0	1.0	140.0	199.0	0.0	0.0	178.0	1.0	1.4	1.0	0.0	7.0	1
u_{10}	48.0	1.0	2.0	130.0	245.0	0.0	2.0	180.0	0.0	0.2	2.0	0.0	3.0	1
u_{11}	54.0	0.0	2.0	132.0	288.0	1.0	2.0	159.0	1.0	0.0	1.0	1.0	3.0	1
u_{12}	71.0	0.0	3.0	110.0	265.0	1.0	2.0	130.0	0.0	0.0	1.0	1.0	3.0	1
u_{13}	70.0	1.0	4.0	130.0	322.0	0.0	2.0	109.0	0.0	2.4	2.0	3.0	3.0	2
u_{14}	56.0	1.0	3.0	130.0	256.0	1.0	2.0	142.0	1.0	0.6	2.0	1.0	6.0	2
u_{15}	59.0	1.0	4.0	110.0	239.0	0.0	2.0	142.0	1.0	1.2	2.0	1.0	7.0	2
u_{16}	64.0	1.0	1.0	110.0	211.0	0.0	2.0	144.0	1.0	1.8	2.0	0.0	3.0	1
u_{17}	67.0	1.0	4.0	120.0	229.0	0.0	2.0	129.0	1.0	2.6	2.0	2.0	7.0	2
u_{18}	51.0	0.0	3.0	120.0	295.0	0.0	2.0	157.0	0.0	0.6	1.0	0.0	3.0	1
u_{19}	64.0	1.0	4.0	128.0	263.0	0.0	0.0	105.0	1.0	0.2	2.0	1.0	7.0	1
u_{20}	57.0	0.0	4.0	128.0	303.0	0.0	2.0	159.0	0.0	0.0	1.0	1.0	3.0	1
u_{21}	71.0	0.0	4.0	112.0	149.0	0.0	0.0	125.0	0.0	1.6	2.0	0.0	3.0	1
u_{22}	53.0	1.0	4.0	140.0	203.0	1.0	2.0	155.0	1.0	3.1	3.0	0.0	7.0	2
u_{23}	47.0	1.0	4.0	112.0	204.0	0.0	0.0	143.0	0.0	0.1	1.0	0.0	3.0	1
u_{24}	58.0	1.0	3.0	112.0	230.0	0.0	2.0	165.0	0.0	2.5	2.0	1.0	7.0	2

Granules covering training system by random choice:
$$g_{0.462}(u_2) = (u_2, u_3, u_4, u_5, u_9, u_{23}),$$
$$g_{0.539}(u_3) = (u_2, u_3, u_5),$$
$$g_{0.462}(u_6) = (u_4, u_6, u_{16}, u_{20}, u_{21}),$$
$$g_{0.462}(u_8) = (u_7, u_8, u_{13}),$$
$$g_{0.385}(u_{12}) = (u_1, u_{11}, u_{12}, u_{18}, u_{20}),$$
$$g_{0.385}(u_{14}) = (u_{14}, u_{15}, u_{24}),$$
$$g_{0.539}(u_{17}) = (u_7, u_{15}, u_{17}),$$
$$g_{0.385}(u_{18}) = (u_1, u_2, u_6, u_{10}, u_{12}, u_{18}, u_{20}, u_{21}, u_{23}),$$
$$g_{0.615}(u_{19}) = (u_{19}),$$
$$g_{0.462}(u_{21}) = (u_3, u_5, u_6, u_{21}, u_{23}),$$
$$g_{0.615}(u_{22}) = (u_{22}),$$
Granular decision system from above granules is as follows (Table 2):

Table 2. Granular decision system formed from covering granules

	a_1	a_2	a_3	a_4	a_5	a_6	a_7	a_8	a_9	a_{10}	a_{11}	a_{12}	a_{13}	d
$g_{0.462}(u_2)$	65.0	1.0	4.0	120.0	177.0	0.0	0.0	140.0	0.0	0.4	1.0	0.0	7.0	1
$g_{0.539}(u_3)$	65.0	1.0	4.0	120.0	177.0	0.0	0.0	140.0	0.0	0.4	2.0	0.0	7.0	1
$g_{0.462}(u_6)$	53.0	0.0	4.0	142.0	226.0	0.0	2.0	111.0	1.0	0.0	2.0	0.0	3.0	1
$g_{0.462}(u_8)$	60.0	1.0	4.0	140.0	293.0	0.0	2.0	170.0	0.0	1.2	2.0	3.0	7.0	2
$g_{0.385}(u_{12})$	74.0	0.0	2.0	120.0	269.0	0.0	2.0	159.0	0.0	0.0	1.0	1.0	3.0	1
$g_{0.385}(u_{14})$	56.0	1.0	3.0	130.0	256.0	0.0	2.0	142.0	1.0	0.6	2.0	1.0	7.0	2
$g_{0.539}(u_{17})$	60.0	1.0	4.0	140.0	293.0	0.0	2.0	170.0	1.0	1.2	2.0	2.0	7.0	2
$g_{0.385}(u_{18})$	71.0	0.0	4.0	120.0	269.0	0.0	2.0	121.0	0.0	0.0	1.0	0.0	3.0	1
$g_{0.615}(u_{19})$	64.0	1.0	4.0	128.0	263.0	0.0	0.0	105.0	1.0	0.2	2.0	1.0	7.0	1
$g_{0.462}(u_{21})$	59.0	1.0	4.0	112.0	234.0	0.0	0.0	161.0	0.0	0.5	2.0	0.0	3.0	1
$g_{0.615}(u_{22})$	53.0	1.0	4.0	140.0	203.0	1.0	2.0	155.0	1.0	3.1	3.0	0.0	7.0	2

4   Random Forest

Random forest algorithm developed by [1,2] is an ensemble method for classification boosting. The general principle of this technique is to create an ensemble of decision trees formed from random attributes. The percentage of attributes drawn to the model is determined experimentally depending on the data we work on. In this technique, similarly to the Adaptive Boost method, the individual classifiers do not have to work perfectly, the important thing is that when combined into a committee they give one effective classifier. The effectiveness of such models can be explained by modelling the decision-making problem in different dimensions of data description, which leads to supporting correct solutions. Below is the pseudo-code of the model used for measuring the classification accuracy.

```
function run_experiment(data, n_times=1, gran_enabled=False):
    """ data - full original dataset
        n_times - number of experiments
        gran_enabled - False used for Nil case, True for homogeneous
        granulation case
    """
    results = []

    for n in range(n_times):
        splitted_data = cv5_split(data)
        # configuring classifier with parameters
        classifier = RandomForestClassifier(n_estimators=100,
        max_features=None, random_state=None)

        for i in range(5):
            tst = splitted_data[i]
            trn = splitted_data <> tst
            # optional granulation if enabled
            if gran_enabled:
                trn = homogeneous_granulation(trn)

            features = trn attributes without decision class
            labels = trn decision class
            classifier = classifier.fit(features, labels)
            result = classifier.score(tst attributes, tst labels)
            results.append(result)

    return results
```

Listing 1: Pseudocode for Random Forest classification using CV5 split

5   Experimental Session

Our experiments were run to compare classification and approximation performance of following approaches:

- **nil case** - Random Forest classification on the original data
- **case 1** - Random Forest classification on training data granulated using homogeneous technique
- **case 2** - Random Forest classification on granulated data (homogeneous) reduced by least important attributes chosen from Random Forest classification statistics.

For each case the Cross Validation 5 split was used to bring up the train and test subsets. The attribute importance threshold was set arbitrary to 5 %. That means that the attributes used during Random Forest classification (first run) that had less than 5% impact on model performance were dropped out from the dataset which is then granulated.

Random forest implementation from Scikit Learn library was used. For each CV5 split 100 random trees were built using all features from tested datasets. Additionally to bring more randomness in the whole process bootstraps were also enabled during tree building process. Bootstrapping procedure selects a random sample with replacement from the training set and fits trees to these samples. This leads to a better performance and lowers the over-fitting rate of the trees by training each tree on different randomly sampled subset of the original data.

We have carried out a series of experiments for data from UCI Repository [16] - see Table 3. In the Figs. 1, 2, 3, 4, 5 and 6 we have the results of classification and approximation level for respectively Iris, Australian credit, Pima Indians diabetes, Heart Disease, Wine quality and Breast cancer Wisconsin data sets. In addition, a visualization of classification results is presented. Finally in Table 4 we have collected some more information about approximation level for each tested case.

Random forests work very satisfactorily on granular data, e.g.. for the Iris system, with a 66 % reduction of the number of objects, the accuracy is 0.935 compared to 0.953 on the original data. When comparing number of features, the approximation is even higher reaching 91% of reduction comparing the nil case vs. case 2 with classification accuracy of 0.953 to 0.93. Detailed results for each tested dataset can be found in Table 4.

Table 3. Data sets description - see [16]

Name	Attr type	Attr no.	Obj no.	Class no.
Iris	*integer, real*	5	150	3
Australian − credit	*categorical, integer, real*	15	690	2
Pima Indians Diabetes	*categorical, integer*	9	768	2
Heart − disease	*categorical, real*	14	270	2
Wine quality	*integer, real*	13	178	3
Breast Cancer Wisconsin	*real*	30	569	2

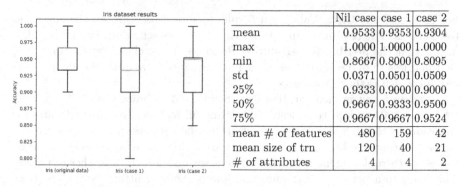

	Nil case	case 1	case 2
mean	0.9533	0.9353	0.9304
max	1.0000	1.0000	1.0000
min	0.8667	0.8000	0.8095
std	0.0371	0.0501	0.0509
25%	0.9333	0.9000	0.9000
50%	0.9667	0.9333	0.9500
75%	0.9667	0.9667	0.9524
mean # of features	480	159	42
mean size of trn	120	40	21
# of attributes	4	4	2

Fig. 1. Results for Iris dataset (5 times CV5), basic parameters and - box plot visualizing accuracy and its deviation

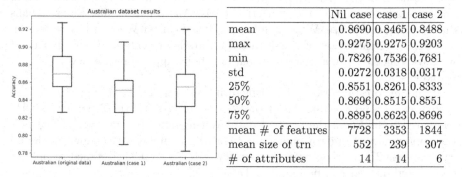

	Nil case	case 1	case 2
mean	0.8690	0.8465	0.8488
max	0.9275	0.9275	0.9203
min	0.7826	0.7536	0.7681
std	0.0272	0.0318	0.0317
25%	0.8551	0.8261	0.8333
50%	0.8696	0.8515	0.8551
75%	0.8895	0.8623	0.8696
mean # of features	7728	3353	1844
mean size of trn	552	239	307
# of attributes	14	14	6

Fig. 2. Results for Australian credit dataset (5 times CV5), basic parameters and - box plot visualizing accuracy and its deviation

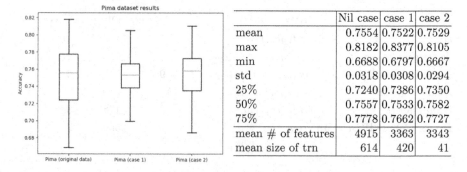

	Nil case	case 1	case 2
mean	0.7554	0.7522	0.7529
max	0.8182	0.8377	0.8105
min	0.6688	0.6797	0.6667
std	0.0318	0.0308	0.0294
25%	0.7240	0.7386	0.7350
50%	0.7557	0.7533	0.7582
75%	0.7778	0.7662	0.7727
mean # of features	4915	3363	3343
mean size of trn	614	420	41

Fig. 3. Results for Pima Indians Diabetes dataset (5 times CV5), basic parameters and - box plot visualizing accuracy and its deviation

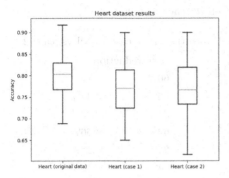

	Nil case	case 1	case 2
mean	0.8020	0.7719	0.7721
max	0.9180	0.9000	0.9000
min	0.6885	0.6500	0.6167
std	0.0483	0.0553	0.0574
25%	0.7676	0.7243	0.7333
50%	0.8033	0.7705	0.7667
75%	0.8299	0.8133	0.8189
mean # of features	3151	1175	849
mean size of trn	242	90	106
# of attributes	13	13	8

Fig. 4. Results for Heart Disease dataset (5 times CV5), basic parameters and - box plot visualizing accuracy and its deviation

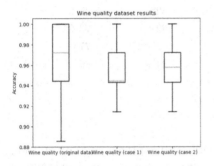

	Nil case	case 1	case 2
mean	0.9651	0.9501	0.9493
max	1.0000	1.0000	1.0000
min	0.8857	0.8333	0.8333
std	0.0317	0.0381	0.0430
25%	0.9444	0.9429	0.9429
50%	0.9722	0.9444	0.9579
75%	1.0000	0.9722	0.9722
mean # of features	1851	1450	431
mean size of trn	142	112	108
# of attributes	13	13	4

Fig. 5. Results for Wine quality dataset (5 times CV5), basic parameters and - box plot visualizing accuracy and its deviation

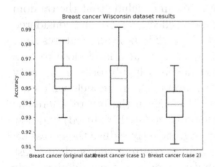

	Nil case	case 1	case 2
mean	0.9591	0.9539	0.9367
max	0.9912	0.9912	0.9649
min	0.9204	0.8860	0.8684
std	0.0140	0.0229	0.0224
25%	0.9496	0.9386	0.9298
50%	0.9561	0.9561	0.9386
75%	0.9649	0.9649	0.9474
mean # of features	13656	10408	1518
mean size of trn	455	347	380
# of attributes	30	30	4

Fig. 6. Results for Breast Cancer Wisconsin dataset (5 times CV5), basic parameters and - box plot visualizing accuracy and its deviation

Table 4. Approximation levels for each tested case

Dataset	Nil case	Case 1 (mean)	Case 2 (mean)	Nil vs. case 1	Nil vs. case 2
	# of objects			% of reduction	
Iris	120	40	21	66%	82%
Australian	552	239	307	56%	44%
Pima	614	420	418	31%	32%
Heart	242	90	106	62%	56%
Wine	142	112	108	22%	24%
Breast	455	347	380	24%	17%
	# of features			% of reduction	
Iris	480	159	42	66%	91%
Australian	7728	3353	1844	56%	76%
Pima	4915	3363	3343	32%	32%
Heart	3151	1175	849	62%	73%
Wine	1851	1450	431	22%	77%
Breast	13656	10408	1518	24%	89%

6   Conclusions

In this work we conducted an experimental verification of the possibility of using the ensemble model, random forests, to boost the classification based on granular data reflections. As a reference granulation technique we used recently discovered the homogeneous granulation method, the basic positive feature of which is the lack of necessity to estimate optimal granulation parameters of approximation. From the experiments carried out in this work we can conclude that the random forest technique fits very well with granular data reflections. On the considered data with a reduction in the number of objects from 22 to 66% and features from 22 to 91% we obtained results of classification accuracy at a level close to that of the original data. Levels of approximation depends highly on the diversity of the dataset. Possible implementation of this approach are models which are pre-trained on current data and need to be re-learned in the future where the new data is collected. Re-learning can be done on granulated (reduced) and new data instead of original + new data which can significantly reduce the necessary computation time. In our upcoming work we plan to confront the random forest technique with our Ensemble of random granules model - also considering their hybrid combination.

Acknowledgements. The research has been supported by grant 23.610.007-000 from Ministry of Science and Higher Education of the Republic of Poland.

References

1. Ho, T.K.: Random decision forests. In: Proceedings of the 3rd International Conference on Document Analysis and Recognition, Montreal, QC, 14–16 August 1995. pp. 278–282 (1995). Archived from the original (PDF) on 17 April 2016. Retrieved 5 June 2016
2. Breiman, L.: Random forests. Mach. Learn. **45**, 5–32 (2001). https://doi.org/10.1023/A:1010933404324
3. Ropiak, K., Artiemjew, P.: A study in granular computing: homogenous granulation. In: Damaševičius, R., Vasiljevienė, G. (eds.) ICIST 2018. CCIS, vol. 920, pp. 336–346. Springer, Cham (2018). https://doi.org/10.1007/978-3-319-99972-2_27
4. Ropiak, K., Artiemjew, P.: On granular rough computing: epsilon homogenous granulation. In: Nguyen, H.S., Ha, Q.-T., Li, T., Przybyła-Kasperek, M. (eds.) IJCRS 2018. LNCS (LNAI), vol. 11103, pp. 546–558. Springer, Cham (2018). https://doi.org/10.1007/978-3-319-99368-3_43
5. Ropiak, K., Artiemjew, P.: Homogenous granulation and its epsilon variant. Computers **8**(2), 36 (2019)
6. Artiemjew, P., Ropiak, K.: A novel ensemble model - the random granular reflections. In: Proceedings of the 27th International Workshop on Concurrency, Specification and Programming, CEUR, Berlin (2018)
7. Artiemjew, P., Ropiak, K.: Missing values absorption based on homogenous granulation. In: Damaševičius, R., Vasiljevienė, G. (eds.) ICIST 2019. CCIS, vol. 1078, pp. 441–450. Springer, Cham (2019). https://doi.org/10.1007/978-3-030-30275-7_34
8. Polkowski, L.: A model of granular computing with applications. In: Proceedings of IEEE 2006 Conference on Granular Computing GrC06, Atlanta, USA, pp. 9–16. IEEE Press (2006)
9. Mani, A.: Comparative approaches to granularity in general rough sets. In: Bello, R., Miao, D., Falcon, R., Nakata, M., Rosete, A., Ciucci, D. (eds.) IJCRS 2020. LNCS (LNAI), vol. 12179, pp. 500–517. Springer, Cham (2020). https://doi.org/10.1007/978-3-030-52705-1_37
10. Polkowski, L.: Formal granular calculi based on rough inclusions. In: Proceedings of IEEE 2005 Conference on Granular Computing GrC05, Beijing, China, pp. 57–62. IEEE Press (2005)
11. Polkowski, L., Artiemjew, P.: Granular Computing in Decision Approximation. ISRL, vol. 77. Springer, Cham (2015). https://doi.org/10.1007/978-3-319-12880-1
12. Polkowski, L.: Granulation of knowledge in decision systems: the approach based on rough inclusions. The method and its applications. In: Kryszkiewicz, M., Peters, J.F., Rybinski, H., Skowron, A. (eds.) RSEISP 2007. LNCS (LNAI), vol. 4585, pp. 69–79. Springer, Heidelberg (2007). https://doi.org/10.1007/978-3-540-73451-2_9
13. Polkowski, L.: A unified approach to granulation of knowledge and granular computing based on rough mereology: a survey. In: Pedrycz, W., Skowron, A., Kreinovich, V. (eds.) Handbook of Granular Computing, pp. 375–400. Wiley, Chichester (2008)
14. Polkowski, L.: Approximate Reasoning by Parts. An Introduction to Rough Mereology. Springer, Heidelberg (2011). https://doi.org/10.1007/978-3-642-22279-5
15. Kleinberg, E.M.: Stochastic discrimination. Ann. Math. Artif. Intell. **1**, 207–239 (1990). https://doi.org/10.1007/BF01531079
16. Irvine Machine Learning Repository, University of California. https://archive.ics.uci.edu/ml/index.php

Orchestration Security Challenges in the Fog Computing

Nerijus Šatkauskas⬤, Algimantas Venčkauskas$^{(\boxtimes)}$ ⬤, Nerijus Morkevičius$^{(\boxtimes)}$ ⬤, and Agnius Liutkevičius

Kaunas University of Technology, Studentų g. 50, Kaunas, Lithuania
{nerijus.satkauskas,algimantas.venckauskas}@ktu.lt,
nerijus.morkevicius@ktu.edu

Abstract. Fog Computing is a new paradigm which is meant to solve some new challenges in IoT like a wide-spread geographical distribution and mobility of the devices, multiple nodes, heterogeneity of the hardware capabilities and communication technologies. A Fog Computing Orchestration enables the control of multiple devices connected to the Fog Computing network. It offers some new application areas like a smart home, smart grid, smart vehicles, or health data management. Since security issues of both the Fog Computing and Orchestration are not fully explored yet, it poses different challenges. This review paper firstly aims to identify the Fog Computing security challenges as it is the environment for an Orchestration. It reviews some proposed Orchestration solutions as well. Secondly, Orchestration challenges are identified themselves by reviewing over 150 papers. The results suggest that security/privacy is among the top concerns.

Keywords: Fog Computing · Fog Orchestration · Orchestration Security · Fog Computing Security Challenges · Internet of Things · IoT

1 Introduction

As media claims, 5G network will soon become available. The advantages of 5G network are high speed and low latency. It will give a rise to multiple people and things connected to the internet. All that will make up the Internet of Things (IoT). It is feared though that the new technology may pose new security challenges which yet are not fully explored.

There are different paradigms for the Internet of Things (IoT) like Cloud Computing, Mobile Computing, Edge Computing or Fog Computing. The Fog Computing as the OpenFog Consortium [1] defines is "A horizontal, system-level architecture that distributes computing, storage, control and networking functions closer to the users along a cloud-to-thing continuum". Bonomi et al. [2] suggests that the Fog Computing is one of the best solutions to meet specific IoT requirements. It may include the edge of the network placement, a very large number of nodes, mobility etc. Fog Computing may fulfill certain IoT requirements; however its security threats or orchestration security challenges should not be overlooked.

© Springer Nature Switzerland AG 2020
A. Lopata et al. (Eds.): ICIST 2020, CCIS 1283, pp. 196–207, 2020.
https://doi.org/10.1007/978-3-030-59506-7_17

Distributed service infrastructure in the Fog layer may be owned by different entities while using different software and hardware which requires effective collaboration and communication solutions. New standards which define how different components of the architecture can communicate are still under development. Fog layer services are often implemented as virtual machines, thus solutions for a lightweight virtual machine lifecycle management (creation, deployment, migration, context preservation etc.) are considerable. Resources are in different locations distributed over various devices. An effective mechanism for service discovery and orchestration is critical in this case. Another big challenge is the mobility of both the end-nodes and Fog Computing devices. It requires specific protocols and solutions which could enable a synchronization of various states of service devices on any heterogeneous infrastructure [3] hosting the Fog services.

The goal of this review paper is to investigate the Fog Computing Security Challenges, Orchestration solutions suitable for the Fog Computing, and Orchestration Security Challenges. As Fog Computing Challenges and Orchestration Challenges are often treated as the same ones in papers, this paper pays an extra attention to tell it apart.

The Sects. 2–4 respectively provide a short review due to a limited space. The chapter No. 2 "Survey of the Fog Orchestration Review Papers" is dedicated to review papers which are up-to-date and thorough enough by their volume to rely on. The chapter No. 3 "Fog Computing Security Challenges" seeks to give a brief overview of the security challenges faced by the Fog Computing as it is the environment for an Orchestrator. A considerable contribution is made by the OpenFog Consortium [1] document as it contains the guidelines proposed on behalf of the Fog Computing by a number of unified companies. The chapter No. 4 reviews the most common Orchestration solutions. It is a more extensive one as it is important in order identify subsequently any orchestration security challenges. The chapter No. 5 "Orchestration Challenges Identification Results" uses a systematic approach to identify any specific Orchestration challenges including the relevance of security and privacy. Over 150 papers that are the most popular on Google Scholar were screened for the right challenge keywords within these documents. A chart is provided because of the findings. The chapter No. 6 gives a summary of the review sections No. 2-4. It is presented as a set of guidelines.

2 Survey of the Fog Orchestration Review Papers

Multiple papers seem to confirm that the Fog Computing paradigm is rather new and insufficiently explored yet. Security and privacy challenges may depend as the paper [4] identifies in this case on location privacy, data privacy, intrusion detection, secure protocols and secure data transfer. As the paper further claims while giving a refence to relevant authors that it is possible to track user's location as he/she moves from one edge cloud to another. However, a solution to this privacy challenge in order to prevent any tracking could be a fake service specifying a fake route. What concerns the data privacy for a vehicular road surface monitoring, referenced authors proposed a certificateless encryption scheme and a data transmission protocol to ensure confidentiality, integrity, privacy, and anonymity. Another challenge could be an intrusion detection. Using Software Defined Network (SDN) switches as the Fog Computing nodes can be a promising idea but if an attacker tampers a fog node, it may become possible to further exploit it to get a control over the network.

Meanwhile, the paper [5] suggests considering the Fog Computing architecture as a three-layered one. The hierarchy according to the authors is made of (1) sensing layer, (2) the middleware (communication medium), and (3) the Fog Computing server. The sensing layer comprises of different sensing devices, such as radio-frequency identification (RFID) tags, wireless sensor networks (WSNs), and near-field communications (NFCs) etc. These end-nodes are to identify relevant physical objects, convert the data and send it to the upper level devices. The middleware is made of the network and transport layers. As the data is received from the bottom layer, it is processed at the middleware and transmitted to a Fog Computing server. The Fog server layer acts as a front end to users. Its main function is to assist with the management of different applications. All these three layers have their typical threats or security challenges. A potential solution to these three-layered threats are immediately prompted but as it is noted in the conclusions section, a fully holistic security is still to be developed.

Orchestration Security plays a significant part as well in relevant papers. As the paper [6] claims, Fog Computing Orchestration applications can simplify the maintenance and increase the security. However, the crucial challenge as the paper further adds is dealing with such service dynamic variations and a transient operational behavior. In order to be more specific, diversity of the Fog Computing nodes is the main challenge. Location, configuration and provided functionalities can dramatically increase it. It leads to a research challenge which is how to optimize a selection of the best Fog Computing components to compose an application processes for such requirements as a security, network latency and Quality of Service (QoS).

Orchestration Security among such other criteria as a scale and complexity, dynamicity, fault diagnosis and tolerance plays an important role. Overall communication integrates multiple sensors, computer chips and communication equipment. Certain services can be made of different components in different geographical locations which increase hack opportunities. Fog Computing end-nodes are extremely vulnerable as the attack can be initiated by human actions in the network infrastructure, and by malicious applications for any data leak. It is even possible to physically tamper the end-nodes.

3   Fog Computing Security Challenges

The Fog Computing paradigm solves several shortcomings of the Cloud Computing by providing a solution in the situations where low latency and jitter, mobility support, constrained devices support, context and proximity awareness is required. On the other hand, the Fog Computing also introduces some new challenges in various fields, including data privacy and security.

Security assuring functions must be installed in every Fog Computing solution to make it responsive, available, survivable and trusted [7]. All the edge paradigms, including Fog Computing, use a lot of different building blocks (such as various wireless communication protocols, constrained devices and networks, distributed and peer-to-peer systems, virtualization platforms, etc.) to comprise the final solution. It is essential to protect the building blocks themselves and to orchestrate diverse security mechanisms [3]. One needs to have a full, unified, and transversal view of all the security mechanisms available in a heterogeneous infrastructure to ensure an effective and secure integration and an interoperability. Moreover, by ensuring a security to all the building blocks individually, one does not necessary ensure a security to the solution itself.

Additionally, the Fog Computing paradigm introduces specific requirements e.g. the security methods and protocols should not be centralized as the central infrastructure may not be available due to strict requirements for latency or it may simply be offline due to malicious attacks. On the other hand, some Fog Computing devices may be constrained enough [8] to support only the simplest authentication protocols and limited connectivity. One not only needs to ensure enough of security in all the building blocks based on different architectures and technologies, but also to ensure a secure global connectivity and accessibility in a heterogeneous ecosystem [9].

According to Puthal's [5] et al. security challenges specific to the Fog Computing, one could group them into three parts by the place of occurrence in the overall Fog architecture: a) security threats in the edge or sensing layer, b) security threats in the network infrastructure, c) security threats in the Fog layer. The remaining part of the Fog architecture, the Fog to Cloud part, doesn't introduce any Fog specific challenges (Table 1).

Table 1. Fog Computing threats [1] as defined by OpenFog Consortium.

Threat categories		Confidentiality	Integrity	Authentication	Availability	Privacy
Attack venue	Intents	Leaking info through a channel	Modifying data/code without authorization	Masquerading one as another	Rendering resources unavailable	Leaking sensitive info
Insider attacks		Data leaks	Data alteration	Identity/key leak	Equipment sabotage	Data/identity leak
Hardware attacks		Hardware, trojans, side channel attacks	Hardware trojans	Hardware trojans	Radio jamming, bandwidth exhaustion	Hardware trojans, side channel attack
Software attacks		Malware	Malware	Malware	DoS/DDos	Malware, social networking
Network attacks		Eavesdrop	Message/transaction replay	Spoofing, Man-in-Middle	DoS/DDos, subnet flooding	Traffic pattern analyses

OpenFog Consortium [1] defines the types of threats for the system to be aware of as it is stated above. Such a threat model does not need to go too much into details of the attacks as it was mentioned. It should however specify whether it considers only operational system threats, or it also includes the attacks caused by an insider. E.g. if a designer creates a back door, it is very hard to prevent it from being exploited later.

4 Fog Orchestration Solutions

As the Orchestration is defined by the OpenFog Consortium [1], it is "Type of composition where one particular element is used by the composition to oversee and direct the other elements". In general, Fog Computing paradigm extends the Cloud Computing and inherits its several important properties such as resource Orchestration, multi-tenancy, elastic provisioning [10], etc. Fog Computing nodes use their computational resources in such implementations to provide required services to the nodes at the edge of the network. If the Orchestration framework is designed correctly, it allows to partition the required services between different Fog Computing nodes and/or some Cloud-based services in such a way, that delay-sensitive tasks are executed by physically close Fog Computing nodes, however the resource-hungry non-real-time tasks are executed by cheap and powerful Cloud services. That process is called an affinity-aware software offloading.

The authors [10] provide an overview of the Fog Computing service Orchestration framework which bridges the gap between the infrastructure and the applications. They propose to use a classic architecture introduced by National Institute of Standards and Technology (NIST) [11] which is already widely adopted in the modern Cloud Computing systems, such as OpenStack. This three-layer Cloud Computing orchestration framework (see Fig. 1) could also be successfully used in the Fog Computing.

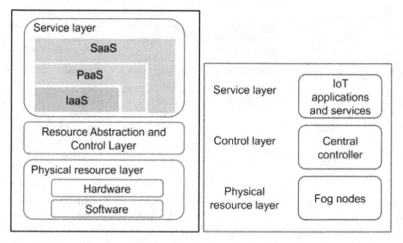

Fig. 1. Cloud Computing architecture (left) [11] to a Fog Orchestrator (right) [10].

A central role in this three-layer architecture is played by the control layer or the central controller which makes decisions on how to efficiently allocate available IoT applications and services to a lower layer of the Fog Computing nodes. Several new challenges specific only to Fog Computing paradigm need to be addressed: scalability of the control layer, affinity-based service provision, and heterogeneous nature of the Fog Computing nodes.

A control layer of the Fog Computing must be able to coordinate any interactions among a massive number of the Fog Computing nodes with entirely different capabilities and constraints forming a physical resource layer. Two methods are used in the Cloud Computing solutions to deal with a scalability of the control layer: hierarchical controller approach (e.g. OpenStack Cells) and the flat controller approach. A hierarchical controller layer uses additional higher-level controllers to form a multi-level structure which helps to minimize computational requirements for the controller layer. The flat controller layer uses a peer-to-peer architecture with a periodic gossiping between different controllers trying to collect information on a global structure of the system and making decisions for a local device management. The flat controller approach is more suitable for Fog Computing systems where nodes are owned by different independent parties (homeowners, public institutions, universities, etc.) with heterogeneous hardware and software resources. On the other hand, a Fog Computing layer may include millions of different nodes to make controllers unable to store and share the information about the whole system. To solve a scalability problem, Jiang et al. [10] propose that each controller should collect and maintain information on the structure of a system in its proximity in order to share the information only with its neighboring controllers. Such a solution ensures that any required Fog Computing services are naturally offloaded to physically close Fog Computing nodes and the amount of the information needed to maintain and share it is significantly reduced. Figure 2 demonstrates a three-layer Fog orchestration framework and its data flows required for an effective Orchestration. Three types of data flows or data exchange interfaces are distinguishable.

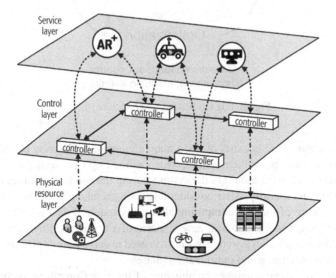

Fig. 2. Fog Computing Orchestration architecture with a flat control layer [10].

The southbound interface connects Fog Computing nodes with an Orchestration controller, and it is used to collect hardware information as well as to offload the required services to corresponding Fog Computing nodes for their physical execution.

The westbound interface is mainly used for communications between neighboring Orchestration controllers in peer-to-peer manner to collect information about the current state of physically closely located Fog nodes in order to exchange any data on service requirements. This interface helps the controllers to form and maintain an aggregated view of their Fog Computing devices in their proximity, as well as to rapidly change the view in the events when Fog Computing nodes move to different locations. Broadcasting information to its neighbors and using peer-to-peer communications prevail in this kind of communications. The northbound interface is used for the access and management of actual IoT applications and services.

Wen et al. [6] discusses possible architectures of a controller or a Fog Orchestrator. The main Fog specific constraints and requirements for a Fog Orchestrator are the following ones: the scale and complexity of a Fog layer; security criticality; inherent properties of the dynamicity of Fog Computing layers; and the need for a fault diagnosis and tolerance. The authors propose their architecture of the Fog Orchestrator summarized in Fig. 3.

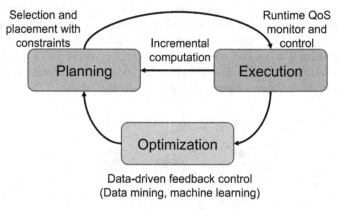

Fig. 3. Fog Orchestrator architecture [6].

The orchestrator there consists of three main elements. A planning element selects appropriate services to place them in the corresponding Fog Computing nodes; an execution monitoring element monitors the system during the runtime assuring a required level of the QoS and security. After considerable changes take place in the system (due to a dynamic nature of the Fog computing elements), required data is collected for an optimization element to find the best new scenario of a service deployment in the Fog Computing nodes. A parallel genetic algorithm is used to solve its optimization problems which arise in the planning and optimization phases.

Brito et al. [12] present another architecture of the Fog Computing orchestrator to demonstrate what modifications of the Fog nodes are necessary for an efficient interaction with the Fog orchestrator (see Fig. 4). A special Fog Orchestration agent is added to each Fog Computing node to make it responsible for communications with the Fog Orchestrator as well as for monitoring of resources in the local Fog Computing node, efficient resource management, security and QoS assurance. The authors use Docker Swarm for a virtualization, and the Open MTC M2M Framework for a communication.

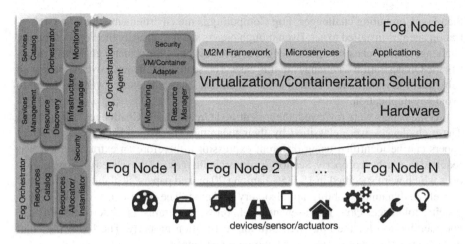

Fig. 4. Fog Orchestrator interaction with a Fog node [12].

Velasquez et al. [13] summarize the challenges specific to the Fog Computing Orchestration. They analyze four already proposed and implemented Fog Orchestration solutions: Supporting the Orchestration of Resilient and Trustworthy Fog Services (SORTS) by Velasquez et al. [13, 14]; The Service Orchestrator Architecture for Fog enabled Infrastructure (SOAFI) proposed by Brito et al. [12]; The reference architecture for Mobile Edge Computing (ETSI IGS MEC) introduced by the ETSI Industry Specification Group [15]; and a Cloud-based architecture for the next-generation cellular systems (CONCERT) by Liu et al. [16].

5   Orchestration Challenges Identification Results

In order to determine the most common Orchestration Challenges and the most common Orchestration Security Challenges inclusively, the academic search engine Google Scholar was used. The keywords below were picked (Table 2).

Table 2. Screening of the paper search results.

Key words	All search results	Checked papers	Picked papers
"Fog Orchestration"	560	100	17
"Fog Orchestration" Challenges	532	10	1
"Fog Orchestrator"	73	50	2

Over 1000 search results were returned and over 150 papers were checked for Orchestration Challenges. As the papers were picked for checking, it was relied on the top results ranked by the search engine for a higher relevance to the highest number of readers. It was also focused mainly on the papers which specify Orchestration Challenges rather than Fog Computing challenges. Fog Computing is the environment where an Orches-tration agent is installed to act. Even though papers seem to identify the Fog Computing challenges and Orchestration Challenges as the same ones, the primary goal was to iden-tify the Orchestration Challenges in this case. The search results were overlapping with subsequent key words to a certain extent; therefore, the same entries were excluded to avoid any duplication.

As the papers were reviewed, their identified Orchestration Challenges were picked. These challenges were classified by their meaning. The same challenge in different papers can be identified using different expressions, therefore an extra attention was required to ascribe it properly. Security/privacy challenges and the related ones are the top ones which were specified in 15 (75%) among 20 picked papers. Scalability/complexity as well as dynamics/mobility are also very common. The other concerns like hetero-geneity, tolerance, QoS, multi-tenancy, reliability, constrains and interoperability are considerable too for the Fog Orchestration to function properly. The following chart gives a general idea of the identified common challenges.

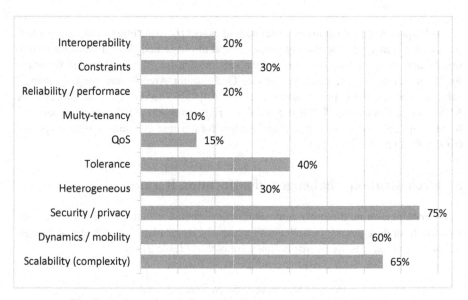

Fig. 5. Orchestration challenge distribution among the picked papers.

Multiple benefits are achieved by getting the system decentralized. However, it can be both good and bad for security. A decentralization enhances the resilience as there is no central point leading to a global failure. Intermediate points are better at detecting different threats. A disadvantage it is recognized for is the added complexity.

6 Evaluation and Discussion

Fog Computing nodes are computational nodes which communicate with different sen-sors and actuators to provide any required services for local data filtering, processing and control as well as they act as intermediaries for a communication with remote cloud-based services. Frequently these Fog Computing services are deployed dynamically into corresponding Fog Computing devices. For example, if a smart vehicle moves from one Fog Computing node to another, service availability should be ensured. It must be assured by using Fog Computing orchestration techniques. Usually a Fog Orchestration is implemented by customizing and adapting already existing Cloud Orchestration solutions [10, 12]. One of very important challenges in such solutions is the QoS assurance and security of the whole system (see Fig. 5).

Mobile nodes may change their location to approach a Fog Computing node which has a different architecture and computational or communication capabilities. Some nodes can be limited devices with strict constrains on available security protocols and communication methods. The service provision in all the cases should be optimally distributed by all the Fog Computing nodes among those in proximity.

Such a continuously changing situation requires an effective Orchestration of services in the Fog Computing nodes, as well as the assurance of a security and QoS. After each significant change in the local situation of a Fog Computing node in its proximity, an optimization problem must be solved to provide the best possible service.

Such an optimization may face the following constraints:

- Security level requirements. Different devices at the edge of a network may collect data of different importance, therefore an adequate data protection must be provided while transferring, storing, and processing it.
- Fog Computing node physical constraints. If a node is constrained, it may not be able to use some of the security and communication protocols due to limitations which are relevant to the processing or transmitting options.
- Communication bandwidth requirements. There is a significant difference in bandwidth requirements between Fog Computing nodes which provide continuous data streaming and one-time sensors (e.g. a real-time video streaming vs. a temperature sensor).
- Communication protocol requirements. Some devices at the edge may need one-way broadcasting while others may require a strict two-way communication with acknowledgements. Some solutions may work using a client/server architecture, and the other ones may communicate in peer-to-peer while using mesh networks.
- Environment requirements [17]. Some Edge nodes may have a short-range high bandwidth (WiFi, ZigBee, BLE, etc.) communication hardware requiring closer proximity to the Fog node, while the others may have a long-range low bandwidth communication hardware (LoRa).

One might need to address the following considerations while implementing an Orchestrator which is able to collect all the security and QoS related information from its neighboring Fog Computing nodes (thus forming a unified view of security and QoS requirements) in order to distribute the required services between any available Fog and Cloud resources in the most efficient way:

- A flat controller (Orchestrator) approach is more suitable due to the constantly changing Fog Computing layers.

- A peer-to-peer architecture with a periodic gossiping is the most suitable for the Fog Computing service orchestrators.
- In order to solve a scalability problem, each controller should collect and maintain information about the infrastructure only in its proximity to communicate it only with its neighboring controllers.
- A Southbound interface (see Fig. 2) communication protocol for exchanging security orchestration specific information among the Orchestrators and Fog Computing nodes must be developed.
- A westbound interface (see Fig. 2) communication protocol for a peer-to-peer gossiping among the neighboring Orchestrators must be developed.

7 Conclusions

The paper reviews Fog Computing challenges, proposed Orchestration solutions and the identified Fog Orchestration Security challenges. As the Fog Computing is the environment where an Orchestrator acts, Orchestration security challenges depend on the Fog Computing itself and on the available Orchestration solutions. Over 150 papers were reviewed while looking for any specified Orchestration challenges. These challenges were classified in order to detect the most relevant ones among the papers. As the results suggest, security/privacy, dynamics/mobility, and scalability/complexity are the most common ones to be addressed. However, a proper functioning requires to consider all of them.

Acknowledgement. This paper is supported in part by European Union's Horizon 2020 research and innovation program under Grant Agreement No. 830892, project "Strategic programs for advanced research and technology in Europe" (SPARTA).

References

1. OpenFog Consortium Architecture Working Group, et al.: OpenFog reference architecture for fog computing. In: OPFRA001, vol. 20817, p. 162 (2017)
2. Bonomi, F., Milito, R., Zhu, J., Addepalli, S.: Fog computing and its role in the internet of things. In: Proceedings of the First Edition of the MCC Workshop on Mobile Cloud Computing, pp. 13–16 (2012)
3. Roman, R., Lopez, J., Mambo, M.: Mobile edge computing, fog et al.: a survey and analysis of security threats and challenges. Future Gener. Comput. Syst. **78**, 680–698 (2018)
4. Yousefpour, A., et al.: All one needs to know about fog computing and related edge computing paradigms: a complete survey. J. Syst. Archit. **98**, 289–330 (2019). https://doi.org/10.1016/j.sysarc.2019.02.009
5. Puthal, D., Mohanty, S.P., Bhavake, S.A., Morgan, G., Ranjan, R.: Fog computing security challenges and future directions [energy and security]. IEEE Consum. Electron. Mag. **8**(3), 92–96 (2019). https://doi.org/10.1109/MCE.2019.2893674
6. Wen, Z., Yang, R., Garraghan, P., Lin, T., Xu, J., Rovatsos, M.: Fog orchestration for Internet of Things services. IEEE Internet Comput. **21**(2), 16–24 (2017). https://doi.org/10.1109/MIC.2017.36

7. Martin, B.A., et al.: OpenFog security requirements and approaches. In: 2017 IEEE Fog World Congress (FWC), October 2017, pp. 1–6. https://doi.org/10.1109/fwc.2017.8368537

8. Bormann, C., Ersue, M., Keränen, A.: Terminology for Constrained-Node Networks. RFC Editor (2014)

9. Roman, R., Zhou, J., Lopez, J.: On the features and challenges of security and privacy in distributed internet of things. Comput. Netw. **57**(10), 2266–2279 (2013)

10. Jiang, Y., Huang, Z., Tsang, D.H.: Challenges and solutions in fog computing orchestration. IEEE Netw. **32**(3), 122–129 (2017)

11. Liu, F., et al.: NIST cloud computing reference architecture: recommendations of the National Institute of Standards and Technology (Special Publication 500-292) (2012)

12. de Brito, M.S., et al.: A service orchestration architecture for Fog-enabled infrastructures. In: 2017 Second International Conference on Fog and Mobile Edge Computing (FMEC), May 2017, pp. 127–132. https://doi.org/10.1109/fmec.2017.7946419

13. Velasquez, K., et al.: Fog orchestration for the Internet of Everything: state-of-the-art and research challenges. J. Internet Serv. Appl. **9**(1), 1–23 (2018). https://doi.org/10.1186/s13 174-018-0086-3

14. Velasquez, K., et al.: Service orchestration in fog environments. In: 2017 IEEE 5th International Conference on Future Internet of Things and Cloud (FiCloud), August 2017, pp. 329–336. https://doi.org/10.1109/ficloud.2017.49

15. Network Functions Virtualisation (NFV) ETSI Industry Specification Group (ISG). ETSI NFV Work Group: Network Functions Virtualisation (NFV); Management and Orchestration (2013). https://www.etsi.org/deliver/etsi_gs/NFV/001_099/002/01.01.01_60/gs_nfv002 v010101p.pdf. Accessed 17 February 2020

16. Liu, J., Zhao, T., Zhou, S., Cheng, Y., Niu, Z.: CONCERT: a cloud-based architecture for next-generation cellular systems. IEEE Wirel. Commun. **21**(6), 14–22 (2014). https://doi.org/10.1109/MWC.2014.7000967

17. Venckauskas, A., Stuikys, V., Toldinas, J., Jusas, N.: A model-driven framework to develop personalized health monitoring. Symmetry-Basel **8**(7), 65 (2016). https://doi.org/10.3390/sym8070065

A Novel Edge Detection Operator for Identifying Buildings in Augmented Reality Applications

Ciprian Orhei$^{(\boxtimes)}$ (ID), Silviu Vert (ID), and Radu Vasiu (ID)

Politehnica University of Timişoara, 300006 Timişoara, Romania
{ciprian.orhei,silviu.vert,radu.vasiu}@cm.upt.ro

Abstract. Augmented Reality is an environment-enhancing technology, widely applied in many domains, such as tourism and culture. One of the major challenges in this field is precise detection and extraction of building information through Computer Vision techniques. Edge detection is one of the building blocks operations for many feature extraction solutions in Computer Vision. AR systems use edge detection for building extraction or for extraction of facade details from buildings. In this paper, we propose a novel filter operator for edge detection that aims to extract building contours or facade features better. The proposed filter gives more weight for finding vertical and horizontal edges that is an important feature for our aim.

Keywords: Augmented reality · Building detection · Edge detection · Edge detection operator · Canny

1 Introduction

Augmented reality (AR) is the process of overlapping computer-generated objects and data over our real, surrounding space [1]. This differs from virtual reality, where the basic elements of the environment are entirely computer-generated in an effort to simulate their existence [2]. Augmented reality is successfully exploited in many domains nowadays, one of the them being culture and tourism, an area in which authors of this paper carried multiple research projects [3–6].

One of the main ways to detect the surrounding space in Augmented Reality is through Computer Vision (CV). This field of research has been developing mathematical techniques for recovery of the 3D shapes and appearances of objects in pictures. In particular, building extraction has been an active research topic in CV as well as digital photogrammetry. Building detection is the process of obtaining the approximate position and shape of a building, while building extraction can be defined as the problem of precisely determining the building outlines, which is one of the critical problems in digital photogrammetry [7]. Building information is extremely important not only for augmented reality applications, but also for urban planning, telecommunication, three-dimensional city modeling, or extraction of unauthorized buildings over agricultural lands [7].

© Springer Nature Switzerland AG 2020
A. Lopata et al. (Eds.): ICIST 2020, CCIS 1283, pp. 208–219, 2020.
https://doi.org/10.1007/978-3-030-59506-7_18

In this paper we present a novel filter operator for edge detection, Sect. 3, that can be combined with an algorithm for contour detection that tries to enhance the topic above mentioned, building extraction. This is the first step towards efficient building detection in augmented reality, a research endeavor that we are currently undertaking as part of the Spotlight Heritage, a cultural project for Timisoara European Capital of Culture 2021 [8].

In Sect. 4 we make a visual comparison with other standard filters similar to the ones we propose: Sobel filter [10], Prewitt filter [11], Scharr filter [12]. Because we are looking for a particular use case, like buildings, we want to look at how the 5×5 extension of the mentioned filters perform. To better understand the capabilities of the filters we will use the Canny algorithm [13] which is one of the most popular algorithms for edge detection.

2 Related Work

In the research literature we can see that applications concerning augmented reality in urban scenes have different approaches. In this section we will present different solutions that we came across that use edge tracking for enhancing their detection.

In [14] they propose a 3d mobile augmented reality solution for urban scenes. The 3D MAR system has two main components: offline database processing, and online image matching, tracking and augmentation. One of the steps presented is the contour extraction that is built upon morphological edge detection by subtracting a 1-pixel erosion.

In [15] the system combines several well-known approaches to provide a robust experience that surpasses each of the individual components alone: an edge-based tracker for accurate localization and gyroscope measurements to deal with fast motions.

In [16] a novel approach for user positioning, robust tracking and online 3D mapping for outdoor augmented reality applications. Robust visual tracking is maintained by fusing frame-to-frame and model-to-frame feature matches. Frame-to-frame tracking is accomplished with corner matching while edges are used for model-to-frame registration.

In [17] they present a methodology to develop immersive AR applications based on the recognition of outdoor buildings. To demonstrate this methodology, a case study focused on the Parliament Buildings National Historic Site in Ottawa, Canada has been conducted.

We believe that using the proposed new operators will improve the quality and number of edges found in each frame by the AR system. This might seem like a small element in the processing chain but this will make the edge tracking better. Improving the edge tracking block will automatically improve the overall performance of an AR application.

3 Preliminaries

In this section we present the filters we would like to compare. The 3×3 Gx kernels for Sobel [10], Prewitt [11] and Scharr [12] are presented in Formula 1.

$$G_{SOBEL} = \begin{bmatrix} -1 & 0 & 1 \\ -2 & 0 & 2 \\ -1 & 0 & 1 \end{bmatrix} \quad G_{PREWITT} = \begin{bmatrix} -1 & 0 & 1 \\ -1 & 0 & 1 \\ -1 & 0 & 1 \end{bmatrix} \quad G_{SCHARR} = \begin{bmatrix} -3 & 0 & 3 \\ -10 & 0 & 10 \\ -3 & 0 & 3 \end{bmatrix} \quad (1)$$

The 5×5 Gx kernels for Sobel, Prewitt and Scharr [18] are presented in Formula 2.

$$G_{SOBEL} = \begin{bmatrix} -5 & -4 & 0 & 4 & 5 \\ -8 & -10 & 0 & 10 & 8 \\ -10 & -20 & 0 & 20 & 10 \\ -8 & -10 & 0 & 10 & 8 \\ -5 & -4 & 0 & 4 & 5 \end{bmatrix} \quad G_{PREWITT} = \begin{bmatrix} -2 & -1 & 0 & 1 & 2 \\ -2 & -1 & 0 & 1 & 2 \\ -2 & -1 & 0 & 1 & 2 \\ -2 & -1 & 0 & 1 & 2 \\ -2 & -1 & 0 & 1 & 2 \end{bmatrix}$$

$$G_{SCHARR} = \begin{bmatrix} -1 & -1 & 0 & 1 & 1 \\ -2 & -2 & 0 & 2 & 2 \\ -3 & -6 & 0 & 6 & 3 \\ -2 & -2 & 0 & 2 & 2 \\ -1 & -1 & 0 & 1 & 1 \end{bmatrix} \quad (2)$$

To determine the exact impact of the filters we use a modified Canny edge detection algorithm [13, 19]:

- **Step 1.** Applying Gaussian Filter on the grey-scale image.
- **Step 2.** Apply Otsu transformation on picture to find threshold value.
- **Step 3.** Finding the magnitude and orientation of the gradient.
- **Step 4.** Non-maximum suppression.
- **Step 5.** Edge tracking by hysteresis using double threshold. Thresholds are found using Step 2 and applying formula (3).

$$\sigma = 0.33$$
$$T_t = max(0, (1.0 - \sigma)) \times val_{ostu} \quad (3)$$
$$T_h = min(255, (1.0 + \sigma)) \times val_{ostu}$$

4 Proposed Filter

We consider that for the use case we are dealing with, extraction of building features, we must try to detect longer edges for a better reconstruction of the contour and with more attention given to the edges that are vertical and horizontal than on the diagonals. This means that the filter that we propose is constructed based on the distance between pixels and with a bigger weight on the 0° and 90° direction of the gradients.

For the first proposed filter we consider the following scheme for creating the weight matrix, that is based on the inverse distance [20], see formulas (4) and (5).

$$w_{ij} = \begin{cases} \frac{1}{d_{ij}^2}, & if\ i \neq j \\ 0, & if\ i = j \end{cases} \tag{4}$$

$$\begin{bmatrix} \frac{1}{2} & \frac{1}{1} & \frac{1}{2} \\ \frac{1}{1} & w & \frac{1}{1} \\ \frac{1}{2} & \frac{1}{1} & \frac{1}{2} \end{bmatrix} \Rightarrow \begin{bmatrix} 1 & 2 & 1 \\ 2 & W & 2 \\ 1 & 2 & 1 \end{bmatrix} \tag{5}$$

We know that we can use linear approximation to estimate the formula (6) [21].

$$J(\alpha, \beta, \gamma) = \sum_{r,c=-(2L+1)}^{2L+1} w_{rc}^2 (\alpha \cdot r + \beta \cdot c + \gamma - 1(r, c))^2 \tag{6}$$

Using the Local Polynomial Approximation for every pixel we can calculate the kernels equivalents for the weight matrix [18, 21]. More detailed calculation in the Appendix A.

$$G_x(r, c) = \frac{\partial I(r, c)}{\partial r} = \alpha \qquad G_y = \frac{\partial I(r, c)}{\partial c} = \beta \tag{7}$$

$$G_x = \begin{bmatrix} -1 & 0 & 1 \\ -4 & 0 & 4 \\ -1 & 0 & 1 \end{bmatrix} \qquad G_y = \begin{bmatrix} -1 & -4 & -1 \\ 0 & 0 & 0 \\ 1 & 4 & 1 \end{bmatrix} \tag{8}$$

Following the scheme presented in formula (4) the 5×5 weight matrix is expanded to result in formula (9).

$$\begin{bmatrix} \frac{1}{8} & \frac{1}{5} & \frac{1}{4} & \frac{1}{5} & \frac{1}{8} \\ \frac{1}{5} & \frac{1}{2} & \frac{1}{1} & \frac{1}{2} & \frac{1}{5} \\ \frac{1}{4} & \frac{1}{1} & w & \frac{1}{1} & \frac{1}{4} \\ \frac{1}{5} & \frac{1}{2} & \frac{1}{1} & \frac{1}{2} & \frac{1}{5} \\ \frac{1}{8} & \frac{1}{5} & \frac{1}{4} & \frac{1}{5} & \frac{1}{8} \end{bmatrix} \Rightarrow \begin{bmatrix} 5 & 8 & 10 & 8 & 5 \\ 8 & 20 & 40 & 20 & 8 \\ 10 & 40 & W & 40 & 10 \\ 8 & 20 & 40 & 20 & 8 \\ 5 & 8 & 10 & 8 & 5 \end{bmatrix} \tag{9}$$

$$G_x = \begin{bmatrix} -25 & -4 & 0 & 4 & 25 \\ -64 & -10 & 0 & 10 & 64 \\ -100 & -20 & 0 & 20 & 100 \\ -64 & -10 & 0 & 10 & 64 \\ -4 & -25 & 0 & 4 & 25 \end{bmatrix} \qquad G_y = \begin{bmatrix} -25 & -4 & -100 & -4 & -25 \\ -64 & -10 & -20 & -10 & -64 \\ 0 & 0 & 0 & 0 & 0 \\ 64 & 10 & 20 & 10 & 64 \\ 25 & 4 & 100 & 4 & 25 \end{bmatrix} \tag{10}$$

We propose the second filter, based on the radial distance weights [20] presented in formula (11). Following the same logic presented above we obtain the formula (12) that represents the 3×3 weight matrix, formula (13) the Gx and Gy kernels for 3×3 and formula (15) the Gx and Gy kernels for 5×5.

$$w_{ij} = \begin{cases} d_{max}, & \text{if } i = 0 \text{ or } j = 0 \\ \frac{d_{max}}{2}, & \text{if } i \neq 0 \text{ and } j \neq 0 \\ 0, & \text{if } i = j \end{cases} \tag{11}$$

$$\begin{bmatrix} 1 & 2 & 1 \\ 2 & w & 2 \\ 1 & 2 & 1 \end{bmatrix} \tag{12}$$

$$G_x = \begin{bmatrix} -1 & 0 & 1 \\ -4 & 0 & 4 \\ -1 & 0 & 1 \end{bmatrix} \quad G_y = \begin{bmatrix} -1 & -4 & -1 \\ 0 & 0 & 0 \\ 1 & 4 & 1 \end{bmatrix} \tag{13}$$

$$\begin{bmatrix} 2 & 2 & 4 & 2 & 2 \\ 2 & 2 & 4 & 2 & 2 \\ 4 & 4 & w & 4 & 4 \\ 2 & 2 & 4 & 2 & 2 \\ 2 & 2 & 4 & 2 & 2 \end{bmatrix} \Rightarrow \begin{bmatrix} 1 & 1 & 2 & 1 & 1 \\ 1 & 1 & 2 & 1 & 1 \\ 2 & 2 & W & 2 & 2 \\ 1 & 1 & 2 & 1 & 1 \\ 1 & 1 & 2 & 1 & 1 \end{bmatrix} \tag{14}$$

$$G_x = \begin{bmatrix} -2 & -1 & 0 & 1 & 2 \\ -2 & -1 & 0 & 1 & 2 \\ -8 & -4 & 0 & 4 & 8 \\ -2 & -1 & 0 & 1 & 2 \\ -2 & -1 & 0 & 1 & 2 \end{bmatrix} \quad G_y = \begin{bmatrix} -2 & -2 & -8 & -2 & -2 \\ -1 & -1 & -4 & -1 & -1 \\ 0 & 0 & 0 & 0 & 0 \\ 1 & 1 & 4 & 1 & 1 \\ 2 & 2 & 8 & 2 & 2 \end{bmatrix} \tag{15}$$

5 Simulation Results

First, we will compare the result we obtain by using the standard formula for calculating the gradient magnitude:

$$|G| = \sqrt{G_x^2 + G_y^2} \tag{16}$$

We will use the kernels presented in Sect. 4 and apply formula (16) and obtain the gradient magnitude that are presented in Figs. 1, 2, 3 and 4.

Visually we can determine from Figs. 2, 3 and 4 that the 3×3 filters produce more concentrated edges than the 5×5 filters. But the 5×5 filters tend to lose a certain amount of detail on behalf of edges relevant for contour extraction.

As stated in Sect. 3 to have a better idea about what edges have added value for a feature extraction based on them we would look over the results we got using the Canny algorithm [13, 19].

To obtain results that we can future use for contour detection or facade detection should be a balance between edges detected from the outer boundary of the building and facade details. The edges that do not belong to the buildings should be preferably

Fig. 1. Original

Fig. 2. Proposed 3 × 3

Fig. 3. Proposed A 5 × 5

Fig. 4. Proposed B 5 × 5

Fig. 5. Canny Sobel 3 × 3

Fig. 6. Canny Proposed A_B 3 × 3

Fig. 7. Canny Sobel 5 × 5

Fig. 8. Canny Proposed A 5 × 5

Fig. 9. Canny Proposed B 5 × 5

Fig. 10. Canny Prewitt 3 × 3

Fig. 11. Canny Prewitt 5 × 5

Fig. 12. Canny Scharr 3 × 3

discarded in this step. As we can see in Figs. 5, 6, 7, 8, 9, 10, 11, 12 and 13 the filters 3 × 3 obtain better results than the 5 × 5 ones.

Figure 7 and 8 show a considerable amount of edges detected that we can consider noise and those edges will strongly affect any future use of those results.

Fig. 13. Canny Scharr 5 × 5   **Fig. 14.** Canny Proposed A   **Fig. 15.** Canny Sobel vs
vs Canny Sobel Canny   Proposed A

Figure 9, 11, 12 and 13 show good results in filtering out edges that are not in our interest but we can observe an extra amount of details on the facade detected that isn't a benefit in future work.

The proposed filters and Sobel 3 × 3 [10] used in the Canny algorithm [13, 19], shown in Fig. 5 and 6, show good results in maintaining a balance between filtering out edges that we can consider noise and edges that we can future use for contour and edges that can be used for facade detection.

Naturally, we desired to better understand our results, so we took a dataset of 30 images that we used for Spotlight Heritage Timisoara project and compared the results obtained between Canny using Sobel 3 × 3 and Canny using our proposed filter. For better representation of the results some images from the dataset are presented in Appendix B.

The first result we saw was the fact that the number of edge pixels was always bigger, a fact that was observed from the images presented in this section. But we wanted to test our statement that the edge pixels we obtain form more and longer edges. To do that we used an eight-neighbor connectivity algorithm [22] and we can observe in Fig. 16 and 17 the results.

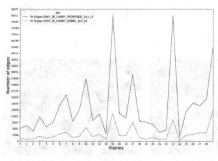
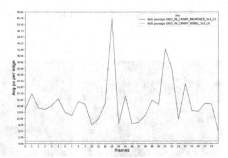

Fig. 16. Number of edges found   **Fig. 17.** Average pixels per edge

In Fig. 16 we observe that in every case our Canny using our proposed filter obtains more edge pixels that formed more edges than the Canny using Sobel filter. This fact alone does not prove that the edges found are useful but if we look on Fig. 17 we can observe that those edges group in longer edges. We can clearly observe that the edges pixels found by the Sobel filter and not by our filter are sporadic pixels.

6 Conclusion and Future Work

It is difficult to design a general edge detection algorithm which performs well in many contexts and captures the requirements of subsequent processing stages. With this research paper, we aimed to find a better fitted first derivative operator for building contour and facade edge detection.

We proposed two filters that have the same kernels for 3 × 3 but with different kernels for 5 × 5. As we can observe from Fig. 15 our proposed filter managed to detect the same edges using the classical Sobel filter when used in the Canny algorithm. In Appendix B we highlight edge pixels that were only discovered by the Canny algorithm using the proposed filter and we conclude that by using the kernels proposed in formula (12) or (19) we obtain more edges in the 0° and 90° direction of the gradients, highlighted by Fig. 16 and Fig. 17.

As future work we plan to try the 3 × 3 filter operator, that obtains the best results, on a bigger data set of pictures with an official benchmarking tool for edge detection so we can assert statistically the improvements the proposed filter brings in this use case. At this point we analyzed the differences this filter brought to edge detection feature, as future work we would like to see the effect it has in contour detection algorithm, respective in facade detection algorithm.

This work will be valuable in improving the augmented reality mobile application of the Spotlight Heritage Timisoara project that the authors of this paper are involved in.

Appendix A

We consider a matrix with $(2L + 1)x(2L + 1)$ dimensions with the upper left corner having the coordinates $(-L, -L)$. From [18, 21] we have the formula (17), where: r,c represent the row, column of matrix, α, β, γ - coefficients of the polynom and η(r,c) a noise function.

$$J(r, c) = \alpha r + \beta c + \gamma + \eta(r, c) \tag{17}$$

Using the least-square procedure, where w is the weight matrix, we obtain formula (17). Afterwards using the least-squares estimation for parameters that will minimize the function derivatives from formula (17) we get the (18)–(21).

$$f(\alpha, \beta, \gamma) = \sum_{r=-L}^{L} \sum_{c=-L}^{L} w_{r,c}^2 \cdot (\alpha \cdot r + \beta \cdot c + \gamma - J(r, c))^2 \tag{18}$$

$$\frac{\partial f}{\partial \alpha} = 2 \sum_{r=-L}^{L} \sum_{c=-L}^{L} w_{r,c}^2 \cdot (\alpha \cdot r + \beta \cdot c + \gamma - J(r, c))r = 0 \tag{19}$$

$$\frac{\partial f}{\partial \beta} = 2 \sum_{r=-L}^{L} \sum_{c=-L}^{L} w_{r,c}^2 \cdot (\alpha \cdot r + \beta \cdot c + \gamma - J(r, c))c = 0 \tag{20}$$

$$\frac{\partial f}{\partial \gamma} = 2 \sum_{r=-L}^{L} \sum_{c=-L}^{L} w_{r,c}^2 \cdot (\alpha \cdot r + \beta \cdot c + \gamma - J(r, c)) = 0 \tag{21}$$

If we expand and do the calculation for (19) we obtain formula (23). But if we take in consideration that the weight matrix is symmetric, see formula (22), we obtain formulas (24)–(26).

$$\sum_{K=-L}^{L} w_{r,c}^2 K = 0 \tag{22}$$

$$\sum_{r=-L}^{L} \sum_{c=-L}^{L} w_{r,c}^2 (\alpha \cdot r + \beta \cdot c + \gamma - J(r,c)) r = 0 \tag{23}$$

$$\sum_{r=-L}^{L} \sum_{c=-L}^{L} w_{r,c}^2 \alpha + \beta \sum_{r=-L}^{L} r \sum_{c=-L}^{L} w_{r,c}^2 c + \gamma \sum_{r=-L}^{L} r \sum_{c=-L}^{L} w_{r,c}^2 - \sum_{r=-L}^{L} r \sum_{c=-L}^{L} w_{r,c}^2 \cdot J(r,c) = 0 \tag{24}$$

$$\sum_{r=-L}^{L} r^2 \sum_{c=-L}^{L} w_{r,c}^2 \alpha - \sum_{r=-L}^{L} r \sum_{c=-L}^{L} w_{r,c}^2 J(r,c) = 0 \tag{25}$$

$$\alpha = \frac{\sum_{r=-L}^{L} r \sum_{c=-L}^{L} w_{r,c}^2 \cdot J(r,c)}{\sum_{r=-L}^{L} r^2 \sum_{c=-L}^{L} w_{r,c}^2} \tag{26}$$

Analog we can do for β and γ see formulas (31), (32).

$$\beta = \frac{\sum_{r=-L}^{L} c \sum_{c=-L}^{L} w_{r,c}^2 \cdot J(r,c)}{\sum_{r=-L}^{L} c^2 \sum_{c=-L}^{L} w_{r,c}^2} \tag{27}$$

$$\gamma = \frac{\sum_{r=-L}^{L} \sum_{c=-L}^{L} w_{r,c}^2 \cdot J(r,c)}{\sum_{r=-L}^{L} \sum_{c=-L}^{L} w_{r,c}^2} \tag{28}$$

If we take L = 1 the 3 × 3 filters (26), (27), (28) become (29), (30), (31).

$$\alpha = \frac{1}{\sum_{r=-1}^{1} r \sum_{c=-1}^{1} w_{r,c}^2} \begin{bmatrix} -w_{-1,-1}^2 & -w_{-1,0}^2 & -w_{-1,1}^2 \\ 0 & 0 & 0 \\ w_{1,-1}^2 & w_{1,0}^2 & w_{1,1}^2 \end{bmatrix} \cdot J \tag{29}$$

$$\beta = \frac{1}{\sum_{c=-1}^{1} c \sum_{r=-1}^{1} w_{r,c}^2} \begin{bmatrix} -w_{-1,-1}^2 & 0 & -w_{-1,1}^2 \\ -w_{0,-1}^2 & 0 & -w_{0,1}^2 \\ -w_{1,-1}^2 & w_{1,0}^2 & w_{1,1}^2 \end{bmatrix} \cdot J \tag{30}$$

$$\gamma = \frac{1}{\sum_{r=-1}^{1} \sum_{c=-1}^{1} w_{r,c}^2} \begin{bmatrix} -w_{-1,-1}^2 & -w_{-1,0}^2 & -w_{-1,1}^2 \\ -w_{0,-1}^2 & w_{0,0}^2 & w_{0,1}^2 \\ w_{1,-1}^2 & w_{1,0}^2 & w_{1,1}^2 \end{bmatrix} \cdot J \tag{31}$$

If we take L = 2 the 5 × 5 filter (26), (27), (28) become (32), (33), (34).

$$\alpha = \frac{1}{\sum_{r=-2}^{2} r \sum_{c=-2}^{2} w_{r,c}^2} \begin{bmatrix} -2w_{-2,-2}^2 & -2w_{-2,-1}^2 & -2w_{-2,0}^2 & -2w_{-2,1}^2 & -2w_{-2,2}^2 \\ -w_{-1,-2}^2 & -w_{-1,-1}^2 & -w_{-1,0}^2 & -w_{-1,1}^2 & -w_{-1,2}^2 \\ 0 & 0 & 0 & 0 & 0 \\ w_{1,-2}^2 & w_{1,-1}^2 & w_{1,0}^2 & w_{1,1}^2 & w_{1,2}^2 \\ 2w_{2,-2}^2 & 2w_{2,-1}^2 & 2w_{2,0}^2 & 2w_{2,1}^2 & 2w_{2,2}^2 \end{bmatrix} \cdot J$$

(32)

$$\beta = \frac{1}{\sum_{c=-2}^{2} c \sum_{r=-2}^{2} w_{r,c}^2} \begin{bmatrix} -2w_{-2,-2}^2 & -w_{-2,-1}^2 & 0 & w_{-2,1}^2 & 2w_{-2,2}^2 \\ -2w_{-1,-2}^2 & -w_{-1,-1}^2 & 0 & w_{-1,1}^2 & 2w_{-1,2}^2 \\ -2w_{0,-2}^2 & -w_{0,-1}^2 & 0 & w_{0,1}^2 & 2w_{0,2}^2 \\ -2w_{1,-2}^2 & -w_{1,-1}^2 & 0 & w_{1,1}^2 & 2w_{1,2}^2 \\ -2w_{2,-2}^2 & -w_{2,-1}^2 & 0 & w_{2,1}^2 & 2w_{2,2}^2 \end{bmatrix} \cdot J$$

(33)

$$\gamma = \frac{1}{\sum_{r=-2}^{2} \sum_{c=-2}^{2} w_{r,c}^2} \begin{bmatrix} w_{-2,-2}^2 & w_{-2,-1}^2 & w_{-2,0}^2 & w_{-2,1}^2 & 2w_{-2,2}^2 \\ w_{-1,-2}^2 & w_{-1,-1}^2 & w_{-1,0}^2 & w_{-1,1}^2 & 2w_{-1,2}^2 \\ w_{0,-2}^2 & w_{0,-1}^2 & w_{0,0}^2 & w_{0,1}^2 & 2w_{0,2}^2 \\ w_{1,-2}^2 & w_{1,-1}^2 & w_{1,0}^2 & w_{1,1}^2 & 2w_{1,2}^2 \\ w_{2,-2}^2 & w_{2,-1}^2 & w_{2,0}^2 & w_{2,1}^2 & 2w_{2,2}^2 \end{bmatrix} \cdot J$$

(34)

Appendix B

See Fig. 18.

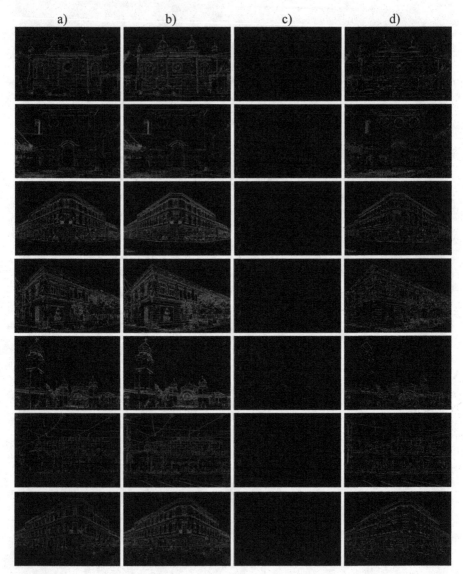

Fig. 18. Rows: a) Canny using Sobel 3 × 3, b) Canny using proposed A 3 × 3, c) Edge pixels found only by a, d) Edge pixels found only by b

References

1. Milgram, P., Kishino, F.: A taxonomy of mixed reality visual displays. IEICE Trans. Inf. Syst. **77**, 1321–1329 (1994)
2. Wright, W.G.: Using virtual reality to augment perception, enhance sensorimotor adaptation, and change our minds. Front. Syst. Neurosci. (2014). https://doi.org/10.3389/fnsys.2014. 00056

3. Vert, S., Dragulescu, B., Vasiu, R.: LOD4AR: exploring linked open data with a mobile augmented reality web application. In: Proceedings of the ISWC 2014 Posters & Demonstrations Track, within the 13th International Semantic Web Conference (ISWC 2014), Riva del Garda, Italy, pp. 185–188 (2014)
4. Vert, S., Vasiu, R.: Relevant aspects for the integration of linked data in mobile augmented reality applications for tourism. In: Dregvaite, G., Damasevicius, R. (eds.) ICIST 2014. CCIS, vol. 465, pp. 334–345. Springer, Cham (2014). https://doi.org/10.1007/978-3-319-11958-8_27
5. Vert, S., Vasiu, R.: Augmented reality lenses for smart city data: the case of building permits. In: Rocha, Á., Correia, A.M., Adeli, H., Reis, L.P., Costanzo, S. (eds.) WorldCIST 2017. AISC, vol. 569, pp. 521–527. Springer, Cham (2017). https://doi.org/10.1007/978-3-319-56535-4_53
6. Vert, S., Andone, D., Vasiu, R.: Augmented and virtual reality for public space art. In: ITM Web of Conferences. EDP Sciences (2019). https://doi.org/10.1051/itmconf/20192903006
7. Elshehaby, A.R., Taha, L.G.E.: A new expert system module for building detection in urban areas using spectral information and LIDAR data. Appl. Geomat. **1**, 97–110 (2009). https://doi.org/10.1007/s12518-009-0013-1
8. eLearning Center: Spotlight Heritage Timișoara. https://elearning.upt.ro/en/project/patrimoniul-sub-reflectoare-timisoara/. Accessed 29 Jan 2020
9. Gong, X.-Y., Su, H., Xu, D., Zhang, Z.-T., Shen, F., Yang, H.-B.: An overview of contour detection approaches. Int. J. Autom. Comput. **15**(6), 656–672 (2018). https://doi.org/10.1007/s11633-018-1117-z
10. Sobel, I., Feldman, G.: A 3 × 3 isotropic gradient operator for image processing. https://www.researchgate.net/publication/285159837_A_33_isotropic_gradient_operator_for_image_processing. Accessed 19 Jan 2020
11. Prewitt, J.M.S.: Object enhancement and extraction. In: Lipkin, B., Rosenfeld, A. (eds.) Picture Processing and Psychopictorics, pp. 75–149. Academic Press, New York (1970)
12. Scharr, H.: Optimal operators in digital image processing [Elektronische Ressource] (2014)
13. Canny, J.: A computational approach to edge detection. IEEE Trans. Pattern Anal. Mach. Intell. (1986). https://doi.org/10.1109/TPAMI.1986.4767851
14. Takacs, G., El Choubassi, M., Wu, Y., Kozintsev, I.: 3D mobile augmented reality in urban scenes. In: 2011 IEEE International Conference on Multimedia and Expo, pp. 1–4 (2011). https://doi.org/10.1109/ICME.2011.6012101
15. Reitmayr, G., Drummond, T.W.: Going out: robust model-based tracking for outdoor augmented reality. In: 2006 IEEE/ACM International Symposium on Mixed and Augmented Reality, pp. 109–118 (2006). https://doi.org/10.1109/ISMAR.2006.297801
16. Karlekar, J., Zhou, S.Z., Lu, W., Loh, Z.C., Nakayama, Y., Hii, D.: Positioning, tracking and mapping for outdoor augmentation. In: 2010 IEEE International Symposium on Mixed and Augmented Reality, pp. 175–184 (2010). https://doi.org/10.1109/ISMAR.2010.5643567
17. Blanco-Pons, S., Carrión-Ruiz, B., Duong, M., Chartrand, J., Fai, S., Lerma, J.L.: Augmented reality markerless multi-image outdoor tracking system for the historical buildings on parliament hill. Sustainability **11**, 4268 (2019). https://doi.org/10.3390/su11164268
18. Levkine, G.: Prewitt, Sobel and Scharr gradient 5x5 convolution matrices (2012). http://www.hlevkin.com/articles/SobelScharrGradients5x5.pdf
19. Fang, M., Yue, G., Yu, Q.: The Study on An Application of Otsu Method in Canny Operator (2009)
20. Fotheringham, A.S., Rogerson, P.A.: The SAGE Handbook of Spatial Analysis. SAGE, Thousand Oaks (2008)
21. Haralick, R.M., Watson, L.: A facet model for image data. Comput. Graph. Image Process. **15**, 113–129 (1981). https://doi.org/10.1016/0146-664X(81)90073-3
22. Bhattacharya, P., Rosenfeld, A.: a-convexity. Pattern Recognit. Lett. **21**, 955–957 (2000). https://doi.org/10.1016/S0167-8655(00)00051-9

Military Vehicle Recognition with Different Image Machine Learning Techniques

Daniel Legendre[✉] and Jouko Vankka

National Defense University, 00860 Helsinki, Finland
dnl.legendre@gmail.com, jouko.vankka@mil.fi
https://maanpuolustuskorkeakoulu.fi/sotatekniikan-laitos

Abstract. Different neural network training systems are studied for image recognition of military vehicles, variable start layer transfer training models and own convolutional neural networks training from scratch. Since, there is limited openly available military recordings, labeled social media images are used for training. Furthermore, expanding the image-set by random data transformation. An implementation is made in terms of image augmentation handling as an internal loop that freezes all numerical parameters of the neural network training, while selecting continuously a slightly larger section of the training set including an increment part of artificial images added to the system. All models where trained for three vehicle and two situational environment classification cases. The transfer learning is based on two of the most widely used recognition networks, ResNet50 and Xception, with a variable number of last trained layers to max. twenty. The first being successfully transfer-trained with validation accuracy values of ≈88%. In contrast Xception resulted on a over-fitted neural network with low validation accuracy and large loss values. Neither of the transferred schemes benefit from image augmentation. Moreover, in variable architecture training of convolutional networks, it was corroborated that different configurations of layers numbers/type/neurons adapt differently. Thus, a tailor-fit neural network combined with data augmentation strategy is the best approach with validation accuracy of ≈86.4%, comparable to large transferred networks with a ≈40 times smaller network architecture. Hence, requiring less computational resources. Data augmentation influenced an increment of validation accuracy values of ≈9.2%, with the least accurate network trained gaining up to 20% on accuracy due inclusion of artificial images.

Keywords: Machine learning · Neural networks · Optimization · Transfer learning · Image augmentation · 3D military machinery

1 Introduction

Several neural networks architectures exist nowadays for image recognition and classification, being one of the most useful for still single image classification,

© Springer Nature Switzerland AG 2020
A. Lopata et al. (Eds.): ICIST 2020, CCIS 1283, pp. 220–242, 2020.
https://doi.org/10.1007/978-3-030-59506-7_19

convolutional neural networks [24]. This has been extensible studied in civilian applications for animal classifications (cats vs dogs from Microsoft [18]), vehicles, face feature recognition, or general object classification [16]. One reason for the success for these recognition tasks are the large data sets available to train, test and validated different models [13,17]. To even further arrange different image recognition competitions with know data sets around the globe [14].

Nevertheless, even if this technology is available for military institutions, different challenges arise due to security and secrecy reasons from different military organizations, as it might not be convenient to share or even to record large databases (images) of diverse military equipment. Thus, arising different challenges in military applications, more centered on how to build a reliable training data base, with sufficient variety, to be used as training/validation set for deep convolutional or recurrent neural networks.

The rest of the present paper is structured as follows: Sect. 2 discusses related published works on the field of recognition of military equipment and applications, Sect. 3 presents the available data for machine learning training and their recollection sources, Sect. 4 explains the methods used in this research for expanding the available training data-sets, Sect. 5 shows the different hyper parameters used for the neural networks training schemes and clarify how it is ensured reproducible results, Sect. 6 explains the transfer learning schemes used and shows their performance to adapted targets, Sect. 7 explain the variable architecture scheme for trained from scratch networks, Sect. 8 presents a proposal on a new method to generate artificial images for different types of vehicles using real life locations and 3D designs, Sect. 9 display the performance of the different trained networks on testing images, to finally in Sect. 10 present an analysis of the different methods used in this investigation to train neural networks for military applications.

2   Related Work

There has been studies to adapt pre-trained models to military applications with limited data sets, such as Hiippala (2017) [11]. The study is mainly centered on variation of hyper-parameters optimal value using random search, yielding high accuracy values of 95% and above average accuracy ≈60% for convolutional network training, using cross-validation in their process, for both designs networks of image recognition. Those results show that training a convolutional neural network from scratch with augmentation is largely outperform by transfer learning architectures ≥35% [11]. Moreover, this paper attempts to take that study a level further and concentrate the training technique not on hyper-parameter optimization, but rather on neural network architecture and how to optimally select levels of training for a transfer learning algorithm and different architecture search for own design neural networks from scratch. Finally, to couple these algorithms with a traditional image augmentation technique [5,11] using Keras [2], and measure the level of influence that artificial created images have on different machine learning configurations. In order to prove that own design architectures can be optimized to obtain high accuracy levels comparable to well transferred models by means of smaller computational requirements. Guo et al. (2016) surveyed the state-of-the art in deep learning algorithms in computer vision, and then briefly describes their applications in diverse vision tasks, such as image classification, object detection, image retrieval, semantic segmentation and human pose estimation [8]. The Convolutional Neural Networks (CNN) is the most extensively utilized and most suitable for images [8].

3   Military Vehicle Image Data Set

As an option to obtain training data from free accessible sources, social media sources are used. For the present task, these images where collected from previous works [11] and different international military conflicts in the middle east. Namely, the Syrian civil war, eastern Ukraine conflict and Afghanistan's war. All images are divided within nine classes, between military vehicles (1–5), environmental situation (6–8) and a final image set (9) featuring other images such as streets and various civilian vehicles: 1) CV 9030 infantry, 2) fighting vehicle, 3) T-72 main battle tanks, 4) Leopard 2A4 main battle tanks, 5) Sisu XA-180 armored personnel carriers, 6) BMP armored personnel carriers, 6) Smoke screen covered tanks, 7) Foliage and camouflage tanks, 8) Tanks firing and 9) Other images.

These images where obtained from diverse social media sources, either as independent shots or as frame extractions from videos [11]. Extracting frames from YouTube videos nearly doubled the volume of data, while also providing images of the vehicles under diverse lighting and weather conditions, and from various angles and distances [11]. Where this data was further labeled to included different vehicles types (Table 1) and situational environments for military machinery (Table 2).

Table 1. Data sources and military vehicles images collected.

	Flickr	Youtube	Web	Total
CV9030	89	262	185	536
Leopard 2A44	124	168	170	462
Sisu XA-180	18	79	143	240
T-72	773	513	171	1457
BMP	182	844	62	1088
Total	1186	1866	731	3783

4   Image Augmentation

Machine learning as an autonomous image classification system has been extensible studied in civilian applications, mainly due the interest of large software developers and the availability of large image data sets to be trained and tested against [13,17]. Large data bases with thousands or even tens of thousands images per class [13]. Although there is a common practice to test and train against known large data sets, in military applications such images banks does not exist due to security and confidential concerns. Thus hindering the development of neural networks tailored to military applications.

Table 2. Data sources and situational military images collected (including other images class).

	Flickr	Youtube	Web	Total
Smoke screen	0	43	79	122
Foliage and camouflage tanks	0	69	98	167
Tanks Firing	0	11	120	131
Other	819	550	108	1477
Total	819	673	405	1897

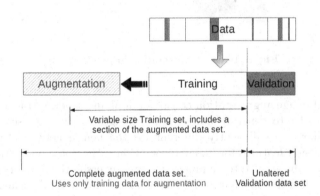

Fig. 1. Data split selection and augmentation set.

In terms of number of images needed to train and validate a convolutional neural network for image classification, the number of images obtained from social media sources fall into the low section of the commonly used. Nevertheless such scenarios have not prevent researchers from finding paths of circumvent issues related with small data sets [11]. As such one approach is to artificially extent the number of images in the data base [26]. To avoid contamination within the validation set and the training data, a special care is made to first shuffle all images in the data base, then split by aleatory selection a 20%/80% portion into Validation/Training data. Further on this artificial image generation is made by exclusively use of the training section of the data, Fig. 1. This can be further described as an internal loop that freezes all numerical parameters of the neural network training, while selecting continuously a slightly larger section of the training set including an increment part of artificial images added to the system. This method allows for comparison of neural network training structures only in terms of the new augmented data set incorporated into the training. Thus the effect on the type and quality of artificial images can be measured and furthermore optimized.

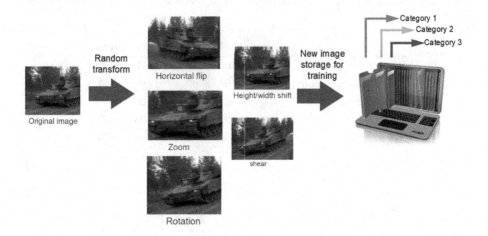

Fig. 2. Image augmentation in practice.

Traditional image augmentation consist of applying random transformations to images in order to generate new training images in the data set [22], that although similar, are sufficiently different for the neural network to learn or refine the necessary features for image recognition. Different type of transformation or filters can be applied to an image to either diversify the data or emphasize certain images features or shapes. Nowadays, there are several means to automatically augment almost every type of data, by either transformations, filters or image concatenations trough neural networks [22]. These techniques have been used successfully in diverse applications, for instance vehicle classification [11], hand writing recognition [26], animal classification [22], among others. Subsequently, proving to increase recognition accuracy and limit the error cause by the neural network recognition, albeit presenting limitations such as artificial images created by random object pasting may hinder accuracy performance [6]. In this investigation the *ImageDataGenerator* class within Keras [2] is used, with different transformation parameters presented in Table 3 and depicted in Fig. 2.

Although this class posses the capability of generate real time data augmentation per batch, a different approach is used on the present research, as from a previously divided training set, a new augmented set is generated with 5000 artificial images. As one of the goals is to evaluate the effect of an augmented

Table 3. Data augmentation: random transformation along with parameters.

Transformation	Parameters
Flip horizontal	True
Rotation	up $\pm$ 10°
Shear	max 20°
Zoom range	up to 1 $\pm$0.1
Height shift range	max 5%
Width shift range	max 20%

data set in different neural networks training schemes, this data split and augmentation is previously done once and remains constant for all training cases in the present manuscript. Moreover, these different training schemes are recalculated for diverse size range of augmented images, from 0 augmented images to 5000 in intervals of 1000 augmented images. This is to illustrate the influence of augmentation of data sets in image recognition algorithms depending on how large is the augmented set.

5 Neural Network Training Numerics

Randomness occurs in neural network training schemes, originated from initialization operations, such as weights initial guesses, regularization such as dropout, optimization such as stochastic optimization or other operations presenting aleatory behaviour [2]. Therefore, in order to ensure reproducible results in all training schemes, all random numbers in python numpy [20] and Tensor Flow [1] are seeded by the numbers 1 and 2 respectively for all calculations. Additionally, taking into account previous works in the topic [11], all networks are trained using the hyper-parameters presented in Table 4. All test runs were executed on a physical server with model HP ProLiant DL360 Gen9. The hardware included:- CPU: Intel(R) Xeon(R) CPU E5-2620 v3 @ 2.40 GHz with 6 physical cores and 12 threads as frequency from 1.2 to 2.4 GHz. L1d cache 32 KByte, L1i cache 32 KByte, L2 cache 256 KByte, L3 cache 15360 KByte.- 32 GB DDR4 RAM-2 TB HDD.

6 Transfer Learning

Two of the most widely use image recognition networks are ResNet50 [10] and Xception [3], although many others exists [23]. Both of this networks present pre-trained weights on ImageNet [13] and are capable to discern images within 1000 classification options (1000 object categories, such as keyboard, mouse, pencil, and many animals, mostly civilian images). The typical approach in cases of small-scale data-sets, (such as the one described above in Sect. 3 of the present manuscript), is to adapt features from existing large trained neural networks onto

Table 4. Neural network hyper-parameters.

Hyper-parameters	Value	Comments
Batch size	64	
Learning rate	1e−3, 1e−4	Decay = 1e−4, 1e−5
Drop out rate	0.2	
Optimizer	Adam	
Image resolution, pixels	224	Optimal for ResNet [2]
Epochs	50	

a new desire target task. To then continue training the network with the available data-set. Transferred neural networks have been already used and adapted to a wide variety of recognition tasks, such as malware recognition using ResNet50 [25] or white blood cell count for disease diagnostics using ResNet50 and Inception [9].

6.1   Transfer Learning Architecture

The architecture on which these networks are based is very different. While ResNet50 is a deep neural network of 50 layers. A compact version of the original 152 layers deep ResNet [10], based on a explicit layer reformulation for learning residual functions in reference with the layer inputs i.e. letting the layers fit a residual mapping. On the counterpart Xception (i.e. Extreme Inception) is a 71 layers deep network developed as an interpretation of Inception, where modules are replaced with depth-wise separable convolutions [3]. Xception is a convolutional neural network where a depth-wise convolution is followed by a point-wise convolution. Of the total amount of layers, 36 are convolutional structured into 14 modules with residual connections [3]. Subsequently, fine-tuned pre-trained deep learning models do not really profit from adding new layers to the system [11,15], as this implies adding a new configuration of layers that does not necessary harmonize with the original architecture philosophy. It is a common task in transfer learning to replace the top layer of a pre-trained neural network with a new top neural network architecture design for the particular new task [9,25]. Thus leaving a new hybrid neural network with a non trainable part, plus new top trainable layers. In the present work, with the objective of no disturb the original optimized architecture of the pre-trained models used, only 3 new dense layers would be added as the new top architecture, distributed as a pyramid configuration of 1024-1024-512 neurons with a drop out rate of 0,2 in the last layer just before the classification *Softmax layer* [1] with the number of nodes equal to the desired classification options.

Moreover, this is taken a step further in the training of the new hybrid neural network, regardless of the pre-trained network used. The new trainable part is optimized as the best classification protocol in terms of model performance for a variable training top layer configuration. In other words, not only the new

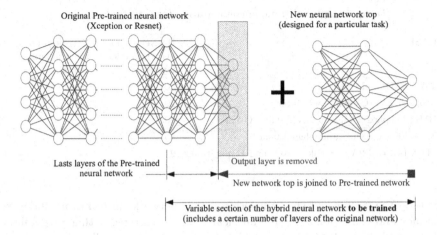

Fig. 3. Transfer Learning architecture.

designed top layers are trained, but also a selected group of layers of the original network using the pre-trained weights as staring conditions for the new training scheme. This is done in a retrospective manner, training different hybrids models with an increasingly training part of the last 5, 10, 15, or 20 layers of the hybrid network, Fig. 3. This training system, not only take advantage of the pre-trained neural network features, but also locates the most suitable trainable layer start that would best adapt this network to the present military application. Further on a cross-validation scheme may be applied to the final transferred network if required.

6.2   Transfer Learning Results

All image classes are separated in five (5) classification cases using both ResNet50 and Xception as base for the transfer learning, Table 5. Where the first three (3) represent image classification in terms of military vehicle type and the final two (2) represent Tanks in different situational environment classification, such as determining if a vehicle is camouflaged or if this vehicle has engage in active fire. All cases present similar behaviour for their respective case and neural network used, therefore only one case would be presented in detail for didactic purposes, CASE: BMP, Leopard 2A4, Sisu XA-180 and Other. Results where oscillating and inconclusive for learning rates values of 1e−3 with decay of 1e−4, after a reduction in these values to 1e−4 and 1e−5 all transferred networks reached stable metrics outlines.

The optimal configuration on number of last trainable layers is selected as the model that provides the highest validation accuracy while still remaining having a relative low Loss value, as seen in Table 5. For the purposes of this paper the Loss function is selected as *sparse categorical crossentropy* [1]. Results for transfer training of ResNet50 and Xception can be seen in Tables 6 and 7 respectively.

Table 5. Optimal training configuration for transfer learning.

CASE	ResNet50: no. last trainable layers	Xception: no. last trainable layers
T-72, BMP and Other	20	15
Leopard 2A4, CV9030 and Other	20	5
BMP, Leopard 2A4, Sisu XA-180 and Other	20	5
Tanks, Foliage and camouflage tanks	15	20
(T72, Leopard 2A4), Smoke screen and Firing Tanks	20	10

To study the stability of the transferred neural networks in terms of validation accuracy and validation loss; all numerical values are filtered with a Savgol filter [21] of window size 9 and polynomial order 3. Furthermore, all approximations are presented with their respective coefficient of determination R^2.

Table 6. Performance on the testing with transfer learning ResNet50.

CASE	Training accuracy	Training loss	Validation accuracy	Validation loss
T-72, BMP and Other	0.99	0.02	0.87	0.94
Leopard 2A4, CV9030 and Other	0.99	0.01	0.90	0.51
BMP, Leopard 2A4, Sisu XA-180 and Other	0.99	0.01	0.95	0.22
Tanks, Foliage and camouflage tanks	0.99	0.01	0.87	0.88
(T72, Leopard 2A4), Smoke screen and Firing Tanks	0.99	0.01	0.81	0.64

In terms of transfer learning for ResNet50, it can be observe that all cases posses not only a high value of validation accuracy between 81%–95% but also low numerical values of validation loss ≤ 0.94. It is important to notice that this represents a well behave neural network only for the optimal number of last trained layers, Table 5. This can be further appreciated in Fig. 4 and 5, where only the optimal configuration (Last 20 Trainable Layers) presents a rather smooth behaviour and the value of R^2 for the filtered function increases as the neural network stabilizes.

In contrast, the transfer learning with Xception presented in Table 7, represents a over-fitted neural network for all levels of trainable layers presented in this research (up to 20), even if this configuration is trained with the same training data and numerical scheme as the previous ResNet50 transfer learning.

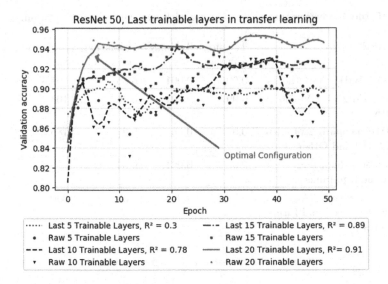

Fig. 4. Transfer learning, ResNet50. CASE: BMP, Leopard 2A4, Sisu XA-180 and Other. Metrics: Accuracy.

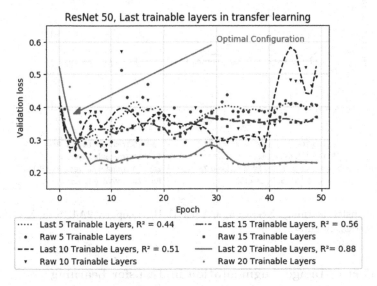

Fig. 5. Transfer learning, ResNet50. CASE: BMP, Leopard 2A4, Sisu XA-180 and Other. Metrics: Loss, sparse categorical crossentropy.

A classical depiction of a over-fitted neural network is present, with a stagnated value of validation accuracy Fig. 6 and a increasing value for validation loss for all configurations with high orders of magnitude in Fig. 7. Not the less, a pseudo optimal configuration or "Best" over-fitted level of training can be selected for further study with data augmentation for every case, Table 5.

Table 7. Performance on the testing with transfer learning Xception.

CASE	Training accuracy	Training loss	Validation accuracy	Validation loss
T-72, BMP and Other	0.99	0.001	0.35	307.8
Leopard 2A4, CV9030 and Other	0.99	0.001	0.36	104.3
BMP, Leopard 2A4, Sisu XA-180 and Other	0.99	0.001	0.27	185.7
Tanks, Foliage and camouflage tanks	0.99	0.001	0.64	9.7
(T72, Leopard 2A4), Smoke screen and Firing Tanks	0.99	0.001	0.39	236.4

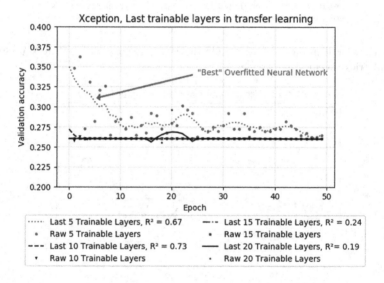

Fig. 6. Transfer learning, Xception. CASE: BMP, Leopard 2A4, Sisu XA-180 and Other. Metrics: Accuracy.

6.3   Effect of Image Augmentation in Transfer Learning

Image augmentation on machinery equipment have prove to be beneficial to image recognition algorithms, although the level of improvement vary depending on the case and algorithm used [26]. In order to measure the level of influence of image augmentation on both trained hybrid neural networks presented, a calculation scheme is build in terms of an incremental number of artificial images feed into the training set. By locking random number generators of the code as previously mentioned, variations on accuracy results can be observe as solely

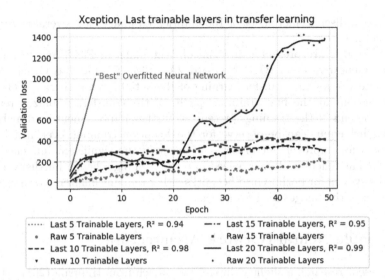

Fig. 7. Transfer learning, Xception. CASE: BMP, Leopard 2A4, Sisu XA-180 and Other. Metrics: Loss, sparse categorical crossentropy.

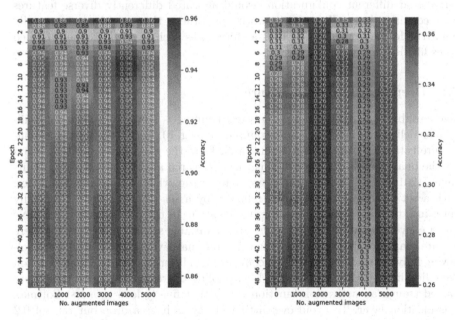

Fig. 8. Transfer learning ResNet50. CASE: BMP, Leopard 2A4, Sisu XA-180 and Other. Effect of image augmentation. Metrics: Accuracy.

Fig. 9. Transfer learning Xception. CASE: BMP, Leopard 2A4, Sisu XA-180 and Other. Effect of image augmentation. Metrics: Accuracy.

influence of a discrete increment of 1000 fabricated images for several re-runs of the hybrid network.

These results are presented in from of heat maps in Fig. 8 and 9, for the same representative case: BMP, Leopard 2A4, Sisu XA-180 and Other. As it can be observed for the transfer learning of ResNet50, even if there are present small variations at the first training epochs of the transfer; stabilized results towards the end of the training, present no further improvement or drawback. A similar behaviour can be observe for the Xception training, even if it has a lot of room for improvement in terms of accuracy, no significant influence can be observed as function of images feed into the training scheme. Further on, the loss of the system for both hybrid networks either remains unaltered or increases as function of the images feed for all cases studied.

7   Variable Neural Network Architecture

In the present research a slightly different approach from Hiippala (2017) [11] is taken, as it is not assumed that a unique neural network architecture would optimally adapt to all features for all the cases of the present study. As it is hypothesized that different configurations would allocated differently diverse features for recognition in small neural networks, hypothesis that would not necessarily hold true for large neural networks architectures such as optimized and refined cases like ResNet and Xception.

7.1   Deep Learning Architecture

The variable architecture neural network training is automated within specifications delineated in Table 8 and exemplify in Fig. 10. Each own designed architecture is trained from a scratch and tailor fit to the particular case in question for the final classification layer. This variable search algorithm is based on Huttunen (2016) [12] basic neural network for recognition of four vehicles types, with a set of convolutional layers followed by a set of Dense layers to finally enter into the final output layer for classification. In the present case, a variable set of convolutional blocks is couple with a variable set of Dense layers. Where feature maps are flattened after the convolutional layers prior entering the following fully connected layers. Each convolutional layer has an activation function "rectified linear" (ReLU) before a Max-pooling operation. All dense layers are passed trough an activation function ReLU that finally lead to a last Softmax classification layer. To avoid over-fitting all layers have a drop out rate of 0.2 as it has proven to be a reliable value in practice. These variable architecture networks have also a flexible number of neurons that oscillates between 64 and 256 neurons.

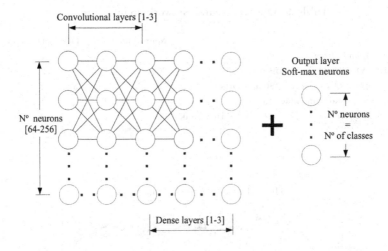

Fig. 10. Neural network architecture.

Table 8. Deep learning neural network architecture.

Neural network element	Optimization search range
Convolution layers	[1-2-3]
Dense layers	[1-2-3]
Number of neurons per layer	[64-128-256]

7.2 Variable Architecture Training Results

Results presented in Table 9 shown that different architectures adapt in a more optimal manner for the different clarification cases. Results prove to be well behaved neural networks for their most optimal configurations, presenting high stabilized validation accuracy results with relative low loss function numerical values. Therefore, in parallel to the transfer learning configuration, only one case would be presented in detail for didactic purposes, CASE: BMP, Leopard 2A4, Sisu XA-180 and Other. Figures 11 and 12 present a few of the tested configurations for the particular case in question. It can be observed that this converged behavior is found within a number of 50 epochs and with a larger learning rate of 1e−3 respective to the transfer learning case. The optimal configuration is selected as the one with the highest stable accuracy value and a relative low Loss function.

Table 9. Optimal Neural Network architecture.

CASE	Neuron no.	Conv. layers	Dense layers
T-72, BMP and Other	64	3	2
Leopard 2A4, CV9030 and Other	64	1	3
BMP, Leopard 2A4, Sisu XA-180 and Other	128	3	2
Tanks, Foliage and camouflage tanks	64	3	1
(T72, Leopard 2A4), Smoke screen and Firing Tanks	256	2	2

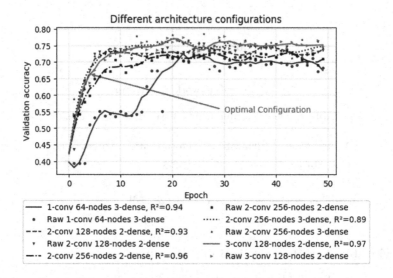

Fig. 11. Own architecture. CASE: BMP, Leopard 2A4, Sisu XA-180 and Other. Metrics: Accuracy.

7.3   Effect of Image Augmentation on Variable Neural Network Architecture Training

Table 10 shows the results for own neural network architecture design with and without image augmentation. It can be appreciated that for the case of training neural networks from scratch, there is an increment in validation accuracy for all cases of ≈10%, with the most accurate neural networks (Val. acc. ≥85%) gaining only a few accuracy points (≤5%) and the least accurate ones (Val. acc. 63%) obtaining an improvement of 20% accuracy due to inclusion of artificial images to the training system.

A detailed influence of how the number of augmented images influence the accuracy of the training process can be observed in Fig. 13 and 14. These represent two different cases in terms of accuracy development. The first case: Tanks,

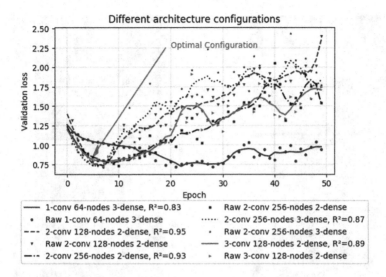

Fig. 12. Own architecture. CASE: BMP, Leopard 2A4, Sisu XA-180 and Other. Metrics: Loss, sparse categorical crossentropy.

Table 10. Performance on the testing with and without data augmentation.

CASE	Validation accuracy	Validation loss	Validation accuracy	Validation loss	Optimal no. aug. img.
	Image augmentation OFF		Image augmentation ON		
T-72, BMP and Other	0.75 ± 0.02	1.3 ± 0.03	0.81 ± 0.01	1.17 ± 0.03	4000–5000
Leopard 2A4, CV9030 and Other	0.87 ± 0.02	$0.41 \pm .02$	0.91 ± 0.03	1.14 ± 0.06	4000–5000
BMP, Leopard 2A4, Sisu XA-180 and Other	0.75 ± 0.02	0.97 ± 0.02	0.85 ± 0.02	0.91 ± 0.04	4000–5000
Tanks, Foliage and camouflage tanks	0.62 ± 0.02	1.34 ± 0.03	0.82 ± 0.02	0.90 ± 0.9	3000–4000
(T72, Leopard 2A4), Smoke screen and Firing Tanks	0.87 ± 0.1	0.62 ± 0.1	0.91 ± 0.01	1.14 ± 0.06	4000–5000

Foliage and camouflage tanks (Fig. 13), portraits how a neural network with a relative low Val. acc. 62% gains large improvements from discrete increments on artificial images, although the increment is not constant and there is a step accuracy decrease to 52% on the first batch of 1000 fabricated images. Nevertheless, reaching its accuracy peak between 3000–4000 augmented images with a top Val. acc. of 83%. The second behaviour can be observe on case: BMP, Leopard 2A4, Sisu XA-180 and Other (Fig. 14); with a rather high Val. acc. (75%). This training system is already stable and shows a slowly but steady accuracy increment towards 4000–5000 artificial images to a sealing value of 86%.

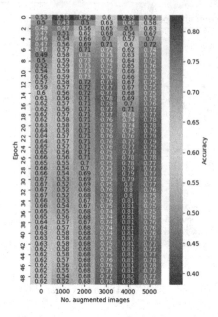

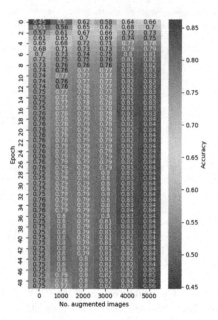

Fig. 13. Effect of image augmentation on neural network training. CASE: Tanks, Foliage and camouflage tanks. Metrics: accuracy.

Fig. 14. Effect of image augmentation on neural network training. CASE: BMP, Leopard 2A4, Sisu XA-180 and Other. Metrics: accuracy.

8   Pseudo-random Placements

In terms of machinery equipment since apparatus models have significantly less discrepancies than biological members of a species, 3D designs and advances in rendering techniques have proven to be useful for creating artificial images [19], that in principle provides limitless number of training data for image analysis algorithms. As a future work recommendation; taking into account the limited number of openly available images of military equipment and the secrecy reservations of military institutions in terms of openly sharing large databases of military equipment in use; the following algorithm is proposed as a manner to produce useful artificial images for machine learning algorithms training.

8.1   Algorithm Description

It has been documented that simply allocating images (2D or 3D) on random backgrounds, where the image allocated and the background does not guard any kind of correlation is detrimental for image recognition machine learning training [6]. In consequence some continuity and harmony must be present between the inserted image/3D render and the surroundings. Some developments in this area have been made by artificially inserting 3D ships on true background images for far top air view of ports, shipyards and seashores on flat air view scenarios [27], accomplishing increasing the quality and quantity of their image training set. Although managing to increase accuracy in their training model, their augmentation algorithm needs further improvement on image overlapping and adequate angles view for the 3D renders, plus adding the necessary model skins to their models for realistic appearance.

A) 3D Military equipment

C) Sphere mapping and level detection

Helsinki (60.164780, 24.949187)

B) 360° Image @ Google [7]

D) Final artificial image

Fig. 15. 3D model placements example.

The algorithm proposed for military vehicles takes advantage of 3D realistic shapes, that in essence can be self drawn/modified with a CAD software from an picture and on top adding camouflage skins and different lighting themes [4] Fig. 15(A). A second step is to obtain from Google maps [7] 360° images through their GPS coordinates Fig. 15(B), these images can be mapped as a sphere projection to set a 360° surrounding, plus adding a plane in tune with the street level of the street view Fig. 15(C). Therefore obtaining a suitable frame to set a military vehicle in this globe surrounding environment Fig. 15(D).

This system has several capabilities such as, various camera angles and flexible zoom focus withing a image background and vehicle pair, diverse illumination configurations, possibility to add fog, rain, fire, snow or sand in the volume around the vehicle plus several backgrounds as street views around the world provided by Google [7] and openly accessible by their GPS coordinates. This algorithm can be added as an extension data set of the augmented images on the different training schemes presented in this paper to measure its influence on the accuracy of different neural networks.

A)
ResNet50:
BMP 100%
Xception:
BMP 100%
Own arch.:
BMP 99.9%

B)
ResNet50:
Leopard 99.9%
Xception:
BMP 99.9%
Own arch.:
BMP 99.1%

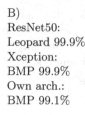

C)
ResNet50:
Sisu 96.4%
Xception:
Sisu 85.5%
Own arch.:
Sisu 88.2%

D)
ResNet50:
Sisu 99.9%
Xception:
Sisu 77.7%
Own arch.:
Other 99.4%

Fig. 16. Accuracy predictions. False predictions market in red. CASE: BMP, Leopard 2A4, Sisu XA-180 and Other. (Color figure online)

9 Recognition Examples

In practice the neural networks described in this research produce as an outcome a probability on how accurate is their prediction. Some examples are presented in Fig. 16 for a vehicle type classification and Fig. 17 for a situational environment classification, these images where not used as training in this paper. It is important to notice that results related to the Xception neural network are expected to be the least reliable since this is an over-fitted network with low accuracy (<64%) and high loss ($\gg$1) values, Table 7. None of the neural networks are capable to make perfect predictions without miss-classifying certain types of vehicles. Although, if the vehicle overall shape can be seen such as in Fig. 16(A),(C), the recognition has higher chances to be on target. On the other hand in 16(B) the own architecture design makes and error, since sharp straight edges and the fact that the tank cannon blend with the pavement lines, makes it somewhat similar to a false prediction of a BMP (canon-less military vehicle). Although this does not mean absolute superiority of the ResNet50 network, even when its Val. acc. is 9% higher than the own architecture design (Tables 6 and 10), there are cases of non military vehicles being miss classified by ResNet50 but correctly allocated by the own architecture design for that particular case, Fig. 16 (D).

The situational environment case: Tanks, Smoke screen and firing tanks is provided as an example in Fig. 17. It is noticed that for ResNet50 Val. acc. $\approx$0.81% and for the case of own architecture design Val. acc. $\approx$0.91%, both being quite accurate models. Although, these models work very well to describe the situation of a military vehicle, with errors related to the color of the smoke or fire. Such as in Fig. 17(C) a miss-prediction is made by ResNet50, since the smoke has certain yellowish tones that produce a false allocation of this image.

It is important to mention that this neural network classification system is in a high degree correlated to the color presented in the image, with yellow/red predominance implying fire and white/gray predominance implying smoke. Nevertheless this case should only be used as a second order recognition system once there is certainty that a military vehicle is located in the figure, since it could produce miss-leading results.

These miss-leading results could be mild, such as mistaking a snow covered civilian car as a smoke cover military vehicle or a military vehicle in a passive state (Basic Tank), Fig. 17 (E). Which in principle does not represent a menace. Or severe errors as miss-labeling a red car with fire-like paintwork as a firing tank, Fig. 17 (D). Since this case would imply an allocated distress situation of a war vehicle engaging in military combat, leading to false information regarding the circumstances of a particular monitored area.

A)
ResNet50:
Basic Tank 99.9%
Xception:
Basic Tank 90.7%
Own arch:
Basic Tank 99.9%

B)
ResNet50:
Firing 99.9%
Xception:
Smoke cover 98.2%
Own arch.:
Firing 99.1%

C)
ResNet50:
Firing 99.9%
Xception:
Smoke cover 95.7%
Own arch.:
Smoke cover 99.9%

D)
ResNet50
Firing 99.9%
Xception:
Basic Tank 99.9%
Own arch.:
Firing 99.9%

E)
ResNet50:
Smoke cover 98.0%
Xception:
Basic Tank 87.4%
Own arch.:
Basic Tank 96.6%

Fig. 17. Accuracy predictions. False predictions market in red. CASE: Basic Tanks (T72, Leopard 2A4), Smoke screen and Firing Tanks. (Color figure online)

10   Conclusions

Two different training schemes of supervised machine learning where studied for classification of military images, variable start layer transfer training models and self design convolutional neural networks training. In terms of transfer learning, ResNet proved to be a well behaved neural network that adapted rapidly to the classification options studied with Val. acc. values on average of 88%. On the other hand, the same transfer-train scheme applied to the Neural network Xception was not successful into adapting to these classification cases, mainly for two reasons, a insufficient large/variable data set and the necessity to train a larger portion of the original network i.e. higher number of last trainable layers.

Moreover, the data augmentation strategy used proved to not have any influence on the accuracy of the transferred machine learning algorithms used. Nevertheless, a new augmentation algorithm is proposed as future work, using 3D renderings of military vehicles in true background 360° images that perhaps could improve the quality and variability of the data to fit pre-trained networks as Xception and many others. The second focus of this investigation is based on variable architecture convolutional network training. Results shown that different architectures are more suitable for different classification cases with average Val. acc. of 86.4%. These are considerable smaller architectures ($\approx$40 times) trained from scratch, and proved to be roughly as reliable as large pre-trained architectures for the purposes of this paper with $\leq$2% difference.

Acknowledgments. The authors wish to acknowledge Ken Riippa, Jani Haapala and Tuomo Hiippala for labeled data and the CSC – IT Center for Science, Finland, for computational resources.

References

1. Abadi, M., et al.: TensorFlow: large-scale machine learning on heterogeneous systems (2015). Software available from tensorflow.org. https://www.tensorflow.org/
2. Chollet, F., et al.: Keras (2015). https://keras.io
3. Chollet, F.: Xception: deep learning with depthwise separable convolutions. In: Proceedings - 30th IEEE Conference on Computer Vision and Pattern Recognition, CVPR 2017, pp. 1800–1807 (2017). https://doi.org/10.1109/CVPR.2017.195
4. Community, B.O.: Blender - a 3D modelling and rendering package. Blender Foundation, Stichting Blender Foundation, Amsterdam (2018). http://www.blender.org. Accessed 09 Mar 2020
5. Bloice, M.D., Stocker, C., Holzinger, A.: Augmentor: an image augmentation library for machine learning. J. Open Source Softw. **2**(19), 432 (2017). https://doi.org/10.21105/joss.00432
6. Dvornik, N., Mairal, J., Schmid, C.: On the importance of visual context for data augmentation in scene understanding, pp. 1–15 (2018). http://arxiv.org/abs/1809.02492
7. Google: Finland google maps. https://www.google.com/maps/@60.1647826,24.9493922,3a,75y,211.07h,75.51t/data=!3m6!1e1!3m4!1swNO3sM2NkZRKrTRN1gqQKg!2e0!7i13312!8i6656

8. Guo, Y., Liu, Y., Oerlemans, A., Lao, S., Wu, S., Lew, M.S.: Deep learning for visual understanding: a review. Neurocomputing **187**, 27–48 (2016)
9. Habibzadeh Motlagh, M., Jannesari, M., Rezaei, Z., Totonchi, M., Baharvand, H.: Automatic white blood cell classification using pre-trained deep learning models: ResNet and inception. In: Tenth International Conference on Machine Vision, Proceedings of SPIE, vol. 1069612, p. 105 (2018). https://doi.org/10.1117/12.2311282
10. He, K., Zhang, X., Ren, S., Sun, J.: Deep residual learning for image recognition. In: Proceedings of the IEEE Computer Society Conference on Computer Vision and Pattern Recognition, pp. 770–778 (2016). https://doi.org/10.1109/CVPR.2016.90
11. Hiippala, T.: Recognizing military vehicles in social media images using deep learning. In: IEEE International Conference on Intelligence and Security Informatics (ISI), pp. 60–65 (2017). https://github.com/DigitalGeographyLab/MilVehicles/
12. Huttunen, H., Yancheshmeh, F.S., Ke, C.: Car type recognition with deep neural networks. In: Proceedings of IEEE Intelligent Vehicles Symposium, pp. 1115–1120 (2016). https://doi.org/10.1109/IVS.2016.7535529
13. Deng, J., Dong, W., Socher, R., Li, L.-J., Li, K., Fei-Fei, L.: ImageNet: a large-scale hierarchical image database. Department of Computer Science, Princeton University, USA (2009)
14. Kaggle: ImageNet Object Localization Challenge — Kaggle. https://www.kaggle.com/c/imagenet-object-localization-challenge/data. Accessed 03 Mar 2020
15. Kornblith, S., Shlens, J., Le, Q.V.: Do better imagenet models transfer better? IEEE/CVF Conference on Computer Vision and Pattern Recognition (CVPR), pp. 2661–2671 (2019). http://arxiv.org/abs/1805.08974
16. Krizhevsky, A., Sutskever, I., Hinton, G.E.: ImageNet classification with deep convolutional neural networks. In: Advances in Neural Information Processing Systems, pp. 1097–1105 (2012)
17. Lin, T.-Y., Maire, M., Belongie, S., Hays, J., Perona, P., Ramanan, D., Dollár, P., Zitnick, C.L.: Microsoft COCO: common objects in context. In: Fleet, D., Pajdla, T., Schiele, B., Tuytelaars, T. (eds.) ECCV 2014. LNCS, vol. 8693, pp. 740–755. Springer, Cham (2014). https://doi.org/10.1007/978-3-319-10602-1_48
18. Microsoft: Download Kaggle Cats and Dogs Dataset from Official Microsoft Download Center. https://www.microsoft.com/en-us/download/details.aspx?id=54765. Accessed 03 Mar 2020
19. Movshovitz-Attias, Y., Kanade, T., Sheikh, Y.: How useful is photo-realistic rendering for visual learning? In: Hua, G., Jégou, H. (eds.) ECCV 2016. LNCS, vol. 9915, pp. 202–217. Springer, Cham (2016). https://doi.org/10.1007/978-3-319-49409-8_18
20. Oliphant, T.: NumPy: A guide to NumPy. USA: Trelgol Publishing (2006). http://www.numpy.org/. Accessed 09 Mar 2020
21. Pedregosa, F., Varoquaux, G., Gramfort, A., Michel, V., Thirion, B., Grisel, O., Blondel, M., Prettenhofer, P., Weiss, R., Dubourg, V., Vanderplas, J., Passos, A., Cournapeau, D., Brucher, M., Perrot, M., Duchesnay, E.: Scikit-learn: machine learning in Python. J. Mach. Learn. Res. **12**, 2825–2830 (2011)
22. Perez, L., Wang, J.: The Effectiveness of Data Augmentation in Image Classification using Deep Learning (2017). http://arxiv.org/abs/1712.04621
23. Redmon, J., Divvala, S., Girshick, R., Farhadi, A.: You only look once: unified, real-time object detection. In: Proceedings of the IEEE Computer Society Conference on Computer Vision and Pattern Recognition, pp. 779–788 (2016). https://doi.org/10.1109/CVPR.2016.91
24. Redmon, J., Farhadi, A.: YOLOv3: an incremental improvement (2018). http://arxiv.org/abs/1804.02767

25. Rezende, E., Ruppert, G., Carvalho, T., Ramos, F., De Geus, P.: Malicious software classification using transfer learning of ResNet-50 deep neural network. In: Proceedings of the 16th IEEE International Conference on Machine Learning and Applications, ICMLA 2017, pp. 1011–1014 (2017). https://doi.org/10.1109/ICMLA.2017.00-19

26. Sato, I., Nishimura, H., Yokoi, K.: APAC: Augmented PAttern Classification with Neural Networks, May 2015. http://arxiv.org/abs/1505.03229

27. Yan, Y., Tan, Z., Su, N.: A data augmentation strategy based on simulated samples for ship detection in RGB remote sensing images. ISPRS Int. J. Geo-Inf. 8(6) (2019). https://doi.org/10.3390/ijgi8060276

Run-Time Class Generation: Algorithm for Decomposition of Homogeneous Classes

Dmytro O. Terletskyi[(✉)]

Taras Shevchenko National University of Kyiv, Kyiv 03022, Ukraine
dmytro.terletskyi@gmail.com

Abstract. An ability to change the internal structure and to correct the behaviour adapting to such change of the working environment as heterogeneity of data is an important feature of modern knowledge-based systems. One of the approaches for achieving the goal is to develop tools for dynamic analysis, modification and generation of knowledge structures and program codes as structural parts of intelligent systems. Therefore, analysis of the class structure in object-oriented programming as well as in object-oriented knowledge representation is presented in the paper. The main result of the paper is developed algorithm for dynamic creation of new classes of objects via decomposition of homogeneous classes of objects to the subclasses. The algorithm performs the decomposition of homogeneous classes of objects creating the set of their semantically correct subclasses via solving corresponding constraint satisfaction problem. It can be adapted and integrated into particular knowledge representation model or programming language.

Keywords: Run-time class generation (RTClG) · Structural atom · Functional atom · Structural molecule · Functional molecule

1 Introduction

Adaptability is one of the crucial features of modern intelligent systems (ISs), which allows systems adapting and effective reacting to challenges of the working environment. Depending on the kind of particular system, such feature can be implemented in different ways, however, the system should be able to change itself, when required, otherwise it will always be restricted by a logic implemented within its program codes. Therefore, to provide high level adaptability, they should be equipped with mechanisms of modifications of its internal structure and functionality, which can be developed using dynamic code generation approach.

According to [7–9,12], the main idea of *dynamic* or *run-time code generation (RTCG)* is to produce new pieces of program code and to execute them within the program run-time. Consequently, programs within run-time can analyse, modify and extend their own source codes or codes of other programs. Using

© Springer Nature Switzerland AG 2020
A. Lopata et al. (Eds.): ICIST 2020, CCIS 1283, pp. 243–254, 2020.
https://doi.org/10.1007/978-3-030-59506-7_20

such opportunities, an IS can form its own reaction to challenges of its working environment and process them respectively. Then, after generation, new pieces of code can be integrated within existed source codes of the system and thus finish the adaptation procedure. Such opportunities for program codes manipulations are implemented mostly within interpreted programming languages with dynamic type system, such as Python, Ruby, JavaScript, etc.

Generally, RTCG can be defined as a generation of particular program constructions of different levels. Within the object-oriented programming (OOP) and object-oriented knowledge representation (OOKR) one of the fundamental constructions is a class, therefore run-time code generation can be interpreted as a *run-time class generation (RTClG)*, as it was proposed in [15,16]. Dynamic generation of new classes of objects can be achieved via development and implementation of different operations, defined over classes. As the result, such operations should dynamically produce new classes of objects during system run-time. A few concepts of such operations were proposed in [15,16] via development of *intersection* and *union of classes*. Another way of run-time class generation is *class decomposition*, that can be implemented as correspondent operation over classes. Let us consider concept of a class and features of its internal structure in more details to achieve this goal.

2   Morphology of Classes

Concept of a class is one of the most significant and widely-used notions in such areas as object-oriented programming, databases and knowledge representation. Classes are fundamental construction blocks for computer programs, relational databases and many of knowledge representation models. Nowadays there are different points of view concerning definition of a class, which propose variety of interpretations for this concept. According to the most known definitions, a class can be considered as:

- *a set of objects that share common structure, common behavior, and common semantics* [2,4];
- *a blueprint or a template for objects* [3,11,19];
- *a data type equipped with a possible partial implementation* [4,10];
- *a factory-like entity which creates objects* [4,11];
- *a program structure or module* [4,10].

As we can see, all of the mentioned definitions are quite general and do not provide clear notion of the *class structure*. Instead of this, they consider a class externally and pay much attention to different ways of its practical application, mostly in programming. Nevertheless, clear understanding of the class internal structure and its features is critically important for development of class decomposition methods. Let us consider concept of a class in terms of its internal structure and features within object-oriented programming and such knowledge representation model as object-oriented dynamic networks (OODNs) which was proposed in [17,18] and then generalized in [14].

2.1   Classes in Object-Oriented Programming

Within object-oriented programming (OOP) a class can be interpreted as some conceptual container for modeling of concrete essences – *objects*, from particular domains within the computer programs [4]. Usually internal structure of such containers can be splitted in two conceptual parts – *structural* and *behavioural*.

Structural part consists of slots, called *attributes* or *fields*, which store particular *static* or *dynamic properties* of the class of objects [2,19]. Static properties are once-defined and immutable, while dynamic ones can be computed by the request or changed for some reason during the objects lifetime. Properties themselves, implement some distinct features, which form structure (body) of all objects of a class. Set of attributes, initialized by particular set of values, forms some *configuration* of an object of a class, defining its *internal state*.

Behavioral part of a class consists of operations, called *methods*, which provide access to states of objects and (or) opportunity to change them in defined way, according to particular program scenarios [2,4,19]. According to [2], there are five most widely-used kinds of methods:

- *Selectors*, which provide access to the state of an object without its changing.
- *Iterators*, which implement access to all components of an object in some defined order.
- *Modifiers*, which allow altering of the state of an object.
- *Constructors*, which create objects and (or) initialize their initial state.
- *Destructors*, which free the state of objects and (or) destroy them.

However, such classification is typical mostly for compiled statically-typed programming languages, while interpreted dynamic-typed languages provide additional opportunities for managing objects states. The main and distinct feature is an ability to change the structure of a class and its objects during program execution. As the result modifiers can be divided on *values modifiers* and *structure modifiers*. In the same time, structural modifiers can be divided on *attribute add methods*, which can inject (integrate) new fields or (and) methods to a class or any of its objects, and *attribute delete methods*, which can remove existed fields or (and) methods from a class or any of its objects. Set of methods implements some *typical behaviour* for all objects of a class, which defines managing of their internal state and external interaction with other objects within the program.

Structural and behavioural parts of a class are strictly connected with each other, because methods of a class provide computation of values for dynamic properties and implement external client interface for managing objects states. Moreover, a class defines the same structure and behaviour for all its objects, therefore classes within the OOP can be called *homogeneous* ones.

2.2   Classes in Object-Oriented Dynamic Networks

Within the OODNs, a class can be defined as an abstract prototype for creation of objects of particular type. Similarly to OOP, internal structure of a class generally can be divided on *structural* and *functional* part.

Structural part of a class consists of its *quantitative* and *qualitative properties*, where the first ones represent some apparent numerical or symbolic characteristics of modelled essences, while the second ones represent more complex and not obvious their features, usually, defined using other properties and methods of the same class [14,17,18].

Functional part of a class within the OODNs, as a behavioural part of a class in the OOP, consists of methods defined over properties and (or) other methods of the class. According to [14], there are four main kinds of methods within OODNs:

- *Selectors*, which provide access to slots of the internal structure of a class, without its modification.
- *Exploiters*, which use classes and objects as parameters for creation of new objects, classes of objects, sets and multisets of objects.
- *Modifiers*, which change objects or classes of objects by modifying their structure and (or) functionality.
- *Generators*, which create sets and multisets of objects and their classes.

Exploiters are similar to constructors within the OOP, however some of them are polymorphically universal and can be applied to any objects or classes of objects regardless their types, for example exploiters of union, intersection, difference, symmetric difference, cloning etc. Concepts of such exploiters were described in [14,17,18], then algorithms for implementation of intersection and union of classes were proposed in [15] and [16].

Modifiers are similar to modifiers within the OOP. They can change the values of properties and modify the structure of a class in six different ways. Therefore as it was described in [17,18] and extended in [14], modifiers can be full, partial, generative, destructive, commutable and combined.

Generators can be interpreted as a special kind of exploiters, however they produce only sets or multisets of objects and their classes. Similarly to exploiters, there are universal generators of sets and multisets of objects, which also were described in [17] then extended in [14].

Similarly to the OOP, structural and functional part of a class within OODNs are strictly connected with each other and define structure and behaviour for all objects of the type defined by the class.

2.3   Internal Structure of Classes

Let us consider simple class aggregation, which defines general concept of triangle on the plane, as the example.

$$\text{Point} = (x = (v_x, \mathbb{R}),\ y = (v_y, \mathbb{R}),\ \text{get\_x}(p, \mathbb{R}) = v_x(p),\ \text{get\_y}(p, \mathbb{R}) = v_y(p),$$
$$\text{set\_x}(p, (x, \mathbb{R})) = (v_x(p) := x),\ \text{set\_y}(p, (y, \mathbb{R})) = (v_y(p) := y))$$
$$\text{Triangle} = (\text{point\_1} = (v_1, \text{Point}),\ \text{point\_2} = (v_2, \text{Point}),\ \text{point\_3} = (v_3, \text{Point}),$$
$$\text{get\_point}(\text{tr}, (n, \mathbb{Z}^+), \text{Point}) = \text{tr.point\_n},$$
$$\text{set\_point}(\text{tr}, (n, \mathbb{Z}^+), (x, \mathbb{R}), (y, \mathbb{R})) =$$

$$= (\text{tr}.p_n.\text{set\_x}(x), \text{tr}.p_n.\text{set\_y}(y)),$$

$$\text{get\_side\_length}((p_a, \text{Point}), (p_b, \text{Point}), \mathbb{R}^+) =$$

$$= \sqrt{(p_a.\text{get\_x}() - p_b.\text{get\_x}())^2 + (p_a.\text{get\_y}() - p_b.\text{get\_y}())^2}$$

$$\text{get\_perimeter}(tr, \mathbb{R}^+) =$$

$$= \text{get\_side\_length}(\text{tr.get\_point}(1), \text{tr.get\_point}(2)) +$$

$$+ \text{get\_side\_length}(\text{tr.get\_point}(2), \text{tr.get\_point}(3)) +$$

$$+ \text{get\_side\_length}(\text{tr.get\_point}(3), \text{tr.get\_point}(1)),$$

$$\text{is\_a\_triangle}(v f_4($$

$$s_1 = \text{get\_side\_length}(\text{tr.get\_point}(1), \text{tr.get\_point}(2)),$$

$$s_2 = \text{get\_side\_length}(\text{tr.get\_point}(2), \text{tr.get\_point}(3)),$$

$$s_3 = \text{get\_side\_length}(\text{tr.get\_point}(3), \text{tr.get\_point}(1)), v_4) =$$

$$= ((s_1 + s_2 > s_3) \wedge (s_1 + s_3 > s_2) \wedge (s_2 + s_3 > s_1)))$$

Now let us analyse internal structure of the class Triangle in more details. Let us denote it as Tr, point_1 as p_1, point_2 as p_2, point_3 as p_3, get_point as f_1, set_point as f_2, get_side_length as f_3, get_perimeter as f_4 and is_a_triangle as p_4.

As we can see, quantitative properties p_1, p_2 and p_3 define vertices of the triangle, and each of them is defined independently from other properties or methods of the class. Methods f_1 and f_2 depend on properties p_1, p_2 and p_3, because they use them to get and set coordinates of the triangle's vertices. Method f_3 depends on properties p_1, p_2 and p_3, because it uses them to compute the length of triangle's sides. Method f_4 depends on methods f_3, f_1 and properties p_1, p_2, p_3, because it uses them to compute the triangle's perimeter. And finally, qualitative property p_4 depends on methods f_3, f_1 and properties p_1, p_2, p_3, because it uses them to check triangle inequality.

Analysing considered example, we can conclude that internal structure of the class consists of semantically independent and (or) dependent properties and methods. Such structure of relations is conceptually similar to connections among atoms and molecules in chemical compounds. Therefore, we can consider internal structure of a class as a set of connected or independent *atoms* and *molecules*. Since attributes and methods of a class are its smallest and independent parts, we can define two kinds of atoms – *structural* and *functional*.

Definition 1. *Structural atom or structural independent component of a class of objects T is a property $p_i \in P(T)$ defined as $p_i()$, where $P(T)$ is specification of the class T.*

The notation $p_i()$ means that property p_i is defined without using any other properties and (or) methods of the class T. In the OOP such atoms can be static attributes, while in the OODNs they are quantitative properties.

Definition 2. *Functional atom or functional independent component of a class of objects T is a method $f_i \in F(T)$ defined as $f_i()$, where $F(T)$ is signature of the class T.*

Similarly to the *structural atom*, the notation $f_i()$ means that method f_i is defined without using any other properties and (or) methods of the class T. It means that method f_i does not use as the input parameters or as a part of its internal implementation any properties of the class T and invocations of its other methods. In the OOP such atoms can be structural modifiers (attribute add methods) or readers or printers methods, while in the OODNs – modifiers or generators.

Since a class structure can contain attributes and methods which are defined using other attributes and (or) methods of the same class, we can define two kinds of molecules of a class – *structural* and *functional.*

Definition 3. *Structural molecule or structural connected component of a class of objects T is the collection $SM_i(T) = (p_i, x_{j_1}, \ldots, x_{j_n}) \subseteq P(T) \cup F(T)$, such that p_i is defined as $p_i(x_{j_1}, \ldots, x_{j_n})$, where $1 \leqslant j_1 \leqslant \cdots \leqslant j_n \leqslant |P(T) \cup F(T)|$, $1 \leqslant i \leqslant |P(T) \cup F(T)|$ and $P(T)$ is a specification of the class T, while $F(T)$ is its signature.*

The notation $p_i(x_{j_1}, \ldots, x_{j_n})$ means that property p_i is defined using other properties and (or) methods of the class T and therefore forms the *structural molecule*, where $x_{j_1}, \ldots, x_{j_n}$ are atoms or smaller molecules. In the OOP such molecules are dynamic attributes, while in the OODNs – qualitative properties.

Definition 4. *Functional molecule or functional connected component of a class of objects T is the collection $FM_i(T) = (f_i, x_{j_1}, \ldots, x_{j_n}) \subseteq P(T) \cup F(T)$, such that f_i is defined as $f_i(x_{j_1}, \ldots, x_{j_n})$, $1 \leqslant j_1 \leqslant \cdots \leqslant j_n \leqslant |P(T) \cup F(T)|$, $1 \leqslant i \leqslant |P(T) \cup F(T)|$ and $P(T)$ is a specification of the class T, while $F(T)$ is its signature.*

Similarly to the *structural molecule*, the notation $f_i(x_{j_1}, \ldots, x_{j_n})$ means that method f_i is defined using other properties and (or) methods of the class T and therefore forms the *functional molecule*, where $x_{j_1}, \ldots, x_{j_n}$ are atoms or smaller molecules. It means that method f_i can use $x_{j_1}, \ldots, x_{j_n}$ as the input parameters or as a part of its internal implementation.

Molecules of a class form internal connections among its atoms. If a constructed class is a precise model of some real essence from the particular domain, then internal connections of a class should model the internal semantic nature of this essence. Therefore, internal connections created by molecules can be noted as *semantic connections* among atoms of a class.

Since a class is a collection of semantically connected attributes and methods, it can be defined using definitions of structural and functional atoms and molecules.

Definition 5. *A class T is a collection*

$$T = (SA, FA, SM_{i_1}, \ldots, SM_{i_n}, FM_{j_1}, \ldots FM_{j_m}),$$

where SA and FA is a collection of structural and functional atoms of the class T, while SM_{i_k}, $k = \overline{1, n}$ and FM_{j_w}, $w = \overline{1, m}$ is its structural and functional molecules.

The term collection can be interpreted as a set in compiled programming languages and as a tuple in interpreted ones.

Using definition of atoms and molecules of a class, we can represent internal structure of the considered above class Tr in the following way

$$SA = \{p_1, p_2, p_3\}, \ FA = \{\}, \ SM_4 = (p_4, \{p_1, p_2, p_3, f_3, f_1\}),$$
$$FM_1 = (f_1, \{p_1, p_2, p_3\}), \ FM_2 = (f_2, \{p_1, p_2, p_3\}),$$
$$FM_3 = (f_3, \{p_1, p_2\}, \{p_1, p_3\}, \{p_2, p_3\}), \ FM_4 = (f_4, \{f_3, f_1, p_1, p_2, p_3\}),$$

where SA and FA is a set of structural and functional atoms of the class Tr correspondingly, SM_4 is its structural molecule, while FM_i, $i = \overline{1,4}$ are its functional molecules.

3   Decomposition Analysis of Classes

Generally term of decomposition can be defined as the process of splitting something into smaller or the smallest parts, therefore decomposition of a class can be interpreted as its splitting into subclasses. Nevertheless, the splitting procedure should take into account internal connections formed by molecules of a class, otherwise, the created subclasses will be models of meaningless or unreal essences within a considered domain. Another important aspect of a class decomposition is to interpret term collection of attributes and method. If a collection is interpreted as a set, then decomposition procedure should not consider the order of atoms inside the created subclasses, because different combinations of the same group of atoms are the same set. However, if a collection is interpreted as a tuple, then different combinations of the same group of atoms can determine subclasses, which are syntactically incorrect or cannot be defined in the terms of particular interpreted programming language.

For development of decomposition procedure for a class, the notion of subclass should be defined. According to [4], within the OOP terms a class and a type means the same concept, however within the OODNs they are not equivalent ones. Within the OODNs there are two kinds of classes – *homogeneous* and *inhomogeneous (or heterogeneous)*, where in the first case a class defines a type, while in second one, a class defines at least two types. Therefore concept of a subclass within the OODNs is defined based on the notion of a subtype [14]. The procedures for checking of the equivalence of class specifications and signatures were proposed in [15].

Subclass relation $\subseteq$ defined over arbitrary set of classes $C = \{T_1, \ldots, T_n\}$ is a partial order relation over this set, that was proven in [14, Assert. 2.3.3]. According to [13, Th. 1] and [14, Th. 2.6.1], quantity of all possible subsets created from the set C is equal to $2^n - n - 1$, where $n = |C|$. Moreover, as it was proven in [13, Th. 2] and [14, Th. 2.6.2], the set of homogeneous classes of objects C, extended by all its possible subsets, together with universal union exploiter $\cup$ define a join-semilattice with 1 maximum element $\{T_1, \ldots, T_n\}$.

All these results can be useful to develop decomposition procedure of a class, because if a class T is interpreted as a set of its properties and methods, i.e.

$T = \{p_1, \ldots, p_n, f_1, \ldots, f_m\}$, then the power set of this set $B(T)$ is a set of all formally possible subclasses of the class T. Since $B(T)$ is a partially ordered set, it together with a universal union exploiter $\cup$ define a join-semilattice with 1 maximum element, which is a class T. In other words, all formally possible subclasses of a class T together, form a join-semilattice with 1 maximum element. Consequently, the quantity of all possible non empty subclasses of the class T is equal to $2^n - 1$, where $n = |P(T) \cup F(T)| = |T|$.

Let us consider the class Tr, described in the previous section, as a set of its properties and methods $Tr = P(Tr) \cup F(Tr) = \{p_1, p_2, p_3, p_4, f_1, f_2, f_3, f_4\}$. As we know, the cardinality of its power set $|B(Tr)|$ is equal to $2^n = 2^8 = 256$, where 255 subclasses are non empty ones. Let us compute the quantity of all possible subclasses of the class Tr which have a defined cardinality, i.e.:

$$C_8^8 = 1, \ C_8^7 = 8, \ C_8^6 = 28, \ C_8^5 = 56, \ C_8^4 = 70, \ C_8^3 = 56, \ C_8^2 = 28, \ C_8^1 = 8.$$

Taking into account obtained results, we can conclude that decomposition of the class Tr is reduced to generation of all its semantically correct subclasses among all 255 formally possible ones. It means, that decomposition procedure should consider all internal connections of the class Tr, formed by its structural and functional molecules.

3.1   Decomposition Problem

Since semantically correct subclasses of a class defines particular systems of restrictions over the atoms and molecules of the class, the selection of such subclasses can be interpreted as finding of solutions of the correspondent *constraint satisfaction problem (CSP)*. According to [5,6], CSP can be defined as a tuple $P = (Y, D, C)$, where Y is a finite sequence of variables $Y = (y_1, \ldots, y_n)$, $n > 0$, which are defined on the respective domains from a finite sequence $D = (D_1, \ldots, D_n)$, such that $y_1 \to D_1, \ldots, y_n \to D_n$, where $D_i = \{x_1, \ldots, x_w\}$, $w > 0$, $i = \overline{1, n}$ is a set of all possible values for the variable y_i, and C is a finite sequence of constraints $C = (c_1, \ldots, c_k)$, $k > 0$, where constraint c_i, $i = \overline{1, k}$ is a pair $c_i = (S_i, R_i)$, where $S_i \in Y$ is a scope of the constraint, i.e. $S_i = (y_{i_1} \in D_{i_1}, \ldots, y_{i_n} \in D_{i_n})$ and $R_i \in D_{i_1} \times \cdots \times D_{i_n}$ is a relation defined on the S_i. According to [1], an n-tuple $X = (x_1, \ldots, x_n) \in D_1 \times \cdots \times D_n$ satisfies the constraint $c_i \in C$, where $c_i = (S_i, R_i)$, if and only if $(x_1, \ldots, x_n) \in S_i$. Therefore, an n-tuple $X = (x_1, \ldots, x_n) \in D_1 \times \cdots \times D_n$ is the solution of the CSP if and only if it satisfies $\forall c_i \in C$. Consequently, CSP is consistent or satisfiable if it has at least one solution and inconsistent or unsatisfiable otherwise.

Let us formulate the CSP for decomposition of the class Tr, considered in the previous sections. As it was shown above, if we consider the class Tr as a set of its properties and methods $P(Tr) \cup F(Tr)$, then during its decomposition we can create subclasses of different cardinality. Thus, for decomposition of the class Tr we need to consider all definitions of the sequence of variables Y, i.e. $Y = (y_1)$, $Y = (y_1, y_2)$, $\ldots$, $Y = (y_1, \ldots, y_7)$.

For all possible definitions of the set Y, all its variables are defined on the same set $D = P(Tr) \cup F(Tr) = \{p_1, p_2, p_3, p_4, f_1, f_2, f_3, f_4\}$. After recognition of all structural and functional atoms and molecules of the class Tr, what was done in the previous section, the situation, when $Y = (y_1)$ becomes the trivial one. Since we need to create all semantically correct subclasses of the class Tr, which have cardinality 1, the sequence of constraints C should include only single unary constraint $C = (c_1)$, which selects form the set D elements which are structural or functional atoms of the class Tr.

In all other cases when $Y = \{y_1, y_2, \dots\}$, we need to create all semantically correct subclasses of the class Tr, which have corresponding cardinality, the sequence of constraints should include two constraints, i.e. $C = \{c_1, c_2\}$, where c_1 guarantees that each possible solution $X_i = (x_1, x_2, \dots)$, $i = \overline{1, q}$ of the CSP consists of only unique elements, while c_2 provides creation of $X_i = (x_1, x_2, \dots)$ as all possible semantically correct unions of structural and (or) functional atoms of the class Tr and (or) its structural and (or) functional molecules.

Since a CSP is considered over a Cartesian product of sets, then in general case its highest complexity is bounded by cardinality of the Cartesian product. Therefore, decomposition of the class Tr in the worst case required to find all its semantically correct subclasses among $n + n^2 + \dots + n^7 = 2396744$ formally possible tuples of Cartesian products, where $n = |Y|$. To reduce the complexity we can consider join-semilattice of the class Tr, where we need to analyse only 255 tuples, that in almost 9399 times less then in the case of Cartesian product.

4   Classes Decomposition Algorithm

Taking into account all previous remarks, let us develop the algorithm for decomposition of homogeneous classes of objects, which analyzes the power set of the class and finds the solutions for the corresponding CSP. Therefore, the algorithm should generate all elements of the power set, defined over the collection of attributes and methods of the class, and then verify the satisfiability of the sequence of constraints for each created subclass.

As we can see, the Algorithm 1 uses homogeneous class T, integer number k and set of constraints C as the input data and returns the set of all semantically correct subclasses of the class T as the result of its decomposition. The condition, written in the fifth line of the algorithm, checks how many 1 are present in the binary form of the integer number i and is this quantity equal to parameter k, which specifies the cardinality of required subclasses. Another condition, located in the eleventh line of the algorithm, invokes the Procedure 1, which verifies the satisfiability of each subclass $t \subseteq T$ according to the sequence of constraints C. The verification procedure returns $true$ as the result, if a subclass $t \subseteq T$ satisfies all constraints from the sequence C and returns $false$ in opposite case, however if a subclass t does not contain the first element of the particular constraint c, then Procedure 1 returns $None$.

Developed algorithm can be used in two modes. In the first one it can generate all subclasses of the class T, which satisfy the set of constraints C. In the second mode, the algorithm can generate all subclasses of the class T, which have cardinality k and satisfy the set of constraints C.

Algorithm 1. Decomposition of homogeneous classes of objects.

Require: T is a HC, k is a cardinality of subclasses, C is a sequence of constraints.
Ensure: $T^k = \{T_1 \subseteq T, \ldots, T_n \subseteq T\}$, $|T_1| = \cdots = |T_n| = k$
 1: **if** $1 \leqslant k < |T|$ **then**
 2:     $T^k := \{\}$;
 3:     $t := \{\}$;
 4:     **for** $i = 1, \ldots, 2^{|T|} - 1$ **do**
 5:         **if** binary(i).count$(1) = k$ **then**
 6:             **for** $j = 1, \ldots, |T|$ **do**
 7:                 **if** $i \,\&\, (1 << j) > 0$ **then**
 8:                     t.add$(T[j])$;
 9:             satisfy := **true**;
10:             **for all** $c \in C$ **do**
11:                 **if** is_correct$(t, c) = $ **false then**
12:                     satisfy := **false**;
13:                     **break**;
14:             **if** satisfy = **true then**
15:                 T^k.add(t);
16:             $t := \{\}$;
17:     **return** T^k;

In other words, we can generate all elements of a join-semilattice defined over the attributes and methods of the class T, as well as any horizontal layer of this semilattice. For usage of the Algorithm 1 in the first mode, the filtration condition from the fifth line should be removed.

Procedure 1. is_correct(t, c)

Input: t is a HC; c is a constraint.
Output: {true, false, None}
 1: **if** $c[0] \in t$ **then**
 2:     satisfy := **false**;
 3:     **for** $i \in 1, \ldots, |c|$ **do**
 4:         **for all** $j \in c[i]$ **do**
 5:             **if** $j \in t$ **then**
 6:                 satisfy := **true**;
 7:             **else**
 8:                 satisfy := **false**;
 9:                 **break**;
10:         **if** satisfy = **true then**
11:             **return** satisfy;
12:     **return** satisfy;

The Algorithm 1 was implemented using Python 3 programming language and used for decomposition of different homogeneous classes, including the class Tr, considered in the previous sections. As the result of decomposition of the class Tr, the algorithm built 49 subclasses of cardinality $k = \overline{1,7}$, which satisfy the set of constraints C described in the Sect. 2.

Analyzing Algorithm 1, we can conclude that generation of all possible subclasses of the class T requires consideration of all elements of power set of the class, namely $2^n - 2$, where $n = |T| = P(T) \cup F(T)$, in the worst case. Another source of complexity appears during verification of the constraints in Procedure 1. Verification of each constraint requires 1 check of the membership for first element of the constraint in the subclass $t \subseteq T$ and if it so, k_i additional checks of the membership for the rest elements of the constraint, where i is a number of constraint. Consequently, the verification of whole sequence of constraints C requires $(k_i + 1)w$ checks of the membership of elements of the constraint c_i in the subclass t, where $i = \overline{1,w}$ and $w = |C|$. Therefore, the time complexity of proposed algorithm is equal to $O(2^n - 2) \cdot O((k_i + 1)w) \approx O(2^n q)$. Despite this, the algorithm also requires p memory for temporal storing of each subclass, consequently the space complexity of the Algorithm 1 is equal to $O(p)$.

5   Conclusions

The adaptability of intelligent systems can be implemented as appropriate internal mechanisms for producing system reaction on the changes of the environment. One of such mechanisms is a run-time class generation, therefore the algorithm for decomposition of homogeneous classes of objects was developed and presented in the paper. It generates all semantically correct subclasses of a class as the solutions of constraint satisfaction problem, formulated over the structural and functional atoms and molecules of the class. The algorithm has exponential time and linear space complexity and implements concept of universal decomposition exploiter of classes. Consequently it can be applied to any homogeneous class of object regardless its type. However, despite all benefits, developed algorithm requires further analysis and improvements.

References

1. Apt, K.R.: Principles of Constraint Programming. Cambridge University Press, New York (2003)
2. Booch, G., et al.: Object-Oriented Analysis and Design with Applications. Object Technology Series, 3rd edn. Addison-Wesley Professional, Boston (2007)
3. Bruce, K.B.: Foundations of Object-Oriented Languages: Types and Semantics. The MIT Press, Cambridge (2002)
4. Craig, I.D.: Object-Oriented Programming Languages: Interpretation. UTCS. Springer, London (2007). https://doi.org/10.1007/978-1-84628-774-9
5. Dechter, R.: Constraint Processing. Morgan Kaufmann Publishers, San Francisco (2003)
6. Freuder, E.C., Mackworth, A.K.: Constraint satisfaction: an emerging paradigm. In: Rossi, F., van Beek, P., Walsh, T. (eds.) Handbook of Constraint Programming, chap. 2, pp. 13–27. Elsevier, Amsterdam (2006)

7. Kamin, S.: Routine run-time code generation. ACM SIGPLAN Notices **38**(12), 208–220 (2003). https://doi.org/10.1145/966051.966059
8. Keppel, D., Eggers, S.J., Henry, R.R.: A case for runtime code generation. Technical Report 91-11-04, University of Washington, Department of Computer Science and Engineering, January 1991
9. Leone, M., Lee, P.: Lightweight run-time code generation. In: Proceedings of ACM SIGPLAN Workshop on Partial Evaluation and Semantics-Based Program Manipulation, pp. 97–106. Orlando, FL, USA, June 1994
10. Meyer, B.: Object-Oriented Software Construction, 2nd edn. Prentice Hall, Santa Barbara (1997)
11. Mezini, M.: Variational Object-Oriented Programming Beyond Classes and Inheritance. The Springer International Series in Engineering and Computer Science, vol. 470. Springer, Boston (1998). https://doi.org/10.1007/978-1-4615-5627-5
12. Sheard, T.: Accomplishments and research challenges in meta-programming. In: Taha, W. (ed.) SAIG 2001. LNCS, vol. 2196, pp. 2–44. Springer, Heidelberg (2001). https://doi.org/10.1007/3-540-44806-3_2
13. Terletskyi, D.O.: Exploiters-based knowledge extraction in object-oriented knowledge representation. In: Suraj, Z., Czaja, L. (eds.) Proceedins of the 24th International Workshop, Concurrency, Specification & Programming, CS&P 2015, vol. 2, pp. 211–221. Rzeszow University, Rzeszow (2015)
14. Terletskyi, D.O.: Object-Oriented dynamic model of knowledge representation within intelligent software systems. Ph.D. thesis, Faculty of Computer Science and Cybernetics, Taras Shevchenko National University of Kyiv, Kyiv, Ukraine, April 2018
15. Terletskyi, D.O.: Run-time class generation: algorithms for intersection of homogeneous and inhomogeneous classes. In: Proceedings of IEEE 2019 14th International Scientific and Technical Conference on Computer Sciences and Information Technologies (CSIT), pp. 272–277. Lviv, Ukraine, September 2019. https://doi.org/10.1109/STC-CSIT.2019.8929736
16. Terletskyi, D.O.: Run-time class generation: algorithms for union of homogeneous and inhomogeneous classes. In: Damaševičius, R., Vasiljevienė, G. (eds.) ICIST 2019. CCIS, vol. 1078, pp. 148–160. Springer, Cham (2019). https://doi.org/10.1007/978-3-030-30275-7_12
17. Terletskyi, D.O., Provotar, O.I.: Mathematical foundations for designing and development of intelligent systems of information analysis. Sci. J. Probl. in Program. **16**(2–3), 233–241 (2014)
18. Terletskyi, D.O., Provotar, O.I.: Object-oriented dynamic networks. In: Setlak, G., Markov, K. (eds.) Computational Models for Business and Engineering Domains, IBS IS&C, vol. 30, pp. 123–136. ITHEA, 1 edn. (2014)
19. Weisfeld, M.: The Object-Oriented Thought Process. Developer's Library, 5th edn. Addison-Wesley Professional, Boston (2019)

Twitter Based Classification for Personal and Non-personal Heart Disease Claims

Ghita Amrani[1(✉)], Fadoua Khennou[2], and Nour El Houda Chaoui[2]

[1] IASSE Laboratory, National School of Applied Sciences, USMBA, Fez, Morocco
ghita.amrani@usmba.ac.ma
[2] TTI Laboratory, Higher School of Technology, USMBA, Fez, Morocco

Abstract. The popularity of Twitter has created a massive social interaction between users that generates a large amount of data containing their opinions and feelings in different subjects including their health conditions, these data contain important information that can be used in disease monitoring and detection, therefore, Twitter has attracted the attention of many researchers as it has proven to be an important source of health information on the Internet.

In this work, we conducted a systematic literature review to discover state-of-the-art methods used in the analysis of Twitter posts related to health, then we proposed an approach based on machine learning, sentiment analysis methods and Big Data technologies to ensure optimal classification of the health status of a population related to cardiovascular diseases in a Twitter environment.

Keywords: Twitter · Machine learning · Cardiovascular diseases · Sentiment analysis · Health

1 Introduction

The advances in artificial intelligence (AI) combined with big data are constantly opening up new perspectives. Machine learning and specifically predictive analysis is a powerful approach, which helps, by combining data from different sources, to predict the impact of phenomena or to invent new services. It improves diagnostics, and allows accurate predictions of how a patient's health is changing.

Patient data is therefore represented as a gold mine for analysts, it gives them the opportunity to implement adequate algorithms and propose novel predictive approaches.

Currently, social networks like Facebook or Twitter are becoming an inseparable part of human life and generate a huge amount of data that includes opinions, feelings, information about health conditions or general information about anything of interest to the community.

In Twitter, the online microblogging site, text messages called tweets whose size is limited to a maximum of 280 characters can be posted by a user, which is visible by its "followers" or by the public. Twitter being text-oriented and limited in character length, can be used as an effective communication tool, especially in smartphone environments where memory, bandwidth and display size are limited.

© Springer Nature Switzerland AG 2020
A. Lopata et al. (Eds.): ICIST 2020, CCIS 1283, pp. 255–269, 2020.
https://doi.org/10.1007/978-3-030-59506-7_21

There are many research papers that were focused on the use of Twitter in disease surveillance [2–4, 9, 13, 14, 17, 19], detection of the onset and spread of epidemics [5, 7, 8, 10, 12, 16], measurement of public concern for diseases [20] and study of spatio-temporal evolution of a disease [11, 15]. This is due to its great popularity and the profitable value of tweets that provide indicators on public health in general.

After an in-depth analysis of the research carried out while using twitter datasets, there are very few studies that focused on the prediction of health status in relation to cardiovascular diseases and which constitute, according to the World Health Organization (WHO) [1], the first cause of death in the world.

In this article, we conducted a systematic literature review to discover state-of-the-art methods used in the analysis of Twitter posts applied in the above-mentioned applications, then we proposed an approach based on machine learning and sentiment analysis methods to ensure optimal classification of the health status of a population related to cardiovascular disease in a Twitter environment.

2 Related Work

Twitter, is an important source of data in the health field. This is due to the interest of several research studies in its use in disease surveillance and detection. Indeed, Articles [2] and [3] focused on the detection of influenza-related tweets from a database of geolocated historical tweets extracted via Twitter API and filtered by keywords related to influenza; in [2], Medtex (medical text analysis platform) was established to extract the relevant features of these tweets that were used by automatic learning algorithms: Naive Bayes, linear logistic regression, multinomial logistic regression, SVM and decision trees. The algorithms that have performed best are logistic and SVM regression. In [3] the TF-IDF method was used to extract the features that constituted an input for the SVM automatic learning algorithm and which gave an accuracy rate of 67%.

In article [4], researchers used Ebola and MERS disease tweets extracted from the AIDR (Artificial intelligence for disaster response) platform to build an automatic classification approach to inventory the different tweets: those related to health and those in relation to death, treatment and transmission of diseases and those that prevent symptoms. The methods used for feature extraction are first Bag-of-words (BOW) where unigrams are considered as features that have been processed by the Twitter Pos Tagger, then transmitted as input to MetaMap, which returns the set of words present in the tweet as concepts in UMLS (the medical knowledge base) with their corresponding semantic type and which are provided as input for the algorithms: SVM, Naive Bayes and logistic regression, the latter has shown the best performance.

In [5], in order to visualize an outbreak, the goal was to detect its occurrence and spread using geo-located tweets extracted in real time using Tweepy the python library and filtered by keywords related to different diseases. All letters in the tweets were then converted to lowercase and empty words and punctuation marks were removed. Finally, the Kibana tool was used to visualize, explore and analyze the data. This prototype was very useful because it provided real-time monitoring of diseases compared to disease control and prevention centers, which take between one to two weeks between the diagnosis of the patient and the availability of data.

The researchers in [6] studied the spatial and temporal evolution of influenza to assess the extent to which this disease is present over time in a specific region. This was implemented by analyzing geo-located twitter data collected using the Tweepy library and the Twitter Stream API. This aims to extract tweets with health-related content where there is at least one medical term present using SNOMED-CT (International System of Clinical Terminology) as well as a list of informal medical terms. Its objective is to use an unsupervised learning approach using the natural language processing package (NLTK chunking, which identifies the nominal and verbal sentence clusters). Then, the verbal sentences that will be used to assess the extent to which influenza is present using linguistic methods of analyzing feelings based on a list of positive and negative verbs.

In [7], the purpose is to automatically analyze feelings towards contagious diseases, mental health problems and clinical science in order to evaluate the Measure of Concern (MOC) expressed by Twitter users using a database of tweets collected through the Twitter API and the Twitter4J library. All these tweets were processed by removing the retweets and one member from each pair containing the same words in the same order. In addition, these tweets are classified in personal and non-personal tweet using a hybrid approach combining a method based on linguistic rules and automatic learning classifiers: Multinomial Naïve Bayes and SVM. In the first classification step, Naive Bayes obtained the best performance and sentiment analysis was applied to personal tweets to predict their polarity using the same automatic learning algorithms. In this second stage, Naive Bayes had the best performance again. Finally, the measurement of public concern about diseases was quantified based on the number of negative personal tweets per day and was represented by geographic distribution.

Based on the PRISMA methodology, 20 articles matched our inclusion criteria and are relevant to our research purpose.

In Table 1, the studies contained in the "research article" type have been summarized by mentioning the sources, volumes and periods of data extraction used, the objective of the study and the methods used to achieve it.

Table 1. Description of included studies

Goal of the study	Dataset	Extraction period	Methods
Detection of flu-related tweets [2]	13.5 million tweets	May–August 2011	Medtex (medical text analysis platform) Naive Bayes, linear logistic regression, multinomial logistic regression, SVM and decision trees
Geolocated data mining for influenza surveillance [3]	NA	2012–2013	SVM
Automatic classification related to health associated with death, treatment and transmission of diseases and symptoms prevention [4]	Ebola: 5.08 million tweets MERS: 0.215 million tweets	August 6, 2014–January 19, 2015 April 27–July 16, 2014	SVM, logistic regression and Naive Bayes
Detection of the outbreak and spread of the influenza epidemic [5]	NA	In real time	The Kibana open-source tool
Classify health-related tweets [6]	NA	NA	Streaming Twitter API Continuous Bag-of-Words Statistical test of the Chi-Square SVM CNN (Convolutional Neural Networks)
Classification of tweets related to mosquito-borne diseases in India [7]	Twitter and news articles	September–November 2016	Twitter API SVM and Naive Bayes (NB) Geography RSS (Rich site summary)
Prediction of the influenza epidemic [8]	1800 Tweets	November–December 2015 October–December 2016	Python crawler using the Twitter API Apache Spark, MapReduce and Hive programming
Extraction, surveillance, real-time classification of infectious diseases (influenza, HIV/AIDS, malaria, measles, poliomyelitis, tuberculosis and plague) [9]	4,000 tweets And news data from the Washington Post website	June 5, 2018–July 9, 2018	R language tf-idf method The fuzzy algorithm Eclass1-MIMO
Prediction of outbreaks of contagious diseases [10]	NAVER	NA	Data from the Korean NAVER platform: via Naver Trends SPSS
Study the spatial and temporal evolution of influenza and assess the presence of the disease [11]	178,000 tweets	March 2015	Tweepy and the Twitter Stream API SNOMED-CT terminology NLTK chuncking
Detect influenza epidemics in each region and season [12]	7 million tweets	August 2, 2012–March 1, 2016	Twitter Streaming API Natural language processing The geocoding service provided by Google Maps. Model LINEAR TRAP model
Extraction of topics and trends from disease data [13]	Naver and Twitter	In real time	String similarity checks (Sift4) OpenKoreanTextProcessorJava CCA (Canonical correlation analysis) ranking algorithm dataTables.js, D3.js and chart.js.
Detect personal health status mentions on Twitter [14]	250 million tweets	May 7, 2014–July 23, 2014	Twitter API Streaming API Multinomial Naïve Bayes (MNB)

(continued)

Table 1. (*continued*)

Goal of the study	Dataset	Extraction period	Methods
Explore the spatio-temporal relationship between the evolution of dengue fever and associated Weibo posts Model the propagation of dengue fever in space and time [15]	25000 Weibo post and official data	June 1, 2014–November 2, 2014	Web crawler Kalman filter Latent Dirichlet allocation (LDA)
Classify health-related tweets. Detect epidemics [16]	466,896,997 tweets 2,669,235 news items 49 CDC reports	June 20, 2016–March 2, 2017	Cosine similarity, Glove, FastText Convolutional Neural Network (CNN) Long Short Term Memory Network (LSTM)
Classify stress and relaxation tweets [17]	12107 tweets 222 million geolocated tweets	July 9, 2014–July 14, 2014 September 30, 2013–February 10, 2014	Twitter API Naive Bayes and SVM Bag-of-words
Classification of Tobacco tweets [18]	7362 tweets	December 2011–July 2012	n-gram Naïve Bayes KNN SVM
Classification of tweets in relation to cancer [19]	876,855 individual account tweets 887,774 tweets from the organization's accounts	NA	Tweepy (Python library) LSTM network (Long Short-Term Memory) naive Bayes Textblob Decision Tree K nearest neighbour (KNN) Decision tree (DT) Random forest (RF) GloVe
Classify tweets related to contagious diseases, mental health problems and clinical science problems. Evaluate the Measure of Concern (MOC) [20]	1882,172 tweets	March 13, 2014–June 29, 2014	Twitter4J Multinomial Naïve Bayes and SVM
Describe the volume and content of tweets associated with cardiovascular disease and the characteristics of Twitter users [21]	550 338 tweets	July 23, 2009–February 5, 2015	UMLS Twitter decahose and Twitter spritzer NVIVO

3   Methods

3.1   Prisma

The PRISMA Method "Preferred Reporting Items for Systematic Reviews and Meta-Analyzes" is a method that aims to improve the quality of reporting systematic review [22]. It attempts to collect all empirical data in a particular area and obtain conclusions that summarize the results of the review.

A review protocol describing each step of the systematic review, including eligibility criteria, was developed prior to commencing the literature search and data retrieval.

Research Question
The research question must be formulated in a clear and precise formula, as it determines the goal of the systematic review. The main research questions considered in this review are:

Table 2. Eligibility criteria

Exclusion criteria	Inclusion criteria
Conferences	Type of publication: "Article" AND "Review OR Survey"
Other languages than English	English
Before 2015	From 2015 to 2019
Images datasets Signals datasets (ECG)	Approaches based on classifying tweets in relation to health OR detecting diseases from tweets using machine learning methods and Big Data technologies

Q1-To what extent has machine learning been applied to the prediction of heart disease?

Q2-What datasets have been used for the prediction of heart disease?

Q3-Which machine learning methods have been applied?

Q4-What are the main machine learning algorithms that help accurately to predict heart disease?

Q5-What are the limits of the current work?

Q6-What are the potentially profitable directions that remain unexplored?

Eligibility Criteria

Once the research question has been defined, it is necessary to specify the eligibility criteria for the studies. These specifications are used to select the studies to be included in the systematic review. The eligibility criteria considered in this review are presented in Table 2.

Research Strategy

The research was applied to the Science Direct and Web of Science databases. The conducted research strategy must allow for exhaustive research, in order to collect the largest number of studies and to reduce selection biases.

Table 3. Research strategy

Database	Research strategy
Science direct	Topic: (disease detection OR disease prediction OR disease monitoring OR sentiment analysis of health care tweets OR classification of health care tweets OR infodemiology OR infoveillance) AND Twitter Title, abstract or key words: disease detection OR disease prediction OR disease monitoring OR sentiment analysis of health care tweets OR classification of health care tweets OR infodemiology OR infoveillance
Web of Science	(TS = Topic) TS = ((disease detection OR disease prediction OR disease monitoring OR sentiment analysis of health care tweets OR classification of health care tweets OR infodemiology OR infoveillance) AND twitter)

The search strategy must be based on a list of keywords and synonyms according to a specific logic. Our search strategy is described in Table 3.

Study Selection

The resulted references were imported into Rayyan [23] a web application that help in organizing and implementing a research strategy of systematic reviews. It is very easy to use for screening large amounts of references.

"Rayyan" has been specially designed to speed up the initial screening process by allowing items to be filtered out and duplicates to be eliminated automatically. Then, it was used to review the titles and abstracts of the studies to eliminate those that did not fit the research question. The results of each phase are presented in the PRISMA diagram of Fig. 1. According to our search strategy, 245 items were retrieved.

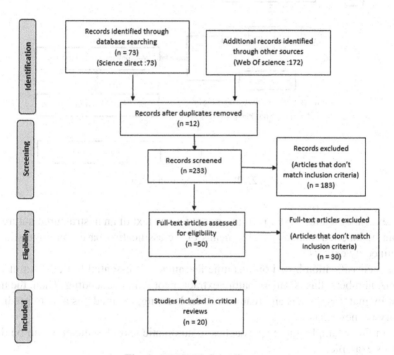

Fig. 1. PRISMA flow diagram

Using Rayyan in the next step, 12 duplicate studies were removed and 233 related articles remained. Summaries and titles of all remaining articles were examined based on the inclusion and exclusion criteria that are described in Table 2, and 183 references were excluded. Subsequent revisions of the full text excluded 30 articles. Overall, 20 articles met our inclusion criteria that are relevant to the studied questions in this systematic review.

3.2 Classification Models

Text classification is the process of assigning labels or categories to the text according to its content. This is one of the fundamental tasks of natural language processing (NLP) with extensive applications such as sentiment analysis, subject labelling, spam and intentions detection.

Unstructured text data is everywhere: emails, chats, web pages, social networks, etc. Text can be an extremely rich source of information, but extracting information from it can be difficult and time-consuming because of its unstructured nature. Figure 2 shows a simplified schema of the steps involved in classifying the text using different approaches.

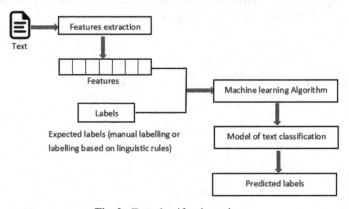

Fig. 2. Text classification scheme

A text classification system has as an input a raw text of an unstructured nature. The text can be labelled manually or by means of a classification based on linguistic rules determined by experts.

For a classification based on machine learning, it is essential to transform it into a vector of numbers, this is called feature extraction or feature encoding. Then, the model is built by matching labels and features. After learning, the model is able to predict the category for new texts.

From this example, three approaches to automatic text classification can be drawn from this example:

- Rules-based approaches.
- Approaches based on automatic learning.
- Hybrid approaches that combine the two previous approaches in order to improve results.

Rule-based approaches classify the text into organized groups using a set of handmade language rules. These rules instruct the system to use the semantically relevant elements of a text to identify the relevant categories according to its content. Instead of relying on manually developed rules, systems based on machine learning teaches how to make classifications based on past observations.

3.3 Feature Extraction

Count Vectors
Count Vectors is a matrix notation of the data set in which each row represents a document in the corpus, each column represents a term in the corpus, and each cell represents the number of frequencies of a particular term in a particular document.

TF-IDF (Term Frequency-Inverse Document Frequency)
The TF-IDF score represents the relative importance of a term in the document and in the entire database. The TF-IDF score is composed of two terms: the first calculates the normalized frequency of terms (TF), the second is the frequency of inverse documents (IDF) calculated as the logarithm of the number of documents in the corpus divided by the number of documents where the specific term appears.

TF(t) = (Number of times the term t appears in a document)/(Total number of terms in the document)
IDF(t) = log (Total number of documents/Number of documents containing the term t)

Then the TF-IDF value of a term is calculated as follows: TF $\times$ IDF

Word Embedding
It is a representation of text where words with the same meaning have a similar representation. In addition, the position of a word in the vector space is both learned from the text and based on the words that surround the word when it is used. In other words, it represents words in a coordinate system where linked words based on a corpus of relationships are placed closer together. The most popular methods of Word Embedding are: Word2vec and GloVe.

4 Proposed Approach

The proposed approach is based on 4 main steps, as described in Fig. 3:

- The extraction of English tweets located in the United States using Twitter API and based on keywords related to cardiovascular disease.
- Tweets cleaning consists in eliminating impertinent terms such as links, emoticons and punctuation marks. Then, this cleaning aims to eliminate retweets and transform the letters of the tweets into lowercase letters.
- The classification of tweets into personal and non-personal then the classification of personal tweets into negative and positive using machine learning algorithms: SVM, multinomial Naive Bayes, random forest and logistic regression using TF-IDF methods and count vectors for the extraction of relevant characteristics.
- The evaluation of twitter as a source of data on cardiovascular disease.

4.1 Tweet Extraction

The purpose of this step is to develop a python crawler that will extract the tweets according to:

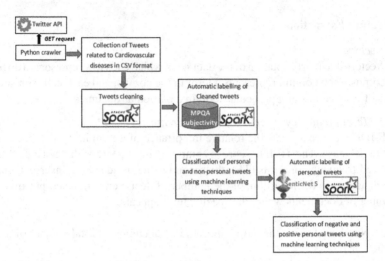

Fig. 3. Proposed model

- Keywords related to cardiovascular disease (heart disease OR cardiovascular OR heart failure OR coronary OR ischemic).
- Location: United States of America.
- The language: English.
- Specific periods (from 2016 to May 2019).

We use the products 'full archive' and '30day endpoint' from twitter and we make the GET request. The results identified count exactly 11,100 tweets.

4.2 Data Cleaning

Data cleaning was applied to the 'text' field of tweets consisting of less than 140 characters and to the 'full_text' field of tweets consisting of more than 140 characters. It consists of:

- Removing links, user references (@username), hashtag (#), punctuation and emoticons using the python library "re" (Regular expression Operations), which provides operations on regular expressions that specify a set of character strings that match it; the functions of this module allow to check if a particular string matches a given regular expression.
- Eliminating retweets to avoid redundancy, this step was performed with Spark using the map transformation applied to the RDD containing the CSV file of the tweets. This transformation took as a parameter the split function () which allowed us to collect a list containing the tweets and each tweet is a list containing these words. Then, we performed a test on the first item on the list to see if it is equal to 'RT'.
- Normalizing the data by transforming all tweets into lowercase and using the lower () function on the list of previously obtained tweets to transform them into lowercase.

After these cleaning operations, only 10,059 tweets remain, they are then stored in a CSV file.

4.3 Personal/Non Personal Classification

The objective of this step is to classify tweets into personal and non-personal (subjective/objective). A personal tweet is a tweet that transmits the author's private states. A private state can be a feeling, an opinion, an evaluation, an emotion, a judgment, an impression, and so forth. Example:

- *"over the last week I ve had a mild heart attack partial kidney failure and extremely low calcium I was in icu for 2 day then moved to a medical icu for 3 days the lord protected me once again I wanna thank all my family and friends for the prayers"*
- *"I have heart failure and to say the least I went to cardiac arrest twice and they brought me back"*
  A non-personal tweet is a tweet that states an objective fact. Example:
- *"the researchers carried out an extensive review of the scientific literature and concluded that both plants based and soya eating patterns reduce the risk of diseases such as diabetes cardiovascular disease stroke and certain cancers diets containing soya were best"*

The MPQA (Multi Perspective Question Answering) lexicon was constructed from human annotations of a corpus of 10,657 sentences in 535 documents that contain news in English from 187 different sources in a variety of countries. The MPQA corpus contains a total of 8,221 words, including 3,250 adjectives, 329 adverbs, 1,146 words of all positions, 2,167 nouns and 1,322 verbs.

Of all the words, 5,569 are strongly subjective words, and the remaining 2,652 are weakly subjective (objective) words. Each tweet was split into a list of words using the Spark map transformation and each word was compared with the MPQA corpus.

By performing several iterations with different thresholds and manually checking the results, the classifier gave the best classification performance by assuming that if the number of strongly subjective words is greater than or equal to 2, the tweet is considered personal, otherwise it is a non-personal tweet.

A problem with text modeling is that it is messy, and techniques such as machine learning require well-defined fixed-length inputs and outputs and cannot work directly with plain text; text must be converted into numbers, more precisely into vectors of numbers, this is called feature extraction or feature coding. In this step, the plain text data will be transformed into characteristic vectors and new characteristics will be created using the existing data set. In our case, we implemented two methods of extracting characteristics: TF-IDF and Count Vectors

Because our data labelling strategy is used to calculate the number of occurrences of words of a certain type so that we can assign a suitable label without regard to word order or context. This strategy is very similar to the two methods TF-IDF and Count Vectors.

By studying the limitations and advantages of the automatic learning algorithms and according to the literature review carried out, the most commonly used algorithms, adapted to the text classification and which have given good results in terms of accuracy rates are: Multinomial Naive Bayes, Logistic regression, Support Vector Machine (SVM), Random Forest

4.4 Positive and Negative Classification

The objective of this step is to classify tweets into negative and non-negative personal tweets. For our problematic, we will be interested in negative personal tweets because they provide essential information on the user's state of health or on the degree of his or her concern about cardiovascular diseases. SenticNet provides the polarity associated with 50,000 natural language concepts. A polarity is a floating number between −1 and +1, the less one is an extreme negativity, and the more one is an extreme positivity. The classifier analyzes each tweet and breaks it down into words and compares them with SenticNet concepts. By performing several iterations with different thresholds and manually checking the results, the classifier gave the best classification performance by assuming that if the number of negative words is greater than 3, the tweet is considered negative, otherwise it is a non-negative tweet.

In this step, the plain text data will be transformed into characteristic vectors and new characteristics will be created using the existing data set. For the same reasons as the previous extraction of characteristics, we implemented TF-IDF, Count Vector and the Model construction.

For the same reasons as the previous classification, we implemented four models: Multinomial Naive Bayes, Logistic regression, Support Vector Machine (SVM), Random Forest Results.

In order to evaluate the performance of the implemented machine learning algorithms we used the "test and validation" cross-validation technique with a stratified repartition.

Then to compare the implemented ML algorithms, we made statistical comparisons of the performance of trained classifiers on specific data sets. The automatic learning models for predicting tweets subjectivity and polarity were built and tested according to two parameters:

– The stratified distribution of learning and test sets.
– Methods for extracting relevant characteristics (TF IDF and count Vectors)

Figure 4 shows the performance of SVM, logistic regression, random forest and Naive Bayes algorithms using TF-IDF and count vectors as feature extraction methods that formed the input elements of the algorithms. In case of subjectivity classification using TF-IDF and Count vectors for feature extraction with 80% distribution for training and 20% for testing, the best performance was 90% for logistic regression and 89% for SVM.

For polarity classification using TF-IDF and Count vectors for feature extraction, the results of classifying the polarity of personal tweets gave better results with 80% distribution for training and 20% for testing, and by using Count Vectors as a method of extracting characteristics with a performance of 89% for both SVM and logistic regression.

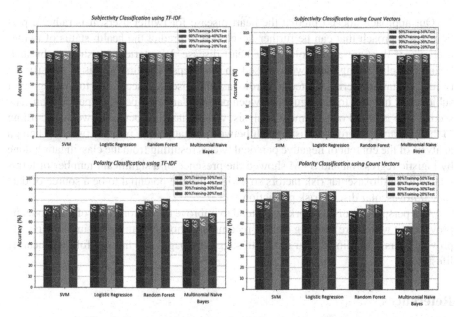

Fig. 4. Tweets subjectivity and polarity classification results

We were unable to compare these results with other studies because there are no actual other proposed approaches that address the classification of personal negative or non-personal classification using a Big Data environment for the heart disease study purpose. The comparison was therefore made between the SVM automatic learning algorithms, logistic regression, random forest and Naïve Bayes by varying two parameters:

– The stratified distribution of learning and test sets.
– The methods of extraction of the relevant characteristics (TF IDF and count Vectors).

According to the classification results, the logistic regression showed the best performance with 89% for the classification of tweets subjectivity, and with 90% for the classification of tweets polarity using the count Vectors feature extraction method. This is because logistic regression is a discriminatory classifier that learns the types of input characteristics most useful for distinguishing between different classes. In addition, logistic regression is essential to understand the influence of several independent variables on a single outcome variable.

5   Conclusion

Twitter remains an important source of information that undoubtedly highlights, via the Internet, the health status of people with cardiovascular complications. It is well known to be a valid and operational communication tool that makes it possible to highlight in an unambiguous and relevant way the risks of diseases, the possible interventions to achieve healthy lifestyles and to dictate adequate and compatible health policies.

Our approach doesn't predict the heart disease for twitter users, it is rather a preliminary approach that can be further developed to predict the health status of twitter users i.e. if they are at risk of having heart disease. We started our strategy by analyzing and classifying their tweets based on two steps; The first step is to classify the tweets, containing terms related to cardiovascular diseases, according to the degree of subjectivity in order to distinguish between personal and non-personal publication. The second step is based on sentiment analysis, which classifies personal tweets according to their polarity in order to distinguish between negative and positive tweets. Then an analysis of the content of negative personal tweets resulting from the classification done by logistic regression and SVM showed the presence of a significant number of terms related to cardiovascular risk factors so Twitter has the potential to be a source of data for cardiovascular disease risk prediction.

As a perspective of this work, we intend to improve the performance of our model by providing it with more learning data. A recommendation system can be implemented to provide users at cardiovascular risk with suggested pages and links to follow a healthy lifestyle.

References

1. Cardiovascular diseases. https://www.who.int/westernpacific/health-topics/cardiovascular-diseases. Accessed 28 Feb 2020
2. Zuccon, G., Khanna, S., Nguyen, A., Boyle, J., Hamlet, M., Cameron, M.: Automatic detection of tweets reporting cases of influenza like illnesses in Australia. Health Inf. Sci. Syst. **3**, S4 (2015). https://doi.org/10.1186/2047-2501-3-S1-S4
3. Allen, C., Tsou, M.-H., Aslam, A., Nagel, A., Gawron, J.-M.: Applying GIS and machine learning methods to twitter data for multiscale surveillance of influenza. PLoS ONE **11**, e0157734 (2016). https://doi.org/10.1371/journal.pone.0157734
4. Rudra, K., Sharma, A., Ganguly, N., Imran, M.: Classifying and summarizing information from microblogs during epidemics. Inf. Syst. Front. **20**(5), 933–948 (2018). https://doi.org/10.1007/s10796-018-9844-9
5. Jiménez-Zafra, S.M., Plaza-del-Arco, F.M., García-Cumbreras, M.Á., Molina-González, M.D., Ureña López, L.A., Martín-Valdivia, M.T.: Monge: geographic monitor of diseases. Procesamiento del Lenguaje Natural **61**, 193–196 (2018). https://doi.org/10.26342/2018-61-30
6. Kuang, S., Davison, B.: Learning word embeddings with chi-square weights for healthcare tweet classification. Appl. Sci. **7**, 846 (2017). https://doi.org/10.3390/app7080846
7. Jain, V.K., Kumar, S.: Effective surveillance and predictive mapping of mosquito-borne diseases using social media. J. Comput. Sci. **25**, 406–415 (2018). https://doi.org/10.1016/j.jocs.2017.07.003
8. Al Essa, A., Faezipour, M.: MapReduce and spark-based analytic framework using social media data for earlier flu outbreak detection. ICDM 2017. LNCS (LNAI), vol. 10357, pp. 246–257. Springer, Cham (2017). https://doi.org/10.1007/978-3-319-62701-4_19
9. Jahanbin, K., Rahmanian, F., Rahmanian, V., Jahromi, A.S., Hojjat-Farsangi, M.: Application of twitter and web news mining in monitoring and documentation of communicable diseases, 9 (2018)
10. Seo, D.-W., Shin, S.-Y.: Methods using social media and search queries to predict infectious disease outbreaks. Healthc. Inform. Res. **23**, 343 (2017). https://doi.org/10.4258/hir.2017.23.4.343

11. Carchiolo, V., Longheu, A., Malgeri, M.: Using twitter data and sentiment analysis to study diseases dynamics. In: Renda, M.E., Bursa, M., Holzinger, A., Khuri, S. (eds.) ITBAM 2015. LNCS, vol. 9267, pp. 16–24. Springer, Cham (2015). https://doi.org/10.1007/978-3-319-227 41-2_2

12. Wakamiya, S., Kawai, Y., Aramaki, E.: Twitter-based influenza detection after flu peak via tweets with indirect information: text mining study. JMIR Public Health Surveill. **4**, e65 (2018). https://doi.org/10.2196/publichealth.8627

13. Yoon, J., Kim, J.W., Jang, B.: DiTeX: Disease-related topic extraction system through internet-based sources. PLoS ONE **13**, e0201933 (2018). https://doi.org/10.1371/journal.pone.020 1933

14. Yin, Z., Fabbri, D., Rosenbloom, S.T., Malin, B.: A scalable framework to detect personal health mentions on twitter. J. Med. Internet Res. **17**, e138 (2015). https://doi.org/10.2196/ jmir.4305

15. Ye, X., Li, S., Yang, X., Qin, C.: Use of social media for the detection and analysis of infectious diseases in China. IJGI **5**, 156 (2016). https://doi.org/10.3390/ijgi5090156

16. Şerban, O., Thapen, N., Maginnis, B., Hankin, C., Foot, V.: Real-time processing of social media with SENTINEL: a syndromic surveillance system incorporating deep learning for health classification. Inf. Process. Manag. **56**, 1166–1184 (2019). https://doi.org/10.1016/j. ipm.2018.04.011

17. Doan, S., Ritchart, A., Perry, N., Chaparro, J.D., Conway, M.: How do you #relax when you're #stressed? A content analysis and infodemiology study of stress-related tweets. JMIR Public Health Surveill. **3**, e35 (2017). https://doi.org/10.2196/publichealth.5939

18. Myslín, M., Zhu, S.-H., Chapman, W., Conway, M.: Using twitter to examine smoking behavior and perceptions of emerging tobacco products. J. Med. Internet Res. **15**, e174 (2013). https://doi.org/10.2196/jmir.2534

19. Zhang, L., Hall, M., Bastola, D.: Utilizing twitter data for analysis of chemotherapy. Int. J. Med. Inform. **120**, 92–100 (2018). https://doi.org/10.1016/j.ijmedinf.2018.10.002

20. Ji, X., Chun, S.A., Geller, J.: Knowledge-based tweet classification for disease sentiment monitoring. In: Pedrycz, W., Chen, S.-M. (eds.) Sentiment Analysis and Ontology Engineering. SCI, vol. 639, pp. 425–454. Springer, Cham (2016). https://doi.org/10.1007/978-3-319-30319-2_17

21. Sinnenberg, L., et al.: Twitter as a potential data source for cardiovascular disease research. JAMA Cardiol. **1**, 1032 (2016). https://doi.org/10.1001/jamacardio.2016.3029

22. PRISMA. http://www.prisma-statement.org/. Accessed 29 Feb 2020

23. Rayyan QCRI, the Systematic Reviews web app. https://rayyan.qcri.org/welcome. Accessed 29 Feb 2020

Information Technology Applications - Special Session on Smart e-Learning Technologies and Applications

Escape the Lab: Chemical Experiments in Virtual Reality

Airidas Janonis, Eligijus Kiudys, Martynas Girdžiūna, Tomas Blažauskas(ID),
Lukas Paulauskas(✉), and Aleksandras Andrejevas

Kaunas University of Technology, 44249 Kaunas, Lithuania
lukas.paulauskas@ktu.lt

Abstract. Virtual Reality (VR) technology introduce new ways to teach students about STEM subjects. Using developed virtual environments students can experience things that would otherwise be dangerous to showcase. We've developed a virtual reality educational escape room game in which the player solves problems based on realistic chemical experiments to advance in the game. The game was showcased in a study fair event where people of various ages and backgrounds had an opportunity to test and complete one of the game's levels. Based on the observations made during the study fair, the overall conclusion is that the VR technology can be a useful tool in education bringing more entertainment and engagement into the learning and teaching processes.

Keywords: Virtual reality · Educational game · Chemical experiments

1 Introduction

Since the appearance of consumer-available virtual reality (VR) headsets, technology was often seen as a tool mostly used for entertainment. However, a lot of industries have seen the advantages of VR and its potential for various types of training. In some cases, training in a virtual environment could be more efficient, where training in a real-world could require expensive equipment, or could be dangerous, where a potential mistake would mean financial losses, injury or even death.

VR technology can bring new ways of learning various subjects. VR can be used for different educational purposes such as knowledge learning, exploration, experimentation and skill training [1]. Just like in various training situations, some subjects' concepts can be difficult or dangerous to demonstrate in a classroom environment, like natural science subjects. A different, more fun way of learning new things engages the students more and they find joy in completing the tasks given to them [5]. VR provides immediacy with the virtual environment and trough visual and audible senses makes one perceive that they are in the virtual environment. This allows for a more engaging, kinesthetic learning process. Kinesthetic learning is described as learning through action, interactions with the real world [3]. People that prefer this kind of learning like to learn through real-world examples that are demonstrated through practice, simulations, videos, they value their

© Springer Nature Switzerland AG 2020
A. Lopata et al. (Eds.): ICIST 2020, CCIS 1283, pp. 273–282, 2020.
https://doi.org/10.1007/978-3-030-59506-7_22

own experiences more so than others. A lot more information is retained, when new things are learned through action and doing things.

The aim of this work was to make kinesthetic learning possible through VR, where learning otherwise can be dangerous or difficult.

2   Related Works

The amount of adoption of serious VR applications is increasing in all kinds of fields. In the medical field, an application simulating trauma decision-making was developed for Oculus VR [4]. Within the application, a single scenario was developed, presenting a virtual patient with blunt thoracic trauma. The simulation has several critical and non-critical decisions. To complete the simulation correct actions, need to be made. Another study tested the application of distance team-based learning for pharmacy in VR using HTC Vive headset and SteamVR Home application, where the participants had to complete the exercise communicating only through VR [2]. In both studies responses to VR were positive and the conclusions were that VR is a viable technology to be used for medical-simulation. Another educational VR game "HoloLAB Champions" is a laboratory practice game presented as a game. The game allows to interact with the virtual environment and safely work with laboratory equipment, users perform various tasks to progress in the game.

Nersesian et al. [6] analyzed the next generation of educational technologies (ET), such as monitor-based (MB) and virtual reality (VR) applications, which are still in their infancy, they do show promise for improving education. In this study, we compared MB and VR educational technologies as alternative supplemental learning environments to traditional classroom instruction using lectures, textbooks, and physical labs.

Open Laboratory usually used for learning program by a student in the school was presented by Khairudin et al. [7]. To support the limited number of facilities in the real laboratory, then a breakthrough in simulation technology is needed before students conducted a real practice in the real laboratory. Especially simulation technology through smartphones.

However, traditional medical education has many drawbacks, such as residency working hour restrictions, patient safety conflicts with the learning needs, and the lack of hands-on workshops. The MedTRain3DModsim Project aimed to produce 3-dimensional (3D) medical printed models, simulations, and innovative applications for every level of medical training using novel worldwide technologies. It was aimed herein to improve the interdisciplinary and transnational approaches and accumulate existing experience for medical education, postgraduate studies, and specialty training [8].

3   Escape the Lab Game Design Methodology

Initially the game was developed as monolithic experience set in a sandbox model world (laboratory in this case). It means the complete freedom to do whatever players wish which mimics the real world. The ideal walkthrough leads players through experiments in an ordered manner: easy to understand experiments are performed first and the more complex experiments (possibly requiring knowledge from previous experiments) are performed later. Unfortunately, during the first demonstration in "GameOn" convention, we have observed that people do not follow the ideal plan and most people fail to complete the objectives during the given time. Therefore, we decided to redesign the game and make it guide the player through the experiments. The methodology which we follow is described by Fig. 1.

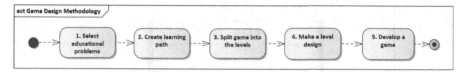

Fig. 1. The design methodology of the game.

The first two phases mostly are related to the pedagogical aspects of the game. In our case - the educational problems are the three chemical experiments: mixing dry ice with liquid, "blue fire" experiment (mixing hydrogen chloride (HCL), copper sulfate (CuSO4) and aluminum (Al) inside a container, then exposing the compound to fire to cause a chemical reaction) and a "chameleon" (mixing potassium permanganate (KMnO4) with sodium hydroxide (NaOH) and sugar). To the chemistry subject educational problems, we added the game mechanics learning activity which also can be considered as an educational problem. In this case, we designed a very simple learning path (See Fig. 2).

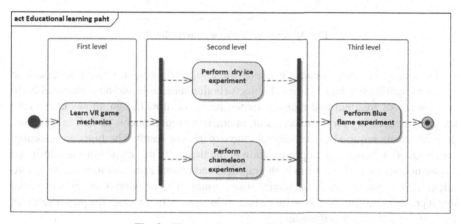

Fig. 2. The learning path split into levels

Splitting learning path activities into the levels is more of an art because it requires the experience of the designer to find a balance of various criteria such as size and complexity of the level, level creation effort, the importance of activities, and many others. Figure 2 shows how our design team split activities into levels. Learning the game mechanics is a required prerequisite in order to start any experiment activity therefore this activity is placed on a separate level. Dry ice and chameleon experiments are quick to perform and they are not related together therefore they are placed into a second level. Grouping them also allows sparing efforts on developing two different levels. The blue flame experiment is the most complex one and the experience from the two previous experiments is handy therefore it is separated into a final level.

Figure 3 shows essential level design activities.

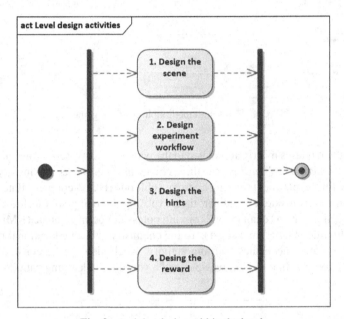

Fig. 3. Activity design within the levels

Designing the scene means designing the level environment, objects necessary to perform experiments, and additional objects (both interactable and non-interactable) to add a sense of freedom and realism. Experiment workflow design allows identifying the objects necessary for the experiment, interactivity requirements as well as computer graphic effects required to demonstrate the experiment result. The hints are essential for progress - it is a gamified presentation of the theory. In our game hints are designed as instructions on leaflets put in both graphical and textual representations. The reward might include gamification mechanics (like earning stars or points), but it is essential that it provides information to advance further in a game. In our case, the player receives parts of the code to open the door.

The activities are shown in Fig. 3 are interrelated. For example, the scene design (level environment and objects), as well as hints, depends on the experiment workflow. The design might be updated iteratively.

The development stage of our game is covered in Sect. 4.

4   Escape the Lab Development

The application was developed on Windows 10 64-bit, using Unity 3D Integrated Development Environment (v2018.3), HTC Vive, and SteamVR (v1.2.3) Utilities. For the modeling of the 3D objects seen in the virtual environment Blender (v2.8) was used. For a more immersive and engaging experience, the audio was integrated into the virtual environment.

The base environment concept was taken from the laboratory facilities of Kaunas University of Technology Chemistry faculty and developed within the Unity 3D Video Game engine. With additional features, these facilities have been turned into a gamified VR escape room type experience which is based on real chemical experiments. The images from recreated laboratory as well as some interaction mechanics are shown in Fig. 4.

Fig. 4. Virtual reality environment images

The goal is to escape the laboratory within a given amount of time. Inside the virtual environment, players must look for various clues and perform chemical experiments to progress further ahead. After completing the required experiment or other tasks, the player is awarded a part of a three-digit code. After collecting all the required parts of the code, the player can type the code on a virtual console and complete the scenario. Additionally, to make the experience more immersive and simulative, the virtual environment is developed to allow the player to interact with every object in the scene.

The internal structure of the game is provided in Fig. 5.

In the package diagram (See Fig. 5) it is shown that the application consists of Interactivity, Virtual Reality API and Game Manager packages. The Game Manager package includes functions such as Menu settings adjustment, Level loading, saving, and game controlling. The system is compatible with Oculus VR, Steam VR, Unity XR, and Windows MR API's. Most of the application functionality resides in the Interactivity package, which consists of three kinds of experiments (Blue flame, Chameleon, and Dry ice), and main gameplay mechanics, such as player movement, hands controls, scoring system, and interactivity between different kinds of objects.

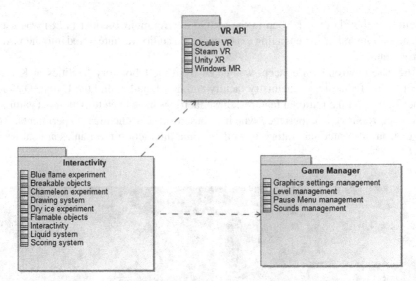

Fig. 5. The structure of the game

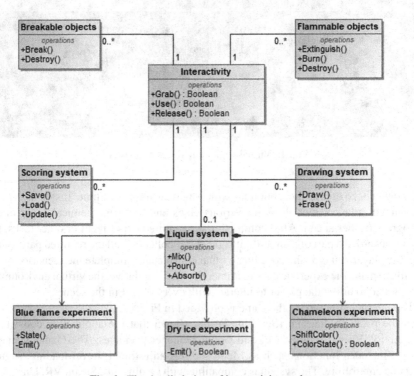

Fig. 6. The detailed view of interactivity package

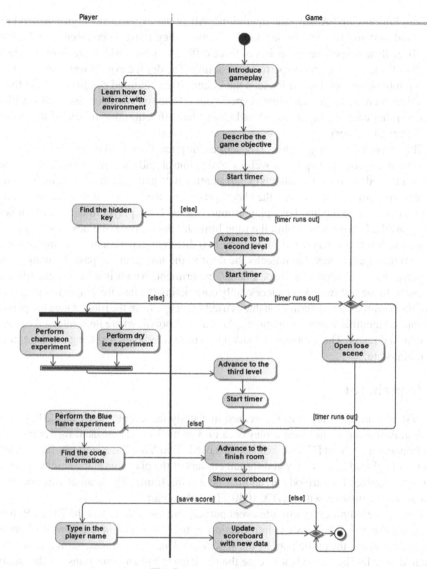

Fig. 7. Game flow diagram

The class diagram (See Fig. 6) takes a closer look at the Interactivity package that was mentioned in the previous diagram. The Interactivity component consists of base mechanics, such as Object grabbing, releasing and/or using. The game objects are separated into different categories - Unbreakable, Breakable (Destroyable), and Flammable objects. The burning objects could also be extinguished, or burnt until they are destroyed. Additional systems that are built upon Interactivity are Drawing (with Drawing and Erasing operations) and Scoring (with saving, loading and updating operations). The liquid system is connected to basic interactions as well because they are required to perform

Mixing, Pouring, and Absorption operations. All of the experiments highly depend on the liquid system. To perform any kind of action, they must be connected to the liquids. Blue flame experiment consists of three different states - which are three different ingredients that are required to perform the action. The dry ice experiment consists of an Emission boolean variable, which tells the system if the required conditions to perform the actions were met. The chameleon experiment is based on two operations - ShiftColor (function that changes liquid color) and ColorState (function that reveals if the liquid has changed its color).

This activity diagram (See Fig. 7) describes the game flow. First of all, the player gets acquainted with the gameplay as well as basic control and movement mechanics. The player is placed in a room that allows experimenting with game mechanics. After learning the basic interactivity mechanics, the player gets introduced to the game objective. Then, the timer starts, and the first level playthrough begins. If the player finds the hidden key and opens the locked door within the time limit, he passes on to the next level. During the second level, the player has to perform two different experiments (Chameleon and Dry ice) to acquire a key that unlocks the door to the last level. To pass the final scene the player has to complete a "Blue Flame" experiment, which is a harder experiment compared to the last two. After successfully completing the task the player has to gather all of the required code information that is used to escape from the room. Once the player has entered the final room, the game displays a scoreboard, where he is allowed to save his achieved result. The data gets uploaded into the leaderboard and the game is reset to the initial state.

5 Experiment

The VR educational game was showcased in a study fair event "Study Fair 2020". For the demonstration, at the stand a play area of 3 m by 3 m was isolated for room-scale functionality and the HTC Vive headset was used. Two Vive Base Stations, facing each other, were placed transversely at different corners of the play area at the height of about 2 m, one mounted on a tripod and another on a stand frame. The headset was powered by a desktop computer with a GTX 1080 TI graphics card.

During the event, every eligible event participant was able to test the game. Before trying out the VR game, a short introduction of the game, and instructions on how to play were given to the participant by the supervisor. During the tryout, participants were watched over by the supervisor in case the participant had any questions for the safety of the participant, in case of any accidents during testing.

This VR experience attempts to combine gamification and education. The principle aim of this experience is to present educational material in the form of a game, making the learning process more entertaining and immersive.

The educational game has confirmed its appeal. Because of its interactivity within the virtual environment and the gameplay, it attracted the attention of different background individuals during its presentation at the study fair event. The participants approached the game from their own unique points of view. Children mostly enjoyed playing around with the virtual environment objects. Meanwhile, during the VR experience, adults and teenagers tried to complete the game by collecting clues and performing chemical experiments.

Non-personal data of the 56 game sessions were gathered during the event. The records include level completion times as well as discovered items leading to finishing the levels. The average age of the audience is unknown because personal data were not recorded. On the other hand, it is known that the game was played mostly by the senior pupils as it was the study fair event. The results are shown in Fig. 8.

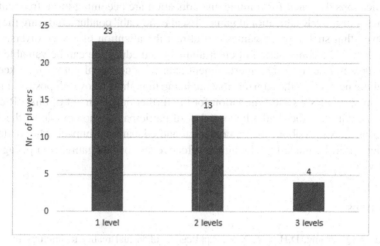

Fig. 8. Number of players who completed the game levels

The first level was finished by half of the participants (23). The second level was completed by 13 players. Only 4 players managed to finish all three levels conducting all the chemical experiments. The main question is related to a small number of people who finished all three levels - is the educational game too complex for the people? The authors observed that only several people during the experiment new how to use HTC Vive equipment. Still - half of the participants completed the first level which was designed to master VR mechanics. Also, the game was designed in a way to ensure replayability. Therefore, it is challenging to keep the motivation of the player and at the same time replaying the game to advance further means repeating the knowledge and concepts learned by a player.

The VR experiences could be used as a complementary tool for teaching and assessments in fields of chemistry. Because the game is based on real chemical experiments, it simulates how various chemical compounds reacts to each other. For teaching, chemical reactions could be showcased within the virtual environment without wasting real compounds avoiding safety concerns.

Still, during the showcasing of the VR game, some safety concerns arose. Some participants displayed cases where, while playing, they got too immersed into the VR experience and forgot about their real surroundings, ignoring the safety bounds drawn in the virtual environment or even perceiving virtual objects as real, trying to lean on them and fall over. However, these safety concerns could mostly depend on the personal experience of the participants, have they tried VR beforehand. Other than that, the game provides a safe environment for all kinds of chemical experiments without causing any harm to the user.

6 Conclusions

VR applications designed for training and education are becoming more frequent. The experiments of the VR educational game "Escape the Lab" conducted during the study fair showed that such type of games can attract the attention of a very diverse range of individuals. The combination of entertainment and education can be valuable to the learning process, because the entertainment side of educational games may keep the learner more invested in the subjects that are being thought. The overall positive opinion of the game provides a solid foundation for the further development of this VR educational game. On the other had a low number of participants who completed the whole game raises questions about the game design and educational impact. More extensive experiments will be made to validate the effectiveness of this game from pedagogical point of view.

References

1. Chang, X.Q., Zhang, D.H., Jin, X.X.: Application of virtual reality technology in distance learning. Int. J. Emerg. Technol. Learn. (iJET) **11**(11), 76–79 (2016)
2. Coyne, L., Takemoto, J.K., Parmentier, B.L., Merritt, T., Sharpton, R.A.: Exploring virtual reality as a platform for distance team-based learning. Curr Pharm Teach Learn **10**(10), 1384–1390 (2018)
3. Gilakjani, A.P.: Visual, auditory, kinaesthetic learning styles and their impacts on English language teaching. J. Stud. Educ. **2**(1), 104–113 (2012)
4. Harrington, C.M., et al.: Development and evaluation of a trauma decision-making simulator in Oculus virtual reality. Am. J. Surg. **215**(1), 42–47 (2018)
5. Kalyani, D., Rajasekaran, K.: Innovative teaching and learning. J. Appl. Adv. Res. **3**(1), 23–25 (2018)
6. Chang, X.Q., Zhang, D.H., Jin, X.X.: Integration of virtual reality in secondary STEM education. In: 2019 IEEE Integrated STEM Education Conference (ISEC), pp. 83–90 (2019)
7. Khairudin, M., Triatmaja, A.K., Istanto, W.J., Azman, M.N.A.: Mobile virtual reality to develop a virtual laboratorium for the subject of digital engineering (2019)
8. Tatar, I., Huri, E., Selçuk, I., Moon, Y.L., Paoluzzi, A., Skolarikos, A.: Review of the effect of 3D medical printing and virtual reality on urology training with MedTRain3DModsim' Erasmus + European Union Project. Tur. j. med. sci. **49**(5), 1257–1270 (2019)

The VOIL Digital Transformation Competence Framework. Evaluation and Design of Higher Education Curricula

Klaus North[1], Andreas Hermann[2], Isabel Ramos[3], Nekane Aramburu[4],
and Daina Gudoniene[5(✉)]

[1] Wiesbaden Business School, Bleichstraße 44, 65183 Wiesbaden, Germany
[2] University of Münster, Schlossplatz 2, 48149 Münster, Germany
[3] University of Minho, R. da Universidade, 4710-057 Braga, Portugal
[4] Deusto Business School, Hermanos Aguirre Kalea, 2, 48014 Bilbo, Spain
[5] Kaunas University of Technology, Studentu 50, 51367 Kaunas, Lithuania
daina.gudoniene@ktu.lt

Abstract. This paper presents a framework to evaluate and develop curricula for higher education in the context of digital transformation. Developing well guided learning journeys for the digital transformation is still a major challenge for educators. The proposed VOIL competence framework is grounded in dynamic capability theory. The VOIL competence framework has been developed by relating the DIGROW digital maturity framework to the European e-competence framework. The foundational architecture and rationale of the VOIL competence framework link learning objectives to the specific challenges of digital transformation of small and medium businesses. The authors also discuss the application of the VOIL competence model for evaluating and designing self-directed and personalized learning journeys.

Keywords: Digital transformation framework · Competence model · Curriculum development · Self-directed learning · Higher education

1 Introduction

Digital technologies are bringing about unprecedented change to business models, products, and services, transforming how people work and interact with customers, partners, and competitors [6, 7]. The resulting digital transformation (DT) is not a recent trend but an ongoing paradigm leading to a digital change of society and economy at all levels [2]. For the individual organization, DT can be regarded as a process, which comprises incremental and disruptive changes enabled by digital technology. Vial [19] describes digital transformation as a process where digital technologies create disruptions triggering strategic responses from organizations that seek to alter their value creation paths, while managing the structural changes and organizational barriers that affect the positive and negative outcomes of this process.

© Springer Nature Switzerland AG 2020
A. Lopata et al. (Eds.): ICIST 2020, CCIS 1283, pp. 283–296, 2020.
https://doi.org/10.1007/978-3-030-59506-7_23

This point of view is aligned with conceptual approaches considering that digitalization transcends technology. As pointed out by several authors [1], DT implies the embeddedness of IT throughout organization, organizational processes and functions. Also, IT strategy becomes integrated with business strategy, giving rise to the novel concept of "digital strategy". According to Bharadwaj et al. [1] "the time is right to rethink the role of IT strategy, from that of a functional-level strategy—aligned but essentially always subordinate to business strategy—to one that reflects a fusion between IT strategy and business strategy. This fusion is herein termed digital business strategy". This view is also supported by other authors [12, 20]. In words of Kahre et al. [12] "digital business strategy reflects a new logic of competitive strategy where boundaries between business and IT strategy become blurred. Dynamically synchronized, business and IT are mutual drivers of strategic change, business value and ultimately competitive advantage". On the other hand, several authors argue that digital strategy relies on organizational capabilities [10, 20]. "The dynamism and complexity of the business and technology environment suggest that digital strategy is emergent, iterative, and influenced by evolving organizational capabilities" [20].

Such profound changes triggered by the speed of technological change requires an agile development and deployment of relevant skills and competencies of managers and staff. Workers must be able to interconnect the organizational challenges with the potentials of technology to come up with innovations that meet the business goals [9]. According to the European E-Skills Forum (2004), digital skills are understood to be the skills and capabilities that enable businesses to exploit opportunities provided by ICT, to ensure more efficient and effective performance, to explore new ways of conducting business and to establish new businesses.

With digital technologies also the way how people are learning is changing [15]. E-Learning allows ubiquitous and self-directed learning "everywhere" by choosing the time, place, media and content that best meets the learners goals, intention and wishes [11]. Data driven identification of learning gaps are the basis for creating personalized learning experiences increasingly based on open education resources available on mobile devices [5]. In this context the role of trainers, coaches and educators is changing. Šereš et al. [16] highlight the importance of preparing students for the challenges of digital transformation, especially those studying business informatics. Therefore, higher education agents need clear roadmaps for the most effective way to develop advanced digital skills that meet organizations' digital transformation needs.

In order to meet the needs for preparing students and staff in firms, particularly in SMEs this paper presents a digital transformation competence framework based on dynamic capabilities theory as will be explained below.

The development of the framework is part of the ongoing VOIL – Virtual Open Innovation Lab www.voil.eu. The project is implemented by partners from different European countries with the purpose of supporting small and medium enterprises (SME) to address the challenges of the digital transformation from a (dynamic) capability and competence perspective. The main objectives of the project are the following: 1) to provide a set of artefacts (i.e. tools, models, methods, etc.) that SMEs can apply to foster and propel their own digital transformation; 2) to provide a digital transformation competence framework and curriculum for higher education in order to guide the development of learning journeys aimed at acquiring and developing digital competences; 3) to disseminate these artefacts, the framework and curriculum to higher education students and SMEs via a dedicated digital platform.

The VOIL Digital Transformation Competence Framework and Curriculum is a tool to support educators in the higher education system, trainers and coaches as well as entrepreneurs, professionals and learners at large interested in designing and evaluating personalized and self-directed training that best fits the needs of their company and workers. The proposed curriculum is grounded in pedagogical strategies of self-directed learning [13]. It therefore represents an approach to customize personalized learning paths aligned with the needs and interests of the learners within a competence framework, linking organizational and individual perspectives of digital transformation. Instead of imposing a one-size-fits-all curriculum a guidance is provided to develop motivating self-directed learning experiences. The VOIL framework is thought to be a guide for educators who want to either evaluate existing programs or to (re)design training programs focusing on the development of advanced digital skills.

In the following, this paper will first develop an understanding of digital transformation as a learning process related to dynamic capability theory. Subsequently the DIGROW digital maturity framework and the European e-competence framework will be explained and linked as a basis to create the VOIL Digital Transformation Competence Framework. The rationale of each of the four competence areas will be pointed out. Examples of learning objectives and possible learning journeys enabled by the Virtual Open Innovation Lab (VOIL) are provided. Section four sketches how to design self-directed and personalized learning journeys.

2   Digital Transformation as a Learning Process

Digital transformation is a learning process that requires integrating technology, business and learning strategies in an entrepreneurial-oriented organization. To understand such technology driven transformation processes Fountain's [8] technology enactment framework differentiates between objective and enacted technologies. Objective technology incorporates innovations such as analytics or the Internet, whereas enacted technology entails the use, design, and perception of those technologies by individuals within the organization. The role of technology, therefore, is dependent on the organization and what individuals within the organization make out of it. This observation is particularly relevant for SMEs where technology decisions depend on few people, their level of digital competencies and attitudes. Therefore, a competence framework for digital transformation and the related learning and development strategies have to allow an individualized appropriation of transformation capabilities related to an overall framework of digitally enabled growth.

Yeow et al. [20] found that as an organization shifts towards a digital strategy, misalignments between the emergent strategy and resources give rise to tension and requires alignment actions. These iteratively reconfigure organizational resources and refine strategy to respond to both changes in the environment and internal tensions. The dynamic capability approach provides a suitable analytical framework for organizations to purposefully align internal resources, processes, and structures to adapt to a changing environment. Sunday et al. [17] argue that using the concept of dynamic capabilities to examine the process of information communication technologies (ICT) adoption helps to unveil the recursive nature of the process. Following Teece [18] "For analytical purposes, dynamic capabilities can be disaggregated into the capacity (1) to sense and shape opportunities and threats, (2) to seize opportunities, and (3) to maintain competitiveness through enhancing, combining, protecting and, when necessary, reconfiguring the business enterprise's intangible and tangible assets" [18]. To act, a first step is to raise awareness of managers, workers, and students as future workers towards required capabilities, as well as opportunities/threats. Central to a successful transformation is the creation of a shared understanding of what "digitally enabled growth" means for the firm and subsequently develop and communicate a strategy.

In this transformation and learning journey individuals and organizations look for orientation, which can be provided by maturity models or frameworks. Maturity models allow the assessment of the current situation of a company as well as the identification of reasonable improvement measures [3] and serve as a guide through the transformation journey. Maturity can be defined as a measure to evaluate the capabilities of an organization regarding a certain discipline. Digital maturity means that a company has the necessary organizational capabilities to succeed in the digital transformation.

The VOIL competence framework is based on the DIGROW-Framework of digital maturity [14] which is visualized as a wheel of digitally enabled growth (see Fig. 1). The DIGROW-Framework serves to:

1. Raise awareness of owners, managers and employees of SMEs and students towards required capabilities, as well as opportunities/threats.
2. Create a shared understanding of what digitally enabled growth or digital transformation means.
3. Develop and communicate a strategy.
4. Anchor pilot initiatives in an overall "picture" of digitalization.
5. Compare own level of digital maturity with other firms.
6. Define learning objectives.

The theoretical foundation of the framework is Teece's [18] model of dynamic capability development. In their empirical study, Pavlou and El Sawy [21] deepened the understanding of how dynamic capabilities are developed and they proposed four steps: sensing, learning, integration, and coordination. These steps highlight the importance of managing knowledge and learning in digital transformation and of coping with turbulent and disruptive environments. A shortcoming in SMEs is that owners and managers are aware of growth potentials but often lack an explicit strategy, and if they have a strategy, they do not communicate that strategy to employees. That is why in the proposed model an intermediate step is inserted between Teece's "sensing" and "seizing": the step of strategy development and communication, which is related to Pavlou and El Sawy's [21] learning and integration.

The "DIGROW" framework, therefore, contains four dimensions, which can be seen as challenges (e.g. what are our challenges to sense digitally enabled growth potentials?) or competence areas or capabilities (e.g. do we have the capability to sense digitally enabled growth potentials?). Both views are useful in a self-assessment or in developing personalized learning paths. Along the lines of Teece's [18] micro-foundations of enterprise performance, North et al. [14] have defined four capacities for each of the four competency areas. Each of these capacities can be evaluated at five levels described by an anchor statement. It thus serves as an initial self-assessment as the basis for defining learning objectives.

The "DIGROW" framework is structured as follows:

1. Sensing digitally enabled growth potentials: Searching for digitally enabled growth opportunities, understanding, and developing digital customer needs, sensing technology driven opportunities, use of external sources for digital innovation.
2. Developing a digitally enabled growth strategy and mindset: Digitally enabled growth strategy, digital leadership, digital mindset (attitudes & behavior's), empowered employees.
3. Seizing digitally enabled growth potentials: Digitally enabled business models, digital market presence, digital customer experience, agile implementation/deployment of digitization initiatives.
4. Managing resources for digital transformation: Digital skills & learning, digital processes, digital technology & security, digital investments.

3   The VOIL Digital Transformation Competence Framework: Relating the DIGROW Framework to the European e-Competence Framework

The European e-Competence Framework (e-CF) version 3.0 [4] provides a reference of 41 competencies as required and applied at the Information and Communication Technology (ICT) workplace, using a common language for competences, skills and capability levels that can be understood across Europe. In the framework 'Competence is a demonstrated ability to apply knowledge, skills and attitudes for achieving observable results. The structure of the 41 competencies follows a logic of an ICT project with the phases plan – build – run – enable – manage. The framework, therefore, does not fully cover competencies needed for the digital transformation of companies.

For the VOIL Digital Transformation Competency Model the DIGROW dimensions have been matched to the 41 e-competencies. The result is displayed in Fig. 1. The result shows that the e-competencies are not evenly distributed across the DIGROW sections. Business and transformation related competencies are underrepresented in relation to ICT development and deployment. For the sections "Digital mindset" and "digitally empowered employees" there are no corresponding e-competencies. We therefore propose 4 additional competencies related to developing a shared vision, commitment, autonomy in decision making and self-organization. Educators are invited to customize the repertoire of competencies according to their specific curricular needs, i.e. add further business relevant competencies or delete competencies.

Based on the above foundations the following architecture of the VOIL competence framework is proposed:

- **Competence areas** are the highest-level categorization of competencies and are, therefore, more stable over time. The VOIL curriculum focuses on four competency areas:

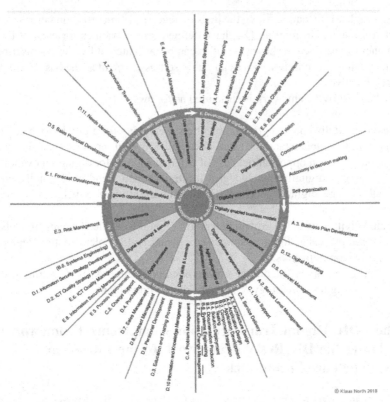

Fig. 1. European e-competence framework 3.0 related to the wheel of digitally enabled growth.

"Sensing digitally enabled growth potentials", "Developing a digitally enabled growth strategy and mindset", "Seizing digitally enabled growth potentials & transformation" and "Managing resources for digital transformation".

- **Competence categories** specify the actual competencies to be developed. The VOIL curriculum includes eight competency categories that must be attained at least at the Awareness level (knowledge needs to be recalled when needed) and desirably at the Novice level (the learner needs to have experienced situations and cases). These categories are the basis for defining the learning objectives of the training modules.
- **Competence** is a demonstrated ability to apply knowledge, skills, and attitudes for achieving observable results (European e-Competence Framework). It is an integrative concept that refers to cognitive and metacognitive skills as well as values and attitudes. Since competencies tend to be more vulnerable to changes in technology and, therefore, less stable, the competencies are listed in this document as examples (Table 1).

In the following, we will explain the rationale of each of the four competence areas, relate these to competencies of the European e-competence framework and propose

Table 1. The VOIL digital transformation competence framework.

Areas	1 Sensing digitally enabled growth potentials	2 Developing a digitally enabled growth strategy and mindset	3 Seizing digitally enabled growth potentials & transformation	4 Managing resources for digital transformation
Categories	1.1. Understand and monitor digital technologies and their business potentials 1.2. Develop digital customer needs	2.1. Review and design digital business strategy and business models 2.2. Develop a digital transformation culture	3.1. Transform the organization 3.2. Design/implement digital market presence and customer experience	4.1. Implement and manage digital processes 4.2. Manage digital risks and cybersecurity
Competencies	A.7. Technology trend monitoring E.1. Forecast development D.11. Needs identification D.5. Sales proposal development	A.1. IS and business strategy alignment A.3. Business plan development A.4. Product/ service planning A.8. Sustainable development E.9. IS governance D.9. Personnel development D.3. Education and training provision	E.7. Business change management E.2. Project and Portfolio management D.10. Information and knowledge management C.4. Problem management B.4. Solution deployment (see also M7) E.4. Relationship management D.12. Digital marketing D.6. Channel management	A.5. Architecture design A.6. Application design B.1. Application development B.2. Component integration B.3. Testing B.4. Solution deployment B.5. Documentation production B.6. Systems engineering D.1. Information security strategy development D.2. ICT quality strategy development E.6. ICT quality management E.8. Information security management E.3. Risk management

learning objectives. Examples of possible learning journeys enabled by the Virtual Open Innovation Lab (VOIL) are given.

3.1 Sensing Digitally Enabled Growth Potentials

To sense digitally enabled growth potentials, firms would need an intention to seek out and understand external information in order to identify new opportunities. In operational terms, SMEs must implement mechanisms and processes for scanning, observing and understanding changes in the business environment. Learning objectives relate to understanding the main digital technologies & applications, assess their business potentials and monitor technology trends. Digitally enabled innovation and growth opportunities arise from understanding and developing digital customer needs and from identifying technology-driven opportunities. A particularly fruitful source can be the use of external knowledge for digital innovation: (potential) customers, universities, research centres, "the crowd", partners in the "ecosystem". This competence area encompasses two competence categories: Understand and monitor digital technologies and their business potential and understand and develop digital customer needs (Table 2).

Table 2. Competencies and learning objectives to sense digitally enabled growth potentials

Categories	Related competencies of European e-competence framework	Learning objectives	Examples of learning journeys enabled by the VOIL platform
Understand and monitor digital technologies and their business potentials	A.7. Technology trend monitoring	Understand the main digital technologies & applications, assess their business potentials, monitor technology trends	DIGROW-assessment, simulators
Understand and develop digital customer needs	E.1. Forecast development D.11. Needs identification D.5. Sales proposal development	Identify and develop digital needs and expectations of (potential) customers, search for new value generation and growth opportunities	DIGROW-assessment, simulators

3.2 Developing a Digitally Enabled Growth Strategy and Mindset

Based on the exploration of possible futures, firms will have to develop an understanding of how digital solutions will help to deliver the firm's objectives and to review their strategy regarding digitalization. The question of how SMEs can succeed in the digital environment requires understanding what strategic orientation best equips SMEs to compete in that environment.

It is crucial that leaders (owner and/or managers of SMEs) recognize the potential of digitally enabled growth. Creating a shared understanding of how the digital world "ticks" is a prerequisite for motivating employees and developing a forward-looking attitude towards digitalization followed by a broad development of new behavior's ("digital mindset"). In such a digitally oriented organization, employees are empowered and encouraged to experiment with digital initiatives. This competence area includes the following competence categories: Review and design digital business strategy and business models and develop a digital transformation culture (Table 3).

Table 3. Competencies and learning objectives to develop a digitally enabled growth strategy and mindset.

Categories (modules)	Related competencies of European e-competence framework	Learning objectives	Examples of learning journeys enabled by the VOIL platform
Review and design digital business strategy and business models	A.1. IS and business strategy alignment A.3. Business plan development A.4. Product/service planning A.8. Sustainable development	Analyze current position of firm, develop a digital strategy, review & modify existing business models, creation of new business models, develop a business plan	DIGROW-self-assessment, co-creation canvas, procedure model
Develop a digital transformation culture	E.9. IS Governance E.2. Project and portfolio management E.3. Risk management E.7. Business change management D.9. Personnel development D.3. Education and training provision D.10. Information and knowledge management C.4. Problem management	Digital leadership, development of a digital mindset, empower employees for digital initiatives	"Learning to grow" methodology co-creation canvas

3.3 Seizing Digitally Enabled Growth Potentials and Transformation

To exploit identified opportunities or mitigate threats of digitalization, SMEs have to revise business strategies and decide whether to adapt current business models or develop new ones. This is linked to investment choices and preparedness to enter into new fields, such key elements are digital market presence and digital customer experience leading to new ways of value creation, value capture and value offer. Depending on their current stage of development, SMEs might perceive business potentials of digitalization but acknowledge their current unpreparedness for implementing the required new technologies. Therefore, the ability to deploy digitalization initiatives is crucial to seizing perceived opportunities. This might include small pilot projects and/or methodologies for agile product and service development, such as design thinking. The competence categories that this competence area integrates are as follows: Transform the organization and Design/implement digital market presence and customer experience (Table 4).

Table 4. Competencies and learning objectives to seize digitally enabled growth potentials & transformation the organization

Categories	Related competencies of European e-competence framework	Learning objectives	Examples of learning journeys enabled by the VOIL platform
Transform the organization	E.7. Business change management B.4. Solution deployment (see also M7) E.4. Relationship management	Change management, process model of digital transformation, digitalization road map, co-creation, collaboration with external partners, agile deployment of initiatives	DIGROW-self-assessment, Co-creation canvas, procedure model "Learning to grow" methodology
Design/implement digital market presence and customer experience	D.12. Digital marketing D.6. Channel management	Business analytics, digital marketing, channel management	

3.4 Managing Resources for Digital Transformation

Managing threats and transforming the organization requires, the continuous alignment and realignment of resources such as knowledge of people, technologies which are embedded in processes and financial investments. Finally, this competence area encompasses the following competence categories: Implement and manage digital processes comprising the capacity to digitalize the organization's processes in order to achieve higher efficiency and efficacy in the execution of the business goals. As well as competencies to manage digital risks and cybersecurity, i.e. the adoption of technologies that guarantee the security in business processes, data, and customers, against possible external attacks and/or an inadequate use of data (Table 5).

4 Outlook: Designing Self-directed and Personalized Learning Journeys

As the main focus of this paper is to present and explain the foundations of the VOIL competence framework in this section we will provide an outlook how this framework can be used by educators or instructional designers and learners to design customized learning paths (CLP). CLP allow learners to co-design their learning with educators rather than simply comply with the directions and expectations of a traditional education process. Customized learning path help learners in taking ownership of their learning, finding greater meaning and purpose, and becoming increasingly independent in their learning skills.

Table 5. Competencies and learning objectives to manage resources for digital transformation.

Categories	Related competencies of European e-competence framework	Learning objectives	Examples of learning journeys enabled by the VOIL platform
Implement and manage digital processes	E.7. Business change management A.5. Architecture design A.6. Application design B.1. Application development B.2. Component integration B.3. Testing B.4. Solution deployment B.5. Documentation production B.6. Systems engineering	Design and deployment of new processes in different areas of the firm	Procedure model
Manage digital risks and cybersecurity	(B.6. Systems engineering) D.1. Information security strategy development D.2. ICT quality strategy development E.6. ICT Quality management E.8. Information security management E.3. Risk management	Deal with digital risks and improve information security and reliability	Simulators

The VOIL competence model is constructed in a way that it enables the design of these personalized learning journeys. To allow this kind of configurability, a component-based architecture of the competence model is needed. Similar to the idea of decoupling applications in software engineering, the competence model aims at decoupling its elements into layers of different levels of abstraction. This layered component-based structure allows two things. First, components can be replaced, extended, or adjusted if changes in the context of the digital transformation occur, for instance, if new technologies demand the development of new Competences. Second, this structure sets the foundation for a flexible design of curricula. Thereby, tailored competence collections can be designed and implemented. Depending on the needs of a study program, a firm or an individual learner relevant competence can be selected and related to educational resources. Let us consider an example: Results of the DIGROW digital maturity assessment might point to the need to better "understand and monitor digital technologies and their business potentials" in the case of block chain. On the VOIL platform learners might use the block chain simulator to understand how block chain works and guided by educators or interacting with peers might learn to assess concrete business potentials.

Through the application of a set of strategies and guidelines for deriving tailored competence collections, a specific instance of the competence model can be created. These strategies and guidelines help educators in their task of creating their own digital transformation curriculum in a structured way. The competence model together with strategies and guidelines to apply the model and derive curricula compose the so-called Meta Level. This level can be interpreted as a generic configurable reference perspective. By applying strategies and guidelines, educators are equipped with a toolset to compile customized curricula. This instantiation leads to the definition and selection of actual modules, learning objectives, learning experiences and courses, which together make up the Instance Level (see Fig. 2).

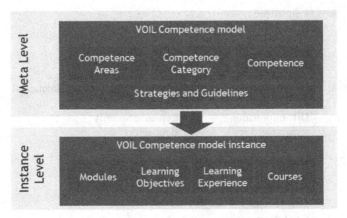

Fig. 2. Two levels of customized curricula design.

The instantiation process leads to the creation of these personalized learning journeys, which are tailored to an organization's needs and starting point. Instead of being confronted with a one-size-fits-all curriculum and learning material, learners are equipped with their personal need-based curriculum.

Therefore, a plethora of different learning journeys will exist. On the VOIL platform these journeys shall be augmented by selected material in form of simulators, tools, methods, etc. Therefore, competence framework and the concept of instantiating it set the foundational architecture for the VOIL platform.

5   Conclusions

The VOIL Digital Transformation Competence Framework links two established frameworks: The DIGROW Framework of digital maturity and the European e-Competence

Framework. In the matching of both frameworks it became obvious that the European e-Competence Framework in particular business and transformation related competencies are underrepresented in relation to ICT development and deployment. Therefore, additional competencies have been proposed, which still need to be validated. The VOIL Competence Framework fills a gap of research as it overcomes two deficits of systematic skill compilations for digital transformation. Firstly, it has a wholistic business focus representing all phases of digitally enabled growth. Secondly it is grounded in dynamic capability theory, which currently is the accepted basis to explain sustainable competitiveness in turbulent environments. As the VOIL project is initial phase test of the frameworks have not yet been performed. Furthermore, the above sketched instantiation approach to define and select competence collections, learning objectives and to create learning experiences and courses needs still to be matured.

Acknowledgments. The paper is developed as part of the project VOIL - "Virtual Open Innovation Lab", the European Union program Erasmus+ (2019-1-DE01-KA203-005021). www.voil.eu.

References

1. Baradhwaj, A., El Sawy, O.A., Pavlou, P.A., Venkatraman, N.: Digital business strategy: towards a next generation of insights. MIS Q. **37**(2), 471–482 (2013)
2. Bounfour, A.: Digital Futures Digital Transformation. Springer, Heidelberg (2016)
3. Becker, J., Knackstedt, R., Pöppelbuß, J.: Developing maturity models for IT management. Bus. Inf. Syst. Eng. **1**(3), 213–222 (2009)
4. CEN: European Norm (EN) 16234-1 European e-Competence Framework (e-CF) (2016). https://www.ecompetences.eu/
5. EAEA: The future of adult learning in Europe. Background paper - European Association for the Education of Adults (2019). https://eaea.org/wp-content/uploads/2019/12/The-future-of-adult-learning-in-Europe.pdf. Accessed 21 Apr 2020
6. European E-Skills Forum: E-Skills for Europe: Towards 2010 and beyond (2004). https://www.bvekennis.nl/Bibliotheek/09-0484_e-skills-forum-2004-09-fsr.pdf
7. EU (European Commission): Digital Transformation Scoreboard 2018 (2018). https://op.europa.eu/en/publication-detail/-/publication/683fe365-408b-11e9-8d04-01aa75ed71a1
8. Fountain, J.E.: Prospects of the Virtual State. University of Tokyo 21st Century COE program "Invention of Policy Systems in Advanced Countries" (2004)
9. IDC-SAP: The next steps in digital transformation. How small and midsize companies are applying technology to meet key business goals (2017). http://news.sap.com/wp-content/blogs.dir/1/files/SAP_IDC_infobrief_SMB_DX_102016.pdf
10. Galliers, R.D.: Further developments in information systems strategizing: unpacking the concept. In: Galliers, R.D., Currie, W.L. (eds.) The Oxford Handbook of Management Information Systems: Critical Perspectives and New Directions, pp. 329–345. Oxford University Press, Oxford (2011)
11. Haenisch, S.: The Future of Learning – Top 7 Predictions for 2030 (2017). https://blogs.sap.com/2017/11/22/the-future-of-learning-top-7-predictions-for-2030/. Accessed 15 Apr 2020
12. Kahre, C., Hoffmann, D., Ahlemann, F.: Beyond business-IT alignment - digital business strategies as a paradigmatic shift: a review and research agenda. In: Proceedings of the 50th Hawaii International Conference on System Sciences, pp. 4706–4715 (2017)

13. Knowles, M.S.: Self-Directed Learning. Association Press, New York (1975)
14. North, K., Aramburu, N., Lorenzo, O.: Promoting digitally enabled growth in SMEs: a framework proposal. J. Enterp. Inf. Manag. **33**(1), 238–262 (2019). https://doi.org/10.1108/JEIM-04-2019-0103
15. OECD: The Future of Education and Skills. Education 2030, p. 4 (2018). https://www.oecd.org/education/2030/E2030%20Position%20Paper%20(05.04.2018).pdf. Accessed 20 Apr 2020
16. Šereš, L., Tumbas, P., Matkovic, P., Pavlićević, V.: Embedding digital competencies in business informatics curriculum. In: 2nd Conference on Innovative Teaching Methods (ITM 2017), 28–29 June 2017, University of Economics Varna, Bulgaria (2017)
17. Sunday, C.E., Vera, C.: Examining information and communication technology (ICT) adoption in SMEs: A dynamic capabilities approach. J. Enterp. Inf. Manag. **31**(2), 338–356 (2018)
18. Teece, D.J.: Explicating dynamic capabilities: the nature and microfoundations of (sustainable) enterprise performance. Strateg. Manag. J. **28**(4), 1319–1350 (2007)
19. Vial, G.: Understanding digital transformation: a review and a research agenda. J. Strateg. Inf. Syst. **28**, 118–144 (2019)
20. Yeow, A., Soh, C., Hansen, R.: Aligning with new digital strategy: a dynamic capabilities approach. J. Strateg. Inf. Syst. **27**, 43–58 (2018)
21. Pavlou, P.A., El Sawy, O.A.: Understanding the elusive black box of dynamic capabilities. Decis. Sci. **42**(1), 239–273 (2011)

Gamified Evaluation in Game-Based Learning

Pavel Boytchev[1]([⊠]) [iD] and Svetla Boytcheva[2] [iD]

[1] Faculty of Mathematics and Informatics - KIT, Sofia University "St. Kliment
Ohridski", Sofia, Bulgaria
boytchev@fmi.uni-sofia.bg
[2] Institute of Information and Communication Technologies, Bulgarian Academy
of Sciences, Sofia, Bulgaria
svetla.boytcheva@gmail.com

Abstract. Gamification is the processes of introducing game-specific
elements into a non-game context. It allows the application of the Game-
based Learning approach in traditional educational contexts. This paper
presents our efforts in gamification of students' evaluation. The learning environment Meiro, used for demonstration and exploration in the
domain of Computer Graphics, is extended with modules for students'
evaluation. The paper presents these models and discusses the preliminary results of end-users tests.

Keywords: Gamification · Gamification in evaluation · Meiro
environment · 3D models

1 Gamification in Evaluation

Gamification is defined as the set of processes and activities, which introduce
game-specific elements into a non-game context. Game-specific elements range
from scoring achievements and use of gaming visuals to competitions, teaming
and rankings. The usage of this term exploded about 10 years ago, according
to data from Google Trends. Figure 1 shows the popularity of *gamification* since
2004. Additionally, the 8 terms most closely related to gamification are *learning,
marketing, classroom, application software, training, motivation, gamification of
learning* and *e-Learning*. This paper is related to all of them except for the
marketing.

A learning approach based on games is called Game Based Learning (GBL)
and it could be implemented with or without gamification. Learning activities,

The research is partially supported by the National Scientific Program "Information
and Communication Technologies in Science, Education and Security" (ICTinSES)
financed by the Ministry of Education and Science; and by Sofia University "St. Kliment
Ohridski" research science fund project N80-10-18/18.03.2020 "Use of high-tech tools
for development of competency models in training". The authors do not thank the
Scientific Research Centre (NIS).

A. Lopata et al. (Eds.): ICIST 2020, CCIS 1283, pp. 297–308, 2020.
https://doi.org/10.1007/978-3-030-59506-7_24

which are designed from scratch as game-like activities, do not need explicit gamification. Gamification is needed when some existing non-GBL entity is converted into the corresponding GBL entity. In respect to education there is a huge amount of educational knowledge, which is non-GBL, but its gamification is supposed to be advantageous to learning. One of the most praised benefit of the GBL is that its approaches allow blending of learning and evaluating into a single activity, much like games, and in contrast to the traditional education.

This paper presents our efforts and experience with introducing gamification in university education. Our focus is targeted at the evaluation process. The rest of this section presents a short overview of gamification in evaluation research at other institutions. Section 2 describes our educational environment, which is used for teaching and learning, but is not extended to cover students' evaluation. Section 3 provides short reviews of the specially developed software models, which handle the gamified evaluation. The preliminary results of end-users tests are discussed in Sect. 4 and the last Sect. 5 lists our future plans.

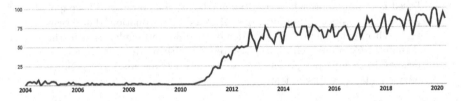

Fig. 1. Popularity of *gamification* according to Google Trends (data retrieved 03'2020 from https://trends.google.com/trends/explore?date=all&q=%2Fm%2F0cm8xv9)

During the years of popularity the term *"Gamification"* evolves, and there are different perceptions, aspects and definitions related to it. Landers et al. present the history of gamification [9] and argue for a different perception of the term in business and education. In sales practices the term seems to tend to have a more negative impact and is highly criticised, as opposed to teaching methods, where it is considered a more advanced method of education. Raczkowski [13] presents different aspects of gamification and refers back to 60s term "token economies" as one of the early attempts for using behaviouristic methods for influencing the human behaviour. Huotari and Hamari [5] study different definitions of gamification, based on a service metaphor and classify game conditions used in it.

These aspects and perspectives also depend on the particular applications of gamification. Dicheva et al. [3] present an overview of gamification applications in various levels and subjects in education. More close to our research is the application of gamification in science, technology, engineering and mathematics (STEM) [6], where the authors analyze success and effectiveness in gamification implementation depending on huge specter of factors, like specifics of the subject thought, the level of education, the educational goals and student needs. The problem of distrust to this method is that in many cases the systems are badly designed with the accent on the technical aspects only, and lack educational purposes, that results to negative experience in students. Rapp et al. [14] present the current challenges of gamification and point out that the main problem is poor game design. The authors of [16] analyze various gaps in the design and implementation of gamification and offer different heuristics of gamification that take into account a wide range of additional factors such as user characteristics, context requirements, system properties, and last but not least – the important role of design.

One of the major objectives of gamification is to increase students' motivation for learning and their interest in the subject. This goal is achieved by active student participation in the educational process. Besides the gamification, the classical methods for active learning are: inquiry based learning, learning by doing, and project based learning. Lister [11] points out that there are different levels of motivation in gamification of weaker and stronger students, and the later one show lower motivation to use it. Some elements of the gamification shows significant impact on the performance and engagement of weaker students. He evaluates the impact and limitations of different game mechanics like points, levels, badges/achievements, leader boards, virtual currency and avatars. In addition, opportunities for sharing the artefacts of game mechanics with peers through social networks or game increases their value especially in multi-agent games [18]. Creation of catalogues of some patterns in gamification [1] can be beneficial for their further implementation.

Despite the many problems mentioned so far with the difficulties of applying gaming, it is gratifying that there are also a number of examples of successful application of gamification in STEM university courses. It worth to mention as best practices some STEM courses, which topics and objectives are related to courses discussed in this paper like: Software Engineering course [8], Computer Programming course [15], and Computer Graphics with WebGL course [17].

When applying gamification to the training, one basic question arises – this is about assessing the trainees during the course and making a final assessment of the course. Naturally, the application of sophisticated training techniques also implies the use of more complex assessment mechanisms. In many cases the gamification is used in blended learning format, where self-assessment evaluation methods and classical teacher monitoring are combined [7]. Hamari and Eranti [4] define a framework for student achievements in gamification that can help further development of other achievements.

Unlike multi-agent gaming systems, the proposed solution in this paper does not allow grades and tasks to be shared among students/agents, and in addition – no cooperation in solving problems is allowed. The students are assigned individual tasks and no collisions are possible during their journey in the game. Such idea is investigated by Polar and Woźniak [12] and they propose an approach for avoiding students/agents collisions in gamification, based on planning method for their moves, inspired by the simulated annealing algorithm idea. Our approach is based on generating an individual *sand-boxed* gaming environment for each student.

2   The Educational Environment Meiro

The educational environment Meiro is created to provide a game-like experience for CS students enrolled in the Fundamentals of Computer Graphics (FCG) course at Faculty of Mathematics and Informatics, Sofia University [10]. It is visualized as a maze with configurable complexity – Fig. 2.

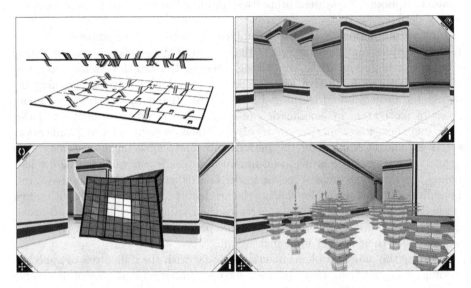

Fig. 2. A floor plan and an empty hall of the Meiro maze (*top row*) and two models inside the maze (*bottom row*).

Initially Meiro is used for two activities:

– In-class *demonstration* of concepts from the domain of computer graphics;
– Out-class *exploration* of these concepts to support self-studying

These activities are supported by virtual models, which are located inside the maze. When used during classes, it is possible to isolate individual models and incorporate them in the presentation materials. To complete the process of gamification, we started to enrich the environment with 10 models for students' evaluation, as the process of learning and the process of evaluation naturally happen concurrently in a game. These efforts are an improvement to our earlier experience with more traditionally oriented evaluation approaches [2]. These models are tested with over 100 students in 2019/2020 and the students are surveyed. The analyses of the tests and the surveys are to be completed by mid-2020, so that there is time to improve the evaluation models and to use them for real since October 2020.

Meiro is a multilevel 3D maze environment and a software framework for defining Meiro models. Currently there are almost 300 interactive 3D models covering all topics included in the lectures of FCG – Fig. 3.

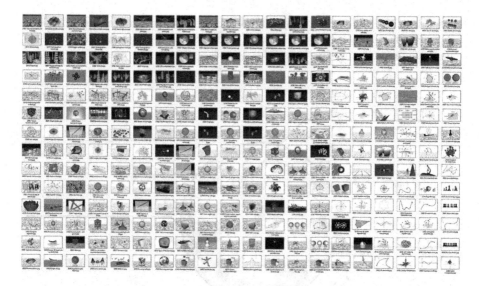

Fig. 3. The collection of 3D models used for demonstration and exploration. Each model is referenced in the lecture notes of FCG.

Turning Meiro into an evaluation environment is completed by extending its architecture with *evaluation models*, supporting the same interface as all other 3D models; a *model configurator* that customizes the models to a desired difficulty level; and a *streaming evaluation*, converting students' interactions into evaluation-ready values.

The gamified evaluation requires changes in the fabrics of scores. A gameplay generates a continuous stream of scores across 17 predefined competences, stored as a vector. This vector is used to capture, store and process both students' and problems' competences. It is visualized as a radar competence diagram via one of the evaluation models – i.e. this model is responsible for in-game visualization of the vectored score. The streaming aspect of vector scores leads to a situation, when a student has multiple (hundreds or more) individual scores for each of the 17 competences. For example, for a given competence X the gameplay generates n scores $\{x_1, x_2, \ldots, x_n\}$ aggregated into a single score X_n. As LMS aggregation functions are not suitable for such type of aggregation, we use own aggregation functions called *temporal average*. It supports easy incremental calculation as new scores arrive; it respects individual scores, but suppresses incidental fluctuations; and it captures score tendencies over time. The temporal average X_n is represented recurrently as a liner combination between the previous aggregated score X_{n-1} and the new individual score x_n: $X_n = (1 - \alpha)x_n + \alpha X_{n-1}$, where $X_0 = 0$, and $\alpha \in (0, 1)$ controls the sensitivity to fluctuations and the impact of time distance (i.e. the weight factor for old scores).

The intended application of temporal average is to aggregate streaming vector scores of the same competence vectors – this is when the same student solves multiple times one or more problems with compatible competence profiles.

A scenario where temporal average should not be applied is when the scores of a group of students are aggregated. In this case individual vectors do not represent achievements along the time axis.

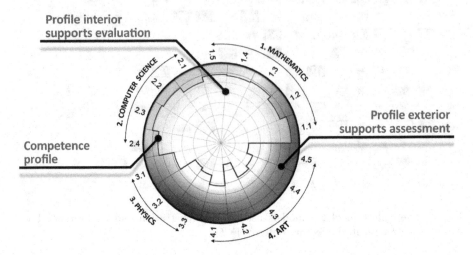

Fig. 4. Using competence radar diagrams to shape the competence profiles of students and to support both evaluation and assessment of students.

The proposed gamified evaluation generates sufficient data to build the radar competence diagram of a student, similar to Fig. 4. The competence profile is the boundary of the white area in the diagram, which extends to the level of gained competence in each of the 17 individual competence. Thus the area inside the profile is used for the evaluation of the student, while the outside area supports assessment decisions.

3   The Evaluation Models

The design of the evaluation models is a balance of two entities – interface compatibility with Meiro and the goal of gamified evaluation. The evaluation models are interactive 3D models resembling reallife objects and inheriting some of their functionalities. The models provide general game-like interactivity like navigation and orbiting, but also support specific interactivity, controlling the game mechanics of the model. Pedagogically, the design of the evaluation models spreads on four mutually complementing features:

- providing subtle clues that provoke decision creativity;
- supporting random configuration within controlled difficulty;
- streaming feedback of vector scores based on gameplay;
- building and testing theoretical knowledge, practical skills and intuition.

The first developed evaluation model is *The CMY reservoir*. It is a tank with colour pipes that add cyan, magenta or yellow water in the tank and an additional drainage pipe – Fig. 5, left. The challenge is to fill the tank with water with the same colour as a plate inside the tank. The model is designed with several subtle hints, like the colour ring for colour composition, the tile-based ruler on the frame, the marks on the tank glass. Thus, students may solve the challenge by either experimenting with different inks, or by calculating their proportions. One of the possible ways to verify the correctness of the solution is to check the visibility of the colour plate – if its colour is the same as the colour of the water, it becomes practically invisible.

The right image in Fig. 5 is a snapshot of *The Dome of difference*. This is a glass jar with several jumping jelly balls. The goal of the model is to identify which ball is different from the others. The difference could the in the ball size, the height of the jump or the frequency of the bouncing. Students may follow several strategies, but the most employed one is to use the air stoppers to freeze some balls. Sometimes differences can be heard rather than seen. For example, the sound of bouncing creates an acoustic pattern. A change in this pattern is an indication of different jumping frequencies.

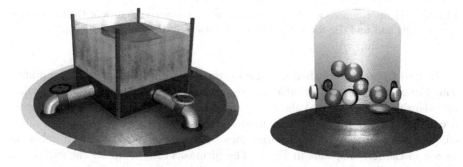

Fig. 5. The CMY reservoir explores color generation (*left*), while the Dome of difference is used to practice comparison of objects' properties (*right*)

The Constructive solid geometry is a method for describing complex geometrical shapes as algebraic expressions on primitive geometrical data. *The geometric cipher* model is a device that can build such expressions – Fig. 6, left. The primitive shapes are circles named after the Eastern four elements (earth, water, fire and wind). More complex shaped can be generated by using parentheses, however, nesting parentheses is not allowed. This is intended behaviour to force students to transform deep algebraic expressions into shallow one.

For simplicity, the exploration of constructive solid geometry is limited to flat shapes. For 3D objects we developed another model, called *The Euler's grill*. The task is to determine the most important topological invariant of polyhedra – the Euler characteristics χ defined by the extended Euler's polyhedron formula: $\chi = V - E + F = 2 - 2T$, where V is the number of vertices, E is the number of edges, F is the number of faces and T is the number of tunnels. The model is a rotating barbeque grilling a complex 3D shape – Fig. 6, right. There are different approaches for finding χ – from using brute force and counting the number of faces, edges and vertices to using polyhedron formula. The model is open for further research and experimentation, because the equation for χ is for tunnels that do not intersect or touch each other, while some of the more complex configurations of the grill use exactly such type of topology.

Fig. 6. Students compose algebraic expressions for geometric shapes in the Geometric cipher (*left*) and find the topological characteristic χ in the Euler's grill (*right*)

In 1967 Cohen and Sutherland develop an algorithm for efficient line clipping. *The Cohen-Sutherland's thimble* model explores the bitmasks associated with this algorithm. The original algorithm is designed for rectangular clipping region framed by 4 lines, but the Meiro model extends the challenge by adding more clipping lines forming curved subregions. The model looks like a thimble as shown in the left snapshot in Fig. 7. The bitmasks are set up on the surface of the thimble. Two of the randomly generated layout are shown in the central snapshots. The challenge for the students is to invent how to apply the original algorithm in a different situation.

The last image in Fig. 7 is a snapshot of *The Pick's plates* model. There are two vertical plates and sliders bound to polygon vertices. The problem is to reshape the polygons to achieve equal areas. The difficulty in this model is that the plate and the sliders are generated in a way, that the polygons are "incompatible". As with the other evaluation models, students may try different approaches – from calculating the areas from coordinates to using the Pick's theorem. There is an audio hint as a Geiger counter, which beeps faster when the areas are closer in size.

Matrices are widely used in computer graphics. They implement translation, scaling, rotation, mirroring and various types of projections. *The matrix carousel* model shows several coordinate systems riding a carousel – Fig. 8, left. Each coordinate system represents a specific matrix transformation, which is also written on the floor. The student plays the model by spinning the carousel and stopping

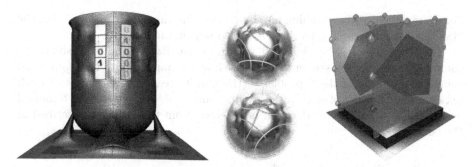

Fig. 7. A side view of the Cohen-Sutherland's thimble (*left*), its interior of intersecting areas (*center*) and the Pick's plates for constructing polygons (*right*)

it so that each coordinate system is above its corresponding matrix. The transformations are visualized as animations – there is a cube in each coordinate system, that is continuously changing its shape via some matrix.

The eighth evaluation model in Meiro is *The Loop's torus* – a 3D shape with a mesh net on its surface. An example of the mesh is shown in Fig. 8, right. The goal is to determine the location of a new vertex for a marked fragment if the mesh is subdivided by the Loop's algorithm. The mesh for every instance of the model is generated randomly. Depending on the desired difficulty, the mesh is mapped onto cylinders, torii or more complex shapes, like trifoliums.

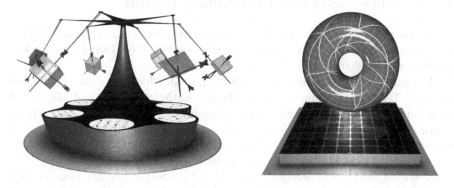

Fig. 8. The Matrix carousel in motion over matrices stamped on the floor (*left*) and the Loop's torus for manual subdivision (*right*)

The last Meiro model build for evaluation is *The butterfly flight*. Students design the DNA of a butterfly to perform a flight through a maze – Fig. 9, left. The DNA is composed of colour-coded series of avionic rotations around the normal, transverse and longitudinal axes of the butterfly. The difficulty of the model is controlled by the size of the maze and by the set of available rotations.

For example, a positive pitching motion (i.e. raising the "nose" and lowering the "tail") can be represented as three negative pitching motions.

The tenth model, shown in Fig. 9, right, is a visualization model. It shows the competence profile of a student (the whitish area) mapped onto the aggregated competence profile of the 9 problems (the bluish area). The model can switch between three metrics of aggregated results – maximal, average and our temporal average. The data for this diagram is collected from the log files, described in the next section.

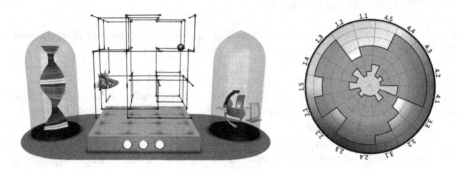

Fig. 9. The Butterfly flight model with a 3D maze and DNA structure (*left*) and the in-game radar diagram for accumulated vector score (*right*)

4   Students' Tests and Preliminary Results

In December 2019 the evaluation Meiro models are given to CS students for end-user testing. There are three sets of data that are collected during these tests – log files, students' surveys and a forum participations.

The gameplay of each model generates log data, which are stored for further analysis. These data include general playing statistics (number of clicks, test duration, ...), system information (model number, student ID, ...) and scoring information (difficulty level, competence vector, ...). Apart from the evaluation, the data from the log files is used to identify possible cheats.

According to the log files 186 students took part in the end-user testing – 121 of them used the LMS to access the models and the rest 65 worked anonymously. We collected data for 19 thousands gameplays for almost 400 h and with over 1 million mouse clicks or taps.

All students were asked to take part in a survey and to express openly their observations about the models. The survey was implemented as a quiz activity in Moodle. Traditionally the Faculty of Mathematics and Informatics, Sofia University conducts students' surveys about the quality of education. The average participation for the FCG course is between 10% and 25%, thus we expected a similar activity for the Meiro survey. To our surprise we received 125 filled surveys about the 3D models, which accounts for 83% student's activity. We received almost 800 individual answers worth 68 continuous pages of text.

The students' observations were focused on technical, interaction and pedagogical issues. We asked the students to work with their personal computers and mobile devices in order to test the applicability of the mobile 3D technology. Only a few problems were reported, mostly related to the initial configuration of the devices. We got some really nice suggestions for the user interface to make it more friendly to mobile or touch-screen users.

Most of the students expressed their enthusiasm of using 3D gaming environment instead of traditional tests. However, they asked for more information about temporal average, as they are not accustomed to its properties.

During the test period we opened an online forum for the students to share their experience with the models as a mutual aid. We also encouraged them to share hints and tricks, and as a side effect we learned a lot about how students approach problems and what information is really helpful to them.

5 Conclusion and Further Work

This paper presents our overall approach to gamify the evaluation of university students in a computer-graphics related course. The approach consists of implementation of competence profiles and temporal average aggregation metric for streaming vector scores; and a set of interactive 3D models for handling the actual gamified evaluation.

Presented are the preliminary results of end-user tests with over 100 undergraduate CS students, conducted from December 2019 to January 2020. The results confirm the positive impact of our approach and the increased students' motivation.

The preliminary results inspire us to continue our work on the gamified evaluation in several aspects. We will first complete the analysis of all data, especially in respect to the development of *computer graphics soft skills* (some of the soft skill covered by our models are identifying similarity of colours, estimating or approximating properties, using non-visual senses, determining motion synchronisation, spacial memory and chaining geometrical transformations).

Then we will improve the evaluation models considering the result of our analyses and the students' recommendations; and we will embed them in the next FCG course starting October 2020. Until January 2021 the models will be used for exploration, self-studying and evaluation. In addition we plan improve the models with mobile augmented reality.

References

1. Arango-López, J., Ruiz, S., Taborda, J.P., Gutiérrez Vela, F.L., Collazos, C.A., et al.: Gamification patterns: a catalog to enhance the learning motivation (2017)
2. Boytchev, P., Boytcheva, S.: Evaluation and assessment in tel courses. AIP Conf. Proc. **2048**(1), 020035 (2018)
3. Dicheva, D., Dichev, C., Agre, G., Angelova, G.: Gamification in education: a systematic mapping study. J. Educ. Technol. Soc. **18**(3) (2015)

4. Hamari, J., Eranti, V.: Framework for designing and evaluating game achievements. In: Digra Conference. Citeseer (2011)
5. Huotari, K., Hamari, J.: A definition for gamification: anchoring gamification in the service marketing literature. Electron. Markets **27**(1), 21–31 (2016). https://doi.org/10.1007/s12525-015-0212-z
6. Kim, S., Song, K., Lockee, B., Burton, J.: Gamification cases in education. Gamification in Learning and Education. AGL, pp. 117–123. Springer, Cham (2018). https://doi.org/10.1007/978-3-319-47283-6_10
7. Kim, S., Song, K., Lockee, B., Burton, J.: Gamification Cases in Education, pp. 117–123. Springer, Cham (2018). https://doi.org/10.1007/978-3-319-47283-6_10
8. Kiper, J.: Gamification in SE courses (2019)
9. Landers, R.N., Auer, E.M., Collmus, A.B., Armstrong, M.B.: Gamification science, its history and future: definitions and a research agenda. Simul. Gaming **49**(3), 315–337 (2018)
10. Lekova, M., Boytchev, P.: Virtual learning environment for computer graphics university course. In: Proceeding of 12th International Technology, Education and Development Conference, IATED Academy, pp. 3301–3309 (2018)
11. Lister, M.: Gamification: the effect on student motivation and performance at the post-secondary level. Issues Trends Educ. Technol. **3**(2) (2015)
12. Połap, D., Woźniak, M.: The impact of the cost function on the operation of the intelligent agent in 2D games. In: Damaševičius, R., Vasiljevienė, G. (eds.) ICIST 2018. CCIS, vol. 920, pp. 293–302. Springer, Cham (2018). https://doi.org/10.1007/978-3-319-99972-2_23
13. Raczkowski, F.: Making points the point: towards a history of ideas of gamification. In: Fuchs, M. (ed.) Rethinking Gamification, pp. 141–160 (2014)
14. Rapp, A., Hopfgartner, F., Hamari, J., Linehan, C., Cena, F.: Strengthening gamification studies: current trends and future opportunities of gamification research (2019)
15. Rojas-López, A., Rincón-Flores, E.G., Mena, J., García-Peñalvo, F.J., Ramírez-Montoya, M.S.: Engagement in the course of programming in higher education through the use of gamification. Universal Access Inf. Soc. **18**(3), 583–597 (2019). https://doi.org/10.1007/s10209-019-00680-z
16. van Roy, R., Zaman, B.: Why gamification fails in education and how to make it successful: introducing nine gamification heuristics based on self-determination theory. In: Ma, M., Oikonomou, A. (eds.) Serious Games and Edutainment Applications, pp. 485–509. Springer, Cham (2017). https://doi.org/10.1007/978-3-319-51645-5_22
17. Villagrasa, S., Duran, J.: Gamification for learning 3D computer graphics arts. In: Proceedings of the First International Conference on Technological Ecosystem for Enhancing Multiculturality, pp. 429–433. ACM (2013)
18. Winnicka, A., Kęsik, K., Połap, D., Woźniak, M., Marszałek, Z.: A multi-agent gamification system for managing smart homes. Sensors **19**(5), 1249 (2019)

Hyperparameter Tuning Using Automated Methods to Improve Models for Predicting Student Success

Bogdan Drăgulescu(✉) and Marian Bucos

Politehnica University Timişoara, Timişoara, Romania
{bogdan.dragulescu,marian.bucos}@upt.ro

Abstract. Predicting student failure is an important task for educators and a popular application in Educational Data Mining. However, building prediction models is not an easy task and requires time and expertise for feature engineering, model selection, and hyperparameters tuning. In this paper, a strategy of automatic machine learning is used to assess the impact on the performance of prediction models. A previous experiment was modified to include hyperparameter tuning with an autoML method for hyperparameters tuning. The data cleaning, preprocessing, feature engineering and time segmentation approach part of the experiment remained unchanged. With this approach, the correct impact on model performance by hyperparameter tuning can be measured on models that were carefully built. The results show improved performance especially for Decision Tree, Extra Tree, Random Forest Classifiers. This study shows that even carefully planned educational prediction models can benefit for the use of autoML methods and could help non-expert users in the field of EDM to achieve accurate results.

Keywords: Automatic machine learning · Educational data mining · Predicting student performance

1 Introduction

Increase usage of information technologies in the educational process has led to the accumulation of metadata about the process itself. This led to the adaptation of Data Mining methods (association, classification, regression, clustering, density estimation) towards exploring this data for enhancing the quality and efficiency of the educational process. These objectives are addressed in the research field of Educational Data Mining (EDM) [1].

One popular application of Data Mining in education is the prediction of students' performance [2]. Peña-Ayala argued that many indicators of performance are worthy to be modelled, for example [1]: evaluation, efficiency, competence, correctness, etc. According to the author, the primary goal of performance modelling is to estimate the student capability to complete a given task. Researchers approached this problem with different methods: comparing classification models to predict student success or failure

© Springer Nature Switzerland AG 2020
A. Lopata et al. (Eds.): ICIST 2020, CCIS 1283, pp. 309–320, 2020.
https://doi.org/10.1007/978-3-030-59506-7_25

[3, 4], using regression models to predict the final marks [5], or predicting final grades of students by a Recurrent Neural Network [6].

Higher education institutions are interested in modelling student academic performance to improve the quality of the educational process and increase the retention rate [7]. Most of the methods used for modelling student performance require tasks as feature engineering and reduction, model selection and hyperparameters tuning which are not straightforward and require knowledge and expertise. To be effective in practice, systems have to automatically resolve the previously mentioned tasks [8]. Recent works have started to tackle this problem in automated machine learning (autoML). Although autoML addresses all the steps mentioned above the central focus is on the hyperparameter optimization part of the machine learning process. Hyperparameters are the parameters of the machine learning algorithm whose values are set before the learning process begins (e.g. the depth of the tree in a Decision Tree Classifier).

In this paper, we focus on evaluating the impact on prediction model performance by employing an autoML strategy for hyperparameters tuning. Given the difficulty of the task to optimize the hyperparameters we estimate that this approach will even improve the performance of prediction models that are carefully built. To test this hypothesis, we reuse a previous experiment in which we developed models to predict students at risk [9] and added autoML methods for hyperparameters optimization.

Previous work in this field of applying autoML in EDM was done by Tsiakmaki [10] that showed very good results. The authors focused on comparing autoML with classical classification and regression algorithms for predicting students' performance. Our study differs by using data collected in 9 consecutive academic years versus just one, allowing us to evaluate the generalization of the models over the years. Second, the better performing framework auto-sklearn [8] is used versus the Auto-Weka tested by Tsiakmaki.

The paper is structured as follows. Next section outlines the methodology for the experiment, describing the main difference between the old and the new approach and how autoML is employed. Section 3 contains the experiments carried out and the results. Section 4 is dedicated to the discussion part of this work, and finally, in Sect. 5, the conclusions and possible future works are outlined.

2   Methodology

To test the hypothesis the process used in the first experiment was reused and extended. The Data Mining process consists of multiple steps employed for knowledge discovery [11, 12]: data collection, preprocessing, data mining, and interpretation of the results.

The original work aimed to reveal student academic performance in distributed examination courses, based on models developed using five common classification algorithms implemented in the popular Scikit-learn framework [13] (Decision Tree CART, Extra Trees Classifier, Random Forest Classifier, Logistic Regression, and C-Support Vector Classification).

Each model was evaluated using two cross-validation techniques: stratified tenfold cross-validation and leave-one-group-out (the old leave-one-label-out). It was a binary classification problem were the positive class represented the students that passed, and the negative class the students that failed the course. The Scikit-learn package version 0.19 was used in the first experiment.

In this context, the goal of this study is to evaluate the impact of an autoML method for hyperparameter tuning on the performance of the models. The same data, preprocessing, list of algorithms, and evaluation strategies were used. Matter of fact, the only difference from the original process is the hyperparameter tuning block visible in Fig. 1.

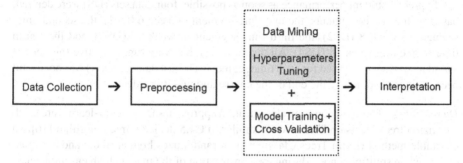

Fig. 1. The four steps used in knowledge discovery. The difference from the original version is highlighted in green. (Color figure online)

2.1 Reuse of the Previous Experiment

Data Collection. The data used in this study was gathered over nine years, from 2009 to 2017, for a single course, Object-Oriented Programming, held by the same tutor. Following the university regulations, course examination for this course was in a distributed examination pattern. The study material was split into two parts, and two examinations are provided for each part to test knowledge, skills and abilities acquired by a student.

In the course considered for this study student participate in 9 course sessions, 14 face-to-face practical activity meetings, and 4 examinations (two of which are re-examinations). The marking is a 10-grading system, where 1 is the lowest, and 10 is the highest grade attainable. To pass in this course the student needs a mark greater or equal than 5 for each examination and the average activity mark. The final course mark is computed as the sum of 50% of the average activity mark and 50% the average examination mark.

Preprocessing. The data set contains 1077 student records, each with 43 attributes, and the output class: 1 (for students who completed the course), and 0 (for those who failed). In the preprocessing step, 169 student records were discarded for this data set due to incomplete information or duplicate information (students who repeated the course). The data was cleaned (filling in missing values, correcting inconsistencies), the categorical attributes were converted to numerical value do to the requirements of some classification algorithms (C-Support Vector Classification) [14], and to avoid cases in which predictor attributes have different weight in the decision process standard normalization (z-score) was applied [15].

The attributes that were not relevant to the problem were discarded reducing the data set to 908 × 12 data points. Furthermore, feature selection based on a univariate statistical test was performed reducing the data set to 908 × 7. The final attributes used for the classification models were the following: student membership to the advanced study group (MG), number of credits earned in the previous year (CR), average activity mark (AA), the number of attendances in practical activity meetings (NA), average examination mark (AE), number of examinations (NE), and final course status (SP).

To predict student performance as soon as possible, four data sets (DS) were derived, based on four time-segments: the first time-segment in week 6 (DS1), the second time-segment in week 8 (DS2), the third time-segment in week 12 (DS3), and the fourth time-segment in week 14 (DS4). All the attributes that were time-sensitive (number of attendance) were computed for each time segment. The last data set (DS4) was not useful because it corresponds to the end of the course and was discarded.

Data Mining. The most common classification approaches from Scikit-learn were used: a decision tree (Decision Tree CART) similar to C4.5 decision tree algorithm [16]; an ensemble method (Extra Trees Classifier) that randomizes both attribute and cut-point choice when splitting a node during the construction of the tree [17]; an ensemble classifier (Random Forest Classifier) using the perturb-and-combine technique for decision trees [18]; a linear model (Logistic Regression Classifier, or logit) for classification using a logistic function [19]; an implementation of support vector machine (C-Support Vector Classification) for classification based on libsvm [20].

The class distribution in the data set is imbalanced with 30% of the data points with the minority class. Imbalance in the class distribution may cause a significant deterioration in classification performance [21]. This problem was addressed by assigning weights to classes during classification.

In the context of predicting academic performance the following metrics were used: true positive (TP rate, recall) – students which have correctly been classified as passed; true negative (TN rate, specificity) – students which have correctly been classified as failed; accuracy (ACC) – the proportion of the total number of students predictions that were correct; precision (PRE) – the proportion of correctly identified students that passed; f-score (f1) – a weighted harmonic average of precision and recall.

To build an accurate model with a limited amount of data, and to ensure that the model is not overfitting, an evaluation strategy is needed [22]. Two cross-validation methods were applied: stratified tenfold cross-validation and leave-one-group-out (the old leave-one-label-out). The first strategy partitions the data into ten equal-sized folds, each class has equal representation [23]. The folds are used for training and testing (9 for training and one for testing) 10 times, and the metrics are averaged. The second strategy differs in the way the folds are created: the data is split by a label or a group, in this case, the academic year. In this case there were 9 groups (9 academic years), used for training and testing 9 times, and the metrics are averaged.

The experiment was split in two. In the first part, the stratified cross-validation was used to evaluate the models trained over the 3 data sets (DS1, DS2, DS3) and find the best performing algorithm. In the second the leave-one-group out was used to evaluate and train the models.

In the current experiment, all the steps mentioned above were kept. Small adaptation of the code was needed by using the newer version of Scikit-learn 0.21.3. After the corrections were implemented the results remained identical.

2.2 AutoML

In this experiment, to evaluate only the hyperparameter tuning the steps described in the previous section remained intact. One step was inserted just before the evaluation strategy employed in both experiments.

This step consists of using an autoML strategy to optimize the performance of the algorithms. The auto-sklearn toolkit was used first because it is built on top of the Scikit-learn library, and second it performs better against the previous state of the art in autoML [24].

The AutoSklearnClassifier was used, limiting the search space to only one estimator (classification algorithm) per run to not modify the rest of the process. All preprocessing on the data was disabled, to not modify the data on which the models are trained. For resampling strategy, the one defined for the experiment was used: stratified 10-fold cross-validation or leave-one-group-out.

We change the default metric for optimization (accuracy) to balance accuracy which is better on imbalanced datasets, like in our case [25].

The software finds the best hyperparameters value in the amount of time permitted for each run. It can tune 4 parameters for the decision tree algorithm, 5 for Extra Trees Classifier, 5 for Random Forest Classifier, 10 for Linear Classifier, and 4 for Support Vector Classification [8]. In the original experiment, the default values for hyperparameters were used.

3 Results

The purpose of the experiments was to evaluate the impact on performance by employing autoML techniques in an older approach. By using two cross-validation techniques the experiment was split into two parts: in the first one 10-fold cross-validation was used and in the second leave-one-group-out. In both parts, the same classification algorithms were used to train models for the 3 time-segments datasets.

The original experiment was adapted to the new version of Scikit-learn library and produced identical results as the original. Validating that the code produced the same results was mandatory to ensure that we can compare the original results with the enhanced version of the experiment, that uses autoML hyperparameter tuning.

The modified experiment was run in the same approach as the original, split into two parts, using the same classification algorithms, training models for the 3 time-segments datasets. The time limit for the search of appropriate models done by the AutoSklearnClassifier was left to the default setting of 3600 s. With this setting, the models were computed in approximately 20 h for each part of the experiment (10-fold cross-validation and leave-one-group-out cross-validation). For comparison in the original experiment, the models were computed in just under 20 s on the same hardware.

10-Fold Cross-validation. The prediction results for each time-segment and classification algorithm are shown in Table 1. On the left side is the results from the original experiment and on the right the new version. Five metrics were used: true positive rate (TP rate), true negative rate (TN rate), Accuracy (Acc), precision (Pre), and f-score (F1). With red is highlighted where the original experiment has better results for that specific metric, with green where the new experiment produced better results, and with black, the results are the same in both experiments. The best performing models for a specific metric are highlighted by the grey background colour for those specific cells.

Table 1. Classification results using stratified tenfold cross-validation original vs auto

Segment	Alg	Original					autoML				
		TPR	TNR	Acc	Pre	F1	TPR	TNR	Acc	Pre	F1
DS1	DT	0.84	0.56	0.76	0.82	0.83	0.73	0.82	0.76	0.91	0.81
week 6	ET	0.82	0.62	0.76	0.84	0.83	0.74	0.82	0.77	0.91	0.82
	RF	0.85	0.63	0.79	0.85	0.85	0.78	0.79	0.79	0.9	0.84
	logit	0.72	0.8	0.74	0.9	0.8	0.71	0.8	0.73	0.9	0.79
	SVC	0.72	0.85	0.76	0.92	0.81	0.76	0.86	0.79	0.93	0.84
DS2	DT	0.89	0.74	0.85	0.89	0.89	0.88	0.89	0.88	0.95	0.91
week 8	ET	0.87	0.75	0.84	0.89	0.88	0.89	0.85	0.88	0.94	0.91
	RF	0.9	0.75	0.86	0.9	0.9	0.89	0.88	0.88	0.95	0.91
	logit	0.87	0.85	0.86	0.94	0.9	0.88	0.85	0.87	0.93	0.9
	SVC	0.87	0.84	0.86	0.93	0.9	0.88	0.87	0.87	0.94	0.91
DS3	DT	0.87	0.71	0.82	0.88	0.87	0.83	0.91	0.86	0.96	0.89
week 12	ET	0.87	0.72	0.83	0.88	0.87	0.82	0.94	0.85	0.97	0.89
	RF	0.87	0.78	0.85	0.91	0.89	0.84	0.92	0.86	0.96	0.9
	logit	0.85	0.88	0.86	0.95	0.89	0.85	0.91	0.87	0.96	0.9
	SVC	0.82	0.9	0.84	0.95	0.88	0.86	0.89	0.87	0.95	0.9

As the results indicate, there is a significant variation between the two approaches. The best model in predicting passing students (even from the first time-segment), with more than 85% in the true positive rate, was Random Forest in the original experiment. For this metric, the best algorithm in the original approach outperformed the best algorithm in the hyperparameters tuning version by 9% in the first time-segment (DS1), and only 1% in the second (DS2) and third (DS3). The best algorithm for this metric remains the Random Forest Classifier.

However, predicting student academic performance was most often linked to the classification models that will produce the best results in predicting student failure [26]. According to [27], failing to identify students at risk can be as far costlier than incorrectly identifying someone as a failure. The metric that quantifies the performance of the models for predicting students at risk is the true negative rate. For this metric, the new approach produced far better results than the original, for all algorithm, and in all time-segments. The improvements vary from 1% for SVC in DS1, to 22% for ET in DS3. In the original experiment, SVC produced the best results for this metric. In the new approach, SVC performance remained high for this metric, with marginal improvements for DS1 and DS2. However, in DS2 better true negative rate is obtained by Decision Tree Classifier, and in DS3 by Extra Trees Classifier.

For the metrics that balance the TP rate and TN rate, accuracy and f1-score, the variation between models in a time-segment is low, especially for DS2 and DS3. In this time segments, autoML approach improved the original values by 1% to 3%.

The best accuracy for the first time-segment is achieved using Random Forest Classifier (for original and autoML) and C-Support Vector Classification (for autoML). For the second time segment, the best accuracy was obtained with Decision Tree, Random Forest and Extra Tree in the autoML experiment, obtaining the same score. For the last segment, Logistic Regression Classifier remains the best performer for this metric, but it was matched by C-Support Vector Classification.

In the case of accuracy, we computed a statistical test to verify whether the improvements are statistically significant or not. We applied the t-test with a significance level of 0.05 to compare the accuracy produced in the original experiment versus the autoML version. For the first time segment DS1, the p-value is high and that proves that there is no statistical difference for this metric although the TN rates show large improvements. For DS2 the p-value is 0.0015 and for DS3 p-value is 0.025, and thus we conclude that a statistically significant increase in accuracy is present for the last two time-segments.

Leave-One-Group-Out Validation. A second step in the experiment was conducted to evaluate how the models would generalize to an independent year dataset. To achieve this, a leave-one-group-out cross-validation (the old leave-one-label-out cross-validation) method was used instead of the stratified 10-fold cross-validation. The initial datasets were divided into nine folds, corresponding to the nine academic year records available. Each classifier used eight folds for training and one left-out fold was used for validation. The metrics were computed as an average of the results across nine iterations. Table 2. presents the results obtained for each classification algorithm, time-segment and experiment (original vs autoML). The results were marked in the same manner as in the previous table.

The results are comparable to those obtained in the first step of the experiment. Regarding the true positive rate, the original experiment outperforms the autoML with high variation in the first time-segment, and lower variation in the second and third. For this metric Random Forest Classifier remains strong for all time-segments. TP rate for DS2 in the new approach has very low variance.

TN rate, like in the first half of the experiment, is greatly improved over the original scores for Decision Tree Classifier, Random Forest Classifier, and Extra Tree Classifier. Accuracy score and f-score are improved in DS2 and DS3, however, for DS1 they suffer a decline. The best accuracy for the first time-segment is achieved using Random Forest Classifier (for the original experiment). For the second time segment, the best accuracy

Table 2. Classification results using leave-one-group-out cross-validation original vs auto

Segment	Alg	Original					autoML				
		TPR	TNR	Acc	Pre	F1	TPR	TNR	Acc	Pre	F1
DS1	DT	0.81	0.54	0.74	0.81	0.81	0.59	0.94	0.69	0.96	0.72
week 6	ET	0.82	0.54	0.75	0.82	0.82	0.73	0.79	0.75	0.9	0.8
	RF	0.85	0.6	0.78	0.84	0.84	0.76	0.77	0.76	0.89	0.81
	logit	0.71	0.8	0.74	0.9	0.78	0.68	0.81	0.72	0.91	0.77
	SVC	0.7	0.79	0.73	0.9	0.78	0.73	0.83	0.76	0.92	0.81
DS2	DT	0.89	0.7	0.84	0.88	0.88	0.87	0.87	0.87	0.94	0.9
week 8	ET	0.88	0.76	0.84	0.89	0.88	0.88	0.88	0.87	0.93	0.9
	RF	0.9	0.77	0.86	0.9	0.9	0.87	0.87	0.87	0.93	0.9
	logit	0.87	0.87	0.86	0.93	0.9	0.86	0.86	0.86	0.93	0.89
	SVC	0.87	0.85	0.86	0.93	0.9	0.87	0.87	0.86	0.93	0.9
DS3	DT	0.87	0.69	0.82	0.86	0.86	0.82	0.91	0.85	0.96	0.89
week 12	ET	0.89	0.73	0.84	0.88	0.89	0.8	0.92	0.84	0.96	0.87
	RF	0.88	0.75	0.84	0.89	0.88	0.81	0.93	0.85	0.97	0.88
	logit	0.85	0.88	0.86	0.95	0.89	0.85	0.89	0.86	0.95	0.89
	SVC	0.82	0.90	0.85	0.95	0.88	0.85	0.9	0.87	0.96	0.9

was obtained with Decision Tree, Random Forest and Extra Tree in the autoML experiment, obtaining the same score. For the last segment, C-Support Vector Classification in the autoML experiment outperformed the old winner Logistic Regression Classifier.

Regarding the statistical significance of improvements in accuracy for all models just in DS2 p-value has a sufficiently low value of 0.033 to reject the null hypothesis.

4 Discussions

The problem of predicting student academic performance is of great interest to many researchers in the field of educational data mining. Previous approaches addressed predicting student final mark [28, 29], predicting student failure [30], or predicting the completion of a task [31, 32]. The ability to correctly predict students' performance is a significant undertaking and leads to benefits for all parties involved in the educational process [33]. To maximize the impact of a prediction model it must produce the best results possible. In the pursuit to find the best models, the data scientist must complete a large number of tasks to ensure that the data is cleaned, reduce the number of features, the best algorithm is used, and hyperparameters for that algorithm are optimal. This is not an easy task, particularly for an educator or a non-expert user.

In this paper, we set out to explore the possibility of using autoML techniques to improve prediction models for educational data mining. A previous experiment in which models for predicting student academic performance using data generated in a traditional educational environment was reused. By modifying this experiment, we could asses how auto hyperparameters tuning impacts the performance of the prediction models.

The results illustrated in the previous section unveil the effectiveness of this autoML method on the performance of the models. Using autoML strategies for hyperparameter tuning produced better results for true negative rate but poorer performance on the true positive rate. This implies that the new models are better suited to predict students at risk of failure. The large difference for TP rate is noted only for the first time-segment for Decision Tree, Extra Tree, and Random Forest Classifiers. On the other hand, TN rate is significantly improved with autoML for all time-segments and the same three algorithms. Linear Classifier and Support Vector Classification scores are mildly improved in the autoML experiment. The metrics that incorporate true negative and true positive rate, accuracy and f1-score, are greater in most cases in the second and third time-segments.

Although the hyperparameter tuning improved the performance for most models, the best outcome is that the metrics for all algorithm in time-segment 2 are very close to each other with a variation of only 1%. Therefore, the practitioner can choose an algorithm that can provide higher interpretability without losing performance.

In this experiment, we optimized the hyperparameters for balanced accuracy to compensate the imbalanced in the dataset. This is the reason for the improvements in the true negative rate metric. Balanced accuracy was used to keep the same scenario of the original experiment where a strategy of assigning weights to classes has been employed to address the imbalanced dataset problem. Optimizing the models for a different scenario is a problem of finding the correct metric to use in the hyperparameter tuning process.

We have shown that using autoML techniques can improve performance in prediction models that were carefully produced. Tasks like preprocessing, data normalization, feature selection were reused and only the hyperparameter tuning functionality of auto-sklearn was added. Nevertheless, accuracy and f1-score are improved by up to 4%. If all the steps are done by auto-sklearn is possible to obtain even better optimizations as shown in [10]. On this basis, we believe that autoML techniques and tools can help practitioners in education to produce high-quality prediction models regardless of their expertise in data science. To employ these methods some programming skills are needed. However, these techniques can be integrated into the learning management system of choice. Some LMS like Moodle, offer a software framework to allow the development and integration of EDM and LA prediction models [34]. In this manner, the platform administrators can integrate autoML techniques and make them available through a graphical interface to the users. In this scenario, the time needed to train the models must be considered and the optimal setting for maximum execution time must be found based on the hardware and time limitations.

5   Conclusions

Predicting student failure is a difficult task that was addressed by many researchers. The difficulty of this task is in feature engineering, model selection, hyperparameters tuning.

This paper describes a study in improving the metrics of models by using autoML methods for hyperparameters tuning. To facilitate an easy and reliable comparison a previous experiment that used only the expertise of the data scientist was reuse.

The experimental results have shown that models trained in the autoML version of the experiment are performing better. A large improvement was obtained for true negative rate in models trained on Decision Tree, Extra Tree and Random Forest Classifiers. This is particularly important in the scenario that the models are used to correctly classify students at risk of failure and relatively interpretable models are needed. In general, all models for time-segments two and three have better scores for accuracy and f1-score than their counterparts in the original experiment, but the improvements are small (1–3%).

Properly used autoML methods can be used to build high-quality prediction models, and with the possibility of integrating this technique in learning management systems without an ML expert, tutors and students can benefit the most. In future work, we plan to address this issue and research the best approach for this desiderate.

References

1. Peña-Ayala, A.: Educational data mining: a survey and a data mining-based analysis of recent works. Exp. Syst. Appl. **41**, 1432–1462 (2014)
2. Romero, C., Ventura, S.: Educational data mining: a review of the state of the art. Syst. Man Cybern. Part C Appl. Rev. IEEE Trans. **40**, 601–618 (2010)
3. Hämäläinen, W., Vinni, M.: Comparison of machine learning methods for intelligent tutoring systems. In: Ikeda, M., Ashley, K.D., Chan, T.-W. (eds.) ITS 2006. LNCS, vol. 4053, pp. 525–534. Springer, Heidelberg (2006). https://doi.org/10.1007/11774303_52
4. Mueen, A., Zafar, B., Manzoor, U.: Modeling and predicting students' academic performance using data mining techniques. Int. J. Mod. Educ. Comput. Sci. **8**, 36–42 (2016). King Abdulaziz University, Saudi Arabia, Jeddah https://doi.org/10.5815/ijmecs.2016.11.05
5. Sweeney, M., Rangwala, H., Lester, J., Johri, A.: Next-term student performance prediction: a recommender systems approach. J. Educ. Data Min. **8**, 22–50 (2016)
6. Okubo, F., Yamashita, T., Shimada, A., Ogata, H.: A neural network approach for students' performance prediction. In: Proceedings of the Seventh International Learning Analytics & Knowledge Conference, pp. 598–599. Association for Computing Machinery, Vancouver (2017). https://doi.org/10.1145/3027385.3029479
7. Delavari, N., Phon-Amnuaisuk, S., Beikzadeh, M.R.: Data mining application in higher learning institutions. Inform. Educ. Int. J. **7**, 31–54 (2008)
8. Feurer, M., Klein, A., Eggensperger, K., Springenberg, J.T., Blum, M., Hutter, F.: Auto-sklearn: efficient and robust automated machine learning. In: Hutter, F., Kotthoff, L., Vanschoren, J. (eds.) Automated Machine Learning. TSSCML, pp. 113–134. Springer, Cham (2019). https://doi.org/10.1007/978-3-030-05318-5_6
9. Bucos, M., Drăgulescu, B.: Predicting student success using data generated in traditional educational environments. TEM J. **7**, 617–625 (2018). https://doi.org/10.18421/TEM73-19
10. Tsiakmaki, M., Kostopoulos, G., Kotsiantis, S., Ragos, O.: Implementing AutoML in educational data mining for prediction tasks. Appl. Sci. **10**, 90 (2020)
11. Feyyad, U.M.: Data mining and knowledge discovery: making sense out of data. IEEE Exp. **11**, 20–25 (1996)
12. Kurgan, L.A., Musilek, P.: A survey of knowledge discovery and data mining process models. Knowl. Eng. Rev. **21**, 1–24 (2006)

13. Pedregosa, F., et al.: Scikit-learn: machine learning in python. J. Mach. Learn. Res. **12**, 2825–2830 (2011)
14. Lee, N., Kim, J.-M.: Conversion of categorical variables into numerical variables via Bayesian network classifiers for binary classifications. Comput. Stat. Data Anal. **54**, 1247–1265 (2010)
15. Han, J., Pei, J., Kamber, M.: Data Mining: Concepts and Techniques. Elsevier, Amsterdam (2011)
16. Breiman, L., Friedman, J., Stone, C.J., Olshen, R.A.: Classification and Regression Trees. CRC Press, Boca Raton (1984)
17. Geurts, P., Ernst, D., Wehenkel, L.: Extremely randomized trees. Mach. Learn. **63**, 3–42 (2006)
18. Breiman, L.: Random forests. Mach. Learn. **45**, 5–32 (2001)
19. Yu, H.-F., Huang, F.-L., Lin, C.-J.: Dual coordinate descent methods for logistic regression and maximum entropy models. Mach. Learn. **85**, 41–75 (2011)
20. Chang, C.-C., Lin, C.-J.: LIBSVM: a library for support vector machines. ACM Trans. Intell. Syst. Technol. TIST **2**, 27 (2011)
21. Van Hulse, J., Khoshgoftaar, T.M., Napolitano, A.: Experimental perspectives on learning from imbalanced data. In: Proceedings of the 24th International Conference on Machine learning, pp. 935–942 (2007)
22. Arlot, S., Celisse, A.: A survey of cross-validation procedures for model selection. Stat. Surv. **4**, 40–79 (2010)
23. Hens, A.B., Tiwari, M.K.: Computational time reduction for credit scoring: an integrated approach based on support vector machine and stratified sampling method. Exp. Syst. Appl. **39**, 6774–6781 (2012)
24. Feurer, M., Klein, A., Eggensperger, K., Springenberg, J., Blum, M., Hutter, F.: Efficient and robust automated machine learning. In: Advances in Neural Information Processing Systems, pp. 2962–2970 (2015)
25. Brodersen, K.H., Ong, C.S., Stephan, K.E., Buhmann, J.M.: The balanced accuracy and its posterior distribution. In: 2010 20th International Conference on Pattern Recognition, pp. 3121–3124. IEEE (2010)
26. Márquez-Vera, C., Cano, A., Romero, C., Ventura, S.: Predicting student failure at school using genetic programming and different data mining approaches with high dimensional and imbalanced data. Appl. Intell. **38**, 315–330 (2013)
27. Aguiar, E., Chawla, N.V., Brockman, J., Ambrose, G.A., Goodrich, V.: Engagement vs performance: using electronic portfolios to predict first semester engineering student retention. In: Proceedings of the Fourth International Conference on Learning Analytics and Knowledge, pp. 103–112 (2014)
28. Lopez, M.I., Luna, J.M., Romero, C., Ventura, S.: Classification via clustering for predicting final marks based on student participation in forums. In: Proceedings of the 5th International Conference on Educational Data Mining, pp. 148–151. International Educational Data Mining Society, Chania (2012)
29. Romero, C., Espejo, P.G., Zafra, A., Romero, J.R., Ventura, S.: Web usage mining for predicting final marks of students that use Moodle courses. Comput. Appl. Eng. Educ. **21**, 135–146 (2013)
30. Tan, M., Shao, P.: Prediction of student dropout in e-learning program through the use of machine learning method. Int. J. Emerg. Technol. Learn. IJET **10**, 11–17 (2015)
31. González-Brenes, J.P., Mostow, J., Duan, W.: How to classify tutorial dialogue? Comparing feature vectors vs. sequences. In: Proceedings of the 4th International Conference on Educational Data Mining, pp. 169–178 (2011)
32. Drăgulescu, B., Bucos, M., Vasiu, R.: Predicting assignment submissions in a multiclass classification problem. TEM J. **4**, 244–254 (2015)

33. Wolff, A., Zdrahal, Z., Herrmannova, D., Knoth, P.: Predicting student performance from combined data sources. In: Peña-Ayala, A. (ed.) Educational Data Mining. SCI, vol. 524, pp. 175–202. Springer, Cham (2014). https://doi.org/10.1007/978-3-319-02738-8_7

34. Monllaó Olivé, D., Huynh, D.Q., Reynolds, M., Dougiamas, M., Wiese, D.: A supervised learning framework: using assessment to identify students at risk of dropping out of a MOOC. J. Comput. High. Educ. 32(1), 9–26 (2019). https://doi.org/10.1007/s12528-019-09230-1

A Case Study of Applying Gamification in Teaching Project Management

Kristina Magylaitė(✉), Lina Čeponienė, Mantas Jurgelaitis, and Tomas Danikauskas

Information Systems Department, Kaunas University of Technology, Studentų Street 50, Kaunas, Lithuania
{kristina.magylaite,lina.ceponiene,mantas.jurgelaitis, tomas.danikauskas}@ktu.lt

Abstract. Project management subject encompasses several project execution and control techniques which are used to ensure successful project delivery. One of such techniques is Earned Value Analysis. Teaching students of information system engineering the principles of Earned Value Analysis is quite challenging, as mastering Earned Value Analysis requires a thorough understanding of the metrics, repetitive calculations and application of the knowledge to various project situations. Therefore, gamification principles were applied and Earned Value Analysis learning game was implemented. The EVA game is an online board game which also incorporates such game elements as rewards, leaderboard, badges, points, levels and feedback. These game elements aim to stimulate the competition among students, increase motivation and level of engagement and make the learning process more interesting. Although the first experimental assessment of the EVA game involved a relatively small number of participants, it demonstrated that students positively evaluate the introduction of gamification elements into the study process.

Keywords: Gamification · EVA · Project management · Online game

1 Introduction

Gamification is the use of game elements in a non-gaming environment such as education, business, politics, medicine, sports, etc. Currently, gamification is widely used in various areas of education [1]. Teachers at schools and universities recognize the value and effectiveness of game as a tool for improving the learning process [2]. Gamification is a wide term, but while analyzing it more accurately, three different strategies of using games in education can be distinguished: gamification, game-based learning, and serious games [3, 4]. A serious game is more oriented to skill practice, rather than increasing motivation as in gamification. On the other hand, a game is a system in which players are interested in a rule-based, interactive, abstract challenge that has feedback and produces a quantifiable result, often triggering an emotional reaction [5]. A game is a standalone unit that has a clear goal, a defined start and end, a determined win state, the ability

© Springer Nature Switzerland AG 2020
A. Lopata et al. (Eds.): ICIST 2020, CCIS 1283, pp. 321–333, 2020.
https://doi.org/10.1007/978-3-030-59506-7_26

to overcome a challenge in multiple attempts, and consists of game elements [6]. Both gamification and game-based learning can be applied in education as they can help motivate and engage students into the learning process, by challenging, rewarding, and stimulating competition among them [4, 7].

As gamification is based on using game elements, three categories of game elements can be distinguished: components, mechanics and dynamics [8]. Game components are specific structures, like points, badges, leaderboards, levels, quests, virtual goods, teams, etc. [9]. Game mechanics are an essential part of the gamification that affects the player's experience while encouraging to engage and move forward [10]. Various authors [9, 10] identify the following main game mechanics elements: feedback, challenges, customization, chance, competitions, and rewards. Game dynamics encompasses abstract game elements such as narrative, rules, player's experience, emotions, and progression [9]. The interplay of these elements is used to engage players, motivating them to learn and solve problems [5].

In this paper we are presenting the case study of using gamification in a specific area of education – a project management course for undergraduate students of study program "Information System Engineering". As project management encompasses the application of knowledge, skills, tools and methods to satisfying project requirements [11], an important tool in this discipline is Earned Value Analysis (EVA) methodology [12]. This methodology is based on three key metrics: planned value, actual cost and earned value which are used together to determine whether a project is executed as planned [11]. The process of learning Earned Value Analysis encompasses not only studying the material on EVA but also applying formulas to calculate the required metrics. As students may lack the motivation to perform repetitive calculation tasks to master the EVA techniques, we have decided to introduce gamification elements into the learning process. A gamified system was implemented, where students of the course "Information Systems Project Management Technologies" were able to play a game for learning EVA and in tandem prepare for the midterm exam. The gamified system not only explains the concepts, definitions and formulas of EVA but also enables students to apply these formulas and solve tasks in a more engaging and motivating way. Based on [5] we have selected the gamification methods for an EVA game: association, repetition, providing examples and role play. In EVA game, concepts are associated with definitions and vice versa; repeating of certain content is used to help students to memorize EVA concepts, definitions and formulas; examples are provided for explaining the EVA rules and their application; the learner plays a role of project manager and has to apply EVA rules to specific project situations. EVA game is an online board game which encompasses not only a board game with its rules, but also incorporates activities for learning Earned Value Analysis. The player of the game must apply the knowledge of EVA concepts to further progress into the game. The success of the player in the game heavily depends on the selected solutions for various situations and emerging problems in the project and on the accuracy of the answers to the given questions and tasks. Our EVA game was used in the educational process in the course "Information Systems Project Management Technologies" during 2019 autumn semester. We have gathered statistical information about the gameplay and collected the feedback from the students, which indicates that students were interested in the game and found the gamified process more engaging and motivating.

The rest of the paper is organized as follows. The second section analyses research in the area of gamification of teaching project management and software engineering. The third section describes our implemented gamified system for teaching Earned Value Analysis techniques. The fourth section presents performed experimental application of the implemented system in teaching process results. And finally, the last section concludes the research results and outlines future work.

2 Related Work

Nowadays research on gamification of various subjects is widely performed [9]. Gamification in education area become more popular [3] and gamification of project management activities is considered quite effective [13–15]. To analyze the benefits and effects of gamification, researchers attempt to gamify both real-life project management process [13] and the teaching and learning of project management techniques [14–16]. Gamification of teaching and learning project management has a common goal to increase student motivation and engagement into the study process [14].

Some researchers use non-computerized gamification methods. Wangenheim, Savi and Borgatto [14] created a non-computerized game for teaching Earned Value Management (EVM is a project management methodology based on Earned Value Analysis). The researchers presented a board game designed to be played during a single university lecture. Students were divided into teams and each team had to plan the project and participate in its simulated execution. Project execution was simulated by rolling a dice and moving across the game board through various project scenarios, while dealing with risks, monitoring and controlling project execution using EVM. The goal of the game was to deliver a software project to the customer in time and on budget. During the experiment, the board game was used in two project management courses of the undergraduate study program at the Federal University of Santa Catarina to improve motivation, user experience and game's contribution. A survey was created to test a hypothesis that game can increase students' motivation to learn and provide a positive experience and was later confirmed. In total 28 students, which played the game, participated in the survey and the overall feedback from the majority of students was positive.

The researchers of Saints Cyril and Methodius University of Skopje [15] present the results of applied non-computerized gamification approach in the course "Project Management" at the Faculty of Electrical Engineering and IT. In the course, students were divided into teams and had to perform assigned tasks in a limited time. The first part involved choosing the leader of the team, starting a project, defining the scope of the project, describing the mission and criteria for project success, presenting the project proposal and providing comments and remarks for other teams. The teams competed for an incentive of ten points, which they could later add to their exam grade. Other participants were awarded up to two points. After the first phase, the leader of the better team was transferred to the group, which had a lower rank. Afterwards, students were asked to produce a WBS structure of tasks and Gantt chart for the project. The students' feedback was collected using a questionnaire, which showed that using a game in the practical training interested students.

The researchers of Ural Federal University [17] presented a universal gamification pattern which consists of problem definition, game and reflection. The experimental evaluation of this pattern was performed in the project management course on a multi-disciplinary target audience of students. Key project elements, roles and project-related documents were provided to students. The teams had to perform project tasks and resolve non-standard situations. Game elements were used to help familiarize students with the project and teamwork concepts, facilitate team building, role assignment and other project-related activities performance.

The researchers of Federal University of Lavras [18] adapted the gamification system in an introductory software engineering course in the undergraduate study program. Students worked in teams and had to develop a software product. There were three iterations in project execution, at the end of each iteration teams presented the iteration results. Teams were awarded badges for successful task completion. Each badge had a given point value, which was used to calculate team rank and place it in the leaderboard. Student feedback was positive; however, researchers noticed that students were not so eager to compete and instead were more interested in progressing and receiving rewards. Researchers have determined a set of guidelines that can be used to apply gamification elements in software education and concluded that gamification and game-based learning is a useful tool for developing an engaging study process.

While applying non-computerized gamification solutions in education is considered beneficial, the use of computerized gamification provides even more benefits and opportunities. The group of researchers from Brazil Universidade do Vale do Itajai [16] describe how to create serious games and use them for improving the process of teaching the topics related to software engineering. An experiment was conducted with undergraduate students using a serious game for teaching project management. the experiment, "Planager" project management game was used, which was targeted at the audience with little to no experience in project management. The game consisted of five parts: scope, WBS, activity, activity sequencing and critical path. In total 14 students have completed the game and students' feedback showed that the game increased student motivation. Based on the results of the experiment, researchers proposed a set of recommendations for serious game development and adoption in pedagogical activities.

Researchers at Kaunas University of Technology (KTU) created a game called "Hard Nut" to teach fundamentals of entrepreneurship [19]. This computerized game has been used in KTU course "Simulation of business processes" to increase students' motivation to learn and understand the dependencies between the business processes. The game simulates the management of electronic engineering enterprise in a competitive environment and reflects production, sales, marketing and finance activities [20]. Students are divided into teams, where each team is a competing company branch. They had to analyze the current financial situation of the company, formulate a strategy and make management decisions. At the end of the financial year, the team reports on the results and the game determines the market position of the company. The goal of the team is to achieve the biggest capital.

Ašeriškis and Damaševičius [13] analyzed the gamification of project management processes in real life. They introduced the Trogon Project Management System, which contains a gamification component. The following game elements were used in the gamified system: leaderboard, badges and the project forest which is a visualization of project tasks performed by teams. The goal of using this gamified system was to distract employers from monotony in performing project tasks and maintain their motivation over time. The forest has an unoccupied plot, which represents unfinished tasks and areas with trees that represent completed tasks. This information is used by the project manager who can evaluate employers, their skills and the complexity of the tasks by the project forest. In this research, a questionnaire was used to evaluate the usability of the gamified system. During the experiment, 30 information system experts evaluated the system for interface usability, the overall achieved score was 71 out of 100.

The analyzed gamification solutions emphasize the benefits of gamification in various areas associated with project management: both in education and real-life projects. Most of the analyzed papers on gamifying project management education try to simulate project execution to make the learning process more attractive and engaging. The authors of [14] propose introducing gamification into EVA teaching process, but their solution is a non-computerized board game. On the other hand, our gamified EVA learning system is an online board game which has the advantages of a computerized game: can be played anywhere and anytime, provides instant feedback, visualizes the progress and facilitates the application of gamification elements into the study process.

3   Gamified System for Learning Earned Value Analysis

The goal of our work was to motivate students by providing a system which promotes independent learning of EVA and introduces game elements to keep the students engaged. For this purpose, a gamified system for learning earned value analysis (EVA game) was developed.

The EVA game enables players to participate in a game, in which the player is responsible for executing a software implementation project. The player is given the role of a project manager, who has to ensure that that project is finished successfully: it is delivered on time and does not exceed the allocated project budget. At several points in the game, the player is given tasks or combination of tasks corresponding to the project, which need to be solved to progress further into the game.

The game consists of two stages – planning and execution. At the planning stage, the player needs to choose a project, select work assignments and resources. Then each work assignment is allocated to a work resource, based on the resource hourly cost, and in some cases productivity. At the project execution stage, the player begins at the start of 50 squares game board, which represents the planned project execution period. During the game, a Gannt chart diagram is always displayed, which represents work assignments, their dependencies, milestones, assignments' actual and planned durations. On each turn, the player rolls a six-sided die and performs the presented assignment. If the player rolls a number between one and four, a task is presented. The tasks range from simple definition identification task to calculation of several Earned Value metrics. If the player rolls five or six, a risk card must be chosen. Risk cards illustrate risks that range from additional bonuses to time or budget, or penalties which require a player to reschedule the certain assignments, work overtime or deal with other unforeseen complications of the resources. Risk cards are based on Deliver! proposed risks [14] and the most common risks proposed by Arnuphaptrairong [21].

The project is finished when the player completes all the assignments or reaches the last square on the board. A successful project completion awards player more points and is reached once a player completes the project ahead of schedule or exactly on time. And vice versa: the player loses if the allocated budget or time runs out before finishing the project.

3.1 Types of Tasks in EVA Game

Based on gamification methods defined in [5], four types of tasks were implemented in the EVA game – definition, formula, percent and graphic tasks. The types of tasks were created and implemented with increasing difficulty in mind: starting with definition identification tasks, proceeding to EV metrics calculation tasks, problem-solving and graph interpretation tasks. Examples of the task types are presented in Fig. 1 and 2.

The first type of task is the definition identification task where the player has to identify EVA metrics out of given options. The player must associate the earned value metric with its definition or definition with its metric.

The second type of task is the EVA metrics calculation task where the player must calculate specific EVA metric by plugging in metrics from the project. The student must associate appropriate values with the fields to calculate the given metric value correctly.

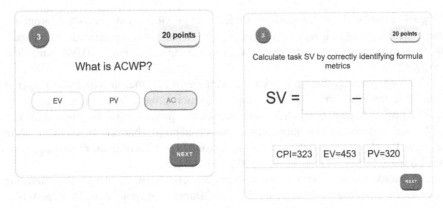

Fig. 1. Definition identification task (left), EVA metrics calculation task (right)

The third type of task is the problem-solving task. The task is based on the work assignment, which is currently in execution, and the task itself is presented in three parts. In the first part, the player identifies planned and earned values of the current assignment. In the second part, the player is asked to identify a correct formula of CV, SV, CPI or SPI metric. Finally, the metric values have to be plugged into the formula.

The last type of task is graph interpretation task which is, in essence, a problem-solving task. The only difference between the two is that the task is presented in graph form instead of text. The student must interpret the graph to choose metric values to plugin into the formula.

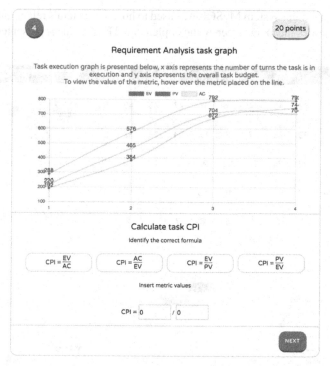

Fig. 2. Graph interpretation task

The type and number of tasks presented to a player depend on which game board square players figure is standing on at the given time. On each turn, a player moves a rolled number of squares and receives a combination of tasks to complete, which get progressively more difficult the further the player is in the game. For the first ten squares, the player is asked to solve three definition identification tasks. From 11th to 20th square, the player is given a definition identification and two EVA metric calculation tasks. Starting from the 21st square and up to 30th square, the player is asked to solve one definition task and a problem-solving task or two, depending on the current work assignment in execution. From 31st to 40th square, the player gets two definition tasks and accordingly a graph interpretation task or two. For the last ten squares, a player is asked to solve two definition tasks and a random selection of the other task types. During the game, once a milestone is reached, a player is asked to fill out a full EVA table, based on the current project executables and all EVA metrics have to be calculated by the player.

3.2 Implementation of the EVA Game

The EVA game was developed using web technologies for easier access and support. The gamified system was developed using React for front-end development and the back end was implemented using Express, a Node.js web application framework. An open-source database management system MySQL was used to host the system's relational database. The overall view of the main screen in the implemented EVA game is presented in Fig. 3.

Fig. 3. The main screen of the EVA game

In addition to the different task types, EVA game system supports other gamification elements for keeping users engaged and motivated based on gamification principles described by Fiona F. Nah [22].

The users of EVA game system are awarded points for successful completion of a task during the game. Accumulated points raise players level and in total there are 15 levels to be reached in the system. Levels and points are used to provide a clear goal orientation. User is also awarded badges for achievements such as placing third in the leaderboard, successfully completing a project or first-time activities as finishing planning stage, distributing resources for project execution and so on. Based on collected points, users are placed in the leaderboard thus encouraging competition between the players. Players names, points and levels are displayed in the leaderboard.

The system uses reinforcement based on players actions. Successful completion of tasks awards player with points and unsuccessful completion provides player instantaneous feedback. Additional feedback and guidance are provided by hints, which explain game rules, guide users to supplementary training material or provides tips on what should the player do next.

4 Findings of Applying EVA Game in Education Process

4.1 Experimental EVA Game Application in Education

In order to measure the effectiveness of the gamified system for learning Earned Value Analysis on student motivation, an experiment was conducted. During the 2019 fall semester, a number of students of "Information Systems Engineering" graduate study program in Kaunas University of Technology were invited to use the EVA system as an extra tool for independent learning. The system was developed as an additional resource for the course "Information Systems Project Management Technologies". Overall, seven students participated in the experiment. The experiment was carried out in two weeks. During the two-week period, students used the EVA game for mastering EVA techniques and preparing for the midterm exam.

At the end of the two weeks, students were asked to anonymously evaluate their experience by filling out a questionnaire which measured their motivation and engagement while playing the game. The questions about participants subjective experience and intrinsic motivation were based on the IMI scale for measuring motivation [23], and the questions about playing experience were based on the MEEGA + model [24] for evaluation of game quality. Four items from each model were selected for the questionnaire. Students were asked to rate the given statements on a scale from one to five, one being not true at all and five being very true. The questions of the questionnaire are presented along with the statistics of the participants' answers in Fig. 4 and 5. After the two weeks period, students also took a part in a midterm exam that encompassed the exercises of Earned Value Analysis.

4.2 EVA Game Application Effectiveness Results

The questionnaire results showed that motivation and game experience were rated above average. Most students responded that they felt more competent after playing the game, which helped them to better prepare for the midterm exam. Based on questionnaire results, 40% of students spent from two to three hours in the EVA game, and the rest (60%) spent between one and two hours.

As the tasks presented during the game were developed to be relatively similar to the tasks in the midterm exam, all of the participants noticed the benefits of the EVA game tasks. As presented in Fig. 4, the results of the motivation assessment showed that the students felt more competent after solving the game tasks, which helped them to better prepare for the exam. Students also assessed that the tasks were interesting. All of the above-mentioned statements were rated on average 4,4. Lastly, the importance to do well was rated lowest out of the group - 3,8 out of 5.

As Fig. 5 shows, game experience was evaluated quite favorably. 60% of students would certainly recommend this game to others. Most of the students had the impression that the game would be easy and found it interesting. Out of all the respondents to the questionnaire, 60% rated the game fun in four or five out five, and only 20% did not feel they had fun with the game.

Both the motivation and game experience were rated quite similarly by the participants. The overall motivation was rated higher than the game experience, but not by

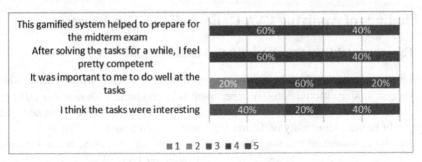

Fig. 4. Results of evaluating motivation

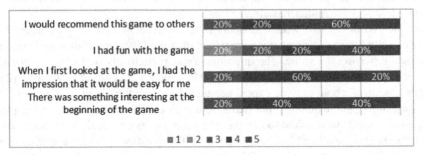

Fig. 5. Results of evaluating the game experience

a lot. The average of score the respondents gave for the motivation questions was 4,15 out of 5. And the average of game experience was measured to be 4,1 out of 5. The comparison of the scores can be found in Fig. 6 boxplot diagram.

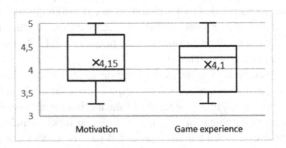

Fig. 6. The results of the student questionnaire

Additionally, student midterm exam scores were compared to evaluate the effectiveness of gamification. Figure 7 represents the three sets of data that were collected and compared. Out of the three sets, two represent the previous year midterm exam results, and the last is for 2019, in which students were given access to the gamified system for learning Earned Value Analysis. All years' exam tasks were of the same type, but variants of initial data for the tasks were different, moreover, even in the same year, there were several variants with different initial data for the tasks. Students knew the types of tasks in advance because analogous tasks were solved during the lectures. Although midterm exams include other tasks, besides EVA (EVA tasks are worth 40% of exam score), student exam results have increased significantly. The average of midterm exam score has risen from 7,4 up to 9,5 out of 10.

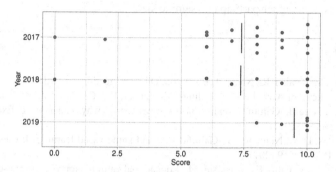

Fig. 7. Plots of the midterm exam score data by year

The results of the experiment are quite promising, as evaluations of motivation and game experience are high and the midterm exam scores have risen compared to previous years. Unfortunately, both data sets for the questionnaire and midterm exam scores are relatively small, and the made conclusions are not entirely reliable. It would be beneficial to repeat the same experiment in the future with a bigger sample of participants.

5 Conclusion

Gamification methods are considered useful in education as they help to increase student motivation and engagement by enhancing the learning process. The process of teaching project management could also benefit from gamification. Project management subject encompasses numerous project execution and control techniques which are used to ensure successful project delivery. One of such techniques is Earned Value Analysis. There exist numerous research papers, analyzing gamification of project management education, which in some degree try to simulate project execution to make the learning process more attractive and engaging. Gamification of teaching EVA is also researched, but it currently is limited to non-computerized board game solution.

Teaching the fundamentals of EVA is challenging, as mastering EVA requires a thorough understanding of the metrics, involves repetitive calculations and knowledge application to various project situations. It was determined that EVA teaching would benefit of gamification approach, therefore a gamified system for learning EVA was developed for increasing student motivation and engagement in learning EVA concepts and their applications. The implemented EVA game is an online board game which also incorporates such game elements as rewards, leaderboard, badges, points, levels and feedback. These game elements aim to stimulate the competition among students, guide students during the independent learning process, motivate students by employing various external motivation techniques, and make the learning process more engaging.

The first experimental assessment of the EVA game demonstrated that students positively evaluate the introduction of gamification elements into the study process. Although the findings are promising, the sample size of participants is relatively small, and the results are not entirely reliable. Therefore, in the future, we are planning to repeat the experiment using a bigger participants sample size.

References

1. Deterding, S., Khaled, R., Nacke, L.E., Dixon, D.: Gamification: toward a definition. In: CHI 2011 Gamification Workshop Proceedings, Vancouver, BC, Canada, vol. 12 (2011)
2. Hammer, J., Lee, J.: Gamification in education: what, how, why bother. Acad. Exchange Qu. 15(2), 146–151 (2011)
3. Karagiorgas, D.N., Niemann, S.: Gamification and game-based learning. J. Educ. Technol. Syst. 45(4), 499–519 (2017)
4. Al-Azawi, R., Al-Faliti, F., Al-Blushi, M.: Educational gamification vs. game based learning: comparative study. Int. J. Innov. Manage. Technol. 7(4), 132–136 (2016)
5. Kapp, K.M.: The Gamification of Learning and Instruction: Game-based Methods and Strategies for Training and Education. Wiley, Hoboken (2012)
6. Kapp, K.M., Blair, L., Mesch, R.: The Gamification of Learning and Instruction Fieldbook: Ideas into Practice. Wiley, San Francisco (2013)
7. Ivanova, G., Kozov, V., Zlatarov, P.: Gamification in software engineering education. In: 2019 42nd International Convention on Information and Communication Technology, Electronics and Microelectronics (MIPRO), pp. 1445–1450. IEEE (2019)
8. Werbach, K., Hunter, D.: For the Win: How Game Thinking Can Revolutionize Your Business. Wharton Digital Press, Philadelphia (2012)
9. Wood, L., Reiners, T.: Gamification in logistics and supply chain education: extending active learning. In: IADIS Internet Technologies & Society, pp. 101–108 (2012)
10. Zichermann, G., Cunningham, C.: Gamification by Design: Implementing Game Mechanics in Web and Mobile Apps. O'Reilly Media Inc., Sebastopol (2011)
11. Project Management Institute: A Guide to the Project Management Body of Knowledge (PMBOK guide), vol. 2. Project Management Inst, Pennsylvania (2000)
12. Lewis, V.: Fundamentals of Project Management: A Worksmart Guide. Amacom, New York (1995)
13. Ašeriškis, D., Damaševičius, R.: Gamification of a project management system. In: Proceedings of International Conference on Advances in Computer-Human Interactions ACHI2014, Barcelona, pp. 200–207 (2014)
14. von Wangenheim, C.G., Savi, R., Borgatto, A.F.: DELIVER!–an educational game for teaching earned value management in computing courses. Inf. Softw. Technol. 54(3), 286–298 (2012)
15. Fustik, V., Rogleva, N.K., Petrova, N.: Gamification for practical engineering education in project and risk management. In: IEEE EUROCON 2019-18th International Conference on Smart Technologies, pp. 1–4 (2019)
16. Raabe, A., Santos, E., Paludo, L., Benitti, F.: Serious games applied to project management teaching. In: Enterprise Resource Planning: Concepts, Methodologies, Tools, and Applications, pp. 1427–1451. IGI Global (2013)

17. Stepanova, N., Davy, Y., Bochkov, P., Larionova, V.: Gamification in project management training. In: European Conference on Games Based Learning, pp. 653–659. Academic Conferences International Limited (2018)
18. Souza, M., Moreira, R., Figueiredo, E.: Playing the project: incorporating gamification into project-based approaches for software engineering education. In: Anais do XXVII Workshop sobre Educação em Computação, pp. 71–80. SBC (2019)
19. Bagdonas, E., Patašienė, I., Patašius, M., Skvernys, V.: Use of simulation and gaming to enhance entrepreneurship. Elektronika ir Elektrotechnika 102(6), 155–158 (2010)
20. Bagdonas, E., Patašienė, I., Skvernys, V.: How to cope with the complexities of a business game. In: International Simulation and Gaming Research Yearbook, vol. 6, pp. 100–109 (1998)
21. Arnuphaptrairong, T.: Top ten lists of software project risks: evidence from the literature survey. In: Proceedings of the International MultiConference of Engineers and Computer Scientists, vol. 1, pp. 1–6 (2011)
22. Nah, F.F.-H., Telaprolu, V.R., Rallapalli, S., Venkata, P.R.: Gamification of education using computer games. In: Yamamoto, S. (ed.) HIMI 2013. LNCS, vol. 8018, pp. 99–107. Springer, Heidelberg (2013). https://doi.org/10.1007/978-3-642-39226-9_12
23. Intrinsic Motivation Inventory (IMI). http://selfdeterminationtheory.org/intrinsic-motivation-inventory. Accessed 16 Mar 2020
24. Petri, G., von Wangenheim, C.G.: A method for the evaluation of the quality of games for computing education. In: Anais dos Workshops do Congresso Brasileiro de Informática na Educação, Rio de Janeiro, vol. 8, no. 1, p. 951 (2019)

Design of the Platform Solutions to Increase the Employability and E-Learning Opportunities for Low Skilled Women

Danguole Rutkauskiene[1](✉) and Greta Volodzkaite[2]

[1] Kaunas University of Technology, Kaunas, Lithuania
danguole.rutkauskiene@ktu.lt
[2] Information Technology Department, Kaunas University of Technology, Kaunas, Lithuania

Abstract. Personal behavioral skills combined with specific technical knowledge are a must in order to assess the labor market in the twenty first century. Individuals, like young women who are not employed, completed compulsory education or assessed any trainings are the ones who have the urgent need to enter labor market as fast as possible and not be excluded out of it. The aim of this paper is to present the best profiling tool approach to improve women employability by assessing alternative and integrated approach. The presented platform is accessible at any time from any of the devices and will direct users towards existing training offers online and face to face. It will identify existing user skills and competencies against identified digital jobs profile to place user in an employment matrix.

Keywords: Profiling · Gap analysis · Adult education · E-learning tools

1 Introduction

A good match between the skills demanded by the labor market and those acquired in training is important for promoting strong and inclusive growth for women [1, 7]. Studies show that female human capital accumulation has a considerable impact on technology adoption, innovation and economic growth and although women are beginning to achieve gender equality and close the gender gap in IT by developing digital fluency, they still remain underrepresented in the workforce in many developed countries [2].

Thus, helping women to access the skills they need to be successful can improve gender equality, promote inclusive growth and affect positively productivity, while also improve the efficiency of human capital allocation [3, 8].

However, the nature of jobs is quickly changing due to automation, social and economic factors, and it is difficult to predict which skills jobs will require in the future, thus threatening to widen the skills gap and making career planning more difficult [4]. In order to overcome this problem, profiling tool is one of the most reliable methods [5]. Systematic approach to setting project priorities carefully analyzing beneficiaries' needs, but in close cooperation with employers and stakeholders to identify current and desired status on important values and best support [6, 9].

© Springer Nature Switzerland AG 2020
A. Lopata et al. (Eds.): ICIST 2020, CCIS 1283, pp. 334–342, 2020.
https://doi.org/10.1007/978-3-030-59506-7_27

Technologies here play the crucial role. It is the easiest way to involve stakeholder, employees and employers into one platform where needs of the labor market will be covered by trainings developed by the professionals [10]. Platforms, consisting traditional learning and virtual learning methodological approaches help to assess the need faster, easier and more accurate. Tools, like profiling tools or gap analysis mechanisms help to match people with the job profiles which are the most related to their behavioral and specific required technical competencies needed for digital jobs profiles [11, 13, 15]. These tools combined together help to empower people to assess their already gained competencies and to gain the missing ones to become future leaders and information and communication technologies specialist [12, 14].

2 Requirements for the Profiling Tool

Digital jobs employability profiling tool is developed to follow a simple four-stage waterfall approach:

1. An online employability profiling tool to identify the user existing skills, competences, attitudes and experience in line with E-Competence framework, Digital Competence, social and working skills framework. These combined with the age, personal goals and formal education will place the user in an employment matrix. A digital employability pathway defines what individual training needs, experiences and work needs to be undertaken to achieve the objectives [15, 16].
2. An employer co-designed customized learning plan. The learning/training is hosted on the platform but will direct the user towards external learning offers if this would be needed. The platform is accessible online anytime from anywhere through any smart device. Face to face courses should also be are a part of the offering [17].
3. The recognition of user training, skills and experience (Prior Experiential Learning (PEL)) [18].
4. A job application and on-boarding support system developed to assist each individual with transitioning from an unemployment status to a successful first step into a digital job-related employment [19].

The aim of the profiling tool is to make a comparison of person's skills/competences/experiences versus the ones, which are required for that digital job.

2.1 Objectives of the Profiling Tool

1. Design profile framework for young women who might in the future search for digital job
2. Develop prototype of the profile environment
3. Design and develop tool for profiles implementation, sharing and delivery for job providers
4. Design and develop tool to perform gap analysis
5. Design and developed tool to build a training roadmap
6. Organize experimental evaluation of the profile and profiling tool
7. Develop methodology for tool users

Design Profile Framework. An analysis of the most appropriate profile structure has been made. Profile structure matches E-Competence framework, Digital Competence, social and working skills framework requirements as well as employer's requirements collected during the need's analysis process. Woman profiles and job profiles have common points to be match able together to be able to perform gap analysis and serve as a reference when build a training roadmap (Fig. 1).

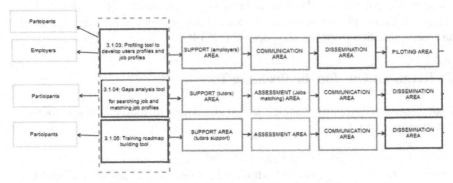

Fig. 1. Framework of the proposed profiling tool.

Development of architecture for Prototype Profile and Profiling Tool. The needs and existing good practices have been analyzed and base data structures and solution architecture for profiles and tools developed. Data structures and solution architecture designed to meet currently known best practices to achieve scalability, performance, code maintainability, quick changes, reduced complexity, adaptability. Data structures normalized, contain data only required to achieve the goals but at the same time be extensible for unforeseen future requirements. Data structures, storage and functionalities designed to meet EU General Data Protection Regulation (GDPR).

Development of Profiling Tools for young Women Searching for Digital Job. Wizard-like self-evaluation test(s) to assist in building personal profile have been created. Profile is used to check skills, competencies and experience gaps and to help to build a roadmap in order to become suitable for selected job profiles. User profiling data is stored privately, and user has a possibility to make the profile data available for other roles to review, perform gap analysis, create a training roadmap and other activities.

Development of Gap Analysis Tool. This tool contains functionality to set goals, create tasks to achieve those goals and track the progress. The roadmap is assigned automatically. Gap analysis tool is prefilled with job profiles containing data to identify required skills/competencies/experience. User profiles automatically matched with job profiles and insights provided in easily comprehensible way. Gap analysis result provide most matching job profiles, list of skills/competencies/experience user is matching and mismatching, some recommendations which skills/competencies/experience is recommended to gain by analyzing how often this skill/competence/experience is required in job profiles or taking into account other criteria, for example, it's the only skill/competence/experience what is missing to perfectly match one of the job profiles.

Development of Training Roadmap Building Tool. This tool contains functionalities to set goals, create steps to achieve those goals and to monitor the progress. Search engine finds courses and learning objects related to the requested keyword. Training roadmap is created for every user personally. Roadmap specifies what training is needed in order to potentially fit a desired job role, also, provides tools to monitor the progress, allow to set deadlines, tasks, completion status. The roadmap is an employer co-designed customized learning plan.

Experimental Evaluation and Recommendations for Improvement. The evaluation was organized using different methods and forms. The conclusions and suggestions for improvements have been adapted to the final project. Experimental evaluation has been conducted using a Software-Implemented Fault Injection tool (Xception) and both realistic programs and synthetic workloads (to focus on specific features) have been used. The results provided a comprehensive picture of the impact of faults and contributed to the key features (process scheduling and the most frequent system calls), data integrity, error propagation, application termination, and correctness of application results, virtualization, web application, communication, storage. Collected data was analyzed, features, types of virtualization and web application were discussed, and storage possibilities reviewed.

Design Methodology to Use Profiles and Profiling Tool. The methodology was designed with the aim to describe easily accessible, understandable functionality for profiling tool, for young women with low digital skills. Moreover, it is easy to use without additional help and serves as a user guide to using Profiles and profiling tool. Visual display of personal data associated with a specific user was presented. A description of profile refers the explicit digital representation of a person's identity, skills, competences and is presented online. Profiling is presented in the form of automated processing of personal data to evaluate certain personal aspects relating to a natural person, in particular to analyze or predict certain aspects concerning that natural person's performance at work.

3 Development of the Profiling Tool

A profiling tool performs as an assessment of the individual's skills, competencies and experience via an intuitive self-evaluation test and present the results to the individual. First of all, the collection of the requirements was done using already existing

data, followed by analysis of all the data acquired. Digital job profiles requirements were specified to create requirements specification (Fig. 2).

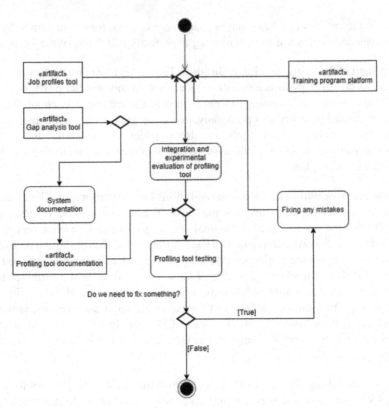

Fig. 2. Realization process and training phases during the development of the profiling tool.

Profiling tool design consists of requirements specification, which leads to creation of job profiles design prototype. Simultaneously Gaps analysis tool and training program platform were designed. After the designing phase, profiling tool was integrated and broken down into three graphs: Job profiles tool, gaps analysis tool and training program platform.

The realization process starts off when all the tools are created and implemented. Those tools were experimentally evaluated and profiled only then the profiling tool as whole begins. Before the testing, system documentation was created to guide testing process. In case any mistakes occurred, those specific tools had to be fixed and the whole cycle repeated. Implementation process gathers all the tools created and tested and checks if any mistakes were made, if none, the implementation is deemed as successful.

3.1 Data Streams

The purpose of this chapter is to define data sources for Profiling Tool. Profiling Tool is fed with taxonomies from ESCO, DigComp or e-CF. Job analysis results, including job level and work context, employers' and stakeholders' perceptions regarding existing and future trends as well as current job holders' experiences could also be considered when linking existing classification frameworks with evidence from the different national settings. Prioritization of suggestions could also consider job seeker preferences and employers' attitudes/values regarding specific competences. Taxonomies from different sources for profiling tool were pre-loaded by hand or like in ESCO case, by using single or multiple API's. Pre-loading with taxonomies is displayed in the diagram below (Fig. 3).

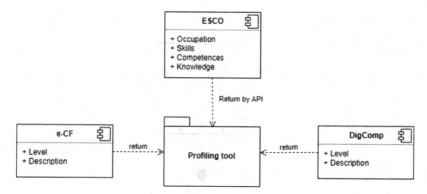

Fig. 3. Taxonomy of data pre-loading into the profiling tool

After the launch of the profiling tool, all data sources were gathered from Employers and Job Seekers excluding the need of constant taxonomy update and return from external sources. This leads to more stable tool and a more practical view of what the employers and job seekers need.

4 Architecture for the Gap Analysis Tool

The profiling tool and gap analysis tool were integrated and providing matching data results. The gap analysis tool measures the actual competencies for job profile and gives a feedback on: 1) women actual profile (skills and competences) and 2) gaps - where the competences are below the "norm" by suggesting the new training roadmap to gain new necessary skills and competences. Purpose of the Gap analysis tool is to match Job Seeker profile with occupations and Job Profiles to give insights on jobs woman is matching best. Best match means current woman knowledge, skill and knowledge is closest to the market needs and will probably take the minimum amount of effort to fill the gaps and get a job. Principal schema is demonstrated below (Fig. 4).

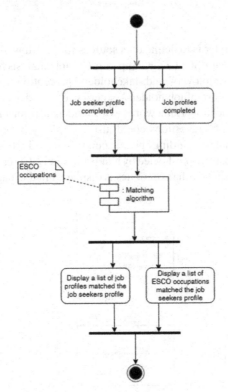

Fig. 4. The base structure of the proposed gap analysis tool

Gap analysis tool is fully automated and don't require any extra intervention or data but the Job Seeker profile and Job Profiles. To provide best possible results occupations from ESCO are also taken into consideration. This way Gap analysis tool will provide double results - matching to existing Job Profiles on the Profiling tool and matching to all ESCO specified occupations. This allows to not be restricted to current available jobs but also for prospects on other occupations and encourage for proactive job seeking.

5 Training Roadmap Builder

The purpose of the Training roadmap is to fill the gaps to get the job. Job Seeker, considering Gap Analysis results, existing Job Profiles and ESCO occupations where relevant builds a task list to achieve a goal (Fig. 5).

The profiling tool and gap analysis tool are integrated and providing matching data results. The gap analysis tool measures the actual competencies for job profile and gives a feedback on 1) women actual profile (skills and competences) and 2) gaps - where the competences are below the "norm" by suggesting the new training roadmap to gain new necessary skills and competences. The learning/training is the mostly hosted on the platform but direct the user towards external learning offers if this needed.

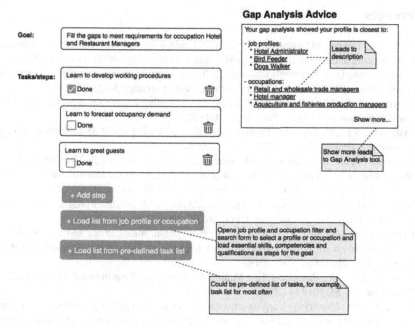

Fig. 5. The base structure of the proposed gap analysis tool

6 Conclusion

In this paper, we presented a detailed discussion of the best profiling tool integrated into the learning and training platform approach. The profiling tool and gap analysis tool are integrated and providing matching data results. The platform is accessible by individual women, who will use it in a self-paced mode but also could be used by a group of individuals in one location participating in a guided session. The best model to reach women, assess their competencies and train for future work requires these several methods: profile framework, profiling tool, gap analysis tool, training road map and collaboration with the target groups. Profile framework matches E-Competence framework, Digital Competence, social and working skills framework requirements as well as employer's requirements collected during the need's analysis process. Profiling tool, to check skills, competencies and experience gaps and to help to build a roadmap in order to become suitable for selected job profiles. Gap analysis tool, to set goals, create tasks to achieve those goals and track the progress. Training roadmap specifies what training is needed in order to potentially fit a desired job role, also, provides tools to monitor the progress, allow to set deadlines, tasks, completion status. Collaboration with the target groups allow us to combine the competencies needed in the labor market from the employers and stakeholders position, best training practices from the training providers and young women abilities to participate in the labor market. By targeting these practices, young women who are at the edge of exclusion from the labor market will be employed in the fastest and most involving way possible.

References

1. Assadi, A., Lundin, M.: Street-level bureaucrats, rule-following and tenure: how assessment tools are used at the front line of the public sector. Public Adm. **96**(1), 154–170 (2018)
2. Winsborough, D., Chamorro-Premuzic, T.: Talent identification in the digital world: new talent signals and the future of HR assessment. People Strategy **39**(2), 28 (2016)
3. Brayman, S., Grable, J. E., Griffin, P., Finke, M.: Assessing a client's risk profile: a review of solution providers. J. Financ. Serv. Prof. **71**(1) (2017)
4. Evuleocha, S.U., Ugbah, S.D.: Profiling: the efficacy of using social networking sites for job screening. J. Employ. Couns. **55**(2), 48–57 (2018)
5. Gandini, A., Pais, I.: Social recruiting: control and surveillance in a digitised job market. In: Moore, Phoebe V., Upchurch, M., Whittaker, X. (eds.) Humans and Machines at Work. DVW, pp. 125–149. Springer, Cham (2018). https://doi.org/10.1007/978-3-319-58232-0_6
6. Blazquez, M., Herrarte, A., Saez, F.: Training and job search assistance programmes in Spain: the case of long-term unemployed. J. Pol. Model. **41**(2), 316–335 (2019)
7. Considine, M., Nguyen, P., O'Sullivan, S.: New public management and the rule of economic incentives: Australian welfare-to-work from job market signalling perspective. Public Manage. Rev. **20**, 1186–1204 (2018)
8. Greco, F., Polli, A.: Emotional Text Mining: Customer profiling in brand management. Int. J. Inf. Manage. **51**, 101934 (2020)
9. Masse, J., et al.: Identifying learning outcomes for a Canadian pedology field school: addressing the gap between new graduates' skills and the needs of the current job market. Can. J. Soil Sci. **99**(4), 458–471 (2019)
10. Ahmad, N., Siddique, J.: Personality assessment using Twitter tweets. Procedia Comput. Sci. **112**, 1964–1973 (2017)
11. Persson, A.: Implicit bias in predictive data profiling within recruitments. In: Lehmann, A., Whitehouse, D., Fischer-Hübner, S., Fritsch, L., Raab, C. (eds.) Privacy and Identity 2016. IAICT, vol. 498, pp. 212–230. Springer, Cham (2016). https://doi.org/10.1007/978-3-319-55783-0_15
12. Ras, E., Wild, F., Stahl, C., Baudet, A.: Bridging the skills gap of workers in Industry 4.0 by human performance augmentation tools: challenges and roadmap. In Proceedings of the 10th International Conference on PErvasive Technologies Related to Assistive Environments, pp. 428–432, June 2017
13. McDonald, P., Thompson, P., O'Connor, P.: Profiling employees online: shifting public–private boundaries in organisational life. Hum. Resource Manage. J. **26**(4), 541–556 (2016)
14. ESF Transnational Platform: Tackling Long-Term Unemployment through Risk Profiling and Outreach (2018)
15. Sienkiewicz, Ł.: Professionalization of vocational roles of public employment services employees in europe through competency profiling. Problemy Zarządzania **14**(3(61)), 110–128 (2016)
16. Starr, S.B.: Testing racial profiling: empirical assessment of disparate treatment by police. University of Chicago Legal Forum, p. 485 (2016)
17. Arcidiacono, C., Tuozzi, T., Procentese, F.: Community profiling in participatory action research. In: Handbook of Methodological Approaches to Community-Based Research: Qualitative, Quantitative, and Mixed Methods, pp. 355–364 (2016)
18. Sztandar-Sztanderska, K., Zielenska, M.: Changing social citizenship through information technology. Soc. Work Soc. **16**(2) (2018)
19. Wasi-ur-Rahman, M., Islam, N.S., Lu, X., Shankar, D., Panda, D.K.D.: MR-Advisor: a comprehensive tuning, profiling, and prediction tool for MapReduce execution frameworks on HPC clusters. J. Parallel Distrib. Comput. **120**, 237–250 (2018)

Information Technology Applications - Special Session on Language Technologies

Cross-lingual Metaphor Paraphrase Detection – Experimental Corpus and Baselines

Martin Víta[✉]

NLP Centre, Faculty of Informatics, Masaryk University,
Botanická 68a, 602 00 Brno, Czech Republic
info@martinvita.eu

Abstract. Correct understanding to metaphors is an integral part of natural language understanding. It requires, among other issues, the ability to decide whether a given pair of sentences – such that the first one contains a metaphor – form a paraphrase pair. Although this decision task is formally analogous to a "traditional paraphrase detection" task, it requires a different approach. Recently, a first monolingual corpus (in English) for metaphor paraphrasing was released – together with several baselines. In this work we are going to shift this task to a cross-lingual level: we state a task of cross-lingual metaphor paraphrase detection, introduce a corresponding experimental cross-lingual corpus (English-Czech) and present several approaches to this problem and set the baselines to this challenging problem. This cross-lingual approach may allow us to deal with tasks like multi-document summarization involving texts in different languages as well as enable us to improve information retrieval tools.

Keywords: Paraphrasing · Metaphor · Cross-lingual setting · Metaphor paraphrase corpus · Textual entailment

1 Introduction

The task of detecting pairs of sentences that convey the same (or almost the same meaning), i.e., paraphrase detection, is one of the important tasks in NLP with many downstream applications – including text summarization, sentence compression, plagiarism detection, question answering and others, see [1,4]. Generally, it can be stated as a binary classification task over sentence pairs and it can be seen as a mutual (bidirectional) textual entailment.

Paraphrase detection is intensively studied problem for a relatively long period – a survey paper from 2010 [4] covers many "traditional" approaches (including surface string similarity, syntactic similarity, logic based approaches etc.). Currently – similarly to other fields of NLP – the major approaches to paraphrase detection are based on deep learning methods [1].

© Springer Nature Switzerland AG 2020
A. Lopata et al. (Eds.): ICIST 2020, CCIS 1283, pp. 345–356, 2020.
https://doi.org/10.1007/978-3-030-59506-7_28

Although we can observe a growing interest in metaphor detection (recently, a special Workshop on Figurative Language Processing was organized as a co-located event of NAACL conference [13]), the issues linking the notions of paraphrasing and metaphor are extremely rare. However, correct understanding to metaphors and their correct interpretation require the ability of detecting paraphrases also among sentences that contain metaphorical expressions. There are only a few papers and resources focused on metaphor paraphrases, like [7] (unsupervised approach) and [18] (focused on creating the corpus for a single word paraphrasing identification task). Nevertheless, these two works focus on particular cases of dealing with metaphors.

To best of our knowledge, there currently exists just only one corpus for metaphor paraphrase detection that covers a wider range of metaphor types [6]. The authors propose also a DNN architecture and set several baselines. We will introduce this corpus in a more detailed way in the next subsection.

Figurative and metaphoric expressions are naturally present in narratives as well as in many common documents being automatically processed – like newspaper articles, especially headlines (*"Republicans are eroding one of the core institutions of American democracy"*, *"Republicans are undermining supreme court"*[1], ...). Cross-lingual paraphrasing (detection) of such expressions allows us – among other tasks – summarizing such texts (like headlines [19]), improve plagiarism detection systems etc.

In this paper we introduce a task of *cross-lingual metaphor paraphrase detection* and describe a corresponding experimental English-Czech cross-lingual annotated corpus.

The task of cross-lingual metaphor detection (English-Czech in particular) can be stated as follows: it is a task to decide whether a given English sentence containing a metaphor convey or not convey the same (or almost the same) meaning as a given Czech sentence with **no metaphorical expressions.**

Notation Remark. For the purposes of this paper, we will follow a common naming convention: a sentence containing a metaphor expression will be called a *premise* and its potential paraphrase sentence candidate (without any metaphorical expression) will be called a *hypothesis*.

As already mentioned, the paraphrase detection task is closely related to a recognizing textual entailment (RTE), nowadays known rather as natural language inference (NLI) task: paraphrases are treated as *bidirectional* entailment relations [4].

To get a better insight into the problem, we provide one positive and one negative example (the first sentence in English contains a metaphorical expression, the second sentence, in Czech, is a potential paraphrase candidate followed by its translation to English) and, finally, the corresponding label (i.e., the result about paraphrasing):

---

[1] https://www.businessinsider.com/obama-says-republicans-are-undermining-supr eme-court-2016-10.

Positive Example

- PREMISE: *The faculty meeting was an easy breeze.*
- HYPOTHESIS: *Schůze fakulty byla klidná.* (transl. to English: *The faculty meeting was calm.*)
- LABEL: TRUE

Negative Example

- PREMISE: *She was the light of my life*
- HYPOTHESIS: *Měla světlo a život* (transl. to English: *She had light and a life*)
- LABEL: FALSE

2   Related Work

This work is related mainly to two fields: metaphor paraphrase detection and cross-lingual paraphrase detection.

2.1   Metaphor Paraphrase Detection

This work primarily shifts the "monolingual" case presented in [6] to cross-lingual level, hence we provide here more subtle focus on this paper. The authors present there a corpus for metaphor paraphrase detection in English (the authors deal there with the notion of *predicting metaphor paraphrase judgements*). The corpus originally consisted of 200 lists of five sentences such that the first sentence contained a metaphor and it is a sentence to be paraphrased. This sentence was followed by four sentences labeled by integers 1–4 that express the degree of being a paraphrase of the first sentence.

These integer labels roughly correspond with the following verbal expressions:

- 1: Two sentences cannot be considered as paraphrases.
- 2: Two sentences cannot be considered as paraphrases, but they show a degree of semantic similarity.
- 3: Two sentences could be considered as paraphrases, although they present some important difference in style or the content (they are not strong paraphrases).
- 4: Two sentences are strong paraphrases.

Analogous annotation scheme is familiar to "SemEval community" at semantic similarity tasks [3]. To have a better idea of this corpus, we provide an illustrative example taken from the second section of [6].

Reference Metaphor Sentence: *The crowd was a river in the street.*

Paraphrase Candidates and Corresponding Labels:

- *The crowd was large and impetuous in the street.* – LABEL: 4

- *There were a lot of people in the street.* – LABEL: 3
- *There were few people in the street.* – LABEL: 2
- *We reached a river at the end of the street.* – LABEL: 1

In other words, the corpus contains sentence pairs annotated with "graded paraphrase" labels – the labels can be viewed as paraphrase rankings.

Reference metaphor sentences were selected manually in order to cover various types of metaphorical expressions (the examples taken again from [6]):

- Noun phrase metaphors (*My lawyer is an angel.*)
- Adjective metaphors (*The rich man had a cold heart.*)
- Verb metaphors (*She cut him down with her words.*)
- Multi-word metaphors (*The seeds of change were planted in 1943.*)

Paraphrase candidates were also manually created by the authors. The overall goal was to have a reference metaphor sentence along with a strong paraphrase, a loose paraphrase and two non-paraphrases, one of them can contain some relevant words from the metaphor involved in the five-sentences set.

The pairs were originally annotated by one of the authors and, later, in order to achieve more reliable results, they were annotated by annotators from Amazon Mechanical Turk: 20 annotations for each sentence pair were collected. As the final gold label, the mean of the annotations was taken. The final corpus after certain cleansing contains 744 labeled items.

These 4-way labels can be easily transformed into a binary setting: sentence pairs with labels greater or equal to 3 are treated as paraphrases (label 1 in binary classification), other sentence pairs (labeled 1 or 2) are considered as non-paraphrases (label 0 in binary classification). In this work, we will elaborate on binary case. The binary corpus contains 373 negative and 371 positive labels, hence "all- negative" baseline achieves 50.13% accuracy on this dataset.

For binary classification as well as the graded case, the authors in [6] use Siamese deep architectures (premise and hypothesis are both encoded in the same way). Sentences are encoded using a sequence of layers depicted on Fig. 1:

The final dimension of the encoded sentence is relatively low (10). These sentence representations are simply concatenated, fed to a dense layer – the final decision is made by a common sigmoid layer.

The detailed description is provided in the paper and it is also available via the source code[2]. It should be noticed that convolutions used are not "standard ones" but *atrous* (delayed) convolutions [9], since they provide non-trivial improvements in accuracy.

The authors reached an average accuracy of 67 % in 12-fold cross-validation reported in the paper. Nevertheless, when reproducing this result, we achieved a lower accuracy approx. 58% (using various word embeddings including Fast-Text [15] and GloVe [16], the best result 58.33% in 12-fold cross validation was achieved with GloVe embeddings[3] – trained in 60 epochs (with a fixed partition

---

[2] https://github.com/yuri-bizzoni/Metaphor-Paraphrase.
[3] https://nlp.stanford.edu/projects/glove/.

the accuracy increased to 69.35%). The lower accuracy may be caused by several factors – including different word embeddings used (originally, the authors used word2vec embeddings) as well as different training parameters and different partitioning for 12-fold cross-validation.

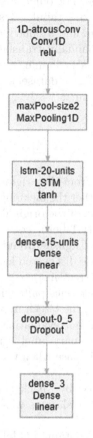

Fig. 1. Sentence encoder architecture.

2.2   Cross-lingual Paraphrase Detection

Unlike the monolingual case, cross-lingual paraphrase settings are less common. As a particular example of such a cross-lingual case, we can point out Vietnamese-English cross-lingual task [12].

The authors introduce an English-Vietnamese paraphrase corpus with 44652 items and they trained Siamese recurrent networks and use mapping bilingual word embeddings, add POS vectors to word embeddings and adjust the POS tagging labels between Vietnamese text and English text. However, their corpus is not focused on metaphorical expressions (hence it was more easy to 40K volume).

3   Data: Creating the Cross-lingual Corpus

The starting point for cross lingual (EN-CZ) metaphor paraphrase corpus development was the original – monolingual – English metaphor paraphrase corpus mentioned in the previous section. For our convenience, these raw corpus data were cleansed and transformed to a tabular (csv) format – this file contains sentence pairs, graded annotation, and a binary classification label.[4]

The hypotheses were than manually translated from English to Czech by a group of four people (graduates in humanities and PhD students, each one translated approx. one fourth of the dataset). The new, cross-lingual corpus basically contains items in the form:

- (EN) premise,
- (CZ) hypothesis,
- (original) binary label.

The binary labels were taken from the original monolingual corpus and subsequently checked manually: whether the meaning of the Czech sentence is equivalent (paraphrase) to the meaning of the original English metaphorical sentence (premise), i.e., whether the binary label is correct or not – with respect to the original metaphoric sentence in English (premise) and the Czech paraphrase candidate (hypothesis). This phase discovered less than one percent of instances with incorrect labels. These incorrect instances (hypotheses) were later manually modified in order to obtain sentence pairs with correct labels: in such cases, premise and label remained fixed, the Czech hypothesis was rewritten.

We should notice that we are *not* evaluating the quality of the translation, but (only) the correctness of the binary label – in other words, generally, we do not reject incorrect translations in case when they are parts of correctly labeled sentence (EN-CZ) pairs.

The dataset was also enriched by "back translations" of Czech sentences (hypotheses) to English. These translations were obtained by a machine translation (MT) system [14].

The final cross-lingual corpus contains 744 labeled instances, the distribution of labels is the same that as in the original corpus (373 negative and 371 positive examples). An example of an item in the corpus is provided below:

- **PremiseID:** premID182
- **HypothesisID:** hypoID725
- **Premise:** *She knew she was burning in shame*
- **Hypothesis in Czech:** *Věděla, že cítíintenzivnípocit hanby.*
- **Original hypothesis:** *She knew she was feeling an intense shame*
- **Binary label:** 1
- **Machine translation of the Czech hypothesis:** *She knew she felt an intense sense of shame.*
- **Degree of being paraphrase:** 4
- **Partition:** 1

---

[4] Available at: https://github.com/martinvita/FigurativeLanguageParaphrasing/blob/master/crossLingualMetaphorParaphraseEN-CZ.csv.

The last (auxiliary) attribute – Partition – is used for 12-fold cross-validation.

Table 1 summarizes the distribution of lengths (i.e., number of tokens) of hypotheses (paraphrase candidates) in Czech.

As can be seen, hypotheses are relatively short – 75% of them have lower or equal to 9 tokens.

BLEU score computed w.r.t. original English hypotheses and MT translation of Czech hypotheses back to English has a value of 0.4596. The impact of quality of translations was not evaluated, however, it may an issue of further research.

Table 1. Distribution of length (number of tokens)

Length	2	3	4	5	6	7	8	9	10	11	12	13	14	15	16	≥17
No. of hypotheses	12	40	85	102	115	96	77	62	47	43	15	18	9	9	5	9

4   Approaches and Models

As mentioned above, in the monolingual case, the authors in [6] presented a DNN Siamese architecture that encodes premise and hypothesis using convolutional NNs (to be more precious, using time-dilated convolutions and max-poolings – the architecture of the network is described above in Related Work section). Input sentences are represented as a sequences of word embeddings in a common way.

Our approaches to the cross-lingual case can be divided into two basic classes:

1. approaches that use *monolingual* tools and machine translation
2. approaches that use *multilingual* tools (e.g., embeddings),

4.1   Monolingual Tools and Machine Translation Approaches

As previously mentioned, we have already performed machine translation on Czech hypotheses. Therefore we can deal with a classification task of sentence pairs in the form of *"original premise* (containing metaphorical expression) and *machine-translated hypotheses* (paraphrase candidate, translated from Czech to English)".

Machine Translation + FastText Word Embeddings on English Approach (MT+FastText): We used the same architecture (sentence encoder) as in the original monolingual work [6] with a little modification: we used FastText embeddings from MUSE project. The network has 41701 trainable parameters in total. It was trained in 130 epochs with RMSprop.

Machine Translation + GloVe Word Embeddings on English Approach (MT+GloVe): The same approach as in the previous case with GloVe embeddings instead of FastText embeddings.

Universal Sentence Encoder Approach (MT+USE): Our second approach is based on Universal Sentence Encoders (USE for short), see [8]. (A brief descriptions of USE family is provided in [5].) USE outputs are 512-dimensional sentence embeddings (generally, embeddings of more-than-one-word pieces of text).[5] Since USE are not available for Czech, we used MT translations again.

Sentence representations (premise and translated hypothesis representations) obtained by USE are merged using a concatenation layer followed by a dense 32-dimensional layer, subsequently followed by a dropout layer and completed with a sigmoid classification layer.

4.2   Multilingual Embeddings Approach

MUSE Word Embeddings Approaches: While the previously introduced approaches fully rely on machine translation, the second set of baseline approaches is based on multilingual word embeddings.

We used precomputed FastText word embeddings (trained on Wikipedia) that are aligned in a single vector space. Therefore the embedding of an English word and the embedding of its corresponding translation are located close in the embedding space. These multilingual embeddings are available for 30 languages *including Czech* within a MUSE project[6].

We used the same sentence encoders and investigated three scenarios:

1. concatenation of encoded premise and Czech hypothesis is subsequently fed to a sigmoid layer (MUSE-EN+CZ),
2. concatenation of encoded premise, encoded Czech hypothesis and encoded English hypothesis (MT from CZ to EN) is subsequently fed again to a sigmoid layer (MUSE-EN+CZ+EN-concat),
3. concatenation of encoded premise and average of encoded Czech hypothesis and encoded English hypothesis (MT from CZ to EN) is subsequently fed again to a sigmoid layer (MUSE-EN+(CZ+EN)-aver).

The last architecture is shown on Fig. 2.

The idea behind the last two scenarios is to exploit both the information contained in the Czech hypothesis and also in the information from the English hypothesis obtained from the Czech by machine translation. The averaging used in the third scenario is possible since we use the same sentence encoders. In all cases, presented architectures are simple, since the volume of the dataset is still not big, hence larger models may be faced with overfitting.

---

[5] We used https://tfhub.dev/google/universal-sentence-encoder/4.
[6] https://github.com/facebookresearch/MUSE.

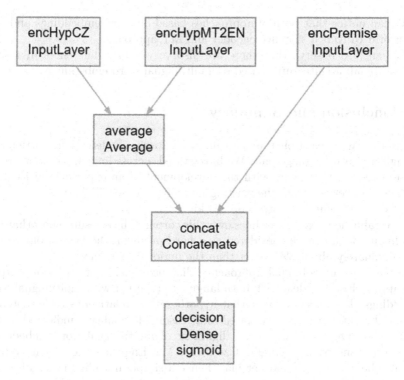

Fig. 2. Architecture based on averaging sentence representations of Czech and MT English hypotheses

5   Results

The results of proposed classifiers are summarized in the following table.

Table 2. Results of considered approaches

Approach	Accuracy
MT+GloVe	0.5671
MT+FastText	**0.5820**
MT+USE	0.5565
MUSE-EN+(CZ+EN)-aver	0.5591
MUSE-EN+CZ+EN-concat	0.5531
MUSE-EN+CZ	0.5534

As accuracy (in the context of Table 2), we mean the mean of accuracies obtained by 12-fold validation – the same concept of 12-fold validation was used in original paper [6].

We can notice that both of approaches based on word embeddings and MT outperform Universal sentence encoder and MT approach.

We can also observe that there are also very subtle differences in results obtained by all architectures based on multilingual word embeddings.

6   Conclusion and Summary

This work was focused on the cross-lingual paraphrase detection, particularly on English-Czech language pair. We have stated a cross lingual metaphor paraphrase detection task along with the development of an experimental English-Czech corpus derived from the existing monolingual one. To best of our knowledge, this is the only one corpus of this kind.

We established several baselines over this corpus. These results show that this cross-lingual task can be considered as a hard problem: the best of our results is approximately about 8% higher than the majority baseline.

In our case, monolingual approaches that use machine translation outperform approaches that deal with both languages together with multilingual word embeddings. The reason may be that hypotheses are relatively simple sentences that can be automatically translated in a reasonable quality – indicated by the BLEU score. On the other hand, alignment of multilingual word embeddings may cause some bias. Averaging Czech and MT English sentence embeddings may also be a source of another bias, hence a simple monolingual architecture outperforms other approaches. Generally, low results are probably caused by a relative small volume of the corpus – the impact of increasing number of training instances will be a subject of further investigations.

6.1   Further Work

Since deep learning approaches generally require large volume of training data, one of the future directions is augmenting this dataset with additional examples. Additional training data allows us to investigate also the impact of size of the dataset. Moreover, larger datasets provide a solid background for stating statistical hypotheses and their testing.

In a similar task of cross-lingual inference, one of the first experimental corpora contained 1332 examples in four languages [2], more widely known XNLI corpus [10] contains 7500 items. The other issue is also adding other languages (i. e., hypotheses in languages different from Czech). Incorporating additional languages other than Czech enables discovering the role of the language and/or possible independence of approaches on a given language.

The other major direction is the development of new models and architectures, including promising approaches based on transformers like BERT [11] and contextualized word embeddings like ELMo [17].

Acknowledgement. The author wants to express thanks to colleagues and friends who contributed to translations of the paraphrase candidates and anonymous referees for their valuable comments and suggestions.

This work contains materials and results achieved in the author's PhD thesis, currently under review.

References

1. Agarwal, B., Ramampiaro, H., Langseth, H., Ruocco, M.: A deep network model for paraphrase detection in short text messages. Inf. Process. Manag. **54**(6), 922–937 (2018)
2. Agić, Ž., Schluter, N.: Baselines and test data for cross-lingual inference. arXiv preprint arXiv:1704.05347 (2017)
3. Agirre, E., et al.: SemEval-2016 task 1: semantic textual similarity, monolingual and cross-lingual evaluation. In: Proceedings of the 10th International Workshop on Semantic Evaluation (SemEval-2016), pp. 497–511 (2016)
4. Androutsopoulos, I., Malakasiotis, P.: A survey of paraphrasing and textual entailment methods. J. Artif. Intell. Res. **38**, 135–187 (2010)
5. Barančíková, P., Bojar, O.: In search for linear relations in sentence embedding spaces. arXiv preprint arXiv:1910.03375 (2019)
6. Bizzoni, Y., Lappin, S.: Predicting human metaphor paraphrase judgments with deep neural networks. In: Proceedings of the Workshop on Figurative Language Processing, pp. 45–55. Association for Computational Linguistics, New Orleans, June 2018. https://doi.org/10.18653/v1/W18-0906. https://www.aclweb.org/anthology/W18-0906
7. Bollegala, D., Shutova, E.: Metaphor interpretation using paraphrases extracted from the web. PLoS ONE **8**(9), e74304 (2013)
8. Cer, D., et al.: Universal sentence encoder. arXiv preprint arXiv:1803.11175 (2018)
9. Chen, L.C., Papandreou, G., Kokkinos, I., Murphy, K., Yuille, A.L.: DeepLab: semantic image segmentation with deep convolutional nets, atrous convolution, and fully connected CRFs. IEEE Trans. Pattern Anal. Mach. Intell. **40**(4), 834–848 (2017)
10. Conneau, A., et al.: XNLI: evaluating cross-lingual sentence representations. arXiv preprint arXiv:1809.05053 (2018)
11. Devlin, J., Chang, M.W., Lee, K., Toutanova, K.: BERT: pre-training of deep bidirectional transformers for language understanding. arXiv preprint arXiv:1810.04805 (2018)
12. Dien, D., et al.: Vietnamese-English cross-lingual paraphrase identification using siamese recurrent architectures. In: 2019 19th International Symposium on Communications and Information Technologies (ISCIT), pp. 70–75. IEEE (2019)
13. Klebanov, B.B., Shutova, E., Lichtenstein, P., Muresan, S., Wee, C.: Proceedings of the Workshop on Figurative Language Processing (2018)
14. Košarko, O., Variš, D., Popel, M.: LINDAT translation service. LINDAT/CLARIN digital library at the Institute of Formal and Applied Linguistics (ÚFAL), Faculty of Mathematics and Physics, Charles University (2019). http://hdl.handle.net/11234/1-2922
15. Lample, G., Conneau, A., Denoyer, L., Ranzato, M.: Unsupervised machine translation using monolingual corpora only. arXiv preprint arXiv:1711.00043 (2017)

16. Pennington, J., Socher, R., Manning, C.D.: GloVe: global vectors for word representation. In: Proceedings of the 2014 Conference on Empirical Methods in Natural Language Processing (EMNLP), pp. 1532–1543 (2014)
17. Peters, M.E., et al.: Deep contextualized word representations. arXiv preprint arXiv:1802.05365 (2018)
18. Shutova, E., Teufel, S.: Metaphor corpus annotated for source-target domain mappings. In: LREC, vol. 2, p. 2. Citeseer (2010)
19. Zhou, L., Hovy, E.: Headline summarization at ISI. In: Proceedings of the HLT-NAACL 2003 Text Summarization Workshop and Document Understanding Conference (DUC 2003), pp. 174–178 (2003)

Deep Learning-Based Part-of-Speech Tagging of the Tigrinya Language

Senait Gebremichael Tesfagergish[(✉)] and Jurgita Kapociute-Dzikiene

Vytautas Magnus University, K. Donelaičio, 44248 Kaunas, Lithuania
senugeb17@gmail.com, jurgita.k.dz@gmail.com

Abstract. Deep Neural Networks have demonstrated the great efficiency in many NLP task for various languages. Unfortunately, some resource-scarce languages as, e.g., Tigrinya still receive too little attention, therefore many NLP applications as part-of-speech tagging are in their early stages. Consequently, the main objective of this research is to offer the effective part-of-speech tagging solutions for the Tigrinya language having rather small training corpus.

In this paper the Deep Neural Network classifiers (i.e., Feed Forward Neural Network, Long Short-Term Memory, Bidirectional LSTM and Convolutional Neural Network) are investigated by applying them on a top of trained distributional neural word2vec embeddings. Seeking for the most accurate solutions, DNN models are optimized manually and automatically. Despite automatic hyper-parameter optimization demonstrates a good performance with the Convolutional Neural Network, the manually tested Bidirectional Long Short – Term Memory method achieves the highest overall accuracy equal to 0.91% .

Keywords: Deep Neural Networks · FFNN, CNN, LSTM, BiLSTM methods · word2vec embeddings · Nagaoka corpus · Tigrinya part-of-speech tagging

1 Introduction

Part-of-speech (POS) tagging is a well-known task in NLP: it represents a process of mapping words in sentences into their corresponding parts-of-speech, based on their context and the meaning. POS tagging is a prerequisite for many NLP tasks such as dependency parsing, machine translation, speech recognition and so many others. To train the accurate POS tagger, a large annotated corpus is required. Unfortunately, for many resource-scarce languages such annotated corpora do not exist. Unsupervised solutions still underperform supervised, therefore, to expect better results the annotated data is crucial. Besides, there is no one right solution that could work for each language: each language is different and difficult in its own way, therefore requires adaptation [6].

Tigrinya belongs to the Semitic language branch of the Afro-asiatic family, along with Hebrew, Amharic, Maltese, Tigre and Arabic. Semitic languages are characterized with the rich derivational and influential morphology which results in the numerous variations of word forms. The distinguishing feature of Semitic languages lies in the 'root-template' morphological pattern that is often composed of trilateral roots. The verb

© Springer Nature Switzerland AG 2020
A. Lopata et al. (Eds.): ICIST 2020, CCIS 1283, pp. 357–367, 2020.
https://doi.org/10.1007/978-3-030-59506-7_29

roots in Semitic languages comprise a sequence of consonants, whereas the templates are the patterns of vowels that are intercalated in between these consonants, forming various stems.

Besides, the resource rich languages such as English have large corpora, well-developed language tools and can continue the research based on finding from the previous studies. On the contrary, the Tigrinya language has only one corpus, available for POS tagging, which is rather small [5]. Open resource corpus (such as Crubadan Corpus Building for Minority Languages[1]) doesn't contain the morphological labels crucial for the POS tagging task. Previous research (presented in [6] and [3] performed with the Tigrinya POS tagging was based on training the traditional supervised machine learning techniques; in particular, the Conditional Random Fields (CRFs) classifier and Support Vector Machines (SVMs). Despite the authors managed to achieve good results they have not tested state-of-the-art techniques yet that could boost the accuracy even further. Consequently, in this research for the Tigrinya POS tagging we focus on the best currently known solutions based on the Deep learning. Seeking for the best model we test several Deep Neural Network (DNN) classifiers (Feed Forward Neural Network – FFNN, Long Short-Term Memory Network – LSTM, Bidirectional LSTM – BiLSTM and Convolutional Neural Network – CNN) by tuning hyperparameters manually and automatically. It resulted in finding the accurate model able to reach the accuracy of ~0.91 using BiLSTM method.

2 The Corpus

The data for the Tigrinya POS tagging is taken from the *Nagaoka University of Japan*[2] [5] and to our knowledge it is the only POS tagged corpus publicly available for the Tigrinya language. The corpus contains newspaper articles, 72,080 tokens from 4656 sentences (the snippet from the corpus can be found in Fig. 1) [5]. Words in the corpus are labelled with 20 POS tags (**V_PRF, UNC, V_AUX, V_IMV, N, PUN, V_REL, ADV, INT, N_V, ADJ, NUM, N_PRP, FW, V, V_GER, CON, V_IMF, PRE, PRO**) making this problem a supervised multi-class classification problem. It is prepared in Geez and English alphabets, but in our experiments only the English alphabet is used.

The corpus was split into training, validation and testing. The statistics can be found in Table 1.

Tigrinya words possess rich morphological information embedded in the form of prefixes, infixes and suffixes [1]. Thus, the Tigrinya language specifics makes us to consider the following features: 1) if a word is the first word in a sentence; 2) if a word is the last word in a sentence; 3) POS tags of 2 words before a target word; 4) a POS tag of 1 word before a target word; 5) POS tags of 2 words after a target word; 6) a POS tag of 1 word after a target word.

---

[1] Available at http://crubadan.org/languages/ti and word list compiled by Biniam Gebremichael's web crawler, available http://www.cs.ru.nl/biniam/geez/crawl.php.

[2] Available at https://eng.jnlp.org/yemane/ntigcorpus.

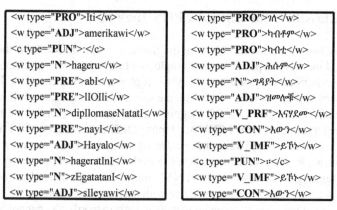

Fig. 1. The snipper from the Nagaoka corpus used for the Tigrinya POS tagging [5]

Table 1. Training, testing and validation splits of the dataset used in Tigrinya POS tagging

Set	Percentage points	Number of tokens	Number of sentences
Training	60%	43,248	2,792
Validation	20%	14,416	931
Testing	20%	14,416	933

3 Vectorization

DNNs can be applied on a top of vectorized words. For this reason, we have selected the novel distributional word embeddings approach, where each word is represented with a real values vector and vectors of the semantically similar words are projected closely in a vector space.

In our experiments we have used word2vec approach, which is a NN trained embedding model. Before training, the text corpus was split into windows containing a focus word (given as a NN input) and its context (given as the output). Since similar focus words appear in the similar context; their word2vec vectors are closer in the vector space. Given enough training data, the position of the word in a vector space is learned correctly.

Since pre-trained and publicly available word embeddings do not exist for the Tigrinya language, we have trained embeddings with 4656 sentences of the Nagaoka corpus with dimensionality = 100. We have set the context window size equal to 3, which means that a context of 3 words before and 3 words after a target word were considered. All the rest parameters were set to their default values. For training the word embeddings we have used python programming language with *gensim* [9]. The pre-trained word embeddings were saved and afterwards used in all our experiments.

4   DNN Classifiers for Tigrinya POS Tagging

Feed Forward Neural Network (FFNN) or multilayer perceptron (MLPs) is the simplest network of all the DNN types, it is very simple and fast compared to the other types of DNN. For the POS tagging problem, FFNN can play a role of a classifier. Despite it, FFNN does not have solutions to work with the sequential data (i.e., words in sentences) that is especially important in the POS tagging; therefore, the sequential information (a context of the target word) to the FFNN was inputted indirectly: in a form of 2 succeeding and 2 preceding words around a target word. Despite contextual information was fed into FFNN in such a fake way, we do not expect the method to demonstrate very good results in the POS tagging task. However, the FNNN method is still selected as the baseline approach to see how far the accuracy can go with such a naïve solution.

However, working with the sequential data (as a text) a word order cannot be ignored. Especially a word order is informative for the Tigrinya language, because changing it in a sentence, the meaning of a sentence also changes. For this reason, Recurrent Neural Networks (RNNs) should be a good choice for our POS tagging task. RNNs are methods having memory units and therefore adjusted to cope with the sequential data. An input of the current time step is an input for the next time step, thus it has two inputs of which the first one is an actual input (i.e., incoming word from a sentence) and the second one is an output of the previous time steps (i.e., generalized information about previous words). Despite RNNs have the memory, they suffer from the vanishing gradient problem. RNNs remember only the recent information and therefore are accurate working with the short-term dependencies. For the longer sequence's LSTMs and BiLSTMs are used instead, because they are refined to remember longer sequences. LSTM memory cell has 3 weighted gates adjusted during training the input, forget and output gates are used to memorize what information to input, forget and output, respectively. LSTM considers information going in only one direction: i.e., from the beginning to the future. However, BiLSTM considers sequences going in both directions: from-the-past-to-the-future and from-the-future-to-the-past. In the POS tagging task, some later words may give important details about the morphological form of the current word and it is especially evident with the Tigrinya language verbs carrying a lot of information about nouns and pronouns, mostly appearing at the end of sentences.

Despite RNNs (as LSTMs, BiLSTM) are adjusted to cope with the sequences of words, sometimes they underperform the other classifiers. Recurrent methods consider the whole context including unrelated to the target word. For this reason, CNNs could be a good solution. Initially these methods were used for the image data, however, recently they are successfully adjusted for the NLP problems. Instead of whole text sequences, CNNs consider only patterns of sequential words (called n-grams) and a width n (usually $n = [2, 5]$ words) of some filter determines how long patterns are worth to explore. CNNs could be a good option for our solving task, because in the Tigrinya language not all the information in text sentences matters, but only some context (in terms of n-grams), usually close to the target word.

5   Experiments and Results

In this research we have experimented with the dataset (described in Sect. 2), using vectorization (in Sect. 3) and the DNN methods (in Sect. 4). For the method implementations we have used python programming language with *TensorFlow* [10] and *Keras* [2].

As the evaluation metrics we have used the accuracy and the loss presented in Eq. 1.

$$\text{Accuracy} = \frac{tp + tn}{tp + tn + fp + fn}, \quad \text{where} \tag{1}$$

tp (true positives) represent + instances with, determined class +;
fn (false negatives) represent + instances, with determined class −;
fp (false positives) represent − instances, with determined class +;
tn (true negatives) represent − instances, with determined class −.

For the POS tagging results to be considered reasonable and appropriate the accuracy (in Eq. 1) must be above calculated random = 0.127 (see Eq. 2) and majority = 0.270 (Eq. 3) baselines.

$$\text{Random baseline} = \sum P(c_i)^2 \tag{2}$$

$$\text{Majority baseline} = \max P(c_i), \quad \text{where} \tag{3}$$

c_i is a probability of a class (where classes represent POS tags).

In this research we have explored different DNNs architectures and hyper-parameters (by tuning manually and automatically), paying specific attention to the activation functions. Activation functions determine the output of DNNs deciding whether it should be activated or not based on each neurons' input and relevancy in prediction. In this paper we have explored 3 types of activation functions [8]: *relu*, *softmax* and *tanh* to determine the best.

5.1   Manually Tuned DNN Architectures and Hyper-parameters

With **FFNN** classifier the following parameters were investigated (Figs. 8 and 9):

- One-hot encoding vectorization;
- 1, 2 and 3 hidden layers and neurons of 256, 512, 1024;
- 100 epochs;
- 256 as the batch size;
- *Tanh, softmax, relu* activation functions.

The highest accuracy (equal to 28%) with the FFNN classifier was achieved with the *softmax* activation function (see Fig. 3) and the architecture presented in Fig. 2[3]. Different numbers of neurons, hidden layers didn't show any significant impact on the accuracy.

With **LSTM** and **BiLSTM** classifiers the following parameters were investigated:

---

[3] For representing this and further models *plot_model* function in Keras was used.

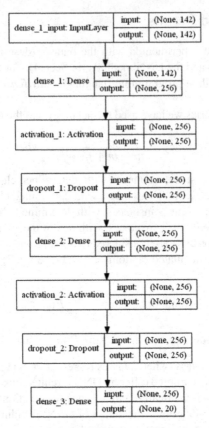

Fig. 2. Architecture of the best determined model with the FFNN classifier

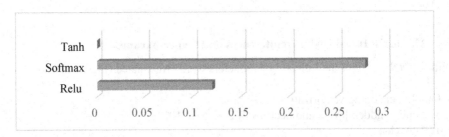

Fig. 3. Accuracies with different activation functions using FFNN

- Word2vec distributional neural embeddings (Sect. 3);
- 1, 2, and 3 hidden layers;
- 32, 64, 128, 256 neurons;
- 100 epochs;
- 32 as the batch size;
- *Tanh, softmax, relu* activation functions.

The best accuracies with different activation functions for LSTM (Fig. 5, Fig. 4) and BiLSTM (Fig. 7, Fig. 6) were achieved with one hidden layer and 64 neurons.

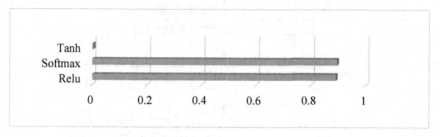

Fig. 4. Accuracies with different activation functions using LSTM

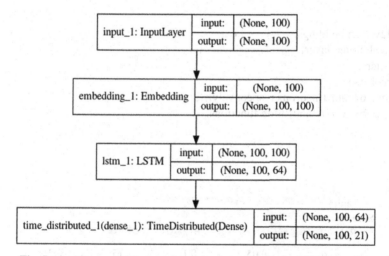

Fig. 5. Architecture of the best determined model with the LSTM classifier

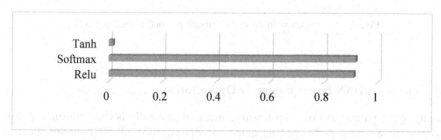

Fig. 6. Accuracies with different activation functions using BiLSTM

With **CNN** classifier the following parameters were investigated:

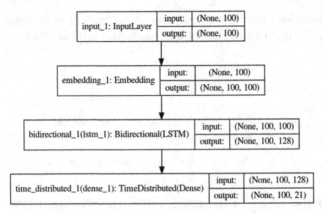

Fig. 7. Architecture of the best determined model with the BiLSTM classifier

- word2vec embeddings;
- 1 convolutional layer;
- 100 filters;
- 3 kernel size;
- 2 layers, 64 and 1 neurons respectively;
- *Tanh*, *softmax*, *relu* activation functions.

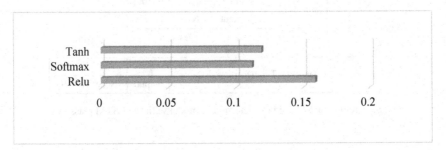

Fig. 8. Accuracies with different activation functions using CNN

5.2 Automatic DNN Hyperparameter Optimization

Tuning hyper-parameters of deep learning methods manually is time consuming. For this reason, we have performed an automatic optimization of the hyper-parameters with python's library Hyperas [4]. The discrete and real hyper-parameter values were tuned automatically searching for the best their options giving the highest accuracy on the validation dataset. LSTM, BiLSTM and CNN classifiers applied on a top of word2vec embeddings with the following options of hyper-parameters were tested in our experiments:

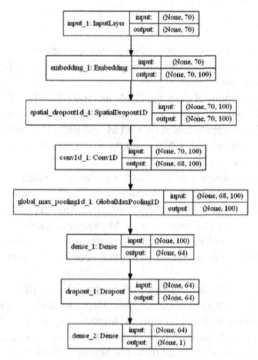

Fig. 9. Architecture of the best determined model with the CNN classifier

- *sigmoid, softmax, tanh, relu, swish, selu* activation functions;
- *adam, sdg, rmsprop* optimizers;
- 32, 64, 128 as the batch size;
- 16, 32, 64, 128 neurons;
- 1, 2, 3 layers

The optimization was performed in 20 iterations tuning hyper-parameters in the directed manner using *tpe.suggest* strategy. The best obtained results are presented in Table 2.

Table 2. Hyperparameter optimization results

Method	Activation	Layers	Neurons	Batch_size	Optimizer	Accuracy
LSTM	Sigmoid	1	32	32	rmsprop	0.89
BiLSTM	Sigmoid	1	64	32	rmsprop	0.91
CNN	Sigmoid, Softmax	1	32	32	adam	0.61

6 Discussion

Zooming into the results allow us to make the following statements. The best results with different classifiers are above random and majority baselines, therefore are considered appropriate and reasonable.

Using the limited amount of data, the DNN methods, FFNN, LSTM, BiLSTM and CNN have been tested with the neural word embeddings. Hyper-parameter optimization has not made significant improvement on LSTM and BiLSTM, however, the accuracy got higher on CNN reaching 0.61. CNN is not the worst option (FFNN is the worst), but it is not efficient with the sequential data.

Either manual or automatic tuning of hyper-parameters revealed the superiority of the BiLSTM classifier reaching the accuracy = 0.91. This result was proved to be significantly the best compared to the other achieved results reported in this paper. The statistical significance was calculated by using McNemar test with the significance level of 95% [7]. BiLSTM considers sequences of words in both direction (from-the-past-to-the-future and from-the-future-to-the-past) that seems to be very important for the Tigrinya language.

In the previous work for the Tigrinya POS tagging the traditional classifiers (CRFs and SVMs) were applied on a top of contextual, morphological and affix features reaching the accuracy of 0.90. In this paper we to improve this result with the DNN. Our research work is important, because it explores the effectiveness of the state-of-the-art DNN methods that are already proved to be the best in various NLP tasks for the other languages.

Since the experiment is done with a rather small corpus, we anticipate that the accuracy of the model could increase even more by adding more representative and diverse sentences to the corpus.

7 Conclusion

In this paper we are solving the part-of-speech tagging problem for the morphologically complex Tigrinya language. The contribution of this research is that for the first time we apply state-of-the-art DNN classifiers (in particular, Feed Forward Neural Network, Long Short-Term Memory, Bidirectional LSTM and Convolutional Neural Network) in the part-of-speech tagging task for the Tigrinya language. Besides, we train and use Tigrinya neural word embeddings. Seeking for the best model for our solving task, we also test different options of hyper-parameter values (by tuning them manually and automatically) for different types of DNNs. The best accuracy of 0.91 is achieved with the Bidirectional LSTM classifier and the *softmax* activation function. The result is considered promising (because much above random and majority baselines); however, to improve the accuracy even more we probably need more training data. This research is important for the Tigrinya language; however, other similar Ethiopic languages (especially resource-scarce) can also benefit from this research: we expect the conclusions about the methods (and hyper-parameters) to be similar.

References

1. Amsalu, S., Gibbon, D.: Finite state morphology of amharic. In: International Conference on Recent Advances in Natural Language Processing, pp. 47–51 (2005)
2. Chollet, F.: Keras: deep learning library for Theano and Tensorflow (2015). https://keras.io/. Accessed Mar 2020
3. Gebregzabiher, T.: Part of speech tagger for tigrigna language. Department of Computer Science, Addis Ababa University, Master thesis (2010)
4. Hyperas: Keras + Hyperopt: A Very Simple Wrapper for Convenient Hyperparameter Optimization. https://github.com/maxpumperla/hyperas. Accessed Mar 2020
5. Keleta, Y., Yamamoto, K., Marasinghe, A.: Nagaoka Tigrinya Corpus: Design and Development of Part-of-Speech Tagged Corpus. The Association for Natural Language Processing, pp. 413–416 (2016)
6. Keleta, Y., Yamamoto, K., Marasinghe, A.: Tigrinya part-of-speech tagging with morphological patterns and the New Nagaoka Tigrinya Corpus. Int. J. Comput. Appl. **146**(14), 33–41 (2016). https://doi.org/10.5120/ijca2016910943
7. McNemar, Q.: Note on the sampling error of the difference between correlated proportions or percentages. Psychometrika **12**(2), 153–157. https://doi.org/10.1007/bf02295996, PMID 20254758
8. Nwankpa, Ch., Ijomah, W., Gachagan, A., Marshall, S.: Activation Functions: Comparison of Trends in Practice and Research for Deep Learning (2018). arXiv:1811.03378v1
9. Řehůřek, R., Sojka, P.: Software framework for topic modeling with large corpora. In: Proceedings of the LREC 2010 Workshop on New Challenges for NLP Frameworks, pp. 45–50 (2010). https://doi.org/10.13140/2.1.2393.1847
10. Tensorflow. https://www.tensorflow.org/. Accessed Mar 2020

Tag Me If You Can: Insights into the Challenges of Supporting Unrestricted P2P News Tagging

Frederik S. Bäumer[1(✉)], Joschka Kersting[2], Bianca Buff[3], and Michaela Geierhos[4]

[1] Bielefeld University of Applied Sciences, Bielefeld, Germany
`frederik.baeumer@fh-bielefeld.de`
[2] Paderborn University, Paderborn, Germany
`joschka.kersting@upb.de`
[3] Bielefeld University, Bielefeld, Germany
`bianca.buff@uni-bielefeld.de`
[4] Research Institute CODE, Bundeswehr University Munich, Munich, Germany
`michaela.geierhos@unibw.de`

Abstract. Peer-to-Peer news portals allow Internet users to write news articles and make them available online to interested readers. Despite the fact that authors are free in their choice of topics, there are a number of quality characteristics that an article must meet before it is published. In addition to meaningful titles, comprehensibly written texts and meaningful images, relevant tags are an important criteria for the quality of such news. In this case study, we discuss the challenges and common mistakes that Peer-to-Peer reporters face when tagging news and how incorrect information can be corrected through the orchestration of existing Natural Language Processing services. Lastly, we use this illustrative example to give insight into the challenges of dealing with bottom-up taxonomies.

Keywords: Tagging · Bottom-up taxonomies · Data cleansing

1 Introduction

Wherever content in larger amounts is created online, many websites make use of tags. Whether the content is created by individual users on a blog or question-and-answer website such as StackOverflow or by professional journalists on a news website, adding relevant keywords to an entry works as a shortcut for handling the mass of data. Furthermore, authors can utilize tags to describe their article on a higher level of abstraction than would be possible by merely composing a concise title. The choice of appropriate tags also makes it possible to categorize the articles and integrate it into the website's contents in a structured manner. Thus, connections to related topics and articles become apparent. On the other side, tags help users browse all the available contents for specific terms

© Springer Nature Switzerland AG 2020
A. Lopata et al. (Eds.): ICIST 2020, CCIS 1283, pp. 368–382, 2020.
https://doi.org/10.1007/978-3-030-59506-7_30

they are interested and to filter the search results to ultimately get just the most important articles regarding their query.

Although at first sight tags seem like a perfect means to semantically structure a website's contents, on closer examination the reality shows a different picture. First, some authors do not choose relevant tags to describe their articles, given that they use only terms that are too general or too precise. Both of these extremes are problematic because badly tagged articles, being difficult for interested users to find, corrupt the purpose of tags as helpful metadata. Furthermore, in general the inventory of tags on websites is incredibly vast: A large German Peer-to-Peer (P2P) news platform, for instance, counts more than 50,000 different tags (in the time period of 2000–2017), including a huge amount of tag synonyms in this number. To name but a few, various forms of the same tags co-exist, such as synonym pairs of singular and plural forms like *"Krankheit"* (illness) and *"Krankheiten"* (illnesses), unnecessary usages of punctuation like *"Fußball"* (football) and *"Fußball:"* and misspellings. Such redundancies of tag synonyms complicate their quantitative and qualitative analysis as well as any further processing and subsequent usage for other applications. We therefore analyze the tags from a P2P news platform, with a special focus on tag synonyms and available cleansing approaches thereof.

The structure of the paper is as follows: In Sect. 2, we provide an overview of the related work, presenting our dataset in Sect. 3. We discuss in Sect. 4 the need for Natural Language Processing (NLP) and the orchestration of NLP services, then ending by presenting a conclusion in Sect. 5.

2   Related Work

The following section gives insight into existing work in this research area. We briefly introduce P2P News (cf. Sect. 2.1) and bottom-up taxonomies (cf. Sect. 2.2) before presenting work on relevant data cleansing approaches (cf. Sect. 2.3).

2.1   Peer-to-Peer News

News portals with high user interaction such as ShortNews, digg or Newsvine are known as "citizen journalism" [13] or "Peer-to-Peer" news [17,18], named after the operation principles of P2P websites. Another well-known term is "social news" [9], which describes websites offering participative journalism. The basic idea of P2P news portals is that every registered user can make his/her own news available to other users. The quality of these articles is often evaluated via quality guidelines and a community-based voting system. To ensure the motivation of the reporters, a point system is used on some pages, which rewards the effort of P2P reporters, who often try to adopt the writing style of professional reporters while at the same time devoting themselves to small, local topics. For example, German P2P platform ShortNews[1] is dedicated to the short, concise presentation of news

---

[1] ShortNews discontinued operations in 2018.

that has already been published on major news portals. In contrast to community news, there is no thematic limitation here, but rather content compression and processing. The idea is to summarize topics in three paragraphs for other users. Moreover, authors are asked to provide some metadata (categories, tags) that help describe an article and allows it to be found by other users [3]. Tags are generally chosen initially by the authors or later on by the community. In this context, bottom-up taxonomies (folksonomies) as well as top-down taxonomies (e.g. controlled vocabulary) are used [3].

2.2 Bottom-Up Taxonomies

The defining feature of a bottom-up taxonomy or folksonomy is that it is generated in collaboration by a whole group of active users (the *folk*). In contrast to a top-down taxonomy, the vocabulary is not predetermined but develops over time, open-ended [3]. Inherent in this system is the opportunity for users to freely choose those tags that they deem most appropriate for their articles. They can introduce new tags if the existing ones do not meet their needs. Thanks to its open nature, a bottom-up taxonomy therefore reflects the users' needs and vocabularies that evolve and vary over time. Since the majority of users are not professional experts, the complexity of the annotated tags is generally on a lower level. As such, a folksonomy should be regarded more as a *categorization* that is less restricted by defined boundaries than a formal and systematic *classification*. In addition, it is not structured hierarchically and does not include explicit relationships between different tags [15].

Websites relying on bottom-up taxonomies often specify guidelines for their users concerning the choice of tags. Good tags are the ones that integrate an article appropriately into the entirety of articles available on a certain website. This means that the tags should describe the articles' content on a level of abstraction that ensures everyone roughly understands what it deals with. Tags should be chosen considering how other people would search for topics they are interested in. For instance, the tags *"woman"*, *"society"* and *"50"* are clearly uninformative, giving no insight into the content of the article and impeding that a user even receives it as a search result on a (tag-based) query. These tags (sometimes called meta-tags) are too general and should therefore be used carefully as, if applied singularly, they cannot describe the article and differentiate it from others properly. Also, websites such as StackOverflow advise their users not to introduce new tags but instead to utilize existing tags consistently, restricting them in their choice of tags.

2.3 Data Processing Approaches for Taxonomies

Even though there are various different ways to construct a taxonomy, e.g. manually, Tsui et al. [19] focus on automatic construction approaches. These typically include clustering (terms that occur in similar linguistic contexts are arranged in groups), similarity based on lexico-syntactic patterns, and knowledge sources (machine-readable dictionaries are used to check for lexical relations between terms). As a different approach, Tsui et al. developed a system that automatically converts tags from a folksonomy into a hierarchical taxonomy, based on heuristic rules and deep syntactic analysis. In order to find hierarchical relations between terms, the authors apply three heuristic rules: First, when "one term is same as the other term and additionally modified by certain words or adjectives" [19], this is classified as an *is-a* relation, meaning that the longer term is part of the shorter term (e.g. *"Fußball Bundesliga"* (national league football) and *"Fußball"* (football)). Secondly, an abbreviation is classified as the neighbour of a term or phrase when it consists of the first letters of that term or phrase (e.g. *"EU"* and *"Europäische Union"* (European Union)). Lastly, a tag combined of two parts with "and" or "or" (e.g. *"TV and entertainment"*) is located hierarchically above the single terms (*"TV"*, *"entertainment"*). Further, Tsui et al. use a concept-relationship acquisition and inference algorithm to map tags (as found in the raw texts) to concepts [19].

In their study about automatic tag clustering, Begelmann et al. [1] also describe how to find related tags, i.e. tags that frequently co-occur as annotations for a single article. They generated a sparse matrix, consisting of all the pairings of tags present in the articles, with each value then being a measure of the degree of co-occurrence of a pair of tags. Subsequently, this data was used to build up undirected graphs, meaning clusters of these co-occurring tags.

Ienco et al. [10] present a clustering algorithm to generate a concept taxonomy based on the most frequent keywords in a document, occurring at least a certain number of times. They use the Ward hierarchical clustering algorithm to determine the clusters, the cluster-evaluation measure Goodman-Kruskal, as well as PageRank to determine the best ranking of the keywords.

Chuang et al. [6] propose an algorithm based on Hierarchical Agglomerative Clustering (HAC) combined with a min-max partitioning method with the aim of turning the binary into a multi-way tree hierarchy. As they use short text segments as input data, they rely on search results from search engines to retrieve additional relevant contextual information. The sparse input is enriched with the most frequent terms of the first hundred search results.

3   Bottom-Up Taxonomies: The Need for Data Cleansing

On P2P platforms, where users are neither restricted in the number of tags they choose or in the introduction of new tags nor (generally) bound to any guidelines, the amount of existing tags quickly increases enormously, leading to redundant co-existing tag synonyms, i.e. dirty data and sparsity of tag space. For subsequent analysis and applications, the underlying data should be as clean, correct and consistent as possible. Consequently, the *a posteriori* cleansing of such an unrestricted tag system is necessary to keep the overall tag quality high enough for further reliable processing. In the following, we will present the peculiarities of the dataset that is the basis of our research (cf. Sect. 3.1) as well as general issues with bottom-up taxonomies (cf. Sect. 3.2).

3.1 Insights into the Dataset

Our dataset consists of 157,748 news articles published on a large German P2P
news site between 2000 and 2017 by a total of 5,216 different users (cf. Table 1).
There are very active and less active users, e.g. the two most active authors alone
have written 27,977 news articles while many (registered) users do not write
articles at all. The news articles cover 13 different sections, the most popular
being the *"Brennpunkte"* (hot topics) section and the *"Entertainment"* section,
which in total contain 34% of the acquired news articles. In addition, we have
acquired 1,081,372 comments that refer to the news articles and allow us to
further analyze the communication behavior and language of authors and users.

Table 1. Overview of the relevant dataset

Year	Articles	Tags	Unique	New	Tag/Article	Unique/Article
2000	1,389	5,798	1,575	1,575	4.2	1.1
2001	2,302	11,402	4,959	3,111	5.0	**2.2**
2002	1,717	7,810	2,427	**0**	4.5	1.4
2003	1,484	7,189	2,240	682	4.8	1.5
2004	1,700	8,680	2,487	680	5.1	1.5
2005	1,638	9,255	2,723	714	5.3	1.7
2006	1,427	8,097	2,446	525	5.7	1.7
2007	1,446	8,305	2,552	482	5.7	1.8
2008	1,486	9,104	2,751	561	6.1	**1.9**
2009	3,022	19,448	5,013	1,413	6.4	1.7
2010	5,009	35,600	9,131	4,630	7.1	1.8
2011	8,348	67,403	15,080	8,276	8.1	1.8
2012	19,134	137,614	23,661	12,259	7.2	1.2
2013	22,830	115,553	16,528	5,042	5.1	0.7
2014	15,966	80,662	14,090	3,286	5.1	0.8
2015	28,087	127,052	17,396	4,269	4.5	0.6
2016	27,310	117,399	15,650	2,496	4.3	0.6
2017	13,453	54,963	8,760	193	4.1	0.7
	157,748			50,194		

However, this paper focuses on tags used by the authors. There are 50,194
unique tags in the dataset (cf. Table 1), of which the most frequent are "football" (9,040), "USA" (6,103), "man" (3,292), "Germany" (3,153) and "woman"
(2,948). On average, 5.5 tags are assigned per article over all years, whereby
1.4 unique tags are added to the taxonomy per article on average. While the
number of tags assigned per article seems quite stable, the number of unique
tags decreases over the years. This may be an indication that certain tags have

become established and are being used more and more, but it may also indicate that certain topics dominate reporting. Since the tags are not predefined or limited by the site operator, the taxonomy potentially grows with each article added. In contrast to "Tags" in Table 1, which reflects the total number of tags assigned within a year, "Unique Tags" provides the number of different tags. "New" in the table shows the number of tags by which the taxonomy has grown in a given year. These are only tags that were not used in previous years. As Table 1 shows, new tags have been added to the taxonomy every year since 2000, with the exception of 2002. In 2002, 1,717 articles were written and 7,810 tags were assigned, but there were no tags that were not already assigned in previous years, which means that the taxonomy was not growing in 2002[2]. Overall, a taxonomy with a very low tag reuse appears: Almost half of the tags were used only once in our dataset and 95% of the tags were used less than 50 times.

However, many of these tags are only mistakenly present as unique, as no normalization takes place. There are many examples of missing normalization. For example, in the year 2012, 12,259 new tags were added to the taxonomy. However, if we take a closer look at the assigned tags, it becomes clear that this number would be smaller if normalization were applied. Tags are often found in which missing or multiple spaces cause them to be known as new (e.g. "1. FC Köln"). Another example is caused by spellings. In 2012, for example, the spelling "El Kaida" for "Al Kaida" (Al Qaeda) can be found in the dataset, although "Al Kaida" already exists in the dataset. However, the difficult handling of the spelling of foreign names is also a challenge for professional journalism. The situation is different for names whose spelling is clear but difficult to type correctly due to reasons such as special characters. Despite the fact that "Jérôme Boateng" already exists in the dataset, both "Jérôme Agyenim Boateng" and "Jerome Boateng" were added in 2012. To learn more about the existing tags, we have taken a random sample of 5,000 tags (10%) spread over all years. We have compared the tags with dictionaries and lexical resources and the results underline the assumed poor quality. Only 31% of the tags are found in the Duden dictionary and 69% can be found in BabelNet [16]. BabelNet achieves a higher coverage here, as this dictionary supports product names and numerous other entities. Since BabelNet also provides information about ambiguity, 51% of the available tags are accordingly ambiguous. We dive into the details of tag processing in Sect. 3.2.

3.2   Issues with Bottom-Up Taxonomies

A bottom-up taxonomy "[...] represents simultaneously some of the best and worst in the organization of information" [15]. It enables and encourages users to actively participate in the structuring of data, using few (if any) formal restrictions. In this subsection, we will introduce some of the issues that arise when

---

[2] Based on the data available to us. It is very likely that new tags have been added this year, but our dataset does not represent this.

dealing with bottom-up taxonomies due to lacking standards, namely variations in the usage of characters and punctuation, tag ambiguity and heterogeneity.

Because bottom-up taxonomies are generally generated by a collection of users who are not professionals, the quality of the data sometimes does not meet a universal standard. When individual users make a typing error or are not aware of the correct spelling of a name or word, they (sometimes inadvertently) produce a variant of the correctly spelled tag and thus dirty data. This includes non-capitalized nouns, which (when taken without further context) might consequently be confused with verbs, such as the noun *"Laufen"* (running) and the verb *"laufen"* (to run).

In the German language, capitalization is the significant feature for identifying a noun. Also leading to different representations of the same information, the ordering of constituent parts can differ, with dates and addresses being the most prominent example. Moreover, among users, inconsistent usage of punctuation may arise, for instance with regard to the usage of special delimiting characters such a hyphen (or not hyphen) between the constituents of a compound [12].

Furthermore, ambiguity is still a core problem for NLP. Considered in isolation, even a simple word such as *"star"* has at least two meanings, the popular celebrity or the luminous object in the sky at night. Besides these different readings of a single word that are naturally inherent to a language, bottom-up taxonomies additionally face the difficulty that users might interpret a certain word in very individual ways depending on their connotations. Acronyms or abbreviations are another source of confusion when different persons use them to refer to different concepts. As there are no guidelines that users have to adhere to, they apply tags to data by relying on their personal associations [3,12,15].

Another problem that arises is when users utilize different tags for the same text or concept, which is referred to as tag heterogeneity. This problem can manifest itself in several ways: On the morpho-syntactic level, variations in word forms can emerge such as singular versus plural forms or different cases. Besides synonyms as lexical alterations, there are different acronyms or abbreviations that people use for the same term, taking their own personal shortcut, differ [15]. Individual users think on a different level of abstraction and consequently generate tags such as *"Angela Merkel"*, *"Merkel"* or even *"Angela Dorothea Merkel"* and *"Bundeskanzlerin Merkel"* (German Chancellor Merkel). These four tags are variants referring to the same person and are therefore heterogeneous [12]. Another difficulty is that multilingual and international websites face the problem of variants of the same concept being expressed in several languages. Consequently, both tag ambiguity and heterogeneity lead to imprecision and inconsistency in the whole tagging system and complicate efficient searches for relevant articles [15].

As a bottom-up taxonomy has a non-hierarchical structure, there are no relationships between tags. The tags are not interconnected via semantic devices such as synonymy, hyperonymy or hyponymy, which is problematic because a query for a specific word will only yield articles annotated with this tag and none annotated with similar, broader or narrower terms. As a possible solution, some websites using bottom-up taxonomies apply clustering algorithms in order to identify related tags and enrich the search results [15].

However, due to tag ambiguity and heterogeneity, it is difficult to work out reliable and sensible hierarchical structures. However, these are just examples of the challenges accompanied with dirty data. A comprehensive overview of the wide range of challenges is shown by Kim et al. [12]. We have selected these challenges as particularly relevant for our work, on the basis of our findings from the random sample in Sect. 3.1.

4   Cleansing and Tagging Approaches

In this section, we will discuss the need for NLP and present our current experiences with approaches to automatically cleanse the tags in our dataset.

4.1   The Need for NLP

Because of their open, unconstrained nature, bottom-up taxonomies such as P2P news portals are very prone to dirty data that are difficult to automatically cleanse in hindsight. Up to now, only a fraction of dirty data could be prevented *a priori* using specific restrictions on user entries (e.g stopword lists). When the complexity of processing unstructured data such as texts increases, NLP is often required, since simple string comparisons, etc. are no longer sufficient. But the normalization and reduction of tags should not be seen exclusively as the task of NLP. After all, many errors in the data could be corrected by simple database operations and similarity searches. NLP becomes necessary, though, if the underlying news texts are to be included or if linguistic resources are needed to solve lexical ambiguity [16]. As an established discipline, NLP can draw on numerous tools and extensive resources. A famous example for a resource is BabelNet – a semantic network that covers 284 languages and about 830 million word senses. However, NLP approaches always find particular strength when they are not considered in isolation but applied as pipelines. "A pipeline consists of components processing input documents one after the other and passing the output on to the next component" [5]. Each individual component contributes a little to the processing of the documents and is in itself an expert in a particular field. The subsequent components can then rely on the output of the previous components. A special form of NLP pipelines are demand-oriented and orchestrated NLP service pipelines. Here, the need for necessary processing steps to achieve a goal (e.g. less variant richness in a tag collection) is automatically determined and independent NLP services are linked together in order to achieve the goal, whereby each service is responsible as an expert for a detached processing task. This approach is borrowed from On-The-Fly Computing, which involves combining independent software services with regard to given software requirements [4,11]. In the following we show an example of how single NLP services can be applied as a pipeline to the problem described here.

4.2   Orchestrated NLP Services

We have defined NLP microservices, which we use in a pipeline to reduce the number of variants in the tags and make use of them (cf. Fig. 1). The individual services build on each other, whereby the complexity of the processing increases.

Fig. 1. Relevant NLP services

Rule-Based Normalization: In NLP, normalization is a process that converts a given vocabulary into a uniform representation. Depending on the data quality, the subsequent processing of the data can be influenced positively – both in terms of the quality of the results and the speed. However, not all normalization steps are suitable for every NLP task. For example, the conversion to lower case is often an important normalization step, but in our case study we use data in German which is the reason why we cannot rely on lowercase conversion. For example, this would introduce many ambiguities. However, since there are well isolatable normalization needs, we have opted for a rule-based, sequential approach. We therefore defined a total of 35 rules that can transform individual tags (e.g. remove characters) as well as a number of selected tags (e.g. merge similar tags). In the following we present two rules to make the procedure more understandable.

The first rule applied to all tags is the normalization of punctuation marks at the end of a tag. Very often there is a question mark or exclamation mark at the end of a tag, and periods and quatation marks also occur (e.g. *"Unfall!"*, engl.

"Accident!"). These characters can be detected by the first and very simple rule and are deleted without replacement. While this is useful in many cases, there are also cases when the rule fails (e.g. tags related to German TV shows such as *"Wer wird Millionär?"* and *"Wetten dass...?"*).

Another rule that applies to all tags but focuses on merging tags is the rule for normalizing apostrophes, such as the tags in *"McDonald's"* and *"McDonald's"*. In these cases, the variants are reduced to the most common spelling. A similar procedure is used for the normalization of spellings, where several word variants result from a word composition using hyphens (*"Dengue-Fieber"* and *"Denguefieber"*). In German, however, composites are usually used because many nouns are written as one word. As a result, dozens of exceptions exist and there are therefore numerous variations in the tags.

Lemma Merging: During the manual analysis of the tags after the normalization we noticed that many tags are still present twice, but in both a singular (*"Ferienwohnung"*, *"Demo"*) and a plural form (*"Ferienwohnungen"*, *"Demos"*) or in a male and a female form. For this reason, a linguistic service must be used that is able to reduce words to a common form and, if possible, to distinguish different word senses. We have chosen Duden, a dictionary of the German language, in order to reduce the existing variants. To lower the number of comparisons, we assume that tags have a common root. We therefore reduce the tags to the word stem and then pass tags with a common word stem in the original to the service.

Entity Matching: Since the underlying texts are news articles, the tags contain a high number of (named) entities that cannot be found in such as the Duden (cf. Sect. 3.2 and Sect. 3.1). We have therefore decided to use BabelNet as a cross-linguistic resource because it reflects world knowledge in addition to linguistic knowledge. The idea is that this NLP microservice can merge existing entities in the tags, even if they are written differently. To ensure good detection quality, entities should be merged only if there are clues in the news article context: for example, if other tags match.

Figure 2 shows an example regarding the Egyptian politician Abd al-Fattah Said Husain Chalil as-Sisi. This politician appears in our data under four different spellings (*"Abdel Fattah al-Sisi"*, *"Abdel Fattah el-Sisi"*, *"Abdel Fattah al Sisi"* and *"Abdel Fattah al sisi"*), two of which were already merged during normalization. The spellings *"Abdel Fattah al-Sisi"* and *"Abdel Fattah el-Sisi"* differ only marginally, but no rule has merged them yet. However, BabelNet knows both spellings and internally assigns a unique BabelID to the named entity (bn:13913047n). Since the context of the messages also overlaps (two other tags are identical), the two tags can be merged at a low risk. As a positive side effect, this also leads to a lexical disambiguation, since the work can now be continued internally with the unique BabelID. We use the same approach to merge abbreviations (e.g. CDU, AfD) and their written-out named entities (e.g. *"Christlich Demokratische Union Deutschlands"*, *"Alternative für Deutschland"*).

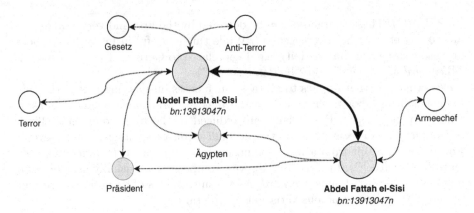

Fig. 2. Entity matching via BabelNet

Lexical Disambiguation: A very efficient way to reduce the number of tags and strengthen the remaining tags in their meaningfulness is lexical disambiguation, which means that the tags are matched with the content (title and article text) and matching tags are disambiguated by the context. The assignment of a unique BabelID results in only one reading for the tag. Furthermore, it is possible to merge synonymous tags, since synonyms can be identified via BabelNet and also mapped to a unique BabelID. An example of this procedure is a news article titled *"Blog veröffentlicht nach dessen Selbstmord FBI-Akte von Hacker Aaron Swartz"* ("Blog publishes FBI file of hacker Aaron Schwartz after his suicide") which was assigned the tags *"Selbstmord"* (suicide), *"Hacker"*, *"Blog"*, *"Akte"* (file), *"FBI"* and *"Aaron Swartz"* by the author.

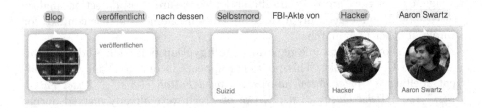

Fig. 3. Lexical disambiguation via babelfy

As shown in Figure 3, five of the ten words from the title could be disambiguated by Babelfy. A comparison of the assigned tags with the disambiguated words from the title results in unique BabelIDs for the tags, which leads to a reduction of variants. This becomes clear with the word *"Selbstmord"* (used 350 times), which is mapped to a BabelID and merged with the synonyms *"Freitod"* (used two times) and *"Suizid"* (used 102 times). Other examples are *"Blog"* and *"Weblog"* or *"Bloggerin"* and *"Blogger"*.

Fuzzy Merging: Merging tags is a task that can be prone to errors: e.g. the Levenshtein distance [14] of two means that two steps are necessary for going from the word *"Chili"* to *"Chile."* Both spellings clearly have an utterly different meaning. The same applies to cases such as *"1. Bundesliga"* and *"2. Bundesliga"*, the first and second German football leagues. That is, the plain string distance is not enough, as it omits the word's semantics. We consequently experimented with word vectors extracted from a pretrained model (BERT [7,8]) and we self-trained vectors on the data using FastText [2]. While such models seek to enrich string data, the result did not solve the issue of merging tags. We did achieve quite good results using Ratcliff-Obershelp similarity, but the error rate is still a concern: The examples above also fail with this approach. The use of fuzzy matching is therefore only an option if at least two tags in direct article comparison support the assumption that the analyzed tags may be merged.

Results and Discussion: Table 2 shows the individual cleansing steps and the effects on our dataset. For performance reasons we have taken a sample of 135,021 news for this paper and apply the presented pipeline to it. The corpus results in 559,097 news-tag relations and 39,330 tags. The range of news-tag relations spans from news with only one tag to news described by 20 tags. It becomes clear that a considerable number of tags has become obsolete due to cleansing. This number could be even larger, but we have limited ourselves to making changes only if we are very sure that we will not introduce new errors into the data or have avoided making decisions where human intervention would be necessary. Nevertheless, it is a significant reduction in the number of tag variants and it makes it possible to experiment with methods that allow for a tag suggestion system and can contribute to making tag selection a little more effective in the future, although paternalism should still not take place.

Table 2. Overview of resulting dataset per processing step

Step	No. input tags	No. output tags	Change
1. Normalization	39,330	30,147	−9,183
2. Lemma merging	30,147	29,176	−2,971
3. Entity matching	29,176	26,166	−3,010
4. Lexical disambiguation	26,166	21,008	−5,158
5. Fuzzy merging	21,008	19,987	−1,021

To understand tag assignment better, we trained neural network transformer models such as BERT [8] in order to automatically assign tags to news texts. Transformers are attention-based language models that learn the semantics of words in a corpus. They can assign word vectors to unknown words and they can be fine-tuned directly on a downstream-task [8,20]. We trained a transformer model on the original P2P news dataset in order to automatically assign tags and we approached the case as a multi-label classification task. The number of labels (i.e., tags) is high and they are sparsely represented, which is why we expected transformer systems as a good approach. They are trained on large amounts of training data and designed for difficult tasks, where they excel due to their broad language model and thus their understanding of language. For example, the German BERT was trained on Wikipedia, legal texts and news articles [7]. As expected, the results were useless and confirm our assumption that the assumed tag quality of the original dataset is very low.

For this reason, we have created a comparative dataset with a much better quality on which we can test the methods in order to understand how they work and we ignore the poor data quality of our P2P dataset for a moment. We therefore crawled a German newspaper website that is a well-known news source. The newspaper articles were written by professional journalists, and so were the tags assigned to them. We found a higher quality in the tag distribution even though they are not entirely clean. Yet, we identified few errors: e.g. among all tags that started with "Rus", only two out of 14 could have been merged (a small number compared to our user-generated news data): namely, *"Russland"* (the German word for Russia) and *"Russlan"* (the same word missing the last letter). But *"Russlan"* can also be a first name. Hence, we regard the newspaper tags as very clean. BERT still had issues learning to assign these tags (fine-tuning with 20 epochs), resulting in a label ranking average precision score (LRAP score) of 0.573. While this alone is not a favorable value, it is a good one for over 21,000 tags. Having seen that, we tried to automatically tag our user-generated news data. As mentioned, this did not work out of the box, so we cleansed the tags and restricted the data on the basis of the appearance of tags. We counted every appearance and excluded tags that did not meet the threshold we set. If this caused news texts to have no tags, we excluded them. We started high and slowly approached a low minimum number of appearances. Using only texts of the category *"Wirtschaft"* (Business) with at least 20 appearances of tags resulted in an LRAP of 0.684, but here we only had 242 tags left. Using the full dataset with tags restricted to at least 30 appearances and thus 113,000 texts with different 2,717 tags, we achieved an LRAP of 0.695 after several epochs which encouraged us to further investigate the case. At least 10 appearances and 6,818 tags resulted in an LRAP of 0.508, five appearances with 11,240 tags in 0.540. That is, excluding tags that only appear very few times enables us to train a system that is able to assign tags automatically. Of course, this can be improved having cleansed tag data. Furthermore, the score of around 50% is not favorable but sufficient for a use case like ours and should, at this point, rather be seen as an outlook and motivation for further work. An automatic tagging system can thus support users and help to avoid as many new tags as possible.

5   Conclusion

In this case study, we intended to show the challenges that P2P news portal operators face when they leave the tagging without rules to their own users and do not perform a quality check. In conclusion, it is evident that bottom-up taxonomies are in theory a satisfactory method for content description. They are easy to understand and allow organizing content quickly. However, they scale poorly if they are not moderated or if other restrictions are introduced.

If such a system has been actively used for years by non-professional users, like in our use case, it is very difficult to normalize the content in an automated way due to ambiguities, spelling errors, and a wide range of word variants. However, we believe that unique tags are still an important tool to sort and thematically classify the mass of daily produced content with a performance-oriented method. In this case we recommend continuing with a validated base of tags to prevent further ambiguities and to introduce unique tag IDs. Classification methods and standards for external linguistic resources allow linking own taxonomies to existing knowledge bases. While writing new articles, authors should already be offered tags selected by the system. We approached this need in Sect. 4.2, which deals with suggesting tags.

In this work, we show that existing tag systems that were never subject to any limitation or set of rules can be automatically cleaned by a variety of isolated NLP services. However, it also became clear that a purely automated approach has significant limitations. For example, some ambiguities cannot be resolved even after an analysis of the titles and contents. Also, there are sometimes contradictions in the tags or neologisms have been introduced, both of which are difficult to detect and correct automatically. We see an opportunity for quality improvement in that a suggestion system will lead to a higher reuse of tags and that some tags will lose relevance and can be removed automatically because they will become obsolete. As we showed, though, building a suggestion system for tags on the basis of low-quality data is challenging. Nevertheless, we were still able to set up such a system that can be used to support authors during tag selection.

Acknowledgements. This work was partially supported by the German Research Foundation (DFG) within the Collaborative Research Centre On-The-Fly Computing (SFB 901).

References

1. Begelman, G., Keller, P., Smadja, F.: Automated tag clustering: improving search and exploration in the tag space. In: Collaborative Web Tagging Workshop at WWW 2006, pp. 15–33, May 2006
2. Bojanowski, P., Grave, E., Joulin, A., Mikolov, T.: Enriching word vectors with subword information **5**, 135–146 (2017). https://doi.org/10.1162/tacl_a_00051
3. Breslin, J.G., Passant, A., Decker, S.: The Social Semantic Web. Springer, Heidelberg (2009). https://doi.org/10.1007/978-3-642-01172-6
4. Bäumer, F.S., Geierhos, M.: Flexible ambiguity resolution and incompleteness detection in requirements descriptions via an indicator-based configuration of text analysis pipelines. In: Proceedings of the 51st Hawaii International Conference on System Sciences, pp. 5746–5755 (2018). https://doi.org/10.24251/HICSS.2018.720

5. de Castilho, R.E., Gurevych, I.: A broad-coverage collection of portable NLP components for building shareable analysis pipelines. In: Proceedings of the Workshop on Open Infrastructures and Analysis Frameworks for HLT, pp. 1–11. ACL and Dublin City University, Dublin (2014). https://doi.org/10.3115/v1/w14-5201

6. Chuang, S.L., Chien, L.F.: Topic hierarchy generation for text segments: a practical web-based approach. ACM J. 1–33 (2005)

7. deepset: deepset - open sourcing German BERT (2019). https://deepset.ai/german-bert. Accessed 28 Nov 2019

8. Devlin, J., Chang, M.W., Lee, K., Toutanova, K.: BERT: pre-training of deep bidirectional transformers for language understanding (2018)

9. Engesser, S.: Die Qualität des Partizipativen Journalismus im Web: Bausteine für ein integratives theoretisches Konzept und eine explanative empirische Analyse. VS Verlag für Sozialwissenschaften, Wiesbaden (2013)

10. Ienco, D., Meo, R.: Towards the automatic construction of conceptual taxonomies. In: Song, I.-Y., Eder, J., Nguyen, T.M. (eds.) DaWaK 2008. LNCS, vol. 5182, pp. 327–336. Springer, Heidelberg (2008). https://doi.org/10.1007/978-3-540-85836-2_31

11. Karl, H., Kundisch, D., Meyer auf der Heide, F., Wehrheim, H.: A case for a new IT ecosystem: on-the-fly computing. Bus. Inf. Syst. Eng. (2019). https://doi.org/10.1007/s12599-019-00627-x

12. Kim, W., Choi, B.J., Hong, E.K., Kim, S.K., Lee, D.: A taxonomy of dirty data. Data Min. Knowl. Disc. **7**(1), 81–99 (2003). https://doi.org/10.1023/A:1021564703268

13. Kopp, M., Schönhagen, P.: Die Laien kommen! Wirklich? Eine Untersuchung zum Rollenselbstbild sogenannter Bürgerjournalistinnen und Bürgerjournalisten. In: Quandt, T., Schweiger, W. (eds.) Journalismus Online- Partizipation oder Profession, pp. 79–94. VS Verlag für Sozialwissenschaften, Wiesbaden (2008)

14. Levenshtein, V.I.: Binary codes capable of correcting deletions, insertions, and reversals. Sov. Phys. Dokl. **10**, 707–710 (1966)

15. Mathes, A.: Folksonomies - cooperative classification and communication through shared metadata. Computer Mediated Communication, LIS590CMC. University of Illinois Urbana-Champaign, Graduate School of Library and Information Science (2004)

16. Navigli, R., Ponzetto, S.P.: BabelNet: the automatic construction, evaluation and application of a wide-coverage multilingual semantic network. Artif. Intell. **193**, 217–250 (2012). https://doi.org/10.1016/j.artint.2012.07.001

17. Neuberger, C.: Wandel der aktuellen Öffentlichkeit im Internet. Ph.D. thesis, Westfälische Wilhelms-Universität, Münster (2004)

18. Neuberger, C.: Das ende des gatekeeper-zeitalters. In: Lehmann, K., Schetsche, M. (eds.) Die Google-Gesellschaft, Bielefeld, pp. 205–211 (2005)

19. Tsui, E., Wang, W.M., Cheung, C.F., Lau, A.S.M.: A concept-relationship acquisition and inference approach for hierarchical taxonomy construction from tags. Inf. Process. Manag. **46**(1), 44–57 (2010). https://doi.org/10.1016/j.ipm.2009.05.009

20. Vaswani, A., et al.: Attention is all you need. In: Proceedings of the 31st Conference on Neural Information Processing Systems, pp. 5998–6008. Curran Associates (2017)

Author Index

Printed in the United States
By Bookmasters